INSTANT POT

COOKBOOK FOR BEGINNERS

650 Quick and Delicious Instant Pot Recipes for Smart People on a Budget

Katherine Jones
Copyright © 2020 by Katherine Jones.
All Right Reserved.

No part of this publication may be reproduced, distributed, or transmitted in any form or by any means, including photocopying, recording, or other electronic or mechanical methods, or by any information storage and retrieval system without the prior written permission of the copyright holder.

Effort has been made to ensure that the information in this book is accurate and complete, however, the author and the publisher do not warrant the accuracy of the information, text and graphics contained within the book due to the rapidly changing nature of science, research, known and unknown facts and internet. The Author and the publisher do not hold any responsibility for errors, omissions or contrary interpretation of the subject matter herein. This book is presented solely for motivational and informational purposes only.

TABLE OF CONTENTS

Introduction 1
- Benefits of Pressure Cooking 2
- Buttons and Time Settings 3
- Pressure Releasing Methods 5
- Parts of Instant Pot 6
- Must Have Accessories 7
- Useful Tips and Tricks 8

Breakfasts 9
- Apple Steel Cut Oats 9
- Sweet Potato Mini Quiche 9
- Blueberry Bliss Bowls 10
- Maple Millet 10
- Cheddar and Broccoli Crustless Quiche 10
- Creamy Sausage Frittata 11
- Tasty Sausage 11
- Sweet Potato Poblano Hash 12
- Tofu & Potatoes Breakfast 12
- Vanilla Polenta 13
- Cheesy Hash Brown 13
- Bircher Bowls with Yogurt 13
- Breakfast Enchiladas 14
- Spiced Fruit 14
- Egg, Ham and Cheese Bake 15
- Breakfast Millet Pilaf 15
- Quinoa and Granola Bowls 16
- Scotch Eggs 16
- Berry Toast Casserole 16
- Breakfast Pudding 17
- Bacon, Egg & Cheese Muffins 17
- Beef Roast 18
- Pumpkin Butter Breakfast 18
- Tofu and Potato Casserole 18
- Sweet Potato Poblano Hash 19
- Potatoes Breakfast Salad 20
- Spinach, Bacon & Eggs 20
- Poached Tomatoes and Eggs 20
- Scrambled Eggs & Bacon 21
- Healthy Tasty Oats 21
- Breakfast Berries Jam 21
- Banana Oat Cake 22
- Tofu Scramble Recipe 22
- Breakfast Bread Pudding 23
- Easy Egg Muffins 23
- Peaches Steel-Cut Oatmeal 24
- Easy and Cheesy Grits 24
- Pumpkin Oatmeal 24
- Strawberry Oats 25
- Granola Bars 25
- Breakfast Huevos Rancheros 26
- Pomegranate Porridge 26
- Chocolate Steel Cut Oats 26
- Sweet Potato Mini Quiche 27
- Sausage and Potato Hash 27
- Veggie Frittatas 28
- Apple Porridge 28
- Cinnamon Cereal Bowls 29
- Breakfast Enchiladas 29
- Italian Shakshuka 30
- Carrot Oatmeal Breakfast 30
- French Toast Casserole 31
- Strawberry Jam 31
- Blueberry Chia Pudding 31
- Banana Quinoa Bowls 32
- Leek Asparagus Frittata 32

Meat Recipes 33
- Mongolian Style Broccoli and Beef 33

Pineapple Pork 33
Tangy Pork with Potatoes 34
Korean style Beef Bowl 34
Delicious Chili Con Carne 35
Pork Tamales 35
Mustard Pork Tenderloin 36
Easy and Tasty Meatloaf 36
Braised Pork Recipe 37
Creamy Pork Chops 37
Beef Stroganoff with Spring Green Peas. 37
Beef and Cabbage 38
Pork Sausages and Mashed Potatoes 38
Pork Chops & Smashed Potatoes 39
Barbacoa Beef 39
Potatoes and Goat 40
Beef Curry 40
Kalua Pork 40
Sausage with Sauerkraut 41
Sour and Sweet Pork 41
Broccoli Beef 42
Pot Roast with Potatoes and Carrots 42
Meatloaf with Mashed Potatoes 43
Easy Veal Dish 43
Meatball Delight 44
Red Beans & Sausage Dish 44
Collard with Bacon 45
Feta & Lamb Meatballs 45
Chinese BBQ Pork 46
Wonton Meatballs 46
Pork Chops & Brown Rice 47
Pork Carnitas 47
Rice & Beef Soup 48
Pork Chile Verde 48
Spiced Pork 49

Taco Casserole 49
Hominy Dish 50
Sausage and Kale Soup 50
Awesome Beef Recipe 51
Meatballs in Tomato Sauce 51
Pasta and Beef Casserole 52
Pulled Pork Dish 52
Pork with Orange and Honey 53
Sloppy Joes. 53
Beef & Broccoli Dish 54
Beef Burgundy. 54
Beef Chili 55
Korean Beef Stew 55
Pork Carnitas. 55
Meatloaf Dish 56
Spiced Pork 56
Delicious Pork Chops 57
Ground Beef and Rice 57
Awesome Beef Recipe 58
Asian Short Ribs 58
Pork Shoulder Tacos 58
Chinese Steamed Ribs 59
Apple Cider Pork 59
Pork Roast with Fennel 60
Pork Chops with Scallion Rice 60
Beef with Cracked Wheat 60
Pulled Pork 61
Hamburger Stew 62
Asian Ground Lamb 62

Poultry Recipes 63
Delicious Duck Chili 63
Chicken and Rice Burrito Bowl 63
Teriyaki Chicken and Rice 64
Mouthwatering Kung Pao Chicken 64

Braised Duck and Potatoes Recipe...............65
Pepper Chicken Soup...............65
Tuscan Chicken with Mashed Potatoes...............66
Stuffed Chicken Breast...............66
Chicken and Brown Rice...............67
Sesame Honey Chicken...............67
Chicken Fajitas...............68
Butter Chicken...............68
Chickpea Chicken Masala...............69
Simple Chicken Delight...............69
Garlic Chicken...............70
Cheering Chicken Wings...............70
Turkey Bolognese with Spaghetti...............71
Italian Chicken...............71
Turkey Bolognese. 72
Chicken Curry...............72
Whole Chicken...............73
Three Cup Chicken...............73
Delicious Chicken in Tomatillo Sauce...............73
Easy Turkey Chili...............74
Awesome Chicken Adobo...............74
Barbeque Honey Chicken...............75
Delicious Chicken Sandwiches...............75
Chicken Curry...............75
Moroccan Chicken...............76
Chicken Salad...............76
Delicious Chicken Cacciatore...............77
Chicken Dish...............77
Chicken Enchilada Casserole...............77
Balsamic Chicken with Vegetables...............78
Delicious Chicken with Cumin-Chile Sauce...............78
Arroz Con Pollo...............79
Potatoes and Chicken...............79
Mushroom Chicken...............80

Three Cup Chicken...............80
Dolma Casserole...............81
Sweet Corn Chicken Soup...............81
Teriyaki Chicken Delight...............82
Garlic Chicken...............82
Asian Chicken...............83
Chicken with Rice...............83
Lemon Piccata Chicken...............84
Creamy Chicken Dish...............84
Sesame Chicken Recipe...............85
Chicken with Rice...............85
Spiced Chicken and Rice Pilaf...............86

Soups, Stews and Chilis...............87
Chicken Chili Soup...............87
Chicken Noodle Soup...............87
Tomato Basil Soup...............88
Veggie Noodle Soup...............88
Beef Stew...............89
Zuppa Toscana Delight...............89
Corn Chowder...............90
Fish Chowder...............90
Peanut Stew...............91
Ground Turkey Chili and Sweet Potato...............91
Tomato Soup...............92
Lasagna Soup...............92
Taco Chili...............93
Lentil Minestrone...............93
Corn Potato Chowder...............94
Chicken Noodle Soup...............94
White Bean and Swiss Chard Stew...............95
Root and Beef Vegetables Stew...............95
Noodle Soup...............96
Cheering Chicken Tortilla Soup...............96
Surprising Sweet Potato Stew...............97

Beef and Mushroom Stew	97
Paprika Lentil Soup	98
Classic Cauliflower Soup	98
Chicken Meatball Soup Recipe	99
Chorizo, Kale and Chicken Soup	99
Cheese and Potato Soup	100
Split Pea Soup	100
Chicken Soup	100
Sweet Potato and Turkey Soup	101
Turkey Stew	101
Bacon and Broccoli Soup	102
Double Bean Chili	102
Baked Potato Soup	103
Double Bean Chili	103
Endive Soup	104
Lasagna Soup	104
Delicious Okra Stew	105
Chicken Stew Recipe	105
Cheesy Broccoli Soup	106
Celery Soup	106
Curried Squash Soup	106
Yummy Tomato Soup	107
Thai Coconut Curry with Tofu	107
Potato Leek Soup	108
Italian Sausage Stew	108
Delicious Beef Stew	108
Beef Goulash	109
Cheesy Broccoli Soup	109
Coconut Carrot Soup	110
Split Pea Soup	110
Beef Chili	111
Beans Chili	111
Wild Rice Soup	112
Veggie Soup	112
White Bean, Sausage and Kale Soup	113
Lamb Stew	113
Chickpeas Stew	113
Mushroom and Wild Rice Stew	114
Broccoli Cream	114
Minestrone Soup	115
Coconut Sweet Potato Stew	115
Simple Fennel Soup	116
Corn Soup	116
Easy Carrot Soup	116
Curried Squash Soup	117
White Bean Soup	117
Italian Stew	118
Cabbage Head Soup	118
Butternut Squash Soup	119
Barley and Beef Soup	119
Veggie Noodle Soup	120
Spinach Stew	120
Asian Peanut Stew	121
Mushroom Cream Soup	121
Classic Lamb Stew	122
White Bean and Swiss Chard Stew	122
Chestnut Soup Recipe	123
Black Bean Chipotle Soup	123
Ginger Carrot Soup	124
Chipotle Sweet Potato Chowder	124
Quinoa Butternut Chili	124
Veg Minestrone with Pasta	125
Tomato Soup	126
Fish and Seafood	**127**
Spicy Salmon Dish	127
Coconut Fish Curry	127
Cajun Dirty Rice	127
Miso Mackerel	128

Mussels and Spicy Sauce	128
Steamed Fish Recipe	128
Shrimp with Tomatoes, Spinach	129
Tuna and Noodle	129
Salmon Burger	130
Surprising Shrimp Delight	130
Almond Cod	130
Salmon Dish	131
Tomato Mussels	131
Shrimp with Herbs and Risotto	131
Poached Salmon Dish	132
Salmon and Veggies Dish	132
Sesame Honey Salmon	132
Garlic Shrimp Scampi	133
Vegetables and Salmon with Butter Sauce	133
Crispy Skin Salmon Fillets	134
Tuna & Pasta Casserole	134
Cheesy Tuna Dish	134
Shrimp Coconut Soup	135
Crab Quiche	135
Shrimp and Grits	136
Steamed Scallion Ginger Fish	136
Crispy Salmon Fillet	137
Seafood Gumbo	137
Simple Clams	137
Crab Legs and Garlic Butter Sauce	138
Delicious Shrimp Paella	138
Seafood Stew	138
Coconut Lime Shrimp	139
Shrimp and Sausage Boil	140
Fish with Orange Sauce	140
Ginger-Soy Salmon with Broccoli	141

Vegetable Recipes **142**

Collard Greens Delight	142
Tuscan Stew	142
Butternut Mac N Cheese	143
Wrapped Asparagus Canes	143
Tomato Basil Pasta	143
Polenta and Kale	144
Tomatoes and Zucchinis	144
Carrots and Turnips	144
Vegetable Stock	145
Maple Glazed Carrots Recipe	145
Layered Casserole	145
Fried Rice	146
Braised Endives	147
Lentil Swiss Chard Soup	147
Sweet & Spicy Cabbage	147
Mushroom Kale Stroganoff	148
Corn Pudding	148
Stuffed Tomatoes Delight	149
Sausages and Cabbage	149
Bacon and Kale	149
Tomato and Beet Salad	150
Cheesy Polenta	150
Hearts of Palm Soup	150
Red Curry Cauliflower	151
Roasted Potatoes	151
Turnips Dish	152
Shrimp and Asparagus	152
Cabbage Rolls	152
Pinto Bean Stew	153
Beet and Orange Salad	153
Instant Steamed Leeks	154
Barbecue Chickpea Tacos	154
Tomatoes and Okra	154
Kimchi Pasta	155
Crunchy Lentil Salad	155

Sweet Potato and Black Bean Tacos 156
Moo Goo Gai Pan 156
Parmesan Eggplant Casserole 157
Vegetable Soup 157
Asian Gobi Masala 158
Thai Farro Salad 158
Barley and Mushroom Risotto 159
Crispy Potatoes Recipe 159
Asian Coconut Rice and Veggies 160
Mucho Burritos 160
Sloppy Janes 161
Cauliflower Mac 'n' Cheese 161
Falafel Wraps 162
Vegetable Salad 162
Black Eyed Peas 163
Thai Stir-Fry 163
Chickpea Kale Korma 164
Walnut Pesto Pasta 165
Stuffed Bell Peppers 165
Collard Greens 166
Corn Chowder 166
Sweet Potato Curry 167
Walnut and Lentil Tacos 167
Greek Style Chickpea Salad 168
Vegetable Bowls 168

Snacks and Appetizers 170

Shrimp Appetizer 170
Zucchini Rolls Recipe 170
Tuna Patties Appetizer 170
Sausage and Shrimp Appetizer 171
Spinach Dip Recipe 171
Cauliflower Dip Recipe 171
Tomatoes Appetizer 172
Spicy Mussels Recipe 172
Shrimp Recipe 172
Asian Squid Appetizer 172
French Endives 173
Instant Chili Dip 173
Black Beans 173
Sweet Potato Slaw 174
Tomato Dip Recipe 174
Mussels and Clams 174
Prosciutto and Asparagus Appetizer 175
Chili Balls 175
Zucchini Dip Recipe 175
Artichokes 176
Tasty Okra Bowls 176
Squash and Beets Dip 176
Delicious Shrimp Appetizer 177
Beet Hummus 177
Stuffed Clams 177
Creamy Corn 178
Stuffed Mushrooms and Shrimp 178
Instant Cod Puddings 178
Artichoke Dip Recipe 179
Baby Carrots 179
Roasted Garlic 179
Simple Baked Potatoes 180
Spicy Salsa 180
Pumpkin and Cinnamon Muffins 180
Mushrooms and Mustard Dip 180
Mussels Bowls 181
Hard Boiled Eggs 181
Simple Baked Potatoes 181
Surprising Oysters 182
Easy Mango Dip 182
Crab and Cheese Dip 182
Avocado Dip Recipe 183

Sweet Potatoes 183
Italian Mussels Appetizer 183
Mushroom Dip 184
Eggplant Spread 184
English Chicken Wings 184
Lentils 185
Perfect Beets 185
Perfect Beets 185
Baby Carrots 186
Italian Dip 186
Sweet Potato Slaw 186
Lemon Broccoli 187
Beet Hummus 187
Ginger Lemon Asparagus 188
Turkey Meatballs 188
Creamy Corn 188
Sesame Noodle Bowls 189
Roasted Garlic 189
Salmon Patties 190
Quinoa 190
Zucchini Appetizer Salad Recipe 190
Lemon Broccoli 191
Cheeseburger Salad with Sauce 191
Appetizing Cranberry Dip 192
Gold Potatoes 192
Broccoli and Carrots 192
Eggroll Bowl 193

Side Dishes 194
Flavored Mashed Sweet Potatoes 194
Mushroom Risotto 194
Mashed Sweet Potatoes 194
Up Mashed Potatoes and Gravy 195
Millet Cornbread 195
Potatoes Side Dish 196

Eggplant Dish 196
Mushrooms & Green Beans Side Dish 196
Poached Fennel Dish 197
Artichokes Dish 197
Cauliflower Mash Dish 197
Onions & Parsnips 197
Black Beans Dish 198
Bulgur Pilaf 198
Green Beans 199
Yummy Not-Fried Pinto Beans 199
Cauliflower "Rice" 200
Potatoes Au Gratin 200
Israeli Couscous Dish 200
Herbed Polenta 201
Applesauce 201
Fava Bean Sauté 201
Mashed Squash 202
Mashed Turnips Dish 202
Special Side Dish 202
Brussels Sprouts Dish 202
Potato Casserole 203
Quinoa Pilaf 203
Easy Veggies Dish 204
Pumpkin Risotto 204
Hummus 204
Vegetable Medley 205
Green Beans Dish 205
Easy Glazed Carrots 206
Bok Choy Dish 206
Parmesan Spaghetti Squash 206

Rice Recipes 208
Steamed Eggs with Rice 208
Rice & Beef Soup 208
Chipotle Rice. 209

Wild Rice & Farro Pilaf 209
Kale and Wild Rice Salad 209
Coconut Sweet Rice 210
Pink Rice 210
Instant Brown Rice 210
Mix-Fruit Wild Rice 211
Grain Rice Millet Blend 211
Wild Rice and Chicken Soup 211
Mexican Basmati Rice 212
Chickpea & Rice Stew 212
Mexican Rice 213
Salmon and Rice 213
Mexican Brown Rice Casserole 213
Pumpkin Rice Pudding 213
Cauliflower & Pineapple Rice 214
Artichokes Rice and Side Dish 214
Easy Risotto 215
Veggie Rice Acorn Squash 215
Black Beans and Rice 215
Cajun Rice 216
Green Rice 216
Fried Basmati Rice 216
French Butter Rice 217
Rice Pudding 217
Lentil & Rice 217
Dolma Casserole 218
Ground Beef and Rice 218
Pineapple Rice 219
Rice and Peas 219
Rice & Veggies Dish 219
Arroz Con Pollo 220
Rice and Chicken 220
Mix Rice Medley 221
Delicious Rice Pudding 221

Rice Bowl 222
Simple White Rice 222
Lentils and Rice 222

Sauce Recipes 223
Guava Sauce Recipe 223
Carrot Sauce Recipe 223
Pineapple Sauce 223
Garden Salsa 223
Mushroom Gravy 224
Orange Sauce 224
Poblano Sauce 225
Cashew Sour Cream 225
Apple sauce 225
Tomato Sauce 226
Red Enchilada Sauce 226
Ginger and Orange Sauce 226
Mushroom Gravy 227
Leeks Sauce Recipe 227
Basil Red Sauce 227
Mustard Sauce Recipe 228
Garlic Red Sauce 228
Peach Sauce Recipe 229
Plum Sauce Recipe 229
Sriracha Sauce 229
Cranberry Sauce 230

Beans, Legumes & Grains 231
Cracked Wheat and Jaggery 231
Cold Quinoa Salad with Pecans and Fruit 231
Cranberry Beans Mix 232
Chickpeas Curry 232
Kidney Beans Curry Recipe 232
Garlic and Chickpeas 233
Mexican Cranberry Beans 233
Creamy White Beans 234

Classic Cranberry Bean Chili 234
Black Eyed Peas with Peanuts 234
Red Beans and Rice 235
Cheesy Barley Dish 235
Green Chile and Baked Beans 236
Asian Lentils Recipe 236
Kidney Beans Dish 236
Pea and Parmesan Risotto 237
Cabbage & Navy Beans 237
Red Lentils with Turmeric 238
Tasty Mashed Sweet Potatoes 238
Veg Quinoa Tabbouleh 238
Delicious Frijoles 239
Spicy Lentils 239
Bacon Butter Beans 239
Basmati Rice 240
Cold Quinoa Salad with Pecans and Fruit 240
Marrow Beans & Lemon Dish 241
Lentils and Tomato Sauce 241
Green Chile Chickpeas 241
Re-fried Pinto Beans 242
Mediterranean Lentils 242
Butternut Lentils 243
Veggie Risotto 243
Black Eyed Peas with Peanuts 244
Asian Rice 244
Lentils and Rice 244
Orange & Bulgur Salad 245
Spanish Style Rice 245
Instant Wheat Berry Salad 246
Healthy Barley Salad 246
Rice and Peas 246
Sticky Mango Brown Rice 247
Coconut Jasmine Rice 247
Chinese Fried Rice 247
Black Beans 248
Hummus 248
Veg Lo Mein 248
Yummy Cauliflower Faux Mashed Potatoes 249
Mexican Style Refried Beans 249
Mushroom and Leek Risotto 250
Veggie Risotto 250
Cilantro Lime Brown Rice 250
Mung Beans 251
Black Bean Soup 251
Sour and Sweet Brussels Sprouts 252
Chickpea Basil Salad 252
Beans with Bacon and Mushrooms 252
Hummus 253
Noodles with Tofu 253
Brown Rice 254
Texas Roma Caviar 254
Mushroom & Barley Risotto 254
Classic Chili Lime Black Beans 255
Rice with Corn and Peas 255
Pasta & Cranberry Beans 255
Lentils Tacos 256
Curried White Bean Broccoli Salad 256
Delicious Frijoles 257
Pepper Lemon Quinoa 257
Veggies Rice Pilaf 258

Yogurt Recipes 259

Pumpkin Spice Yogurt 259
Raspberry Yogurt 259
White Chocolate Yogurt 259
Vanilla Yogurt 260
Kiwi Yogurt 260
Chocolate Yogurt 261

Blueberry Oats Yogurt	261
Slow Cooked Fruity Yogurt	262
Cinnamon Yogurt	262
Mango Yogurt	263
Vegan Soy Yogurt	263
Passionfruit Yogurt	264
Strawberry Yogurt	264

Desserts 265

Chocolate Lava Cake Recipe	265
Instant pot Banana Cake	265
Carrot Cake Recipe	265
Chocolate Cheese cake	266
Crème Brule	266
Mix Berries Compote	267
Poached Pears with Caramel Sauce	267
Pumpkin Chocolate Cake Recipe	268
Instant Pot Key Lime Pie	268
Bourbon Apple Crisp	269
Brown Rice Pudding	269
Berry Jam Recipe	269
Ruby Pears Delight	270
Apple Crumble	270
Caramel Sauce	270
Ginger-Coconut Pudding	271
Delicious Cobbler Recipe	271
Vanilla Applesauce	271
Pears Jam Recipe	272
Sticky Rice and Fruit	272
Delicious Brownies	272
Stuffed Peaches	273
Pina Colada Pudding	273
Delicious Apple Cake	273
Fruit Compote	274
Ginger and Pineapple Risotto	274
Pecan-Cinnamon Coffee Cake	274
Peach Jam Recipe	275
Instant Pot Sweet Carrots	275
Candied Lemon Peel	275
Samoa Cheese Cake Recipe	276
Coconut Rice Pudding	276
Holiday Pudding	277
Instant Pot Baked Apples	277
Lemon Crème Pots	277
Apple Bread	278
Delicious Apple Crisp	278
Zucchini Nut Bread Recipe	278
Ricotta Cake Recipe	279
Peach Compote	279
Quick Raspberry Curd	279
Poached Pears with Caramel Sauce	280
Banana Bread	280
Coconut Rice Pudding	280
Fruit Compote	281
Sticky Rice and Fruit	281
Brownie Cake Recipe	282
Oatmeal Raisin Cookie	282

Introduction

The Instant Pot is revolutionary! You can cook virtually anything in your instant pot - from meats and main courses to rice, vegetables of every description, dessert to even yogurt. Better yet, pressure cooking allows you to prepare foods up to 70 % faster, on average, than conventional cooking methods do, which means you save energy in addition to your precious time!

This beginner's Instant Pot cookbook has a diverse collection of recipes for the amateur home cook who values the convenience of an electric pressure cooker. This collection goes beyond other Instant Pot books and has something for everyone.

This Instant Pot cookbook includes everything you need to revolutionize the way you cook with your favorite machine. This cookbook will teach you to create a variety of healthy, easy-to-make recipes with confidence. Having tasty dinners with loved ones is precious, but the time you need to spend in the kitchen is just exhausting. This is why you need this Instant Pot cookbook.

This Instant Pot cookbook for beginners will take care of your limited cooking time and will allow you to spend more time with your loved one instead of spending in the kitchen. No matter if you'd like to lose weight or just eat a little healthier, this book will make your weeknight dinner routine even simpler with satisfying, all-in-one recipes.

This is truly the ultimate book for gifting or self-purchase… Happy Cooking!

Benefits of Pressure Cooking

Pressure cooking is a very healthy way to cook food to preserve more nutrients and shorten the cooking time for beans, grains, and other foods. And so has the invention of the pressure cooker. It is best kitchen appliance that I know of, it always tops my list of kitchen appliances, whenever, and this is because of some of the fantastic functionalities of the instant pot. So here are some of the key functions

Time-saving: pressure cookers are time savers, and these features come in very handy for everyone, working-class parents, housewives, single parents, aging mothers etc. The pressure cooker has been manufactured with a great cooking speed that it becomes distinctive from every other kitchen appliance. The good news with pressure cookers is that as a cook, you get to spend less time in the kitchen, thereby having more time to achieve other things

Safe and Easy to Operate: the pressure cooker as it name goes cooks at a very high pressure because of heat level it is able to generate within a very short period of time. In order to prevent any sort of explosions, the modern pressure cookers are cooked with different layers of safety. Also, there are numerous other functions that can help to ensure end-user safety. For instance

Comfortability: the pressure cooker has some automated features like, keep warm, countdown, etc. The pressure cooker has a set of default setting with which a user could cook a specific type of meal without having to figure out the manual timing to set. For instance, the pressure cooker could help you cook your meat at a default setting and cook it fine.

You don't have to figure the manual timing to use for cooking that same meat. Apart from that, cooking with the pressure cooker leaves you with less to wash and less cleaning to do as there isn't room for spills or smell in the kitchen.

Energy Saver: the lesser time you have to cook your meal; the more electricity you get to save. It is been established that the pressure cook saves 70 % more energy than any other cooking appliance on the surface of the earth. This does not only save your time; it also saves your money.

Preserving Nutritional Value.: the more time your food spends on heat the more nutritious contents you get to loose from it. The fact that the pressure gives you less cooking time in a tightly enclosed environment, gives you the opportunity to lose fewer nutrients. I mean you don't get to go to your pot every single time in order to check if your meal is well cooked.

The pressure cooker cooks your food in a sealed environment giving no room for nutrients to escape unless you choose to let them. So with this, you have all your nutrients well preserved and waiting to be consumed. For example, steaming food like vegetables with the pressure cooker means that the vegetable gets to retain more nutrients

Delicious cooking: the fact that the pressure cooker cook at an extremely high heat which is extremely higher than what is obtainable with other cooking appliances and this enables it to draw out more flavors from the food and thereby helping to preserve the taste by making it taste a lot much better than usual

Buttons and Time Settings

Manual / Pressure Buttons: This is probably going to be the buttons you use most on the Instant Pot. It will allow you to pressure cook and manually select the time you want – rather than the preset buttons (such as Soup/Stew or Meat buttons). You can adjust the pressure, temperature and time by selecting the "+/-"buttons.

Sauté Button: The "Saute" Button is the second most used function with my Instant Pot. You can do that and basically cook up anything as you would in a skillet or pan. You don't need the 1 cup of liquid. Just press the "Saute" button, add some cooking oil to the inner pot and add food you want to cook like a skillet or pan.

Meat / Stew: Make your favorite stew or meat dish in the Instant Pot. Adjust the settings depending on the texture you want. For instance, the "More" setting is better for fall-off-the-bone cooking. It will default to a High Pressure for 35 minutes. You can adjust for "More" to High Pressure for 45 minutes or "Less" for High Pressure for 20 minutes.

Bean / Chili: One of my favorite things to make in the Instant Pot is beans. It's so much faster (and tastier) with the Instant Pot. When you use the "Bean / Chili" button, it will default to a High Pressure for 30 minutes. You can adjust for "More" to High Pressure for 40 minutes or "Less" for High Pressure for 25 minutes.

Multigrain: The "Multigrain" button is best for cooking brown rice and wild rice, which typically takes longer than white rice to cook. Cook brown rice to a 1:1.25 ratio rice to water and wild rice to a 1:3 ratio rice to water for 22 - 30 minutes.

It will default at the "Normal" setting is 40 minutes of pressure cooking time. Adjust as needed for the "Less" setting is 20 minutes of pressure cooking time, or "More" at 45 minutes of warm water soaking and 60 minutes of pressure cooking.

Slow Cook Button: Use your Instant Pot like a slower cooker with this option. Just add food as you normally would to a slow cooker, close the lid and then press the "Slow Cook" button.

It will default to a 4-hour slow cook time. You can use "+/-"buttons to adjust the cook time.

Steam: Use the "Steam" button to steam vegetables, seafood or reheat food (it's a great alternative to the microwave). Be sure to use the steam rack included with the Instant Pot, otherwise food may burn and stick to the bottom of the inner pot.

Rice: You can cook rice in the Instant Pot in nearly half the time as a conventional rice cooker. White rice, short grain, Jasmine and Basmati rice can all be cooked on this setting in about 4 to 8 minutes. In general, you'll need a 1:1 ratio of rice to water (Basmati is a 1:1.5 ratio).

When you choose the "Rice" button, the cooking duration automatically adjusts depending on how much food you put into the unit and cook on low pressure.

Be sure to add about 10 - 12 minutes to the total cooking time to allow the Instant Pot to come to pressure.

Porridge: Use the "Porridge" button to make rice porridge (congee) and other grains (not regular white or brown rice). It will default to a High Pressure for 20 minutes, which is best for rice porridge. You can adjust for "More" to High Pressure for 30 minutes or "Less" for High Pressure for 15 minutes.

After the porridge is finished, do not use the Quick Release handle. Because it has a high starch content, using the Quick Release will splatter the porridge through the steam release vent. Use the Natural Release.

Poultry: Make your favorite chicken recipes with the "Poultry" button with the Instant Pot. It will default to a High Pressure for 15 minutes. You can adjust for "More" to High Pressure for 30 minutes or "Less" for High Pressure for 5 minutes.

Soup: Use the "Soup" button to make broth, stock or soup. The Instant Pot will control the pressure and temperature so that the liquid doesn't heavily boil. You can adjust the cooking time as needed, typically between 20 - 40 minutes, and the pressure to either low or high.

Egg: This button cooks at High Pressure for 5 minutes. Adjusted to more cooks for 6 minutes. Adjusted to less cooks for 4 minutes.

Cake: This button cooks at High Pressure for 30 minutes. Adjusted to more cooks for 40 minutes. Adjusted to less cooks for 25 minutes.

Central Dial: Unique to the Instant Pot Ultra, you turn this dial to scroll between menu options and push to select.

Delay Start: Select a cooking function and set adjustments, then press Delay Start and use the [+] and [-] buttons to set amount of time you'd like to wait before the Instant Pot starts cooking.

Cancel Button: At any time, you can cancel cooking and return to standby mode by pressing the "Keep Warm" / "Cancel" button. This is a great option if you selected the wrong time for pressure cooking and need to stop to make adjustments to the pressure or time.

Keep Warm Button: When pressure cooking is done, the Instant Pot will beep and automatically go into the "Keep Warm" function. It will display an "L" in front of a number to indicate how long it's been warm – e.g. "L0:30" for 30 minutes. It's a great feature to keep food warm for up to 99 hours, 50 minutes. It's perfect for pot lucks.

Timer Button: Use the Timer button to delay the cooking start time for the Instant Pot. This works for both pressure cooking and slow cook options.

To use this feature, just press the Timer button with 10 seconds of pressing either the Pressure / Manual button or Slow Cook button. Use "+/- "buttons to adjust the delayed hours, then wait a second and press Timer again to set delayed minutes. You can cancel the Timer anytime by pressing the Keep Warm / Cancel button.

Pressure Releasing Methods

Natural Release:

There's really nothing you have to depressurize your pressure cooker. Once the cooking is finished, the pressure will automatically slowly drop inside the electric pressure cooker. Because of this slow drop in pressure and heat, when using natural release, food continues cooking even though active cooking is complete. Your stocks and soups come out cleaner and food are more likely to stay intact.

After the cooking cycle ends, wait until the Floating Valve (metal pin) completely drops before opening the lid.

*(*For Example, In our recipes, you may see "**Release the pressure naturally for 10 minutes**," – this means after the cooking cycle ends, wait for 10 minutes and then release remaining pressure by turning the valve to 'Venting')*

Use this method when cooking meat, foods that increase in volume or foam (like dried beans and legumes), soups, or any other foods that are primarily liquid.

Use Quick release when adding additional ingredients to the pot (like with a stew), or cooking eggs, vegetables, delicate foods, or ingredients that don't benefit from additional cook time.

Quick Release:

Quick release works by turning the valve once active cooking is complete. This process takes an extra degree of care, as a loud burst of steam is released from the valve. Rapid release takes no more than a minute or two, and works best with foods, like eggs, vegetables, or delicate ingredients that don't benefit from any extra cook time.

This method is also helpful when you need to check the doneness of food or add additional ingredients to the pressure cooker, as you might with a stew.

(*It's best to avoid using Quick release when cooking foods that increase in volume, froth, or foam, like legumes, or those that are mostly **liquid**, like **soup**, as the liquid can boil up and vent through the release valve.**)**

Parts of Instant Pot

Silicone Sealing Ring: This is referred to and alluded to as the gasket in a few manuals. What's more, is a fixing ring inside the top of the cooker which keeps the steam inside. For security purposes, consider cleaning it in the wake of cooking, and get it supplanted once old

Cooker Lid: This is the upper piece of your instant pot used for fixing the cooker opening when cooking. To open/evacuate it subsequent to cooking, you should first discharge the pressure from pot using the brisk discharge strategy or using the common discharge technique

Pressure Indicator: The pressure pointer, is typically situated on the cooker top. It's a little stick arranged comfortable top and would regularly go up when the most extreme pressure point (HIGH Pressure) has been come to. A similar bind would drop when the pressure point is truly low showing that it's sheltered to open the cooker. The stick additionally bolts the cooker some of the time, so you can't open the pot when pressure is developed in the IP. A few books or manual may call it "bolt marker

Steam Release Valve: This is the valve used for discharging pressure from your Instant pot rapidly subsequent to cooking (QPR). Or, then again when time to add more fixing to pot/check sustenance for doneness. It's the handle situated on the cover and can be used essentially by swinging to either fixing or venting

Trivet and Steam Basket: Some electric pressure cooker has a trivet alongside a steam wicker bin. This trivet and the steam wicker bin help to keep the nourishment over the pressure cookers base. Individuals use the trivet to bubble eggs or steaming their vegetables to keep the supplement from draining into the fluid.

Steam Condensation Collector: This is a holder generally made of plastic which is situated in favor of the cooker. It helps gathers additional buildup

Must Have Accessories

1. Seals: - the silicone sealing ring absorbs the smells of what you cook. As the Instant Pot heats the next batch of food, those smells from the sealing ring may filter into the new food. At least, you will want a sweet seal and a savory seal.

2. Silicone Baking Cups: - Useful for cakes, muffins, and smaller portions of just about any recipe you can cook in the IP, silicone baking cups are something that no kitchen should be without

3. Springform Pan: - Cheesecake recipes for the Instant Pot abound. For perfect cheesecake, a springform pan is essential. However, this pan is also great for other kinds of pies, lasagna, and meatloaf

4. Tempered Glass Lid: - The great thing about the Instant Pot is that while the pressure cooking options rock, you can also brown, simmer, and slow cook in it. For these types of meals, you do not need the heavier lid that comes with the unit. A tempered glass lid is easier for clean-up, and is a necessity if you plan to stir whatever you are cooking in your Instant Pot today

5. Steamer Basket: - The key to cooking great veggies in the Instant Pot is to steam them above the water rather than cooking them in the water. A steamer basket helps you do make perfect vegetables every time

6. Egg Bite Mold: - Egg bites are a great way to fix breakfast on the go in the Instant Pot. When cooled, egg bites can be put into containers making them easily portable

7. Stackable Steamer Rack: - A stackable steamer rack efficiently doubles the amount of food you can put into your Instant Pot, in some cases. With the addition of a steamer rack, you could cook two different types of food at the same time. Using the steamer rack also cuts down on food sticking to the insert

Useful Tips and Tricks

Experiment with the functions. Your instant pot does so many things, don't just use it for pressure cooking and get other pots and gadgets for the rest. Otherwise what's the point in having it? Use it to shallow fry, boil, steam, bake, etc. The possibilities are plentiful.

Measure your liquids carefully. Your instant pot has two different limits: the pressure limit and the slow cooker limit. Do not exceed the fluid amount for either! Always count things that liquefy, like gelatine or sugar, as a liquid.

Watch out about overfilling. Your instant pot should not be completely filled. Ever! You need space for pressure and/or steam to build up. Whether you are filling it with food or fluid, always make sure there is plenty of space from the top.

Be careful handling steam. Steam and pressure are nothing to joke around with! Never put your hand right in the steam, and always release the pressure according to the instructions manual. Always seal your instant pot properly before building pressure. Always open it when it is ready

Clean it well after each use. Your instant pot will not last if it ends up with a built up film of fat or layer of burnt and sticky food in it. Besides, that is unhealthy. Even if you have "only" used it to steam, remember that steam carries fat particles and creates a greasy film, so it still needs cleaning

Don't Use quick release unless specified. The pressure that can build up in your instant pot is intense. If you release it too fast you could get hurt. Only use quick release when a recipe specifically calls for it.

Don't Fill it with hot oil. This is not a deep fat fryer! Filling it with oil is dangerous and could cause a grease fire. At the very least, you will break your instant pot.

Don't Try and force it open. Again: intense pressure. Forcing it open could cause a seriously painful blast.

Don't Put things in in huge pieces. Even cooking is important, and big pieces do not respond as well to pressure or quick cooking. Leave the whole chickens for slow cooking only

Do not leave the house when it is on. Unlike with a traditional slow cooker, the instant pot reaches high temperatures, can carry a high voltage, and involves literal pressure

Breakfasts

Apple Steel Cut Oats

(Prep + Cooking Time: 43 minutes | **Servings:**8)

Ingredients:
- ¼ cup raisins
- ¼ cup pure maple syrup
- 2 cups uncooked steel-cut oats
- 3⅓ cups water
- 1 tbsp. ground cinnamon
- 1 tbsp. unsalted butter
- 2 red apples, cored and chopped

Directions:
1. Select *Sauté* and place the butter in the inner pot. Once the butter is melted, add the apples and cinnamon and cook for 2 minutes, stirring occasionally
2. Press Cancel. Add the oats, water, and raisins to the pot. Stir to combine.
3. Now, Lock the lid. Select, "Manual or Pressure Cook" and set the pressure to *High* and the time to 8 minutes. Make sure the steam release knob is in the sealed position
4. After completing the cooking cycle, naturally release the pressure for 10 minutes, then quick release any remaining pressure. Unlock and remove the lid. Stir in the maple syrup. Serve hot.

Sweet Potato Mini Quiche

(Prep + Cooking Time: 37 minutes | **Makes:** 7 Quiches)

Ingredients:
- 1 (14-ounce) package firm tofu, lightly pressed
- 1 cup plus 1 tbsp. water
- 1/2 cup shredded sweet potato
- 1/4 cup nutritional yeast
- 1 tbsp. cornstarch
- 1/4 cup nondairy milk
- 1 tsp. kala namak; or sea salt or as your liking
- 1/2 tsp. garlic powder
- 1/2 tsp. onion powder
- 1/2 tsp. ground turmeric
- Handful kale leaves; chopped small
- Nonstick cooking spray; for preparing the mold
- Vegan-buttered toast; for serving
- Freshly ground black pepper

Directions:
1. Lightly coat an 8¼-inch silicone egg-bites mold with nonstick spray and set aside.
2. In a food processor, combine the tofu, milk, yeast, cornstarch, kala namak, garlic powder, onion powder and turmeric. Blend until smooth
3. Select the "Sauté" Low mode on your instant pot. When the display reads "Hot," add the sweet potato, kale and 1 tbsp. of water. Sauté for 1 to 2 minutes
4. Note: You may need to turn off the Instant Pot if the vegetables start to stick to the bottom, but that's okay because it stays hot
5. Stir the veggies into the tofu mixture and spoon the mixture into the prepared mold. Cover the mold tightly with aluminum foil and place on a trivet. Add the remaining 1 cup of water to the inner pot and use the trivet's handles to lower the trivet and mold into the pot.
6. Lock the lid and turn the steam release handle to Sealing. Using the Manual function, set the cooker to High Pressure for 18 minutes
7. After completing the cooking time, let the pressure release naturally for 10 minutes; quick release any remaining pressure
8. Remove the lid carefully. Remove the silicone mold from the Instant Pot and pull off the foil. Leave the mold on the trivet and let cool for a few minutes
9. The bites will continue to firm as they cool. When ready to eat, schmear the tofu bites onto a piece of vegan-buttered toast and top with a little salt and pepper.

Blueberry Bliss Bowls

(Prep + Cooking Time: 22 minutes | **Servings:** 5)

Ingredients:
- 1 cup nondairy milk, plus more as needed
- 1 cup fresh blueberries
- 1 cup millet; rinsed
- 1/2 cup sliced toasted almonds
- 2 ¼ cups water
- 1 tbsp. freshly squeezed lemon juice
- 2 tbsp. maple syrup
- 1/4 tsp. ground cinnamon
- 1/4 tsp. ground nutmeg
- 1/2 tsp. salt or as your liking
- Zest of ½ lemon

Directions:
1. In the Instant Pot, stir together the millet, water, maple syrup, lemon juice, nutmeg, cinnamon and salt
2. Lock the lid and turn the steam release handle to Sealing. Using the Manual function, set the cooker to High Pressure for 10 minutes.
3. After completing the cooking time, let the pressure release naturally for 10 minutes; quick release any remaining pressure
4. Remove the lid carefully and stir in the milk, adding more if you like a creamier texture. Top with the blueberries, almonds and lemon zest before serving

Maple Millet

(Prep + Cooking Time: 22 minutes | **Servings:** 5)

Ingredients:
- 1/4 cup maple syrup
- 1 cup millet
- 1/2 to 1 cup nondairy milk
- 2 cups water
- 1/2 tsp. ground cinnamon
- 1/2 tsp. salt or as your liking
- Fresh berries; for topping

Directions:
1. In the Instant Pot, stir together the millet, water, cinnamon and salt
2. Lock the lid and turn the steam release handle to Sealing. Using the Manual function, set the cooker to High Pressure for 10 minutes.
3. After completing the cooking time, let the pressure release naturally for 10 minutes; quick release any remaining pressure
4. Remove the lid carefully and stir in the maple syrup and as much milk as you need to get the consistency you prefer "more milk makes it creamier".
5. You can add an extra sprinkle of salt, too. Top with the berries and serve

Cheddar and Broccoli Crustless Quiche

(Prep + Cooking Time: 60 minutes | **Servings:** 6)

Ingredients:
- 1 cup chopped broccoli florets
- 1½ cups shredded Cheddar cheese, divided
- ½ cup low-fat milk.
- ½ cup whole-wheat flour.
- Nonstick cooking spray
- 1 cup water.
- 8 eggs
- ¼ tsp. fine sea salt.
- ¼ tsp. freshly ground black pepper.
- Fresh chopped parsley; for garnish. (optional)

Directions:
1. Spray an 8-inch ceramic soufflé dish with the cooking spray
2. Place the trivet in the inner pot, then pour in the water.
3. If needed, make an aluminum sling (see here)
4. In a large bowl, whisk together the eggs, milk, flour, broccoli, 1 cup of the cheese, and the salt and pepper.

5. Pour the mixture into the soufflé dish. Use the sling to lower the soufflé dish onto the trivet
6. Now, Lock the lid. Select, "Manual or Pressure Cook" and set the pressure to *High* and the time to 30 minutes. Make sure the steam release knob is in the sealed position.
7. After completing the cooking cycle, naturally release the pressure for 10 minutes, then quick release any remaining pressure. Unlock and remove the lid. Use the sling to remove the soufflé dish.
8. Sprinkle the remaining ½ cup of cheese on top of the quiche. Using a sharp knife, slice the quiche into 6 wedges. Serve immediately garnished with fresh parsley

Creamy Sausage Frittata.

(Prep + Cooking Time: 40 minutes | Servings: 4)

Ingredients:
- 4 beaten eggs
- 1/2 cup. cooked ground sausage
- 1 ½ cups. water
- 1/4 cup. grated sharp cheddar
- Black pepper to taste
- 2 tbsp. sour cream
- 1 tbsp. butter
- Salt to taste

Directions:
1. Pour water into the Instant Pot and lower in the steamer rack.
2. Grease a 6 - 7-inch soufflé dish
3. In a bowl, whisk the eggs and sour cream together
4. Add cheese, sausage, salt, and pepper. Stir
5. Pour into the dish and wrap tightly with foil all over
6. Lower into the steam rack and close the pot lid.
7. Hit "Manual" and then 17 minutes on "Low" pressure
8. Quick-release the pressure. Serve hot!

Tasty Sausage

(Prep + Cooking Time: 23 minutes | Servings: 5)

Ingredients:
- 1 (8-ounce) package unflavored tempeh
- 1 cup water
- 1 tbsp. olive oil
- 1 tsp. garlic powder
- 1 tsp. dried sage
- 1/2 tsp. dried oregano
- 2 tsp. vegan Worcestershire sauce
- 1 ½ tsp. smoked paprika
- 1 tsp. onion powder
- 1/2 tsp. salt or as your liking
- 1/4 tsp. freshly ground black pepper
- Pinch chili powder

Directions:
1. Select the "Sauté" Low mode on your instant pot. When the display reads "Hot," add the oil and heat until it begins to shimmer
2. With your hands, crumble the tempeh into the hot oil and stir to coat.
3. Add the Worcestershire sauce, paprika, onion powder, garlic powder, sage; oregano, salt, pepper and chili powder. Continue to sauté, stirring as needed, for 6 to 7 minutes more
4. Turn off the Instant Pot and add the water. Use your spoon to scrape up any bits of flavor that have stuck to the bottom of the pot. Stir well.
5. Lock the lid and turn the steam release handle to Sealing. Using the Manual function, set the cooker to High Pressure for 3 minutes
6. After completing the cooking time, quick release the pressure.
7. Remove the lid carefully. Select Sauté Low again and let the remaining liquid cook off. Taste and season with more salt, as needed

Sweet Potato Poblano Hash

(**Prep + Cooking Time:** 2 hours 10 minutes | **Servings:** 5)

Ingredients:
- 1 (14-ounce) package extra-firm tofu, pressed for at least 2 hours, crumbled in a food processor
- 1 small onion; diced
- 1 bell pepper, any color; diced
- 2 poblano peppers, roasted; cut into large dice
- 2 garlic cloves; minced
- 2 sweet potatoes; cut into large dice
- 1 cup water
- 1 to 2 tbsp. oil
- 1 tsp. ground turmeric
- 1/2 tsp. smoked paprika
- 1/2 tsp. kala namak; or sea salt
- 1 ½ tsp. Montreal chicken seasoning

Directions:
1. In the Instant Pot, combine the sweet potatoes and water
2. Lock the lid and turn the steam release handle to Sealing. Using the Manual function, set the cooker to High Pressure for 2 minutes.
3. While the sweet potatoes cook, heat a skillet over medium heat on your stovetop
4. Add the tofu crumbles, turmeric, paprika and kala namak. Cook for 4 to 5 minutes, stirring often, until the tofu gets a little crispy. Remove from the heat.
5. When the cooking time is complete, quick release the pressure
6. Remove the lid carefully and pour the contents of the inner pot into a colander or steamer basket to drain. Return the inner pot to the Instant Pot and set the sweet potatoes aside.
7. Select the "Sauté" Low mode on your instant pot. When the display reads "Hot," add 1 tbsp. of oil. Heat the oil until it shimmers
8. Add the onion and bell pepper. Cook for 2 to 3 minutes. Add the poblanos, garlic and Montreal chicken seasoning and cook for 1 minute more.
9. If the pot looks dry, add the remaining 1 tbsp. of oil. Add the sweet potatoes back to the pot. Cook for 2 to 3 minutes, stirring frequently. Turn off the Instant Pot and stir in the tofu. Mix well to combine and serve warm

Tofu & Potatoes Breakfast.

(**Prep + Cooking Time:** 15 minutes | **Servings:** 4)

Ingredients:
- 3 purple potatoes; cubed
- 1 yellow onion; chopped.
- 1 ½ cups Brussels sprouts
- 2 garlic cloves; minced.
- 1 carrot; chopped.
- 1 ginger root; grated
- 1/2 lb. firm tofu; cubed
- 1 tbsp. tamari
- Mexican spice blend to the taste
- 3 tbsp. water

Directions:
1. Set your instant pot on sauté mode; add onion and brown it for 1 minute.
2. Add potatoes, ginger, garlic, tofu, carrots, tamari, spices, Brussels sprouts and water, close the lid and cook at High for 2 minutes
3. Quick release the pressure, open the instant pot lid; transfer to plates and serve

Vanilla Polenta

(Prep + Cooking Time: 40 minutes | **Servings:** 4)

Ingredients:
- ⅓ cup packed light brown sugar
- 2 cups nondairy milk; or more as needed
- 1 cup polenta
- 2 cups water
- 1 tsp. salt or as your liking
- 1 ½ tsp. vanilla extract
- Fresh fruit; for topping

Directions:
1. In the Instant Pot, combine the polenta, water, milk and salt, stirring well to break up any lumps
2. Lock the lid and turn the steam release handle to Sealing. Using the Porridge function, set the cook time for 20 minutes.
3. After completing the cooking time, turn off the pressure cooker and let the pressure release naturally until the pin drops, about 10 to 15 minutes
4. Remove the lid carefully. There will be liquid on top, but once you stir it in, the polenta will be beautifully creamy!
5. Stir in the brown sugar and vanilla. Taste and add another pinch of salt, if you like, as well as more milk if you want it creamier. Top with the fruit and enjoy

Cheesy Hash Brown.

(Prep + Cooking Time: 10 minutes | **Servings:** 8)

Ingredients:
- 8 eggs
- 6 slices chopped bacon
- 1 cup. shredded cheddar cheese
- 1/4 cup. milk
- 1 tsp. salt
- 1/2 tsp. black pepper
- 2 cups. frozen hash browns

Directions:
1. Turn your Instant Pot to "Sauté" and cook the bacon until it becomes crispy.
2. Add hash browns and stir for 2 minutes, or until they start to thaw
3. In a bowl, whisk eggs, milk, cheese, and seasonings.
4. Pour over the hash browns in the pot, and lock and seal lid
5. Press "Manual" and adjust time to 5 minutes.
6. When time is up, hit "Cancel" and quick-release the pressure
7. Serve in slices.

Bircher Bowls with Yogurt

(Prep + Cooking Time: 23 minutes | **Servings:** 8)

Ingredients:
- 1 cup pure maple syrup
- 2 apples, cored and chopped into bite-size pieces.
- 1 (32-oz.) container low-fat plain yogurt
- ¼ cup unsalted sunflower seeds
- ¼ cup chia seeds
- ¼ cup unsalted pumpkin seeds
- 1 cup low-fat milk.
- ½ tsp. ground cinnamon
- 1 tsp. pure vanilla extract

Directions:
1. Combine the pumpkin seeds, sunflower seeds, chia seeds, apples, milk, vanilla extract, and cinnamon in the inner pot. Stir to combine
2. Now, Lock the lid. Select, "Manual or Pressure Cook" and set the pressure to *High* and the time to 3 minutes. Make sure the steam release knob is in the sealed position.
3. After completing the cooking cycle, quick release the pressure.
4. Unlock and remove the lid. Stir in the maple syrup. Serve the warm seed mixture over the yogurt in individual bowls

Breakfast Enchiladas.

(Prep + Cooking Time: 1 hour 15 minutes | **Servings:** 9)

Ingredients:
For Tofu Scramble:
- 1 small onion; cut into large dice
- 1 (14-ounce) package firm tofu, pressed for 30 to 60 minutes
- 1 medium or large tomato; diced
- 1 bell pepper, any color; cut into large dice
- 1 jalapeño pepper; diced
- 2 garlic cloves; minced
- 1/4 cup nutritional yeast
- 1 tsp. ground cumin
- 1/2 tsp. dried oregano
- 1/2 tsp. kala namak; or sea salt
- 1/2 tsp. ground turmeric
- 1 to 2 tbsp. olive oil
- Few pinches red pepper flakes
- Freshly ground black pepper

For Enchiladas:
- Nonstick cooking spray; for preparing the baking dish
- 1 batch Tempeh "Sausage"
- 12 (6-inch) tortillas; or 10 (8-inch)
- About 1 ¼ cups Red Hot Enchilada Sauce; or 1 (10-ounce) can red enchilada sauce
- 4 scallions, green and light green parts, sliced

To Make Tofu Scramble:
Directions:
1. In a small bowl (or in your tofu press), use a fork to crumble the tofu. Stir in the kala namak and turmeric. Set aside.
2. Select the "Sauté" Low mode on your instant pot. When the display reads "Hot," add the oil and heat until it shimmers.
3. Add the onion, bell pepper and jalapeño. Cook for 2 to 3 minutes, stirring frequently. Turn off the Instant Pot and add the garlic
4. The inner pot will still be hot. Let the veggies cook for another minute or so. Stir in the tomatoes, tofu mixture, nutritional yeast, cumin; oregano and red pepper flakes. Season to taste with salt and pepper.
5. Lock the lid and turn the steam release handle to Sealing. Using the Manual function, set the cooker to High Pressure for 2 minutes
6. After completing the cooking time, quick release the pressure
7. Remove the lid carefully. Select Sauté Low again and cook off the remaining liquid, 3 to 5 minutes, stirring frequently. Taste and adjust the seasonings as desired.

To Make Enchiladas:
1. Preheat the oven to 375°F. Spray the bottom of a 9-by-13-inch glass baking dish with nonstick spray.
2. To build your enchiladas, add 1 spoonful of tempeh sausage to a tortilla, followed by 2 to 3 spoonfuls of tofu scramble "as needed depending on size of tortillas" and roll tightly
3. Place in the prepared baking dish, seam-side down. Repeat for the remaining tortillas
4. Spoon about two-thirds of the enchilada sauce over the top and sprinkle on the scallions
5. Cover the dish with aluminum foil and bake for 20 minutes. Top as desired before serving.

Spiced Fruit

(Prep + Cooking Time: 16 minutes | **Servings:** 6)

Ingredients:
- 1 lb. sliced frozen peaches
- 2 ripe pears, sliced
- ¼ cup pure maple syrup
- 1 lb. frozen pineapple chunks
- 1 cup frozen and pitted dark sweet cherries
- 1 tsp. curry powder, plus more as needed
- Steel-cut oatmeal; for serving (optional)

Directions:
1. Combine the peaches, pineapple, cherries, pears, maple syrup and curry powder in the Instant Pot and secure the lid. Turn the steam release valve to Sealing and select *Manual/Pressure* Cook to cook on *High* pressure for 1 minute
2. Once the cooking cycle is completed, quickly move the steam release valve to Venting to release the steam pressure.
3. When the floating valve drops, remove the lid and stir the mixture well, adding more curry powder if you like it spicy
4. Serve the fruit warm, either as a side dish or as a topping for oatmeal. It is normal for the fruit to be sitting in its juices when this dish is done. Scoop it with a slotted spoon and let the juices drain back into the pot before serving

Egg, Ham and Cheese Bake

(**Prep + Cooking Time:** 60 minutes | **Servings:** 6)

Ingredients:
- 1 cup chopped ham (about ⅓ lb.)
- 1 cup shredded Cheddar cheese, divided.
- ½ cup low-fat milk.
- 8 eggs
- 1 cup water
- Nonstick cooking spray
- ¼ tsp. freshly ground black pepper.
- ¼ tsp. fine sea salt.

Directions:
1. Spray an 8-inch ceramic soufflé dish with the cooking spray
2. Place the trivet in the inner pot, then pour in the water.
3. If needed, make an aluminum sling (see here)
4. In a large bowl, whisk together the eggs, ham, milk, ½ cup of the cheese, and the salt and pepper.
5. Pour the mixture into the soufflé dish. Use the sling to lower the soufflé dish onto the trivet
6. Now, Lock the lid. Select, "Manual or Pressure Cook" and set the pressure to *High* and the time to 30 minutes. Make sure the steam release knob is in the sealed position.
7. After completing the cooking cycle, naturally release the pressure for 10 minutes, then quick release any remaining pressure. Unlock and remove the lid. Use the sling to remove the soufflé dish.
8. Sprinkle the remaining ½ cup of cheese on top of the casserole. Using a sharp knife, slice the casserole into wedges. Serve hot

Breakfast Millet Pilaf

(**Prep + Cooking Time:** 20 minutes | **Servings:** 4)

Ingredients:
- 2 cups organic millet
- 1 bay leaf
- 1-inch cinnamon stick
- 1 white onion; chopped.
- 1 tbsp. ghee
- 1 tsp. cardamom; crushed.
- 3 cups water
- 3 tsp. cumin seeds
- Salt to the taste

Directions:
1. Set your instant pot on sauté mode; add ghee and heat it up
2. Add cumin, cinnamon, cardamom and bay leaf, stir and cook for 1 minute.
3. Add onion; stir and cook for 4 minutes
4. Add millet, salt and water; then stir well. seal the instant pot lid and cook at High for 1 minute
5. Release the pressure naturally, fluff the mix with a fork, transfer to bowls and serve

Quinoa and Granola Bowls

(Prep + Cooking Time: 20 minutes | **Servings:** 4)

Ingredients:
- 1/2 to 1 cup nondairy milk
- 1 cup quinoa; rinsed
- 2 cups granola (any variety)
- 2 cups Fresh Fruit Compote
- 1 ½ cups water
- 2 tbsp. maple syrup
- 1 tsp. vanilla extract
- 1/2 tsp. ground cinnamon
- Pinch salt
- Sliced bananas; for topping (If you like)
- Toasted walnuts; for topping (If you like)

Directions:
1. In the Instant Pot, combine the quinoa, water, maple syrup, vanilla, cinnamon and salt
2. Lock the lid and turn the steam release handle to Sealing. Using the Manual function, set the cooker to High Pressure for 8 minutes
3. After completing the cooking time, let the pressure release naturally for 10 minutes; quick release any remaining pressure.
4. Remove the lid carefully and stir the quinoa. Add enough milk to get the desired consistency.
5. Spoon the quinoa mix into bowls and top with granola, compote and any additional toppings, as desired

Scotch Eggs

(Prep + Cooking Time: 25 minutes | **Servings:** 4)

Ingredients:
- 1 lb. sausage; ground.
- 1 tbsp. vegetable oil
- 4 eggs
- 2 cups water

Directions:
1. Put the eggs in the instant pot, add 1 cup water, seal the instant pot lid and cook at High for 6 minutes
2. Release the pressure naturally for 6 minutes, then release remaining pressure by turning the valve to 'Venting', and carefully open the lid.
3. Remove the eggs and put them in a bowl filled with ice water
4. Peel the eggs and place them on a working surface
5. Divide sausage mix into 4 balls; flatten them, place 1 egg in the center of each sausage piece, wrap meat around each egg and put them all on a plate
6. Set your instant pot on Sauté mode; add the oil and heat it up
7. Add scotch eggs, brown them on each side and transfer them to a plate.
8. Add the rest of the water to your instant pot; arrange the eggs in the steamer basket of the pot, close the instant pot lid and cook at High for 6 minutes more
9. Quick release the pressure; divide the eggs among plates and serve.

Berry Toast Casserole

(Prep + Cooking Time: 30 minutes | **Servings:** 5)

Ingredients:
- 5 cups cubed, stale French bread
- 1 ½ cups fresh blueberries and strawberries (halve or quarter the strawberries)
- 1 cup water
- 1/2 cup applesauce
- 1 tsp. vanilla extract
- 1 tsp. ground cinnamon
- 1/4 tsp. kala namak; or sea salt
- 1/4 cup maple syrup, plus more for topping
- Nonstick cooking spray; for preparing the bowl
- Vegan butter; for topping

Directions:
1. Spray a 7-cup oven-safe glass bowl with nonstick spray. Pour the water into the Instant Pot and place a trivet inside the inner pot
2. In a large bowl, whisk the applesauce, maple syrup, vanilla, cinnamon and kala namak.
3. Quickly toss the bread and berries in the apple mixture, making sure to get even coverage
4. Transfer the mixture to the prepared bowl and cover tightly with aluminum foil. Place the bowl on top of the trivet in the Instant Pot
5. Lock the lid and turn the steam release handle to Sealing. Using the Manual function, set the cooker to High Pressure for 25 minutes.
6. After completing the cooking time, quick release the pressure. Remove the lid carefully and serve with desired toppings

Breakfast Pudding

(**Prep + Cooking Time:** 15 minutes | **Servings:** 4)

Ingredients:
- 1/3 cup tapioca pearls
- 1/2 cup sugar
- 1 ¼ cup whole milk
- 1 ½ cups water
- Zest from 1/2 lemon

Directions:
1. Put 1 cup water in your instant pot
2. Put tapioca pearls in a heat proof bowl add milk, 1/2 cup water, lemon zest and sugar
3. Stir everything, place the bowl in the steamer basket of the pot, close the instant pot lid and cook at High for 10 minutes
4. Quick release the pressure; transfer pudding to cups and serve

Bacon, Egg & Cheese Muffins.

(**Prep + Cooking Time:** 25 minutes | **Servings:** 8)

Ingredients:
- 4 eggs
- 4 tbsp. cheddar or pepper jack cheese, shredded.
- 1 green onion, diced.
- 1 ½ cup. water, for the pot
- 4 slices bacon; cooked and crumbled.
- 1/4 tsp. lemon pepper seasoning

Directions:
1. Pour the water into the Instant Pot container and then put a steamer basket into the pot. In a large-sized measuring bowl with a pour pout, break the eggs.
2. Add the lemon pepper and beat well. Divide the bacon, cheese, and green onion between 4 silicone muffin cups.
3. Pour the egg mix into each muffin cups; with a fork, stir using a fork to combine. Put the muffin cups. onto the steamer basket, close the lid.
4. Set the pressure on "High" pressure and the timer to 8 minutes
5. When the timer beeps, turn off the pot, wait for 2 minutes, and then turn the steam valve to quick release the pressure. Carefully open the pot lid, lift the steamer basket out from the container, and then remove the muffin cups.
6. Serve warm and enjoy!

Tips: These muffins can be stored in the refrigerator for more than 1 week. When ready to serve, just microwave for 30 seconds on "High" to reheat

Beef Roast

(Prep + Cooking Time: 50 minutes | **Servings:** 8)

Ingredients:
- 4 lb. beef roast; cut into small chunks
- 2 tbsp. brown sugar
- 2 ½ tsp. garlic powder
- 2 tsp. mustard powder
- 2 tsp. onion flakes
- 2 tsp. paprika
- 2 tbsp. Worcestershire sauce
- 4 tbsp. butter; soft
- 8 hoagie rolls
- 1 tbsp. balsamic vinegar
- 8 slices provolone cheese
- 3 cups beef stock
- Salt and black pepper to the taste

Directions:
1. Put the meat in your instant pot.
2. Add salt, pepper, paprika, 2 teaspoon garlic powder, mustard powder, onion flakes, stock, vinegar and Worcestershire sauce, stir well, seal the instant pot lid and cook at High for 40 minutes
3. Quick release the pressure, transfer meat to a cutting board, strain the liquid and keep it in a bowl
4. Shred meat and divide among rolls after you've buttered them
5. Add provolone cheese on top, introduce sandwiches in preheated broiler and broil until cheese melts.
6. Dip sandwiches in the sauce from the pot and serve them.

Pumpkin Butter Breakfast

(Prep + Cooking Time: 25 minutes | **Servings:** 18)

Ingredients:
- 30 oz. pumpkin puree
- 3 apples; peeled; cored and chopped.
- 1/2 cup honey
- 12 oz. apple cider
- 1 tbsp. pumpkin spice
- 1 cup sugar
- A pinch of salt

Directions:
1. In your instant pot; mix pumpkin puree with pumpkin spice, apple pieces, sugar, honey, cider and a pinch of salt
2. Stir well, seal the instant pot lid and cook at High for 10 minutes.
3. Release the pressure naturally for 15 minutes, transfer the butter to small jars and keep it in the fridge until you serve it.

Tofu and Potato Casserole

(Prep + Cooking Time: 2 hours | **Servings:** 5)

Ingredients:
- 2 cups frozen hash browns, thawed
- 1 (14-ounce) package firm tofu, pressed for 30 to 60 minutes
- ⅓ cup nutritional yeast
- 1/4 cup nondairy milk
- 1 batch Tempeh "Sausage"
- 1 cup water
- 1/4 tsp. freshly ground black pepper, plus more for seasoning
- 1 tsp. garlic powder
- 1 tsp. ground cumin
- 1 tsp. kala namak; or sea salt
- 1 tsp. onion powder
- 1/2 tsp. dried oregano
- Sliced scallion, green and light green parts; for serving
- Garden Salsa; for serving
- Nonstick cooking spray; for preparing the pan
- Hot sauce; for serving
- Cashew Sour Cream; for serving

Directions:
1. Lightly coat the bottom of a 7-inch springform pan with nonstick spray and set aside. In a large bowl, toss the hash browns with salt to taste and pepper and set aside
2. In a food processor, combine the tofu, yeast, milk, kala namak, onion powder, garlic powder, cumin and oregano. Blend until smooth
3. Add the tempeh sausage to the hash browns along with one-fourth of the tofu mixture. Stir to combine.
4. Layer this mixture on the bottom of the prepared pan. Top with the remaining tofu mixture. Cover the pan with a paper towel and wrap it tightly in aluminum foil
5. Pour the water into your Instant Pot and place a trivet inside the inner pot. Put the springform pan on the trivet.
6. Lock the lid and turn the steam release handle to Sealing. Using the Manual function, set the cooker to High Pressure for 52 minutes
7. After completing the cooking time, quick release the pressure.
8. Remove the lid carefully and remove the pan from the Instant Pot. Take off the foil and paper towel. Let cool before releasing the sides of the pan. Serve topped as desired

Sweet Potato Poblano Hash

(**Prep + Cooking Time:** 2 hours 10 minutes | **Servings:** 5)

Ingredients:
- 1 (14-ounce) package extra-firm tofu, pressed for at least 2 hours, crumbled in a food processor
- 1 small onion; diced
- 1 bell pepper, any color; diced
- 2 poblano peppers, roasted; cut into large dice
- 2 garlic cloves; minced
- 2 sweet potatoes; cut into large dice
- 1 cup water
- 1 to 2 tbsp. oil
- 1 tsp. ground turmeric
- 1/2 tsp. smoked paprika
- 1/2 tsp. sea salt
- 1 ½ tsp. Montreal chicken seasoning

Directions:
1. In the Instant Pot, combine the sweet potatoes and water.
2. Lock the lid and turn the steam release handle to Sealing. Using the Manual function, set the cooker to High Pressure for 2 minutes
3. While the sweet potatoes cook, heat a skillet over medium heat on your stovetop.
4. Add the tofu crumbles, turmeric, paprika and kala namak. Cook for 4 to 5 minutes, stirring often, until the tofu gets a little crispy. Remove from the heat
5. When the cooking time is complete, quick release the pressure
6. Remove the lid carefully and pour the contents of the inner pot into a colander or steamer basket to drain. Return the inner pot to the Instant Pot and set the sweet potatoes aside.
7. Select the "Sauté" Low mode on your instant pot. When the display reads "Hot," add 1 tbsp. of oil. Heat the oil until it shimmers
8. Add the onion and bell pepper. Cook for 2 to 3 minutes. Add the poblanos, garlic and Montreal chicken seasoning and cook for 1 minute more
9. If the pot looks dry, add the remaining 1 tbsp. of oil. Add the sweet potatoes back to the pot. Cook for 2 to 3 minutes, stirring frequently. Turn off the Instant Pot and stir in the tofu. Mix well to combine and serve warm.

Potatoes Breakfast Salad

(Prep + Cooking Time: 15 minutes | **Servings:** 4)

Ingredients:
- 6 potatoes, peeled and cubed
- 1 ½ cups water
- 1 cup homemade mayonnaise
- 1/4 cup onion; finely chopped
- 1 tbsp. dill pickle juice
- 2 tbsp. parsley; finely chopped
- 1 tbsp. mustard
- 4 eggs
- Salt and black pepper to the taste

Directions:
1. Put potatoes, eggs and the water in the steamer basket of your instant pot, close the lid and cook on High for 4 minutes
2. Quick release the pressure, transfer eggs to a bowl filled with ice water and leave them to cool down
3. In a bowl, mix mayo with pickle juice, onion, parsley and mustard and stir well
4. Add potatoes and toss to coat
5. Peel eggs, chop them, add them to salad and toss again.
6. Add salt and pepper to the taste; stir and serve your salad with toasted bread slices.

Spinach, Bacon & Eggs.

(Prep + Cooking Time: 15 minutes | **Servings:** 4)

Ingredients:
- 7 oz. bacon
- 3 tbsp. cream
- 1/2 cup. spinach
- 2 tsp. butter
- 4 eggs, boiled
- 1 tsp. cilantro
- 1/2 tsp. ground white pepper

Directions:
1. Slice the bacon and sprinkle it with the ground white pepper, and cilantro. Stir the mixture
2. Peel eggs and wrap them in the spinach leaves
3. Then wrap the eggs in the sliced bacon
4. Set the Instant Pot mode MEAT/STEW and transfer the wrapped eggs
5. Add butter and cook the dish for 10 minutes.
6. When the time is over - remove the eggs from the Instant Pot and sprinkle them with the cream.
7. Serve the dish hot.

Poached Tomatoes and Eggs.

(Prep + Cooking Time: 15 minutes | **Servings:** 4)

Ingredients:
- 4 eggs
- 1 tbsp. olive oil
- 1 tbsp. fresh dill
- 3 medium tomatoes
- 1/2 tsp. white pepper
- 1/2 tsp. paprika
- 1 red onion
- 1 tsp. salt

Directions:
1. Spray the ramekins with the olive oil inside. Beat the eggs in every ramekin.
2. Combine the paprika, white pepper, fresh dill, and salt together in the mixing bowl. Stir the mixture.
3. After this, chop the red onion.
4. Chop the tomatoes into the tiny pieces and combine them with the onion. Stir the mixture.
5. Then sprinkle the eggs with the tomato mixture.
6. Add spice mixture and transfer the eggs to the Instant Pot.
7. Close the lid and set the Instant Pot mode STEAM
8. Cook the dish for 5 minutes. Then remove the dish from the Instant Pot and chill it little.
9. Serve the dish immediately. Enjoy!

Scrambled Eggs & Bacon.

(**Prep + Cooking Time:** 15 minutes | **Servings:** 4)

Ingredients:
- 7 eggs
- 1/2 cup. milk
- 1 tsp. basil
- 1/4 cup. fresh parsley
- 4 oz. bacon
- 1 tsp. salt
- 1 tsp. paprika
- 1 tbsp. butter
- 1 tbsp. cilantro

Directions:
1. Beat the eggs in the mixing bowl and whisk them well.
2. Then add milk, basil, salt, paprika, and cilantro. Stir the mixture. Chop the bacon and parsley.
3. Set the Instant Pot mode "Sauté" and transfer the chopped bacon. Cook it for 3 minutes
4. Then add whisked egg mixture and cook the dish for 5 minutes more.
5. After this, mix up the eggs carefully with the help of the wooden spoon
6. Then sprinkle the dish with the chopped parsley and cook it for 4 minutes more.
7. When the eggs are cooked - remove them from the Instant Pot.
8. Serve the dish immediately. Enjoy!

Healthy Tasty Oats

(**Prep + Cooking Time:** 24 minutes | **Servings:** 5)

Ingredients:
- 2 cups steel cut oats
- 1/2 cup chia seeds
- 1 cup chopped walnuts
- 1 cup fresh blueberries
- 4 ½ cups water
- 1 cup nondairy milk
- 2 tbsp. agave; or maple syrup; optional
- 1/4 tsp. salt; optional

Directions:
1. In the Instant Pot, stir together the oats and water
2. Lock the lid and turn the steam release handle to Sealing. Using the Manual function, set the cooker to High Pressure for 12 minutes
3. After completing the cooking time, turn off the Instant Pot. Let the pressure release naturally for 10 minutes; quick release any remaining pressure.
4. Remove the lid carefully and add the milk. Stir in the agave and salt and top with the chia seeds, walnuts and blueberries

Breakfast Berries Jam

(**Prep + Cooking Time:** 1 hour and 30 minutes | **Servings:** 12)

Ingredients:
- 16 oz. cranberries
- 4 oz. raisins
- 3 oz. water
- 2 ½ lb. sugar
- 16 oz. strawberries; chopped.
- Zest from 1 lemon
- A pinch of salt

Directions:
1. In your instant pot; mix strawberries with cranberries, lemon zest, and raisins.
2. Add sugar, stir and leave pot aside to 1 hour
3. Add water and a pinch of salt, seal the instant pot lid and cook at High for 15 minutes
4. Quick release the pressure, leave jam aside for 5 minutes; then stir well. pour into small jars and enjoy!
5. Serve with toasted bread slices!

Banana Oat Cake

(Prep + Cooking Time: 65 minutes | **Servings:** 7)

Ingredients:
- 1 cup quick-cooking oats
- ½ cup coconut sugar
- 2 eggs
- ½ cup mashed ripe banana (1 large banana)
- ½ cup almond butter
- ½ tsp. cinnamon
- ¼ tsp. fine sea salt
- ½ tsp. baking soda

Directions:
1. Line a 7-inch round pan with a piece of parchment paper and set it aside. Take a large bowl, combine the banana, almond butter, coconut sugar, eggs, baking soda, cinnamon and salt. Stir well to break up any lumps, then stir in the oats. Pour the batter into the prepared pan and use a spatula to even out the top
2. Pour 1 cup water into the Instant Pot and arrange the trivet (Which comes with your instant pot) on the bottom. Place the pan on top of the trivet.
3. To protect the cake from condensation, cover it with an upside-down plate or another piece of parchment paper
4. Secure the lid and move the pressure valve to Sealing. Select *Manual/Pressure* Cook to cook on *High* pressure for 40 minutes, then let the pressure naturally release for 10 minutes.
5. Turn the steam release valve to Venting to release any remaining steam. When the floating valve drops, remove the lid
6. Use oven mitts to lift the trivet and the pan out of the pot. Let the cake cool completely in the pan to firm up, about 30 minutes, then remove the cake from the pan. Slice and serve at room temperature or chilled

Tofu Scramble Recipe.

(Prep + Cooking Time: 18 minutes | **Servings:** 4)

Ingredients:
- 12 oz. canned tomatoes, diced
- 1 yellow onion; thinly sliced
- 1 tsp. walnut oil
- 3 garlic cloves; minced.
- 1/4 cup veggie stock
- 1 cup carrot; chopped.
- 1 block firm tofu; drained
- 1 tsp. cumin
- 2 tbsp. red pepper; chopped.
- 1 tbsp. Italian seasoning
- 1 tsp. nutritional yeast
- Salt and black pepper to the taste

Directions:
1. Set your instant pot on Sauté mode; add oil and heat it up.
2. Add onion, carrot and garlic, stir and cook for 3 minutes.
3. Crumble tofu, add it to pot and stir
4. Add stock, red pepper, tomatoes, cumin, Italian seasoning, salt and pepper; then stir well. seal the instant pot lid and cook at High for 4 minutes
5. Quick release the pressure, transfer to bowls and serve with nutritional yeast on top.

Breakfast Bread Pudding

(Prep + Cooking Time: 35 minutes | **Servings:** 6)

Ingredients:
- 14 oz. loaf and bread; cubed.
- 1 cup water
- 1 cup Swiss cheese; grated
- 1 cup mushrooms; sliced
- 4 tbsp. butter
- 1 cup onions; thinly sliced.
- 3 eggs; whisked.
- 2 cups half and half
- 1/2 tsp. thyme; dried.
- 1/2 tsp. mustard; dry
- Salt and black pepper to taste
- 1 cup ham; diced.
- 1/4 cup sugar
- Cooking spray

For the sauce:
- 1 ½ tsp. rice wine vinegar
- 1/2 cup mustard.
- 2 tbsp. maple syrup
- Salt and black pepper to taste

Directions:
1. Heat up a pan over medium heat; add butter and melt it.
2. Add onions, stir and cook for 2 minutes.
3. Add ham, stir again, cook for 2 minutes more, take off heat and leave aside
4. Spray a pan with some cooking oil
5. In a bowl; mix eggs with sugar, half and half, thyme, half of the Swiss cheese, salt, pepper, bread cubes, mushroom, ham and onions mix and stir well.
6. Pour this into greased pan, place it in the steamer basket of your instant pot, also add the water in the instant pot, cover with tin foil, close the instant pot lid and cook on High for 25 minutes
7. Meanwhile; heat up a small pot over medium heat, add dry mustard, salt, pepper, vinegar and maple syrup, stir well and cook for 2 - 3 minutes.
8. Release pressure from the pot; uncover, take the pan out, sprinkle the rest of the cheese, introduce in preheated broil and brown for a few minutes.
9. Divide bread pudding on plates; drizzle the sauce on top and serve

Easy Egg Muffins

(Prep + Cooking Time: 20 minutes | **Servings:** 4)

Ingredients:
- 4 eggs
- 4 bacon slices; cooked and crumbled.
- 1 green onion; chopped.
- 1 ½ cups water
- 4 tbsp. cheddar cheese; shredded.
- 1/4 tsp. lemon pepper
- A pinch of salt

Directions:
1. In a bowl, mix eggs with a pinch of salt and lemon pepper and whisk well
2. Divide green onion, bacon and cheese into muffin cups
3. Add eggs and stir a bit
4. Pour the water in your instant pot, add muffin cups in the steamer basket, seal the Instant Pot lid and cook at High for 10 minutes.
5. Quick release the pressure, divide the egg muffins among plates and serve them right away

Peaches Steel-Cut Oatmeal

(Prep + Cooking Time: 34 minutes | **Servings:** 4)

Ingredients:
- 1 lb. frozen sliced peaches
- ¼ cup pure maple syrup
- 2 cups steel-cut oats
- 4 cups water
- ½ tsp. ground cinnamon., plus more for serving. (optional)
- ½ cup full-fat coconut milk, plus more for serving. (optional)

Directions:
1. Combine the steel-cut oats and water in the Instant Pot and give them a stir, then add the peaches, cinnamon and maple syrup
2. Now, Lock the lid and Turn the steam release valve to "Sealing" Position. Select *Manual/Pressure* Cook to cook on *High* pressure for 4 minutes.
3. When the cooking cycle has completed, let the pressure naturally release for 15 minutes to finish cooking the oatmeal
4. Turn the steam release valve to Venting to release any remaining steam pressure. When the floating valve drops, remove the lid. Stir in the coconut milk, then taste and adjust any seasonings. Serve warm

Easy and Cheesy Grits

(Prep + Cooking Time: 20 minutes | **Servings:** 4)

Ingredients:
- 4 oz. cheddar cheese; grated
- 1 ¾ cup half and half
- 2 tbsp. coconut oil
- 1 cup stone ground grits
- 3 cups water
- 2 tsp. salt
- 3 tbsp. butter
- Butter for serving

Directions:
1. Set your instant pot on sauté mode; add grits, stir them for 3 minutes.
2. Add oil, half, and half, water, salt, butter and cheese; then stir well. close the instant pot lid and cook on High for 10 minutes.
3. Release the pressure naturally, leave cheesy grits aside for 15 minutes, transfer to breakfast bowls; add butter on top and serve

Pumpkin Oatmeal

(Prep + Cooking Time: 23 minutes | **Servings:** 6)

Ingredients:
- ½ cup pumpkin purée
- 4 cups low-fat milk
- ¼ cup pure maple syrup
- ¼ cup chopped unsalted almonds
- 2 cups rolled oats
- ⅛ tsp. fine sea salt.
- 1 tsp. pure vanilla extract
- ½ tsp. ground cinnamon

Directions:
1. Combine the milk, oats, pumpkin, vanilla extract, cinnamon, and salt in the inner pot. Mix well
2. Now, Lock the lid. Select, "Manual or Pressure Cook" and set the pressure to *High* and the time to 3 minutes. Make sure the steam release knob is in the sealed position.
3. After completing the cooking cycle, quick release the pressure. Unlock and remove the lid. Stir in the maple syrup and almonds. Serve hot

Strawberry Oats

(Prep + Cooking Time: 45 minutes | **Servings:** 5)

Ingredients:

For Maple-Toasted Walnuts:
- 1/2 cup maple syrup
- 3 cups walnut halves
- 1/2 tsp. salt

For Oats:
- 2 cups strawberries; chopped or sliced
- 2 ½ cups unsweetened nondairy milk; divided
- 1/2 cup packed light brown sugar
- 2 ½ cups water
- 2 cups steel cut oats
- 2 tsp. vanilla extract
- 1/4 tsp. salt

Directions:

To Make Maple-Toasted Walnuts:
1. Cover a heat-resistant flat surface with parchment paper. On your stovetop, heat a skillet over medium-high heat
2. Add the walnuts, maple syrup and salt. Cook for 3 to 4 minutes, stirring frequently; or until the maple syrup has caramelized and the walnuts are toasted.
3. Pour the mixture onto the parchment-covered surface, spreading it out so it doesn't clump into one large piece. Let cool. Break into bite-size pieces

To Make Oats:
1. In the Instant Pot, combine the oats, water, 2 cups of milk, the vanilla and salt. Stir well. Lock the lid and turn the steam release handle to Sealing. Using the Manual function, set the cooker to High Pressure for 12 minutes
2. After completing the cooking time, turn off the Instant Pot. Let the pressure release naturally for 10 minutes; quick release any remaining pressure.
3. Remove the lid carefully and stir in the remaining ½ cup of milk, the strawberries and brown sugar. Top individual servings with the toasted walnuts

Granola Bars

(Prep + Cooking Time: 40 minutes | **Makes:** 10)

Ingredients:
- ⅓ cup dried cranberries or raisins
- ½ cup raw pumpkin seeds (pepitas)
- 1 cup quick-cooking oats
- ⅓ cup pure maple syrup
- ½ cup all-natural peanut butter
- 1 tbsp. extra-virgin olive oil
- ¼ tsp. fine sea salt
- Line a 7-inch round pan with parchment paper.

Directions:
1. Take a large bowl, combine the oats, maple syrup, peanut butter, olive oil and salt and stir well. Fold in the dried fruit and pumpkin seeds, then pour the batter into the prepared pan, using a spatula to press the mixture evenly into the bottom of the pan
2. Pour 1 cup water into the Instant Pot and arrange the trivet (Which comes with your instant pot) on the bottom.
3. Place the pan on top of the trivet. Cover the pan with an upside-down plate or another piece of parchment to protect the granola bars from condensation
4. Secure the lid, moving the steam release valve to Sealing. Select *Manual/Pressure* Cook to cook on *High* pressure for 20 minutes.
5. Release the pressure naturally for 10 minutes, then move the steam release valve to Venting. When the floating valve drops, remove the lid. Use oven mitts to lift the trivet and the pan out of the pot. Let the granola cool completely in the pan, at least 1 hour

6. Cut the cooled granola into 10 pieces. The round pan will make the bars uneven in size, but you can cut them into uniform wedges if you'd prefer. Wrap them individually in plastic wrap

Breakfast Huevos Rancheros

(Prep + Cooking Time: 17 minutes | Servings: 6)

Ingredients:
- 6 corn tortillas
- 6 eggs
- ½ red onion; chopped.
- 1 green bell pepper; seeded and chopped.
- 1½ cups cooked black beans, or one 15-oz. can black beans, drained and rinsed
- 1½ cups prepared salsa, plus more for serving.
- ½ cup water
- 1 tbsp. extra-virgin olive oil
- 1 tsp. ground cumin
- ⅛ tsp. cayenne pepper (optional)
- Fine sea salt and freshly ground black pepper
- Chopped green onions, crumbled feta cheese, sliced avocado and chopped fresh cilantro; for garnish. (optional)

Directions:
1. Press the *Sauté* button and add the olive oil to the Instant Pot. Once the oil is hot but not smoking, add the onion and bell pepper and sauté until tender, about 6 minutes
2. Press *Cancel* Button, then stir in the cumin and cayenne with a wooden spoon or spatula while the pot is still hot.
3. Add the beans, salsa and water to the pot and stir well, scraping the bottom to make sure nothing sticks. Carefully crack the eggs into the salsa, keeping them spaced at least 1 inch apart. Sprinkle salt and black pepper on top of each egg
4. Now, Lock the lid and Turn the steam release valve to "Sealing" Position. Select *Manual/Pressure* Cook and cook on *High* pressure for 0 minutes (Sure set it to 0 minutes).
5. When the pot has come to pressure and the screen reads L0:00, quickly release the pressure by immediately moving the steam release valve to Venting
6. When the floating valve drops, remove the lid and use a slotted spoon to scoop the eggs and some of the salsa mixture onto a tortilla. Top with additional salsa and the garnishes of your choice and serve immediately

Pomegranate Porridge

(Prep + Cooking Time: 8 minutes | Servings: 2)

Ingredients:
- Seeds from 1 pomegranate
- 1 cup porridge oats
- 1 cup water
- 3/4 cup pomegranate juice
- A pinch of salt

Directions:
1. Put oats in your instant pot
2. Add water, a pinch of salt and pomegranate juice; then stir well. seal the instant pot lid and cook at High for 2 minutes
3. Release the pressure naturally; add pomegranate seeds, stir well; divide into bowls and serve.

Chocolate Steel Cut Oats

(Prep + Cooking Time: 25 minutes | Servings: 5)

Ingredients:
- 2 cups steel cut oats
- 2 ½ cups nondairy milk; divided; or more as needed
- 1/4 cup chocolate chips
- 1/4 cup peanut butter
- 2 ½ cups water
- 2 tbsp. agave; or maple syrup
- 1/4 tsp. salt or as your liking

Directions:
1. In Your Instant Pot, combine the oats, water, 2 cups of milk, the salt and chocolate chips. Stir to mix
2. Lock the lid and turn the steam release handle to Sealing. Using the Manual function, set the cooker to High Pressure for 12 minutes.
3. After completing the cooking time, turn off the pressure cooker
4. Let the pressure release naturally for 10 minutes; quick release any remaining pressure.
5. Add the remaining ½ cup of milk "more if you want the oats thinner". Stir in the peanut butter and agave and enjoy

Note: Inner pot of your pressure cooker is never filled more than halfway when cooking oats or the foam may clog the pressure release valve.

Sweet Potato Mini Quiche

(**Prep + Cooking Time:** 37 minutes | Makes: 7 Quiches)

Ingredients:
- 1 (14-ounce) package firm tofu, lightly pressed
- 1 cup plus 1 tbsp. water
- 1/2 cup shredded sweet potato
- 1/4 cup nutritional yeast
- 1 tbsp. cornstarch
- 1/4 cup nondairy milk
- 1 tsp. kala namak; or sea salt or as your liking
- 1/2 tsp. garlic powder
- 1/2 tsp. onion powder
- 1/2 tsp. ground turmeric
- Handful kale leaves; chopped small
- Nonstick cooking spray; for preparing the mold
- Vegan-buttered toast; for serving
- Freshly ground black pepper

Directions:
1. Lightly coat an 8¼-inch silicone egg-bites mold with nonstick spray and set aside
2. In a food processor, combine the tofu, milk, yeast, cornstarch, kala namak, garlic powder, onion powder and turmeric. Blend until smooth.
3. Select the "Sauté" Low mode on your instant pot. When the display reads "Hot," add the sweet potato, kale and 1 tbsp. of water. Sauté for 1 to 2 minutes
4. Note: You may need to turn off the Instant Pot if the vegetables start to stick to the bottom, but that's okay because it stays hot.
5. Stir the veggies into the tofu mixture and spoon the mixture into the prepared mold. Cover the mold tightly with aluminum foil and place on a trivet. Add the remaining 1 cup of water to the inner pot and use the trivet's handles to lower the trivet and mold into the pot
6. Lock the lid and turn the steam release handle to Sealing. Using the Manual function, set the cooker to High Pressure for 18 minutes.
7. After completing the cooking time, let the pressure release naturally for 10 minutes; quick release any remaining pressure
8. Remove the lid carefully. Remove the silicone mold from the Instant Pot and pull off the foil. Leave the mold on the trivet and let cool for a few minutes.
9. The bites will continue to firm as they cool. When ready to eat, schmear the tofu bites onto a piece of vegan-buttered toast and top with a little salt and pepper

Sausage and Potato Hash

(**Prep + Cooking Time:** 45 minutes | **Servings:**6)

Ingredients:
- 1 lb. uncooked chorizo; sliced. into ¾-inch-thick pieces
- 1 cup low-sodium chicken broth.
- 2 garlic cloves; minced.
- 1 yellow onion; diced.
- 6 medium white potatoes, peeled and cut into bite-size pieces.
- 1 tbsp. balsamic vinegar
- 1 tbsp. extra-virgin olive oil.
- ½ tsp. freshly ground black pepper.
- ½ tsp. dried rosemary

Directions:
1. Select *Sauté* and add the olive oil to the inner pot. Once the oil is hot, add the chorizo, garlic, onion, and rosemary. *Sauté* for 3 minutes, stirring occasionally
2. Press Cancel, then pour the broth into the pot. Use a wooden spoon to scrape up any pieces of food stuck to the bottom of the pot. Add the potatoes to the pot and stir to combine
3. Now, Lock the lid. Select, "Manual or Pressure Cook" and set the pressure to *High* and the time to 10 minutes. Make sure the steam release knob is in the sealed position.
4. After completing the cooking cycle, naturally release the pressure for 10 minutes, then quick release any remaining pressure. Unlock and remove the lid. Stir in the black pepper and vinegar. Serve hot

Veggie Frittatas

(**Prep + Cooking Time:** 38 minutes | **Servings:** 4)

Ingredients:
- 1 cup chopped spinach
- ¼ cup crumbled feta cheese
- 6 eggs
- 1 red bell pepper; seeded and chopped.
- 3 green onions, tender white and green parts only; chopped.
- ½ tsp. fine sea salt
- Freshly ground black pepper

Directions:
1. Combine the eggs, salt, bell pepper, green onions, spinach, feta and a few grinds of black pepper in a mixing bowl and stir well
2. Grease four 8-oz. mason jars with olive oil and then divide the mixture evenly among the jars.
3. Pour 1 cup water into the Instant Pot and arrange the trivet (Which comes with your instant pot) on the bottom
4. Place the four jars in a single layer on the trivet and secure the lid. Turn the steam release valve to Sealing and select *Manual/Pressure* Cook to cook on *High* pressure for 8 minutes
5. Release the pressure naturally for 10 minutes, then move the steam release valve to Venting to release any remaining steam.
6. When the floating valve drops, remove the lid. Use oven mitts to remove the jars. Tip the frittatas out of the jars and onto plates to serve warm

Apple Porridge

(**Prep + Cooking Time:** 24 minutes | **Servings:** 4)

Ingredients:
- 1 apple, chopped
- 1/2 to 1 cup nondairy milk
- 1 cup quinoa; rinsed
- 1 ½ cups water
- 2 tbsp. ground cinnamon
- 2 tbsp. maple syrup
- 1/2 tsp. vanilla extract
- 1/2 tsp. salt or as your liking

Directions:
1. In the Instant Pot, stir together the quinoa, water, maple syrup, cinnamon, vanilla, salt and apple
2. Lock the lid and turn the steam release handle to Sealing. Using the Manual function, set the cooker to High Pressure for 8 minutes.
3. After completing the cooking time, let the pressure release naturally for 10 minutes; quick release any remaining pressure
4. Remove the lid carefully and stir in as much milk as needed to make it creamy.
5. If you didn't cook the apples, add them now and put the cover back on for 1 to 2 minutes to warm them

Cinnamon Cereal Bowls

(Prep + Cooking Time: 25 minutes | **Servings:** 6)

Ingredients:
- ¼ cup pure maple syrup
- 2 cups buckwheat groats, soaked for at least 20 minutes and up to overnight
- 3 cups water
- ¼ tsp. fine sea salt
- 1 tsp. ground cinnamon.
- 1 tsp. vanilla extract
- Almond milk; for serving
- Chopped or sliced fresh fruit; for serving

Directions:
1. Drain and rinse the buckwheat, then combine it with the water, cinnamon, maple syrup, vanilla and salt in the Instant Pot and secure the lid
2. Turn the steam release valve to Sealing and select *Manual/Pressure* Cook to cook on *High* pressure for 1 minute.
3. Release the pressure naturally for 10 minutes before moving the steam release valve to Venting. When the floating valve drops, carefully remove the lid and stir the cooked grains
4. Serve the buckwheat right away with almond milk and fresh fruit

Breakfast Enchiladas.

(Prep + Cooking Time: 1 hour 15 minutes | **Servings:** 9)

Ingredients:
For Tofu Scramble:
- 1 small onion; cut into large dice
- 1 (14-ounce) package firm tofu, pressed for 30 to 60 minutes
- 1 medium or large tomato; diced
- 1 bell pepper, any color; cut into large dice
- 1 jalapeño pepper; diced
- 2 garlic cloves; minced
- 1/4 cup nutritional yeast
- 1 tsp. ground cumin
- 1/2 tsp. dried oregano
- 1/2 tsp. kala namak; or sea salt
- 1/2 tsp. ground turmeric
- 1 to 2 tbsp. olive oil
- Few pinches red pepper flakes
- Freshly ground black pepper

For Enchiladas:
- Nonstick cooking spray; for preparing the baking dish
- 1 batch Tempeh "Sausage"
- 12 (6-inch) tortillas; or 10 (8-inch)
- About 1 ¼ cups Red Hot Enchilada Sauce; or 1 (10-ounce) can red enchilada sauce
- 4 scallions, green and light green parts, sliced

To Make Tofu Scramble:
Directions:
8. In a small bowl (or in your tofu press), use a fork to crumble the tofu. Stir in the kala namak and turmeric. Set aside
9. Select the "Sauté" Low mode on your instant pot. When the display reads "Hot," add the oil and heat until it shimmers.
10. Add the onion, bell pepper and jalapeño. Cook for 2 to 3 minutes, stirring frequently. Turn off the Instant Pot and add the garlic
11. The inner pot will still be hot. Let the veggies cook for another minute or so. Stir in the tomatoes, tofu mixture, nutritional yeast, cumin; oregano and red pepper flakes. Season to taste with salt and pepper.
12. Lock the lid and turn the steam release handle to Sealing. Using the Manual function, set the cooker to High Pressure for 2 minutes
13. After completing the cooking time, quick release the pressure.
14. Remove the lid carefully. Select Sauté Low again and cook off the remaining liquid, 3 to 5 minutes, stirring frequently. Taste and adjust the seasonings as desired

To Make Enchiladas:
6. Preheat the oven to 375°F. Spray the bottom of a 9-by-13-inch glass baking dish with nonstick spray
7. To build your enchiladas, add 1 spoonful of tempeh sausage to a tortilla, followed by 2 to 3 spoonfuls of tofu scramble "as needed depending on size of tortillas" and roll tightly.
8. Place in the prepared baking dish, seam-side down. Repeat for the remaining tortillas
9. Spoon about two-thirds of the enchilada sauce over the top and sprinkle on the scallions.
10. Cover the dish with aluminum foil and bake for 20 minutes. Top as desired before serving

Italian Shakshuka

(**Prep + Cooking Time:** 20 minutes | **Servings:** 4)

Ingredients:
- ½ yellow onion; chopped.
- 2½ cups marinara sauce
- 1 cup chopped kale, stems removed
- 4 eggs
- 2 cloves garlic; minced.
- ¼ cup water
- 1 tbsp. extra-virgin olive oil
- Fine sea salt
- Freshly ground black pepper
- Chopped fresh flat-leaf parsley or basil; for garnish. (optional)
- Crumbled feta or grated Parmesan cheese; for garnish. (optional)
- Toast slices; for serving (optional)

Directions:
1. Press *Sauté* and add the olive oil to the Instant Pot. Once the oil is hot but not smoking, add the onion, garlic and a pinch of salt and sauté until softened, about 5 minutes. Add the water, marinara sauce and kale and stir well with a wooden spoon, scraping the bottom of the pot to make sure nothing sticks
2. Press *Cancel* Button. Use the spoon to make four small wells evenly spaced in the marinara sauce, then carefully crack an egg into each well. Season the eggs with salt and pepper.
3. Now, Lock the lid and Turn the steam release valve to "Sealing" Position. Select *Manual/Pressure* Cook to cook on *High* pressure for 0 minutes (Sure set it to 0 minutes)
4. When the pot has come to pressure and the screen reads L0:00, quickly release the pressure by immediately moving the steam release valve to Venting.
5. *This method of cooking produces a hard-cooked yolk when using an 8-quart pot and a slightly softer hard-cooked yolk when using a 6-quart pot. If you prefer runny eggs, you might want to cook them on the stove instead
6. When the floating valve drops, remove the lid and use a slotted spoon to scoop the eggs, sauce and plenty of the cooked veggies into a small serving dish. Top with cheese and chopped parsley and serve immediately

Carrot Oatmeal Breakfast

(**Prep + Cooking Time:** 25 minutes | **Servings:** 6)

Ingredients:
- 1 cup steel cut oats
- 1 cup grated carrots
- 1/4 cup chia seeds
- 1 tbsp. butter
- 3 tbsp. maple syrup
- 4 cups water
- 2 tsp. cinnamon
- 3/4 cup raisins
- 1 tsp. pie spice
- A pinch of salt

Directions:
1. Select the Sauté mode on your instant pot, add butter and melt it
2. Add oats, stir for 3 minutes
3. Add carrots, water, maple syrup, cinnamon, spice and a pinch of salt; then stir well and seal the instant pot lid and cook at High for 10 minutes.
4. Release the pressure naturally for 10 minutes, then release remaining pressure by turning the valve to 'Venting', add raisins and chia seeds; then stir well and leave oatmeal aside for 10 minutes; divide it between bowls and serve right away.

French Toast Casserole

(Prep + Cooking Time: 30 minutes | **Servings:** 5)

Ingredients:
- 6 cups cubed, stale French bread
- 1/4 cup maple syrup, Or more for serving
- 1/4 cup Bailey's Almande Almond Milk Liqueur
- 1 cup water
- Nonstick cooking spray; for preparing the bowl
- 1/4 tsp. kala namak; or sea salt
- 1 tsp. vanilla extract
- 1 large banana, plus more for topping; optional
- Vegan butter; for topping

Directions:
1. Spray a 7-cup oven-safe glass bowl with nonstick spray and set aside. Pour the water into your Instant Pot and place a trivet inside the inner pot
2. In a large bowl, mash the banana with a fork. Stir in the maple syrup, Bailey's, vanilla and kala namak, making sure the banana is completely mixed in.
3. Quickly toss the bread in the banana mixture, making sure to get even coverage.
4. Transfer to the prepared bowl, cover tightly with aluminum foil and place the bowl on top of the trivet in the Instant Pot.
5. Lock the lid and turn the steam release handle to Sealing. Using the Manual function, set the cooker to High Pressure for 25 minutes
6. After completing the cooking time, quick release the pressure. Remove the lid carefully. Serve with toppings as desired and enjoy

Strawberry Jam

(Prep + Cooking Time: 36 minutes | Makes 16 Ounces)

Ingredients:
- 1 lb. frozen strawberries
- 2 tbsp. chia seeds
- ¼ cup pure maple syrup
- Pinch of fine sea salt

Directions:
1. Combine the frozen strawberries, maple syrup and salt in the Instant Pot and secure the lid. Turn the steam release valve to Sealing and select *Manual/Pressure* Cook to cook at *High* pressure for 1 minute
2. Once the cooking cycle is completed, let the pressure naturally release for 10 minutes, then move the steam release valve to Venting to release any remaining pressure.
3. When the floating valve drops, remove the lid and Press *Cancel* Button to stop the cooking cycle
4. Press the *Sauté* button and add the chia seeds. Simmer the jam until it begins to thicken, stirring often to make sure it doesn't stick to the bottom of the pan, about 5 minutes.
5. Once the mixture has thickened slightly, or if the jam starts to stick to the pan, Press *Cancel* Button to stop the cooking cycle. Transfer the jam to a 16-oz. glass jar with a lid and store it in the fridge to thicken as it cools

Blueberry Chia Pudding

(Prep + Cooking Time: 28 minutes | **Servings:**8)

Ingredients:
- 1 (14-oz.) can full-fat coconut milk
- 1 (12-oz.) bag frozen blueberries
- 1 cup rolled oats
- ½ cup pure maple syrup
- 1 cup chia seeds
- 1 cup water
- ½ tsp. pure vanilla extract
- Fresh berries; for garnish. (optional)

Directions:
1. Combine the coconut milk, water, blueberries, chia seeds, oats, maple syrup, and vanilla extract in the inner pot
2. Now, Lock the lid. Select, "Manual or Pressure Cook" and set the pressure to *High* and the time to 3 minutes. Make sure the steam release knob is in the sealed position.
3. After completing the cooking cycle, naturally release the pressure for 5 minutes, then quick release any remaining pressure.
4. Unlock and remove the lid. Pour the pudding into individual serving cups and refrigerate until it sets, about 1 hour. Serve cold garnished with berries

Banana Quinoa Bowls

(**Prep + Cooking Time:** 42 minutes | **Servings:** 6)

Ingredients:
- 1 (15-oz.) can full-fat coconut milk
- 2 medium ripe bananas, peeled and chopped
- ¼ cup pure maple syrup
- 1½ cups quinoa; rinsed.
- 1½ cups water
- 1 tbsp. unsweetened cocoa powder
- 1 tsp. pure vanilla extract
- ¼ tsp. fine sea salt.

Directions:
1. Place the quinoa in the inner pot and add the bananas, coconut milk, water, vanilla extract, and cocoa powder. Stir to combine
2. Now, Lock the lid. Select, "Manual or Pressure Cook" and set the pressure to *Low* and the time to 12 minutes. Make sure the steam release knob is in the sealed position.
3. After completing the cooking cycle, naturally release the pressure for 10 minutes, then quick release any remaining pressure. Unlock and remove the lid. Stir in the salt and maple syrup. Serve hot

Leek Asparagus Frittata

(**Prep + Cooking Time:** 36 minutes | **Servings:** 4)

Ingredients:
- 8 oz. asparagus spears, woody stems removed, cut into 1-inch pieces
- ¼ cup grated Parmesan cheese
- 1 cup thinly sliced leeks
- 6 eggs
- ¼ tsp. fine sea salt
- Freshly ground black pepper
- Chopped green onions; for garnish.
- Fresh flat-leaf parsley; for garnish.

Directions:
1. Grease a 7-inch round pan generously with olive oil to prevent sticking. In a large mixing bowl, combine the eggs, salt and several grinds of black pepper and beat well with a fork. Fold in the asparagus, leeks and Parmesan and pour the mixture into the prepared pan
2. Pour 1 cup water into the Instant Pot and arrange the trivet (Which comes with your instant pot) on the bottom.
3. Place the pan on top of the trivet. Now, Lock the lid and Turn the steam release valve to "Sealing" Position. Select *Manual/Pressure* Cook to cook on *High* pressure for 10 minutes
4. Release the pressure naturally for 10 minutes, then move the steam release valve to Venting to release any remaining pressure. When the floating valve drops, remove the lid.
5. Use oven mitts to lift the trivet and the pan out of the pot. Let the frittata cool for 5 minutes in the pan before cutting and serving

Meat Recipes

Mongolian Style Broccoli and Beef

(Prep + Cooking Time: 41 minutes | **Servings:**6)

Ingredients:
- 2 lbs. skirt steak; cut into thin strips
- 15 ounces broccoli florets, fresh or frozen
- 1 medium yellow onion; chopped.
- ½ cup water
- 2 garlic cloves; minced.
- 1 cup low-sodium beef broth
- ¼ cup reduced-sodium soy sauce
- 2 tbsp. extra-virgin olive oil.
- 2 tbsp. brown sugar
- 2 tbsp. cornstarch
- 2 tbsp. balsamic vinegar

Directions:
1. Take a small bowl, make a slurry by whisking together the cornstarch and water. Set aside
2. Select *Sauté* and add the olive oil. Once the oil is hot, add the steak, onion, and garlic; cook for about 3 minutes, stirring occasionally.
3. Now, press *Cancel* and add the broth, soy sauce, vinegar, and brown sugar; stir to combine. Using a wooden spoon, scrape up any browned bits stuck to the bottom of the pot
4. Now, Lock the lid. Select, "Manual or Pressure Cook" and set the pressure to *High* and the time to 10 minutes. Make sure the steam release knob is in the sealed position.
5. After completing the cooking cycle, naturally release the pressure for 5 minutes, then quick release any remaining pressure. Unlock and remove the lid. Add the broccoli florets
6. Lock the lid into place again. Select, "Manual or Pressure Cook" and set the pressure to *High* and the time to 1 minute (3 minutes if using frozen florets). Make sure the steam release knob is in the sealed position.
7. After completing the cooking cycle, quick release the pressure. Unlock and remove the lid. Select *Sauté*. Use a slotted spoon to transfer the beef and vegetables to a serving bowl
8. Whisk the cornstarch slurry into the liquid. Let it cook, uncovered, for 2 minutes or until the sauce starts to thicken. Press Cancel. Add the beef and vegetables back to the pot and stir to combine. Serve hot.

Pineapple Pork

(Prep + Cooking Time: 45 minutes | **Servings:**6)

Ingredients:
- 2 lbs. pork loin; cut into 1-inch chunks
- 3 garlic cloves; minced.
- 1 (20-oz.) can pineapple chunks in juice
- 1 medium yellow onion; chopped.
- ¼ cup reduced-sodium soy sauce
- 2 red bell peppers, seeded and chopped
- 2 tbsp. brown sugar
- 2 tbsp. extra-virgin olive oil.
- ¼ tsp. chili powder

Directions:
1. Select *Sauté* and add the olive oil to the inner pot. Once the oil is hot, add the pork, onion, and garlic; sauté for 4 minutes, stirring occasionally to brown the pork on all sides
2. Now, press *Cancel* and add the pineapple and its juice. Using a wooden spoon, scrape up any browned bits stuck to the bottom of the pot. Add the bell peppers, soy sauce, brown sugar, and chili powder. Stir to combine
3. Now, Lock the lid. Select, "Manual or Pressure Cook" and set the pressure to *High* and the time to 10 minutes. Make sure the steam release knob is in the sealed position.
4. After completing the cooking cycle, naturally release the pressure for 10 minutes, then quick release any remaining pressure. Unlock and remove the lid. Serve hot

Tangy Pork with Potatoes

(**Prep + Cooking Time:** 70 minutes | **Servings:**6)

Ingredients:
- 1 lb. white potatoes; cut into 1-inch cubes
- 2 lbs. boneless pork shoulder; cut into 1-inch cubes
- 2 garlic cloves; minced.
- 1¼ cups low-sodium chicken broth.
- ½ cup water
- ⅓ cup reduced-sodium soy sauce
- ¼ cup white wine vinegar
- 2 tbsp. honey
- 2 tbsp. cornstarch
- 1 tbsp. extra-virgin olive oil.
- ½ tsp. freshly ground black pepper.

Directions:
1. Take a small bowl, make a slurry by whisking together the cornstarch and water. Set aside
2. Select *Sauté* and add the olive oil. Once the oil is hot, add the pork and garlic and sauté for 3 minutes, stirring occasionally.
3. Now, press *Cancel* and pour in the broth. Using a wooden spoon, scrape up any browned bits stuck to the bottom of the pot. Add the soy sauce, vinegar, honey, black pepper, and potatoes to the pot; stir to combine
4. Now, Lock the lid. Select, "Manual or Pressure Cook" and set the pressure to *High* and the time to 25 minutes. Make sure the steam release knob is in the sealed position.
5. After completing the cooking cycle, naturally release the pressure for 10 minutes, then quick release any remaining pressure. Unlock and remove the lid. Select *Sauté*. Using a slotted spoon, transfer the pork and potatoes to a serving plate.
6. Once the liquid in the pot is bubbling, whisk in the cornstarch slurry. Let the sauce simmer, uncovered, for about 2 minutes or until the sauce starts to thicken. Return the pork and potatoes to the pot and stir to combine. Serve hot

Korean style Beef Bowl

(**Prep + Cooking Time:** 50 minutes | **Servings:**6)

Ingredients:
- 2 lbs. flank steak; sliced. into ½-inch-thick strips
- ½ cup low-sodium beef broth
- ⅓ cup reduced-sodium soy sauce
- 3 garlic cloves; minced.
- ¼ cup white wine vinegar
- ½ cup water
- 1 medium cucumber; sliced.
- 2 red bell peppers; seeded and sliced.
- 4 scallions, white and light green parts only; sliced.
- 1 tbsp. extra-virgin olive oil.
- 2 tbsp. honey
- 2 tbsp. cornstarch
- ¼ tsp. ground ginger
- 2 tsp. Sriracha sauce

Directions:
1. In a small bowl make a slurry by whisking together the cornstarch and water. Set aside
2. Select *Sauté* and add the olive oil to the inner pot. Once the oil is hot, add the steak and garlic and sauté for 3 minutes, stirring occasionally so the beef starts to brown on all sides.
3. Now, press *Cancel* and add the broth. Using a wooden spoon, scrape up any browned bits stuck to the bottom of the pot. Add the soy sauce, vinegar, honey, Sriracha, and ginger; stir to combine
4. Now, Lock the lid. Select, "Manual or Pressure Cook" and set the pressure to *High* and the time to 10 minutes. Make sure the steam release knob is in the sealed position.
5. After completing the cooking cycle, naturally release the pressure for 5 minutes, then quick release any remaining pressure. Unlock and remove the lid. Select *Sauté*. Use a slotted spoon to transfer the beef to a serving plate
6. Once the liquid begins to bubble, whisk in the cornstarch slurry and let the sauce cook, uncovered, for 2 minutes or until it starts to thicken. Return the beef to the pot and stir to combine.
7. Serve each bowl with a few slices of cucumber and red bell pepper and some sliced scallions on top

Delicious Chili Con Carne

(Prep + Cooking Time: 40 minutes | **Servings:** 4)

Ingredients:
- 1 lb. beef, ground.
- 8 oz. canned tomatoes; chopped.
- 4 oz. kidney beans, soaked overnight and drained
- 1 tsp. tomato paste
- 5 oz. water
- 1 yellow onion; chopped.
- 4 tbsp. extra virgin olive oil
- 1 tbsp. chili powder
- 1/2 tsp. cumin, ground.
- Salt and black pepper to the taste
- 2 garlic cloves; minced.
- 1 bay leaf

Directions:
1. Set your instant pot on Sauté mode; add 1 tablespoon oil and heat it up.
2. Add meat, brown for a few minutes and transfer to a bowl
3. Add the rest of the oil to the pot and also heat it up
4. Add onion and garlic, stir and cook for 3 minutes.
5. Return beef to pot, add bay leaf, beans, tomato paste, tomatoes, chili powder, cumin, salt, pepper and water; then stir well. seal the instant pot lid and cook on High for 18 minutes
6. Quick release the pressure, carefully open the lid; discard bay leaf, divide chili among bowls and serve.

Pork Tamales

(Prep + Cooking Time: 1 hour and 45 minutes | **Servings:** 24 pieces)

Ingredients:
- 8 oz. dried corn husks, soaked for 1 day and drained
- 3 lb. pork shoulder, boneless and chopped.
- 1 yellow onion; chopped
- 2 garlic cloves, crushed.
- 2 tbsp. chili powder
- 4 cups water
- 1 tsp. baking powder
- 1 tsp. cumin
- 4 cups masa
- 1/4 cup corn oil
- 1/4 cup shortening
- 1 tbsp. chipotle chili powder
- Salt and black pepper to taste

Directions:
1. In your instant pot, mix 2 cups water with salt, pepper, onion, garlic, chipotle powder, chili powder, and cumin.
2. Add pork, stir, close the instant pot lid and cook at High for 75 minutes
3. Release the pressure naturally for 10 minutes, carefully open the instant pot lid, transfer meat to a cutting board and shred it with 2 forks.
4. Put pork meat in a bowl, add 1 tbsp. of cooking liquid, more salt and pepper, stir and leave aside. In a bowl, mix masa with salt, pepper, baking powder, shortening and oil and stir using a mixer
5. Add cooking liquid from the instant pot and blend again well
6. Add 2 cups of water to your instant pot and place the steamer basket inside
7. Unfold 2 corn husks, place them on a work surface, add 1/4 cup masa mix near the top of the husk, press into a square and leaves 2 inches at the bottom
8. Add 1 tbsp. pork in the center of the masa, wrap the husk around the dough and place standing up in the steamer basket
9. Repeat with the rest of the husks, close the instant pot lid and cook at High for 20 minutes. Release the pressure naturally for 15 minutes, then release remaining pressure by turning the valve to 'Venting', and carefully open the lid.

Mustard Pork Tenderloin

(Prep + Cooking Time: 48 minutes | **Servings:** 6)

Ingredients:
- 2 lbs. pork tenderloin
- ½ cup water
- ¼ cup honey
- 1 cup low-sodium chicken broth.
- 3 garlic cloves; minced.
- 2 tbsp. Dijon mustard
- 2 tbsp. cornstarch
- 2 tbsp. extra-virgin olive oil.
- ¼ tsp. freshly ground black pepper.
- ½ tsp. fine sea salt.

Directions:
1. Take a small bowl, make a slurry by whisking together the cornstarch and water. Set aside
2. Select *Sauté* and add the olive oil to the inner pot. Once the oil is hot, add the pork and brown it for 2 minutes per side.
3. Press Cancel. Using tongs, transfer the pork to a plate
4. Pour the broth into the pot. Using a wooden spoon, scrape up any browned bits stuck to the bottom of the pot. Add the garlic, mustard, honey, salt, and pepper; stir to combine. Place the trivet inside the pot. Use the tongs to place the pork on the trivet.
5. Now, Lock the lid. Select, "Manual or Pressure Cook" and set the pressure to *High* and the time to 8 minutes. Make sure the steam release knob is in the sealed position.
6. After completing the cooking cycle, naturally release the pressure for 10 minutes, then quick release any remaining pressure. Unlock and remove the lid. Select *Sauté*. Using clean tongs, transfer the pork to a cutting board.
7. Whisk the cornstarch slurry into the liquid and cook, uncovered, for about 5 minutes or until the sauce starts to thicken. Carefully pour the sauce into a small pitcher or glass bowl.
8. Using a sharp knife, slice the pork into 6 servings. Serve the pork with the sauce

Easy and Tasty Meatloaf

(Prep + Cooking Time: 50 minutes | **Servings:** 6)

Ingredients:
- 2 lb. ground meat
- 1/3 cup milk
- 1/4 cup ketchup
- 2 eggs, whisked
- 2 cups water
- 1/2 cup panko breadcrumbs
- 1 yellow onion, grated
- Salt and black pepper to the taste

Directions:
1. In a bowl, mix breadcrumbs with milk, stir and leave aside for 5 minutes
2. Add onion, salt, pepper and eggs and stir.
3. Add ground meat and stir very well again.
4. Place this on a greased tin foil and shape a loaf
5. Add ketchup on top.
6. Pour the water in your instant pot, arrange meatloaf in the steamer basket of the pot, seal the instant pot lid and cook at High for 35 minutes.
7. Release the pressure naturally for 10 minutes, then release remaining pressure by turning the valve to 'Venting', carefully open the lid; take meatloaf out, leave it to cool down for 5 minutes, slices and serve it.

Braised Pork Recipe

(Prep + Cooking Time: 1 hour 30 minutes | **Servings:** 6)

Ingredients:
- 4 lb. pork butt; chopped.
- 16 oz. chicken stock
- 16 oz. red wine
- 4 oz. lemon juice
- 2 tbsp. extra virgin olive oil
- 1/4 cup onion; chopped.
- 1/4 cup garlic powder
- 1 tbsp. paprika
- Salt and black pepper to taste

Directions:
1. In your instant pot, mix pork with stock, wine, lemon juice, onion, garlic powder, oil, paprika, salt and pepper, stir, cover and cook on High for 45 minutes.
2. Leave the pot aside for 15 minutes, release the pressure quickly, stir braised pork, divide into bowls and serve

Creamy Pork Chops

(Prep + Cooking Time: 30 minutes | **Servings:** 4)

Ingredients:
- 4 pork chops, boneless
- 1/2 small bunch parsley; chopped.
- 1 cup water
- 2 tbsp. extra virgin olive oil
- 2 tsp. chicken bouillon powder
- 10 oz. canned cream of mushroom soup
- 1 cup sour cream
- Salt and black pepper to taste

Directions:
1. Set your instant pot on Sauté mode; add oil and heat it up.
2. Add pork chops, salt and pepper, brown them on all sides, transfer to a plate and leave aside for now.
3. Add water and chicken bouillon powder to the pot and stir well.
4. Return pork chops, stir, cover and cook at High for 9 minutes
5. Release the pressure naturally, transfer pork chops to a platter and leave aside
6. Set the pot on Simmer mode and heat up the cooking liquid
7. Add mushroom soup, stir, cook for 2 minutes and take off heat. Add parsley and sour cream, stir and pour over pork chops

Beef Stroganoff with Spring Green Peas.

(Prep + Cooking Time: 55 minutes | **Servings:**6)

Ingredients:
- 2 lbs. sirloin steak; cut into thin strips
- 3 garlic cloves; minced.
- 2 shallots; diced.
- ¼ cup chopped fresh dill
- ⅓ cup low-fat plain Greek yogurt
- ½ cup water
- 2 cups button mushrooms; sliced.
- 1 cup low-sodium beef broth
- 2 cups green peas (thawed if frozen)
- 2 tbsp. Dijon mustard
- 2 tbsp. cornstarch
- 2 tbsp. extra-virgin olive oil.
- Juice of 1 medium lemon

Directions:
1. Take a small bowl, make a slurry by whisking together the cornstarch and water. Set aside
2. Select *Sauté* and add the olive oil to the inner pot. Once the oil is hot, use tongs to place the beef strips into the pot. Cook the beef, stirring constantly, for 2 minutes or until it starts to brown. Add the garlic, shallots, and mushrooms and stir to combine.
3. Now, press *Cancel* and add the broth. Using a wooden spoon, scrape up any browned bits stuck to the bottom of the pot

4. Now, Lock the lid. Select, "Manual or Pressure Cook" and set the pressure to *High* and the time to 10 minutes. Make sure the steam release knob is in the sealed position.
5. After completing the cooking cycle, naturally release the pressure for 10 minutes, then quick release any remaining pressure. Unlock and remove the lid. Select *Sauté*
6. Add the peas, cornstarch slurry, and mustard and whisk to combine. Continue whisking for about 2 minutes or until the sauce starts to thicken. Now, press *Cancel* and stir in the dill, yogurt, and lemon juice. Serve hot

Beef and Cabbage

(**Prep + Cooking Time:** 1 hour and 30 minutes | **Servings:** 6)

Ingredients:
- 2 ½ lb. beef brisket
- 4 carrots; chopped
- 1 cabbage heat, cut into 6 wedges
- 6 potatoes, cut into quarters
- 4 cups water
- 2 bay leaves
- 3 garlic cloves; chopped
- 3 turnips, cut into quarters
- Horseradish sauce for serving
- Salt and black pepper to the taste

Directions:
1. Put beef brisket and water in your instant pot, add salt, pepper, garlic and bay leaves, seal the instant pot lid and cook at High for 1 hour and 15 minutes.
2. Quick release the pressure, carefully open the lid; add carrots, cabbage, potatoes, and turnips; then stir well. seal the instant pot lid again and cook at High for 6 minutes
3. Release the pressure naturally, carefully open the lid; divide among plates and serve with horseradish sauce on top

Pork Sausages and Mashed Potatoes

(**Prep + Cooking Time:** 30 minutes | **Servings:** 6)

Ingredients:
For the potatoes:
- 4 potatoes, peeled and cut into cubes
- 1 tbsp. butter
- 1 tsp. mustard powder
- 1 tbsp. cheddar cheese, grated
- 4 oz. milk, warm
- 6 oz. water
- Sat and black pepper to taste

For the sausages:
- 6 pork sausages
- 2 tbsp. extra virgin olive oil
- 1 tbsp. cornstarch mixed with 1 tbsp. water
- 1/2 cup onion jam
- 3 oz. red wine
- 3 oz. water
- Salt and black pepper to taste

Directions:
1. Put potatoes in your instant pot, add 6 oz. water, salt and pepper, stir, cover and cook on High for 5 minutes.
2. Release the pressure quickly, drain potatoes and put them in a bowl.
3. Add warm milk, butter, mustard and more salt and pepper, and mash well
4. Add cheese, stir again and leave aside for now
5. Set your instant pot on Sauté mode; add oil and heat it up.
6. Add sausages and brown them on all sides.
7. Add onion jam, wine and 3 oz. water
8. Add salt and pepper to the taste, close the instant pot lid and cook at High for 8 minutes
9. Release the pressure quickly and divide sausages among plates
10. Add cornstarch mix to the pot and stir well. Drizzle the sauce over sausages and serve them with mashed potatoes.

Pork Chops & Smashed Potatoes

(Prep + Cooking Time: 35 minutes | **Servings:** 6)

Ingredients:
- 6 pork chops, boneless
- 2 lb. potatoes, cut into chunks
- 1 yellow onion, cut into chunks
- 1 bunch mixed rosemary, sage, oregano and thyme
- 2 tbsp. white flour
- 2 cups chicken stock
- 2 tbsp. butter
- 1 tsp. smoked paprika
- 3 garlic cloves; chopped.
- Salt and black pepper to taste

Directions:
1. Put the potatoes in your instant pot. Add garlic and half of the onion. Add herbs and stock
2. Place pork chops on top, add salt, pepper, and paprika. Cover and cook at High for 15 minutes
3. Meanwhile, heat up a pan over medium heat, add butter and heat it up
4. Add flour, stir very well, cook for 2 minutes and take off heat
5. Release the pressure quick, transfer pork to a platter and discard herbs
6. Transfer potatoes to a bowl, add some of the cooking liquid, add salt, pepper, and stir using your hand mixer.
7. Set your instant pot on Simmer mode and cook the cooking liquid for 2 minutes
8. Add butter mix and stir until it thickens. Divide pork chops on plates, add mashed potatoes on the side and drizzle the gravy from the pot all over.

Barbacoa Beef

(Prep + Cooking Time: 65 minutes | **Servings:**8)

Ingredients:
- 2 lbs. beef chuck roast; cut into 2-inch cubes
- 2 garlic cloves; minced.
- 1 (4-oz.) can diced green chiles
- 1 cup low-sodium beef broth
- 1 medium yellow onion; diced.
- 2 tbsp. extra-virgin olive oil.
- ½ tsp. dried oregano
- ½ tsp. chili powder
- 1 tsp. ground cumin
- 1 tsp. fine sea salt.
- ½ tsp. freshly ground black pepper.
- Juice of 2 limes

Directions:
1. Select *Sauté* and add the olive oil to the inner pot. Once the oil is hot, add the beef, garlic, onion, cumin, oregano, chili powder, salt, and pepper; sauté for 3 minutes, stirring occasionally
2. Now, press *Cancel* and pour in the broth, lime juice, and green chiles. Using a wooden spoon, scrape up any browned bits stuck to the bottom of the pot.
3. Now, Lock the lid. Select, "Manual or Pressure Cook" and set the pressure to *High* and the time to 30 minutes. Make sure the steam release knob is in the sealed position.
4. After completing the cooking cycle, naturally release the pressure for 10 minutes, then quick release any remaining pressure
5. Unlock and remove the lid. Stir the mixture. If you want to shred the beef, use two forks to pull apart each piece. Serve hot.

Potatoes and Goat

(Prep + Cooking Time: 60 minutes | **Servings:** 5)

Ingredients:
- 2 ½ lb. goat meat, cut into small cubes
- 5 tbsp. vegetable oil
- 3 tsp. turmeric powder
- 3 cardamom pods
- 3 onions; chopped.
- 2-inch cinnamon stick
- 2 tomatoes; chopped.
- 4 garlic cloves; minced.
- 2 green chilies; chopped.
- 3/4 tsp. chili powder
- 3 potatoes, cut into halves
- 1 tsp. sugar
- 4 cloves
- A small piece of ginger, grated
- Salt and black pepper to the taste
- 2 ½ cups water
- 1 tsp. coriander; chopped.

Directions:
1. Put goat cubes in a bowl, add salt, pepper and turmeric, toss to coat and leave aside for 10 minutes.
2. Set your instant pot on Sauté mode; add the oil and half of the sugar, stir and heat up
3. Add potatoes, fry them a bit and transfer to a bowl
4. Add cloves, cinnamon stick and cardamom to pot and stir
5. Also add ginger, onion, chilies and garlic, stir and cook for 3 minutes.
6. Add tomatoes and chili powder, stir and cook for 5 minutes
7. Add meat, stir and cook for 10 minutes.
8. Add 2 cups water; then stir well. seal the instant pot lid and cook at High for 15 minutes.
9. Quick release the pressure, carefully open the lid; add more salt and pepper, the rest of the sugar, potatoes and ½ cup water, seal the instant pot lid and cook at High for 5 minutes
10. Release the pressure again, carefully open the lid; divide among plates, sprinkle coriander on top and serve.

Beef Curry

(Prep + Cooking Time: 30 minutes | **Servings:** 4)

Ingredients:
- 2 lb. beef steak, cubed
- 3 potatoes, diced
- 1 tbsp. wine mustard
- 2 ½ tbsp. curry powder
- 2 yellow onions; chopped.
- 2 tbsp. extra virgin olive oil
- 2 garlic cloves; minced.
- 10 oz. canned coconut milk
- 2 tbsp. tomato sauce
- Salt and black pepper to the taste

Directions:
1. Set your instant pot on Sauté mode; add the oil and heat it up
2. Add onions and garlic, stir and cook for 4 minutes.
3. Add potatoes and mustard, stir and cook for 1 minute
4. Add beef, stir and brown on all sides.
5. Add curry powder, salt and pepper, stir and cook for 2 minutes.
6. Add coconut milk and tomato sauce; then stir well. seal the instant pot lid and cook at High for 10 minutes.
7. Quick release the pressure, carefully open the lid; divide curry among plates and serve

Kalua Pork

(Prep + Cooking Time: 1 hour 30 minutes | **Servings:** 5)

Ingredients:
- 4 lb. pork shoulder, cut into half
- 1/2 cup water
- 2 tbsp. vegetable oil
- 1 tbsp. liquid smoke
- Steamed green beans for serving
- Salt and black pepper to taste

Directions:
1. Set your instant pot on Sauté mode; add the oil and heat it up.
2. Add pork, salt and pepper, brown for 3 minutes on each side and transfer to a plate.
3. Add water and liquid smoke to the pot and stir.
4. Return meat, stir, cover pot and cook at High for 90 minutes.
5. Release the pressure naturally for 15 minutes, then release remaining pressure by turning the valve to 'Venting', and carefully open the lid.
6. Transfer meat to a cutting board and shred it with 2 forks
7. Divide pork on plates, add some of the sauce on top and serve with steamed green beans on the side

Sausage with Sauerkraut

(**Prep + Cooking Time:** 45 minutes | **Servings:** 6)

Ingredients:
- 1 (32-oz.) jar sauerkraut
- 3 medium red potatoes; chopped into bite-size pieces.
- 1 (12-oz.) package fully cooked Polish sausage; cut into 1-inch-thick slices
- 1 medium yellow onion; chopped.
- 2 garlic cloves; minced.
- 2 cups low-sodium chicken broth.
- 1 apple; chopped.
- 1 tbsp. extra-virgin olive oil.

Directions:
1. Select *Sauté* and add the olive oil to the inner pot. Once the oil is hot, add the onion and garlic and sauté for 3 minutes, stirring occasionally
2. Now, press *Cancel* and pour in the broth. Using a wooden spoon, scrape up any browned bits stuck to the bottom of the pot. Add the sausage slices, sauerkraut, apple, and potatoes; stir to combine
3. Now, Lock the lid. Select, "Manual or Pressure Cook" and set the pressure to *High* and the time to 10 minutes. Make sure the steam release knob is in the sealed position.
4. After completing the cooking cycle, naturally release the pressure for 10 minutes, then quick release any remaining pressure. Unlock and remove the lid. Serve hot

Sour and Sweet Pork

(**Prep + Cooking Time:** 53 minutes | **Servings:** 6)

Ingredients:
- 2 lbs. boneless pork shoulder; cut into 1-inch pieces
- ½ cup water
- 1 medium yellow onion; chopped.
- ⅓ cup reduced-sodium soy sauce
- ¼ cup white wine vinegar
- ¼ cup honey
- 2 garlic cloves; minced.
- 2 red bell peppers; seeded and sliced.
- 1¼ cups freshly squeezed orange juice
- 2 tbsp. tomato paste
- 2 tbsp. cornstarch
- 1 tbsp. extra-virgin olive oil.

Directions:
1. Take a small bowl, make a slurry by whisking together the cornstarch and water. Set aside
2. Select *Sauté* and add the olive oil. Once the oil is hot, add the pork, onion, and garlic and sauté for 3 minutes, stirring occasionally.
3. Now, press *Cancel* and add the orange juice. Using a wooden spoon, scrape up any browned bits stuck to the bottom of the pot. Add the tomato paste, soy sauce, vinegar, honey, and bell peppers; stir to combine
4. Now, Lock the lid. Select, "Manual or Pressure Cook" and set the pressure to *High* and the time to 8 minutes. Make sure the steam release knob is in the sealed position.
5. After completing the cooking cycle, naturally release the pressure for 10 minutes, then quick release any remaining pressure.
6. Unlock and remove the lid. Select *Sauté*. Using a slotted spoon, transfer the pork and vegetables to a serving bowl

7. Whisk the cornstarch slurry into the liquid and let it simmer, uncovered, for 2 minutes or until the sauce starts to thicken. Place the pork and vegetables back in the pot and stir to combine. Serve hot

Broccoli Beef

(**Prep + Cooking Time:** 54 minutes | **Servings:**6)

Ingredients:
- 1 lb. broccoli florets, fresh or frozen (about 3½ cups)
- 2 lbs. flank steak; cut into ½-inch-thick slices
- 3 garlic cloves; minced.
- ½ cup low-sodium beef broth
- ⅓ cup reduced-sodium soy sauce
- ¼ cup white wine vinegar
- ½ cup water
- 2 tbsp. cornstarch
- 1 tbsp. extra-virgin olive oil.
- 1 tbsp. brown sugar
- ¼ tsp. ground ginger
- 2 tsp. Sriracha sauce
- 4 scallions, white and light green parts only; sliced.; for garnish.

Directions:
1. Take a small bowl, make a slurry by whisking together the cornstarch and water. Set aside
2. Select *Sauté* and add the olive oil to the inner pot. Once the oil is hot, add the steak and garlic and sauté for 3 minutes, stirring occasionally so the beef starts to brown on both sides.
3. Now, press *Cancel* and add the broth. Using a wooden spoon, scrape up any browned bits stuck to the bottom of the pot. Add the soy sauce, vinegar, brown sugar, Sriracha, and ginger; stir to combine
4. Now, Lock the lid. Select, "Manual or Pressure Cook" and set the pressure to *High* and the time to 8 minutes. Make sure the steam release knob is in the sealed position.
5. After completing the cooking cycle, naturally release the pressure for 5 minutes, then quick release any remaining pressure.
6. Unlock and remove the lid. Add the broccoli florets
7. Lock the lid into place again. Select, "Manual or Pressure Cook" and set the pressure to *High* and the time to 1 minute. Make sure the steam release knob is in the sealed position.
8. After completing the cooking cycle, quick release the pressure. Unlock and remove the lid. Select *Sauté*. Use a slotted spoon to transfer the beef and broccoli to a serving plate
9. Once the liquid is bubbling in the inner pot, whisk in the cornstarch slurry and let the sauce cook, uncovered, for 2 minutes or until it starts to thicken
10. Return the beef and broccoli to the pot and stir to combine. Serve the dish garnished with the scallions

Pot Roast with Potatoes and Carrots

(**Prep + Cooking Time:** 75 minutes | **Servings:**6)

Ingredients:
- 4 large carrots, peeled and cut into 2-inch pieces
- 1 (2-lb.) beef chuck roast
- 1½ lbs. medium red potatoes; quartered.
- 2 garlic cloves; minced.
- 1 medium yellow onion; diced.
- 2 cups low-sodium beef broth
- 2 bay leaves
- 2 tbsp. extra-virgin olive oil.
- ½ tsp. dried oregano
- 2 tsp. Worcestershire sauce
- 1 tsp. fine sea salt.
- ½ tsp. freshly ground black pepper.

Directions:
1. Select *Sauté* and add the olive oil to the inner pot. Once the oil is hot, add the beef, garlic, and onion and cook for 3 minutes, turning the beef once so it browns on both sides
2. Now, press *Cancel* and pour in the broth. Using a wooden spoon, scrape up any browned bits stuck to the bottom of the pot. Add the carrots, potatoes, oregano, Worcestershire sauce, bay leaves, salt, and pepper; stir to combine.
3. Now, Lock the lid. Select, "Manual or Pressure Cook" and set the pressure to *High* and the time to 40 minutes. Make sure the steam release knob is in the sealed position.

4. After completing the cooking cycle, naturally release the pressure for 10 minutes, then quick release any remaining pressure
5. Unlock and remove the lid. Stir the ingredients. Use tongs to remove and discard the bay leaves. If you want to shred the beef, use tongs to transfer it to a cutting board and two forks to shred the meat. Return the meat to the pot. Serve hot.

Meatloaf with Mashed Potatoes

(Prep + Cooking Time: 60 minutes | Servings: 8)

Ingredients:
- 1 lb. medium russet or Yukon Gold potatoes
- 2 lbs. 90% lean ground beef
- 2 garlic cloves; minced.
- 1 egg
- ½ medium yellow onion; chopped.
- 1 cup low-sodium chicken broth.
- 2 tsp. Worcestershire sauce
- 1 tsp. Dijon mustard
- 2 tbsp. unsalted butter
- 1 tsp. fine sea salt.
- ½ tsp. freshly ground black pepper.

Directions:
1. Place the potatoes and broth in the inner pot
2. In a large bowl, combine the ground beef, onion, garlic, egg, Worcestershire sauce, and mustard. Using your hands, mix the ingredients together thoroughly.
3. Form the meatloaf mixture into a loaf that will fit inside the inner pot
4. Tear off a 2-foot piece of aluminum foil and fold it in half. Turn up the edges so it makes the shape of a square basket that will fit inside the inner pot. Place the meatloaf in the foil basket and place it on top of the potatoes
5. Now, Lock the lid. Select, "Manual or Pressure Cook" and set the pressure to *High* and the time to 30 minutes. Make sure the steam release knob is in the sealed position.
6. After completing the cooking cycle, naturally release the pressure for 10 minutes, then quick release the remaining pressure.
7. Unlock and remove the lid. Carefully remove the meatloaf and the foil from the pot. Add the butter, salt, and pepper to the potatoes, then mash them to your liking with a potato masher or immersion blender. Serve hot.

Easy Veal Dish

(Prep + Cooking Time: 45 minutes | Servings: 4)

Ingredients:
- 2 lb. veal shoulder, cut into medium chunks
- 3.5 oz. button mushrooms, sliced
- 3.5 oz. shiitake mushrooms, sliced
- 17 oz. potatoes; chopped.
- 16 oz. shallots; chopped.
- 9 oz. beef stock
- 2 oz. white wine
- 1 tbsp. white flour
- 1/8 tsp. thyme; dried
- 2 garlic cloves; minced.
- 2 tbsp. chives; chopped.
- 1 tsp. sage; dried
- 3 ½ tbsp. extra virgin olive oil
- Salt and black pepper to the taste

Directions:
1. Set your instant pot on Sauté mode; add 1 ½ tablespoon oil and heat it up
2. Add veal, season with salt and pepper; then stir well. brown for 5 minutes and transfer to a bowl.
3. Add the rest of the oil to the pot and heat it up
4. Add all mushrooms, stir and cook for 3 minutes.
5. Add garlic; then stir well. cook for 1 minute and transfer everything to a bowl.
6. Add wine and flour to the pot, stir and cook for 1 minute.
7. Add stock, sage, thyme and return meat to pot as well.
8. Stir, seal the instant pot lid and cook at High for 20 minutes

9. Quick release the pressure, carefully open the lid; return mushrooms and garlic and stir.
10. Also add potatoes and shallots; then stir well. seal the instant pot lid and cook at High for 4 minutes.
11. Release the pressure again, carefully open the lid; add more salt and pepper if needed, also add chives; then stir well. divide among bowls and serve.

Meatball Delight

(Prep + Cooking Time: 20 minutes | **Servings:** 8)

Ingredients:
- 1 ½ lb. ground pork meat
- 2 tbsp. parsley; chopped.
- one egg
- 2 potatoes, cubed
- 1 bay leaf
- 1/4 cup white wine
- 2 garlic cloves; minced.
- 2 bread slices, soaked in water
- 1/2 tsp. paprika
- 3/4 cup beef stock
- 1/2 tsp. nutmeg
- 1/4 cup flour
- 1 tsp. Worcestershire sauce
- 2 tbsp. extra virgin olive oil
- 2 carrots; chopped.
- 3/4 cup fresh peas
- Salt and black pepper to taste

Directions:
1. In a bowl, mix ground meat with soaked bread, egg, salt, pepper, parsley, paprika, garlic and nutmeg and stir well.
2. Add 1 tbsp. stock and Worcestershire sauce and stir again
3. Shape meatballs and dust them with flour.
4. Set your instant pot on Sauté mode; add oil and heat it up
5. Add meatballs and brown them on all sides.
6. Add carrots, peas, potatoes, bay leaf, stock and wine, close the instant pot lid and cook at High for 6 minutes.
7. Release the pressure, carefully open the instant pot lid, discard bay leaf, divide meatballs mix into bowls and serve.

Red Beans & Sausage Dish

(Prep + Cooking Time: 45 minutes | **Servings:** 8)

Ingredients:
- 1 lb. smoked sausage, sliced
- 1 garlic clove; chopped.
- 2 tbsp. Cajun seasoning
- 1/2 green bell pepper; chopped.
- 1 tsp. parsley; dried
- 1 small yellow onion; chopped.
- 1 celery stalk; chopped.
- 1 lb. red beans, dried, soaked overnight and drained
- 1 bay leaf
- 5 cups water
- 1/4 tsp. cumin, ground.
- Salt and black pepper to the taste

Directions:
1. In your instant pot, mix beans with sausage, bay leaf, Cajun seasoning, celery, salt, pepper, bell pepper, parsley, cumin, garlic, onion and water; then stir well. seal the instant pot lid and cook at High for 30 minutes.
2. Quick release the pressure, carefully open the lid; divide mix into bowls and serve

Collard with Bacon.

(Prep + Cooking Time: 40 minutes | **Servings:** 6)

Ingredients:
- 1/4 lb. bacon, cut into 1-inch pieces
- 1 lb. collard greens, cleaned and then stems trimmed
- 1/2 tsp. kosher salt
- 1/2 cup. water
- Fresh ground black pepper

Directions:
1. Spread the bacon in the bottom of the Instant Pot inner pot.
2. Press the "Sauté" button and cook for about 5 minutes, occasionally stirring until the bacon is crispy and browne
3. Stir in a big handful of collard greens to coat with bacon grease until slightly wilted. Pack in the rest of the collards
4. The pot will be filled –just pack them enough to close the lid since they will quickly wilt.
5. Sprinkle the greens with salt and pour water over everything. Close and lock the lid. Turn the steam release valve to "Sealing", set the pressure to "High", and the timer to 20 minutes
6. When the timer beeps, turn the steam valve to "Venting" to quick release the pressure. Carefully open and remove the lid.
7. Pour the collard into a serving dish
8. Sprinkle with freshly ground black pepper and then serve.

Feta & Lamb Meatballs.

(Prep + Cooking Time: 15 minutes | **Servings:** 6)

Ingredients:
- 1 ½ lb. ground lamb
- 4 minced garlic cloves
- 1 (28 oz.) can of crushed tomatoes
- 6 oz. can of tomato sauce
- 1 chopped onion
- 2 tbsp. chopped parsley
- 2 tbsp. olive oil
- 1 tbsp. chopped mint
- 1/2 cup. crumbled feta cheese
- 1/2 cup. breadcrumbs
- 1 tbsp. water
- 1 tsp. dried oregano
- 1 beaten egg
- 1 chopped green bell pepper
- 1/2 tsp. salt
- 1/4 tsp. black pepper

Directions:
1. In a bowl, mix lamb, egg, breadcrumbs, mint, parsley, feta, water, half of the minced garlic, pepper, and salt
2. With your hands, mold into 1-inch meatballs.
3. Turn your Instant Pot to "Sauté" and add oil.
4. When hot, toss in the bell pepper and onion. Cook for 2 minutes before adding the rest of the garlic.
5. After another minute, mix in crushed tomatoes with their liquid, the tomato sauce, and oregano. Sprinkle in salt and pepper
6. Put the meatballs in and ladle over the sauce before sealing the cooker lid
7. Select "Manual" and adjust time to 8 minutes on "High" pressure
8. When time is up, hit "Cancel" and carefully quick-release
9. Serve meatballs with parsley and more cheese!

Chinese BBQ Pork

(Prep + Cooking Time: 60 minutes | **Servings:** 6)

Ingredients:
- 2 lb. pork belly
- 2 tbsp. dry sherry
- 1-quart chicken stock
- 8 tbsp. char siu sauce
- 2 tsp. sesame oil
- 2 tbsp. honey
- 4 tbsp. soy sauce
- 1 tsp. peanut oil

Directions:
1. Set your instant pot on Simmer mode, add sherry, stock, soy sauce and half of char siu sauce, stir and cook for 8 minutes
2. Add pork, stir, cover and cook at High for 30 minutes.
3. Release the pressure naturally, transfer pork to a cutting board, leave aside to cool down and chop into small pieces.
4. Heat up a pan with the peanut oil over medium high heat, add pork, stir and cook for a few minutes.
5. Meanwhile, in a bowl, mix sesame oil with the rest of the char siu sauce and honey. Brush pork from the pan with this mix, stir and cook for 10 minutes.
6. Heat up another pan over medium high heat, add cooking liquid from the instant pot and bring to a boil. Simmer for 3 minutes and take off heat.
7. Divide pork on plates, drizzle the sauce over it and serve.

Wonton Meatballs

(Prep + Cooking Time: 45 minutes | **Servings:** 4)

Ingredients:
- 1 lb. ground pork
- 2 large eggs, lighten beaten
- 2 cups water
- 1/4 cup chopped fresh cilantro
- 1/4 cup chopped scallions
- 1 tbsp. minced garlic
- 1 tbsp. minced fresh ginger
- 1 tsp. oyster sauce
- 2 tsp. soy sauce, plus more for serving
- 1 tsp. black pepper
- 1/2 tsp. salt or as your liking

Directions:
1. In a large bowl, combine the pork, eggs, scallions, cilantro, ginger, garlic, soy sauce, oyster sauce, pepper and salt. Using your hands, gently mix until all the ingredients are thoroughly incorporated
2. Divide the mixture into 12 equal portions. Place each in the cup of a baby food container (see headnote). Lightly cover with aluminum foil
3. Pour the water into the Instant Pot. Place a steamer rack with handles in the pot. Gently stack the baby food containers on top of the rack.
4. Now secure the lid on the pot and close the valve. Now Press the *Steam* setting and set to cook for 10 minutes. After completing the cooking time, allow the pot to sit undisturbed for 5 minutes, then release any remaining pressure.
5. Using silicone oven mitts, carefully remove the baby food containers. Use a meat thermometer to ensure the meatballs have reached an internal temperature of 160°F. If not, re-secure the lid on the pot and close the pressure-release valve. Cook for an additional 2 to 3 minutes on the "Steam" setting
6. At the end of the second cooking time, allow the pot to sit undisturbed for 5 minutes, then release any remaining pressure. Unmold and serve the meatballs with soy sauce

Pork Chops & Brown Rice

(Prep + Cooking Time: 35 minutes | **Servings:** 6)

Ingredients:
- 2 lb. pork chops
- 2 cups brown rice
- 1/3 cup brown sugar
- 1 tbsp. peppercorns
- 4 garlic cloves, crushed.
- 2 cups water
- 2 bay leaves
- 1/3 cup salt
- 1 cup onion; chopped.
- 3 tbsp. butter
- 2 ½ cups beef stock
- 2 cups ice
- 2 hot peppers, crushed.
- Salt and black pepper to taste

Directions:
1. Heat up a pan over medium high heat with the water.
2. Add salt and brown sugar, stir until it dissolves, take off heat and add ice
3. Add hot peppers, garlic, peppercorns and bay leaves and stir
4. Add pork chops, toss to coat, cover and keep in the fridge for 4 hours
5. Rinse pork chops and pat dry them with paper towels.
6. Set your instant pot on Sauté mode; add butter and melt it. Add pork chops, brown them on all sides, transfer to a plate and leave aside for now.
7. Add onion to your instant pot and cook for 2 minutes. Add rice, stir and cook for 1 minute
8. Add stock, pork chops, close the instant pot lid and cook at High for 22 minutes
9. Release the pressure naturally for 10 minutes, carefully open the instant pot lid, add salt and pepper, divide pork chops and rice among plates and serve.

Pork Carnitas

(Prep + Cooking Time: 1 hour and 10 minutes | **Servings:** 8)

Ingredients:
- 3 lb. pork shoulder; chopped.
- 2 tbsp. extra virgin olive oil
- 1 tsp. oregano
- 3 garlic cloves; minced.
- 1 yellow onion; chopped.
- 1 lb. tomatillos, cut into quarters
- 1 tsp. cumin
- 2 cups chicken stock
- 2 bay leaves
- Salt and black pepper to taste
- 1 jalapeno pepper; chopped.
- 1 poblano pepper; chopped.
- 1 green bell pepper; chopped.
- Flour tortillas for serving
- 1 red onion; chopped for serving
- Shredded cheddar cheese, for serving

Directions:
1. Set your instant pot on Sauté mode; add oil and heat it up
2. Add pork pieces, salt and pepper and brown them for 3 minutes.
3. Add green bell pepper, jalapeno, poblano pepper, tomatillos, onion, garlic, oregano, cumin, bay leaves and stock. Stir, cover and cook at High for 55 minutes.
4. Release the pressure naturally, for 10 minutes, open the instant pot lid and transfer meat to a cutting board.
5. Puree the mix from the pot using a hand blender
6. Shred meat with a fork and mix with the puree. Divide this on flour tortillas, add red onion and cheese and serve

Rice & Beef Soup

(**Prep + Cooking Time:** 25 minutes | **Servings:** 6)

Ingredients:
- 1 lb. beef meat, ground.
- 3 garlic cloves; minced.
- 1 potato, cubed
- 1 yellow onion; chopped.
- 28 oz. canned beef stock
- 14 oz. canned tomatoes, crushed.
- 1/2 cup white rice
- 15 oz. canned garbanzo beans, rinsed
- 12 oz. spicy V8 juice
- 1/2 cup frozen peas
- 2 carrots, thinly sliced
- 1 tbsp. vegetable oil
- 1 celery rib; chopped.
- Salt and black pepper to the taste

Directions:
1. Set your instant pot on Sauté mode; add beef; then stir well. cook until it browns and transfer to a plate.
2. Add the oil to your pot and heat it up
3. Add celery and onion, stir and cook for 5 minutes.
4. Add garlic, stir and cook for 1 minute more
5. Add V8 juice, stock, tomatoes, rice, beans, carrots, potatoes, beef, salt and pepper; then stir well. seal the instant pot lid and cook at High for 5 minutes.
6. Quick release the pressure, open the instant pot lid and set it on Simmer mode
7. Add more salt and pepper if needed and peas; then stir well. bring to a simmer, transfer to bowls and serve hot.

Pork Chile Verde

(**Prep + Cooking Time:** 60 minutes | **Servings:** 8)

Ingredients:
- 2 lbs. pork shoulder roast; trimmed and cut into 6 large pieces
- 2 poblano peppers
- 3 tomatillos, husked and rinsed
- 1 medium tomato; chopped
- 6 garlic cloves
- 3 jalapeños
- 1/4 cup chopped fresh cilantro
- 1 tbsp. fish sauce
- 2 tsp. ground cumin
- Salt as your liking

Directions:
1. In your Instant Pot, combine the tomatillos, tomato, garlic, jalapeños and poblanos. Place the meat on top of the vegetables. Season the meat with the cumin and salt to taste
2. Now secure the lid on the pot and close the valve. Now Press "Manual" and set the pot at "High" pressure for 30 minutes. After completing the cooking time, allow the pot to sit undisturbed until the pressure has released
3. Using tongs, carefully transfer the pork to a platter (the meat is falling apart at this stage, so you have to be a little careful)
4. Add the cilantro and fish sauce to the pot. Using an immersion blender, puree the vegetables directly in the pot until there are no big chunks left. Return the pork to the pot and stir gently to coat with the sauce

Spiced Pork

(Prep + Cooking Time: 1hour 25 minutes | **Servings:** 4)

Ingredients:
- 1-lb. boneless pork shoulder, cut into short ½-inch thick slices
- 1/4 cup water
- 1/4 cup sliced scallions, for garnish
- 2 yellow onions, thinly sliced
- 1 tbsp. soy sauce
- 1 tbsp. rice wine
- 1 tbsp. sesame seeds, for garnish
- 1 tbsp. minced fresh ginger
- 1 tbsp. toasted sesame oil
- 2 tbsp. gochujang (Korean red chile paste)
- 1 tbsp. minced garlic
- 1 tsp. sugar
- 1/4 to 1 tsp. cayenne pepper

Directions:
1. In your Instant Pot, combine the pork, half the sliced onions, the water, gochujang, sugar, ginger, garlic, soy sauce, rice wine, sesame oil and gochugaru. Stir until everything is well combined. Allow pork to stand at room temperature for 30 minutes
2. Now secure the lid on the pot and close the valve. Now Press "Manual" and set the pot at "High" pressure for 20 minutes.
3. After completing the cooking time, allow the pot to sit undisturbed for 10 minutes, then release any remaining pressure
4. Heat a large cast-iron skillet over high heat. Using a slotted spoon, add the pork cubes and the remaining sliced onions to the skillet
5. When the pork and onions are very hot, add ¼ to ½ cup of the sauce from the pot and stir to combine with the pork. Cook until the sauce has thickened and the onions have softened.
6. Sprinkle the meat with the sesame seeds and scallions. Serve with the remaining sauce from the pot

Taco Casserole

(Prep + Cooking Time: 38 minutes | **Servings:** 4)

Ingredients:
- 1 lb. lean ground beef or turkey
- 1 green bell pepper; seeded and chopped.
- 1½ cups cooked black beans, or one 15-oz. can black beans, rinsed and drained
- 1 cup water
- 1½ cups prepared salsa
- ¾ cup bulgur (or quinoa, to make it gluten-free)
- 1 red onion; chopped.
- 1 clove garlic; minced.
- 1 tbsp. extra-virgin olive oil
- 1½ tsp. ground cumin
- 1 tsp. fine sea salt
- 1 tsp. chili powder

Directions:
1. Avocado slices; chopped. fresh cilantro; chopped. lettuce; chopped. tomatoes; chopped. green onions and shredded Cheddar cheese, for topping (optional)
2. Press *Sauté* and add the olive oil, beef, onion and salt to the Instant Pot. Sauté until the meat is browned and cooked through, breaking it up with a wooden spoon as you stir, about 8 minutes. Add the garlic, chili powder and cumin and stir until fragrant, about 1 minute
3. Press *Cancel* Button to stop the cooking cycle. Add the water and salsa and stir well, making sure that nothing is stuck on the bottom of the pot. Without stirring, sprinkle the bulgur over the top, making sure it doesn't touch the bottom of the pot (which might give you a "Burn" error)
4. Scatter the bell pepper and black beans over the bulgur to help it cook evenly, then secure the lid and move the steam release valve to Sealing. Select *Manual/Pressure* Cook to cook on *High* pressure for 1 minute.
5. Once the cooking cycle is completed, let the pressure naturally release for 10 minutes, then move the steam release valve to Venting to release any remaining pressure.

6. When the floating valve drops, remove the lid. Stir the mixture well, then taste and adjust the seasonings as needed. To serve, transfer the mixture to a serving platter and top as desired. Serve warm

Hominy Dish

(Prep + Cooking Time: 40 minutes | **Servings:** 6)

Ingredients:
- 30 oz. hominy, drained
- 1 ¼ lb. pork shoulder, boneless and cut into medium pieces
- 4 cups chicken stock
- 1/4 cup water
- 2 tbsp. cornstarch
- 2 tbsp. chili powder
- 1 white onion; chopped
- 4 garlic cloves; minced.
- Avocado slices for serving
- Lime wedges for serving
- 2 tbsp. vegetable oil
- Salt and black pepper to taste

Directions:
1. Set your instant pot on Sauté mode; add 1 tbsp. oil and heat it up
2. Add pork, salt, and pepper, brown on all sides and transfer to a bowl. Add the rest of the oil to the pot and heat it up.
3. Add garlic, onion and chili powder, stir and sauté for 4 minutes. Add half of the stock, stir and cook for 1 minute
4. Add the rest of the stock and return pork to pot, stir, cover and cook at High for 30 minutes.
5. Release the pressure naturally for 10 minutes, transfer pork to a cutting board and shred with 2 forks
6. Add cornstarch mixed with water to the pot and set on Sauté mode again. Add hominy, more salt and pepper and shredded pork, stir and cook for 2 minutes.
7. Divide among bowls and serve with avocado slices on top and lime wedges on the side

Sausage and Kale Soup

(Prep + Cooking Time: 35 minutes | **Servings:** 4)

Ingredients:
- 1 lb. bulk hot Italian sausage meat
- 1 (12-ounce) package frozen kale
- 3 cups water
- 1/2 cup heavy cream
- 1/2 cup shredded Parmesan cheese
- 2 cups diced potatoes
- 1 cup diced yellow onions
- 6 garlic cloves; minced

Directions:
1. Now Press "Sauté" on the Instant Pot. When the pot is hot, add the sausage. Cook, stirring to break up the clumps, until it is the texture of ground beef, 3 to 4 minutes
2. Add the onions and garlic and stir well to combine. Add the potatoes and kale and stir well to combine. Stir in the water. Now Press "Cancel"
3. Now secure the lid on the pot and close the valve. Now Press "Manual" and set the pot at "High" pressure for 6 minutes
4. After completing the cooking time, allow the pot to sit undisturbed for 5 minutes, then release any remaining pressure.
5. Add the cream and stir well to combine. Divide among four bowls. Top with the Parmesan and serve

Awesome Beef Recipe

(Prep + Cooking Time: 1 hour 10 minutes | **Servings:** 4)

Ingredients:
- 1 lb. skirt steak, cut into 2-inch chunks
- 1 small jalapeño
- 1 (1.2-ounce) package rendang curry paste
- 1/2 cup water
- 1 cup full-fat coconut milk
- ¾ cup finely minced onions
- 1 tbsp. minced fresh ginger
- 1 tbsp. minced garlic
- 2 tbsp. vegetable oil
- 2 tbsp. unsweetened shredded coconut, toasted, for garnish

Directions:
1. Now Press "Sauté" on the Instant Pot. When the pot is hot, add the oil. When the oil is hot, add the onions, ginger, garlic and jalapeño, stirring to coat with the oil. Add the curry paste. Cook, stirring, until the curry paste is lightly toasted, 3 to 4 minutes.
2. Add the steak and cook, stirring to coat with the spices, for about 2 minutes. Pour in ¼ cup of the water and stir to scrape up the browned bits from the bottom of the pot. Add the remaining ¼ cup water and ½ cup of the coconut milk. Now Press "Cancel"
3. Now secure the lid on the pot and close the valve. Now Press "Manual" and set the pot at "High" pressure for 25 minutes
4. After completing the cooking time, allow the pot to sit undisturbed for 10 minutes, then release any remaining pressure
5. If you want the dish a little less saucy, select "Sauté" to cook off some of the water. Add the remaining ½ cup coconut milk and stir well to combine. Now Press "Cancel". Divide among four bowls and garnish with the shredded coconut before serving.

Meatballs in Tomato Sauce

(Prep + Cooking Time: 50 minutes | **Servings:** 6)

Ingredients:
For Meatballs:
- 1 lb. ground beef
- ⅓ cup arborio rice
- 1/2 cup finely chopped yellow onion
- 1/4 cup chopped fresh parsley
- 1 large egg, slightly beaten
- Salt and black pepper to taste

For Sauce:
- 1 (14.5-ounce) can diced tomatoes; undrained
- 1/2 tsp. smoked paprika
- 1/4 tsp. ground cloves
- 1 cup water
- 1 tsp. dried oregano
- 1/2 tsp. ground cinnamon
- Salt and black pepper to taste
- Chopped fresh parsley, for garnish

Directions:
1. For meatballs: In a large bowl, combine the ground beef, egg, onion, rice and parsley and season with salt and pepper. Mix until well combined. Shape the mixture into 8 to 10 meatballs. Place in a single layer in the Instant Pot
2. For sauce: In a medium bowl, combine the tomatoes with their juices, water, oregano, cinnamon, paprika and cloves and season with salt and pepper. Stir to combine and pour over the meatballs
3. Now secure the lid on the pot and close the valve. Now Press "Manual" and set the pot at "High" pressure for 15 minutes. After completing the cooking time, allow the pot to sit undisturbed until the pressure has released.
4. Carefully transfer the meatballs to a serving bowl. Use an immersion blender to puree the sauce directly in the pot until smooth, if desired. Pour the sauce over the meatballs. Garnish with parsley, if desired and serve

Pasta and Beef Casserole

(Prep + Cooking Time: 30 minutes | **Servings:** 4)

Ingredients:
- 17 oz. pasta
- 1 carrot; chopped.
- 1 tbsp. red wine
- 16 oz. tomato puree
- 1 celery stalk; chopped.
- 1 yellow onion; chopped.
- 2 tbsp. butter
- 1 lb. beef, ground
- 13 oz. mozzarella cheese, shredded.
- Salt and black pepper to the taste

Directions:
1. Set your instant pot on Sauté mode; add the butter and melt it.
2. Add carrot, onion, and celery, stir and cook for 5 minutes
3. Add beef, salt and pepper and cook for 10 minutes
4. Add wine, stir and cook for 1 minute more.
5. Add pasta, tomato puree and water to cover pasta; then stir well. seal the instant pot lid and cook at High for 6 minutes
6. Quick release the pressure, carefully open the lid; add cheese; then stir well. divide everything among plates and serve.

Pulled Pork Dish

(Prep + Cooking Time: 1 Hour 30 minutes | **Servings:** 6)

Ingredients:
- 3 lb. pork shoulder, halves
- 2 teaspoons dried mustard
- 11 oz. beer
- 3 oz. sugar
- 2 teaspoons smoked paprika
- 8 oz. water
- Salt to the taste

For the sauce:
- 12 oz. apple cider vinegar
- 2 tablespoons brown sugar
- 4 oz. hot water
- Salt and black pepper to the taste
- A pinch of cayenne pepper
- 2 teaspoons dry mustard

Directions:
1. In a bowl, mix 3 oz. sugar with smoked paprika, 2 tsp. dry mustard and salt to the taste
2. Rub pork meat with this mix and put pieces in your instant pot.
3. Add beer and 3 oz. water, stir, close the instant pot lid and cook at High for 75 minutes
4. Release the pressure quickly, carefully open the instant pot lid, transfer pork to a cutting board, shred with 2 forks and leave aside for now.
5. Discard half of the cooking liquid from the pot.
6. In a bowl, mix brown sugar with 4 oz. hot water, vinegar, cayenne, salt, pepper and 2 tsp. dry mustard and stir well.
7. Pour this over cooking sauce from the pot, stir, cover and cook at High for 3 minutes
8. Release the pressure, divide pork among plates, drizzle the sauce all over and serve

Pork with Orange and Honey

(Prep + Cooking Time: 1 hour 10 minutes | **Servings:** 4)

Ingredients:
- 1 ½ lb. pork shoulder; chopped
- 3 garlic cloves; minced.
- 1 cinnamon stick
- 2 cloves
- 1/2 cup water
- 1 tsp. rosemary; dried
- 2 tbsp. soy sauce
- 1 tbsp. grape seed oil
- 1 tbsp. honey
- 1 tbsp. maple syrup
- 1 tbsp. water Juice from 1 orange
- Salt and black pepper to taste
- 1 yellow onion, sliced
- 1 tbsp. ginger, sliced
- 1 ½ tbsp. cornstarch

Directions:
1. Set your instant pot on Sauté mode; add grape seed oil and heat it up.
2. Add pork, salt and pepper, stir, brown for 5 minutes on each side and transfer to a plate
3. Add onions, ginger, salt and pepper to the pot, stir and cook for 1 minute. Add garlic and cook for 30 seconds,
4. Add orange juice, water, soy sauce, honey, maple syrup, cinnamon, cloves, rosemary and pork pieces.
5. close the instant pot lid, cook at High for 50 minutes and release the pressure naturally.
6. Uncover the pot, discard cinnamon and cloves, add cornstarch mixed with water, stir, set the pot on Sauté mode again and cook until the sauce thickens.
7. Divide pork and sauce among plates and serve.

Sloppy Joes.

(Prep + Cooking Time: 40 minutes | **Servings:**8)

Ingredients:
- 2 lbs. 90% lean ground beef
- 1 (16-oz.) can tomato purée
- ½ cup ketchup
- 1 tbsp. extra-virgin olive oil.
- 2 tbsp. reduced-sodium soy sauce
- 1 tbsp. brown sugar
- ½ tsp. garlic powder
- 1 tsp. chili powder
- 1 tsp. onion powder
- Purple slaw; for garnish. (optional)
- Fresh chopped parsley; for garnish. (optional)

Directions:
1. Select *Sauté* and add the olive oil to the inner pot. Once the oil is hot, add the ground beef and cook for 3 minutes, using a spatula to break up the meat
2. Now, press *Cancel* and add the onion powder, garlic powder, chili powder, tomato purée, ketchup, soy sauce, and brown sugar. Stir to combine.
3. Now, Lock the lid. Select, "Manual or Pressure Cook" and set the pressure to *High* and the time to 10 minutes. Make sure the steam release knob is in the sealed position.
4. After completing the cooking cycle, naturally release the pressure for 10 minutes, then quick release the remaining pressure
5. Unlock and remove the lid. Stir the Sloppy Joe mixture to make sure it's well combined. Serve immediately garnished with purple slaw and parsley, if desired

Beef & Broccoli Dish

(**Prep + Cooking Time:** 20 minutes | **Servings:** 4)

Ingredients:
- 3 lb. chuck roast, cut into thin strips
- 1 lb. broccoli florets
- 1 tbsp. peanut oil
- 2 tsp. toasted sesame oil

For the marinade:
- 1/2 cup soy sauce
- 1/2 cup black soy sauce
- 1 tbsp. sesame oil
- 3 red peppers; dried and crushed.
- 1/2 tsp. Chinese five spice
- 2 tbsp. potato starch
- 1 yellow onion; chopped.
- 1/2 cup beef stock
- White rice, already cooked for servings
- 2 tbsp. fish sauce
- 5 garlic cloves; minced.
- Toasted sesame seeds for serving

Directions:
1. In a bowl, mix black soy sauce with soy sauce, fish sauce, 1 tablespoon sesame oil, 5 garlic cloves, five spice and crushed red peppers and stir well
2. Add beef strips, toss to coat and leave aside for 10 minutes.
3. Set your instant pot on Sauté mode; add peanut oil and heat it up.
4. Add onions, stir and cook for 4 minutes
5. Add beef and marinade, stir and cook for 2 minutes.
6. Add stock; then stir well. seal the instant pot lid and cook at High for 5 minutes
7. Release the pressure naturally for 10 minutes, then release remaining pressure by turning the valve to 'Venting', carefully open the lid; add cornstarch after you've mixed it with 1/4 cup liquid from the pot, add broccoli to the steamer basket, close the lid again and cook for 3 minutes at High
8. Release the pressure again, carefully open the lid; divide beef into bowls on top of rice, add broccoli on the side, drizzle toasted sesame oil, sprinkle sesame seeds and serve

Beef Burgundy.

(**Prep + Cooking Time:** 65 minutes | **Servings:**8)

Ingredients:
- 2 lbs. beef chuck roast; cut into 1-inch cubes
- 1 cup red wine
- 4 carrots, peeled and sliced (about 1 cup)
- 2 garlic cloves; minced.
- 1 medium yellow onion; diced.
- ¼ cup all-purpose flour
- 1 tbsp. tomato paste
- 2 tbsp. extra-virgin olive oil.
- 1 tsp. dried thyme
- 1 tsp. fine sea salt.
- ½ tsp. freshly ground black pepper.

Directions:
1. Place the beef and flour in a zip-top bag. Seal the bag and then use your hands to make sure the beef gets coated with the flour
2. Select *Sauté* and add the olive oil to the inner pot. Once the oil is hot, add the flour-coated beef, garlic, onion, thyme, salt, and pepper; sauté for 3 minutes, stirring occasionally.
3. Now, press *Cancel* and pour in the wine. Using a wooden spoon, scrape up any browned bits stuck to the bottom of the pot. Add the tomato paste and carrots and stir to combine
4. Now, Lock the lid. Select, "Manual or Pressure Cook" and set the pressure to *High* and the time to 30 minutes. Make sure the steam release knob is in the sealed position.
5. After completing the cooking cycle, naturally release the pressure for 10 minutes, then quick release any remaining pressure. Unlock and remove the lid. Serve hot

Beef Chili

(Prep + Cooking Time: 50 minutes | **Servings:** 6)

Ingredients:
- 16 oz. mixed beans, soaked overnight and drained
- 28 oz. canned tomatoes; chopped.
- 17 oz. beef stock
- 12 oz. pale ale
- 1 ½ lb. beef, ground.
- 1 sweet onion; chopped.
- 3 tbsp. chili powder
- 1 bay leaf
- 2 tbsp. vegetable oil
- 4 carrots; chopped.
- 1 tsp. chipotle powder
- 6 garlic cloves; chopped.
- 7 jalapeno peppers, diced
- Salt and black pepper to the taste

Directions:
1. Set your instant pot on Sauté mode; add half of the oil and heat it up.
2. Add beef; then stir well. brown for 8 minutes and transfer to a bowl
3. Add the rest of the oil to the pot and heat it up.
4. Add carrots, onion, jalapenos and garlic, stir and sauté for 4 minutes
5. Add ale and tomatoes and stir.
6. Also add beans, bay leaf, stock, chili powder, chipotle powder, salt and pepper and the beef; then stir well. seal the instant pot lid and cook at High for 25 minutes
7. Release the pressure naturally, carefully open the lid; stir chili, transfer to bowls and serve.

Korean Beef Stew

(Prep + Cooking Time: 45 minutes | **Servings:** 6)

Ingredients:
- 1 lb. beef (preferably a fatty cut), cut into 2-inch cubes
- 1/2 cup sliced scallions, for serving
- 2 cups prepared kimchi
- 2 cups water
- 1 cup chopped yellow onions
- 1 cup dried shiitake mushrooms
- 1 tbsp. toasted sesame oil
- 1 tbsp. dark soy sauce
- 1 tbsp. gochujang (Korean red chile paste)
- 1 tbsp. minced garlic
- 1 tbsp. minced fresh ginger
- 1/2 tsp. cayenne pepper
- 1/2 tsp. sugar
- Salt to taste

Directions:
1. In your Instant Pot, combine the beef, kimchi, water, onions, mushrooms, garlic, ginger, sesame oil, soy sauce, gochugaru, gochujang and sugar
2. Now secure the lid on the pot and close the valve. Now Press "Manual" and set the pot at "High" pressure for 15 minutes.
3. After completing the cooking time, allow the pot to sit undisturbed until the pressure has released. Taste and season with salt. Stir in the scallions and the tofu, if desired and serve

Pork Carnitas.

(Prep + Cooking Time: 1 hour 40 minutes | **Servings:**6)

Ingredients:
- 2 lbs. boneless pork roast; cut into 2 or 3 pieces so it fits inside the pot
- 1 cup low-sodium chicken broth.
- 2 tbsp. extra-virgin olive oil.
- 1 tsp. chili powder
- 1 tsp. ground cumin
- 1 tsp. dried oregano
- ½ tsp. garlic powder
- 1 tsp. fine sea salt.
- ½ tsp. freshly ground black pepper.
- Juice of 2 limes

Directions:
1. Select *Sauté* and add the olive oil to the inner pot. Once the oil is hot, add the pork and brown it for 3 minutes. Turn the pieces over and brown for another 3 minutes
2. Now, press *Cancel* and pour in the broth. Using a wooden spoon, scrape up any browned bits stuck to the bottom of the pot. Add the salt, pepper, cumin, oregano, chili powder, and garlic powder; stir to combine
3. Now, Lock the lid. Select, "Manual or Pressure Cook" and set the pressure to *High* and the time to 60 minutes. Make sure the steam release knob is in the sealed position.
4. After completing the cooking cycle, naturally release the pressure for 10 minutes, then quick release any remaining pressure. Unlock and remove the lid. Stir in the lime juice. Using two forks, shred the pork. Serve hot

Meatloaf Dish

(**Prep + Cooking Time:** 35 minutes | **Servings:** 8)

Ingredients:
- 2 lb. ground beef
- 2 cups water
- 8 bacon slices
- 3 eggs, whisked
- 2 tbsp. parsley; dried
- 1/2 cup BBQ sauce
- 3 bread slices
- 1/2 cup milk
- 3/4 cup parmesan, grated
- Salt and black pepper to the taste

Directions:
1. In a bowl, mix bread slices with milk and leave aside for 5 minutes
2. Add meat, cheese, salt, pepper, eggs and parsley and stir well
3. Shape a loaf, place on a tin foil, arrange bacon slices on top, tuck them underneath and spread half of the BBQ sauce all over.
4. Put 2 cups water in the instant pot, place meatloaf in the steamer basket of the pot, seal the instant pot lid and cook on High for 20 minutes
5. Quick release the pressure, carefully open the lid; transfer meat loaf to a pan and spread the rest of the BBQ sauce over it
6. Introduce in preheated broiler for 5 minutes, transfer to a platter and slice.

Spiced Pork

(**Prep + Cooking Time:** 1hour 25 minutes | **Servings:** 4)

Ingredients:
- 1-lb. boneless pork shoulder, cut into short ½-inch thick slices
- 1/4 cup water
- 1/4 cup sliced scallions, for garnish
- 2 yellow onions, thinly sliced
- 1 tbsp. soy sauce
- 1 tbsp. rice wine
- 1 tbsp. sesame seeds, for garnish
- 1 tbsp. minced fresh ginger
- 1 tbsp. toasted sesame oil
- 2 tbsp. gochujang (Korean red chile paste)
- 1 tbsp. minced garlic
- 1 tsp. sugar
- 1/4 to 1 tsp. cayenne pepper

Directions:
1. In your Instant Pot, combine the pork, half the sliced onions, the water, gochujang, sugar, ginger, garlic, soy sauce, rice wine, sesame oil and gochugaru. Stir until everything is well combined. Allow pork to stand at room temperature for 30 minutes.
2. Now secure the lid on the pot and close the valve. Now Press "Manual" and set the pot at "High" pressure for 20 minutes
3. After completing the cooking time, allow the pot to sit undisturbed for 10 minutes, then release any remaining pressure.

4. Heat a large cast-iron skillet over high heat. Using a slotted spoon, add the pork cubes and the remaining sliced onions to the skillet
5. When the pork and onions are very hot, add ¼ to ½ cup of the sauce from the pot and stir to combine with the pork. Cook until the sauce has thickened and the onions have softened
6. Sprinkle the meat with the sesame seeds and scallions. Serve with the remaining sauce from the pot.

Delicious Pork Chops

(Prep + Cooking Time: 25 minutes | **Servings:** 4)

Ingredients:
- 4 pork chops
- 2 tbsp. parsley; chopped.
- 1 tbsp. white flour
- 2 tbsp. extra virgin olive oil
- 1 garlic clove; minced.
- 2 tbsp. lime juice
- 2 tbsp. butter
- 2 tbsp. cornstarch mixed with 3 tbsp. water
- 1 lb. onions, sliced
- 1/2 cup milk
- 1/2 cup white wine
- Salt and black pepper to taste

Directions:
1. Set your instant pot on Sauté mode; add the oil and butter and heat it up.
2. Add pork chops, salt and pepper, brown on all sides and transfer to a bowl.
3. Add garlic and onion to pot, stir and cook for 2 minutes
4. Add wine, lime juice, milk, parsley and return pork chops to pot.
5. Stir, cover and cook at High for 15 minutes
6. Release the pressure, open the instant pot lid, add cornstarch and flour, stir well and cook on Simmer mode for 3 minutes.
7. Divide pork chops and onions on plates, drizzle cooking sauce all over and serve.

Ground Beef and Rice

(Prep + Cooking Time: minutes | **Servings:** 6)

Ingredients:
- 1 lb. 85% lean ground beef
- 5 cardamom pods,
- 2 cups water
- 1 cup basmati rice; rinsed and drained
- 1 cup sliced yellow onions
- 1/2 cup pine nuts
- 1/2 cup chopped fresh cilantro
- 1 tbsp. minced garlic
- 2 tbsp. vegetable oil
- 1 tsp. ground cinnamon
- 1/2 tsp. freshly grated nutmeg
- 1 ½ tsp. ground allspice
- 1 tsp. salt or as your liking
- 1 tsp. black pepper
- Tzatziki, for serving; optional

Directions:
1. Press "Sauté" on the Instant Pot. When the pot is hot, add the oil. When the oil is hot, add the pine nuts. Cook, stirring, for 1 to 2 minutes
2. Add the onions and garlic and stir to combine. Add the ground beef and cook, stirring just enough to break up the clumps of meat, for 2 to 3 minutes.
3. Add the rice, cardamom, allspice, cinnamon, nutmeg, salt and pepper. Stir well to combine. Stir in the water. Now Press "Cancel"
4. Now secure the lid on the pot and close the valve. Now Press "Manual" and set the pot at "High" pressure for 4 minutes.
5. After completing the cooking time, allow the pot to sit undisturbed for 10 minutes, then release any remaining pressure.
6. Stir gently to fluff up the rice. Sprinkle with the chopped fresh herbs. Serve hot, with a side of tzatziki if you like

Awesome Beef Recipe

(**Prep + Cooking Time:** 1 hour 10 minutes | **Servings:** 4)

Ingredients:
- 1 lb. skirt steak, cut into 2-inch chunks
- 1 small jalapeño
- 1 (1.2-ounce) package rendang curry paste
- 1/2 cup water
- 1 cup full-fat coconut milk
- ¾ cup finely minced onions
- 1 tbsp. minced fresh ginger
- 1 tbsp. minced garlic
- 2 tbsp. vegetable oil
- 2 tbsp. unsweetened shredded coconut, toasted, for garnish

Directions:
6. Now Press "Sauté" on the Instant Pot. When the pot is hot, add the oil. When the oil is hot, add the onions, ginger, garlic and jalapeño, stirring to coat with the oil. Add the curry paste. Cook, stirring, until the curry paste is lightly toasted, 3 to 4 minutes
7. Add the steak and cook, stirring to coat with the spices, for about 2 minutes. Pour in ¼ cup of the water and stir to scrape up the browned bits from the bottom of the pot. Add the remaining ¼ cup water and ½ cup of the coconut milk. Now Press "Cancel"
8. Now secure the lid on the pot and close the valve. Now Press "Manual" and set the pot at "High" pressure for 25 minutes
9. After completing the cooking time, allow the pot to sit undisturbed for 10 minutes, then release any remaining pressure.
10. If you want the dish a little less saucy, select "Sauté" to cook off some of the water. Add the remaining ½ cup coconut milk and stir well to combine. Now Press "Cancel". Divide among four bowls and garnish with the shredded coconut before serving

Asian Short Ribs

(**Prep + Cooking Time:** 60 minutes | **Servings:** 4)

Ingredients:
- 2 green onions; chopped.
- 1 tsp. vegetable oil
- 1/4 cup pear juice
- 1/2 cup soy sauce
- 3 garlic cloves; minced.
- 3 ginger slices
- 4 lb. short ribs
- 2 tsp. sesame oil
- 1/2 cup water
- 1/4 cup rice wine

Directions:
1. Set your instant pot on Sauté mode; add the oil and heat it up.
2. Add green onions, ginger and garlic, stir and cook for 1 minute
3. Add ribs, water, wine, soy sauce, sesame oil and pear juice, stir and cook for 2 - 3 minutes.
4. Cover the pot and cook at High for 45 minutes
5. Release the pressure naturally for 15 minutes, open the instant pot lid and transfer the ribs to a plate.
6. Strain liquid from the pot, divide ribs among plates and drizzle the sauce all over

Pork Shoulder Tacos

(**Prep + Cooking Time:** 30 minutes | **Servings:** 4)

Ingredients:
- 1 ½ lbs. boneless pork shoulder, cut into 5 large pieces
- 1/4 cup water
- 1 tsp. ground cumin
- 1 tsp. onion powder
- 1 tsp. smoked paprika
- 1 tbsp. brown sugar
- 1 tsp. garlic powder
- 1/2 tsp. ancho chile powder
- 1 tsp. salt or as your liking
- 1/2 tsp. black pepper
- Corn tortillas, for serving

Directions:
1. In a large bowl, combine the brown sugar, garlic powder, onion powder, smoked paprika, cumin, salt, ancho chile powder and pepper. Stir well to combine. Add the pork to the bowl and toss to coat, massaging the spices into the meat. Allow to stand at room temperature for 30 minutes
2. Transfer the meat to the Instant Pot. Add the water.
3. Now secure the lid on the pot and close the valve. Now Press "Manual" and set the pot at "High" pressure for 25 minutes
4. After completing the cooking time, allow the pot to sit undisturbed for 10 minutes, then release any remaining pressure.
5. Using two forks, shred the meat, making sure it's submerged under the cooking liquid until ready to serve. Serve the shredded pork in corn tortillas with any desired toppings

Chinese Steamed Ribs

(**Prep + Cooking Time:** 45 minutes | **Servings:** 4)

Ingredients:
- 1 ½ lbs. pork spareribs, cut into individual ribs
- 1/4 cup chopped scallions, for garnish
- 1/4 cup water
- 1 tbsp. Shaoxing wine
- 1 tbsp. dark soy sauce
- 1 tbsp. minced fresh ginger
- 2 tbsp. black bean garlic sauce
- 1 tbsp. honey
- 1 tbsp. vegetable oil
- 1 tbsp. minced garlic
- 1 tsp. toasted sesame oil; optional

Directions:
1. Now Press "Sauté" on the Instant Pot. When the pot is hot, add the oil
2. When the oil is hot, add the garlic and ginger. Cook, stirring continuously, for 30 seconds. Add the black bean sauce, wine, soy sauce, agave and water. Stir well to combine. Now Press "Cancel"
3. Add the spareribs and stir until the ribs are well coated with the sauce.
4. Now secure the lid on the pot and close the valve. Now Press "Manual" and set the pot at "High" pressure for 15 minutes
5. After completing the cooking time, allow the pot to sit undisturbed for 10 minutes, then release any remaining pressure.
6. Using a slotted spoon, transfer the ribs to a serving platter. Drizzle with the sesame oil, if desired, sprinkle with the scallions and serve

Apple Cider Pork

(**Prep + Cooking Time:** 35 minutes | **Servings:** 4)

Ingredients:
- 2 lb. pork loin
- 2 cups apple cider
- 2 tbsp. extra virgin olive oil
- 1 yellow onion; chopped.
- 2 apples; chopped.
- Salt and black pepper to taste
- 1 tbsp. dry onion; minced.

Directions:
1. Set your instant pot on Sauté mode; add the oil and heat it up.
2. Add pork loin, salt, pepper and dried onion, stir and brown meat on all sides and transfer to a plate.
3. Add onion to pot, stir and cook for 2 minutes.
4. Return meat to pot, add cider, apples, more salt and pepper, stir, cover and cook on High for 20 minutes.
5. Release the pressure, open the instant pot lid, transfer pork to a cutting board, slice it and divide among plates
6. Add sauce and mix from the pot on the side and serve

Pork Roast with Fennel

(**Prep + Cooking Time:** 1 hour 30 minutes | **Servings:** 4)

Ingredients:
- 2 lb. pork meat, boneless
- 2 garlic cloves; minced.
- 1 yellow onion; chopped.
- 1 lb. fennel bulbs, sliced
- 2 tbsp. extra virgin olive oil
- 5 oz. white wine
- 5 oz. chicken stock
- Salt and black pepper to taste

Directions:
1. Set your instant pot on Sauté mode; add oil and heat it up
2. Add pork, salt and pepper, stir, brown on all sides and transfer to a plate
3. Add garlic, wine and stock to the pot, stir and cook for 2 minutes.
4. Return pork to pot, cover and cook at High for 40 minutes.
5. Release the pressure, carefully open the instant pot lid, add onion and fennels, stir, cover and cook at High for 15 minutes
6. Release the pressure again, stir your mix, transfer pork to a cutting board, slice and divide among plates.
7. Serve with onion and fennel on the side and with cooking sauce all over.

Pork Chops with Scallion Rice

(**Prep + Cooking Time:** 35 minutes | **Servings:** 4)

Ingredients:
- 4 bone-in pork chops cut into ¼ inch thick
- 1 bunch scallions; sliced
- 1 cup long-grain white rice
- 1 ¼ cups water
- 1 tsp. salted butter, vegetable oil
- 1 ½ tsp. salt or as your liking
- 1 ½ tsp. black pepper

Directions:
1. Season the pork chops with ½ tsp. each of the salt and pepper. Now Press "Sauté" on the Instant Pot. When the pot is hot, add the butter
2. When the butter has melted, add the chops to the pot and cook until browned on each side, about 5 minutes total; when you turn the chops to brown the second side, add the scallions. Transfer the chops to a plate
3. Add the rice to the pot. Stir to coat the rice with the butter and rendered pork fat. Add the water, stirring to scrape up the browned bits at the bottom of the pot. Add the remaining 1 tsp. each salt and pepper and stir to combine. Return the pork chops to the pot. Now Press "Cancel"
4. Now secure the lid on the pot and close the valve. Now Press "Manual" and set the pot at "High" pressure for 5 minutes. After completing the cooking time, allow the pot to sit undisturbed until the pressure has released. Serve the pork chops with the rice

Beef with Cracked Wheat

(**Prep + Cooking Time:** 1 hour 25 minutes | **Servings:** 4)

Ingredients:
For Meat:
- 1 lb. beef cut into 1-inch cubes
- 2 cups thinly sliced yellow onions
- 1/4 cup Ghee
- 4 cups water
- 1/2 cup split chana dal
- 1/2 cup cracked wheat
- 1 tbsp. minced garlic
- 1 tbsp. minced fresh ginger
- 2 tsp. Garam Masala
- 1 tsp. ground cumin
- 1 tsp. ground coriander
- 1 tsp. ground turmeric
- 1 tsp. cayenne pepper

For Serving:
- 1/2 cup chopped fresh cilantro
- 1/4 cup julienned fresh ginger

Directions:
1. For meat: Select "Sauté" on the Instant Pot. When the pot is hot, add the ghee. When the ghee has melted, add the onions and cook, stirring, until browned and crispy, about 10 minutes. Remove half the onions and set them aside for garnish. Now Press "Cancel"
2. Add the beef, water, cracked wheat, dal, ginger, garlic, 1 tsp. of the garam masala, the cumin, coriander, turmeric and cayenne to the pot.
3. Now secure the lid on the pot and close the valve. Now Press "Manual" and set the pot at "High" pressure for 35 minutes. After completing the cooking time, allow the pot to sit undisturbed for 10 minutes, then release any remaining pressure
4. Using an immersion blender, puree the mixture directly in the pot until you have a smooth, thick stew. Add the remaining 1 tsp. garam masala and stir to combine.
5. Divide the meat mixture among four bowls and garnish with the cilantro, ginger and reserved fried onions on top and serve

Pulled Pork

(**Prep + Cooking Time:** 1 hour 15 minutes | **Servings:** 4)

Ingredients:
- 1 lb. boneless pork shoulder, trimmed and cut into cubes
- 1/2 cup water
- 1 onion; sliced
- 4 garlic cloves; sliced
- 2 tbsp. coconut oil
- 1/4 tsp. chipotle chile powder
- 1/4 tsp. smoked paprika
- 1/2 tsp. dried oregano
- 1/2 tsp. ground cumin
- 1/4 tsp. ancho chile powder
- Juice of 1 lemon
- 1 tsp. salt or as your liking
- 1 tsp. black pepper

Directions:
1. In your Instant Pot, combine the onion and garlic and toss to combine. Place the pork in a large bowl. In a small bowl, combine the salt, pepper, oregano, cumin, ancho chile powder, chipotle chile powder and paprika and stir to thoroughly combine. Sprinkle the seasonings over the pork. Drizzle with the lemon juice. Toss until everything is well coated
2. Place the pork on top of the onions and garlic in the Instant Pot. Pour the water into the large bowl and swirl to rinse out the last of the spices; pour the water over the pork
3. Now secure the lid on the pot and close the valve. Now Press "Manual" and set the pot at "High" pressure for 35 minutes. After completing the cooking time, allow the pot to sit undisturbed until the pressure has released. Transfer the pork to a shallow dish.
4. Now Press "Sauté". Allow the sauce to reduce while you finish the dish.
5. Using two forks, shred the meat. Heat the coconut oil in a large cast-iron pan over high heat. Lay the shredded meat in a flat layer in the pan and let it sit undisturbed
6. When it starts to brown, stir, then keep cooking until well crisped. Add a little of the concentrated sauce to the skillet. Select "Cancel". Serve the pork with guacamole, salsa, sour cream, cotija

Hamburger Stew

(**Prep + Cooking Time:** 35 minutes | **Servings:** 4)

Ingredients:
- 5 ounces tomato sauce
- 1 lb. 85% lean ground beef
- 6 cups frozen mixed vegetables (corn, okra, carrots, peas and green beans)
- Juice of 1 lemon
- 1 tbsp. chicken broth base
- 2 tbsp. tomato paste
- 1 tbsp. soy sauce
- 3 tbsp. apple cider vinegar
- 1 tsp. salt or as your liking
- 2 tsp. black pepper

Directions:
1. Now Press "Sauté" on the Instant Pot. When the pot is hot, add the beef and cook, stirring just enough to break up the clumps, for 2 to 3 minutes. Stir in the frozen vegetables, tomato sauce, vinegar, tomato paste, chicken broth base, soy sauce, salt and pepper. Now Press "Cancel"
2. Now secure the lid on the pot and close the valve. Now Press "Manual" and set the pot at "High" pressure for 5 minutes.
3. After completing the cooking time, allow the pot to sit undisturbed for 10 minutes, then release any remaining pressure. Stir in the lemon juice and serve

Asian Ground Lamb

(**Prep + Cooking Time:** 45 minutes | **Servings:** 4)

Ingredients:
- 1-lb. ground lamb
- 1 cup frozen peas, thawed
- 1/2 cinnamon stick, broken into small pieces
- 1/4 cup water
- 1 cup chopped yellow onions
- 4 cardamom pods
- 1 tbsp. vegetable oil
- 1 tbsp. minced fresh ginger
- 1 tbsp. minced garlic
- 1/2 tsp. ground coriander
- 1/2 tsp. ground cumin
- 1/2 tsp. ground turmeric
- 1/2 tsp. cayenne pepper
- 1 tsp. Garam Masala
- 1 tsp. salt or as your liking

Directions:
1. Now Press "Sauté" on the Instant Pot. When the pot is hot, add the ghee. When the ghee has melted, add the cinnamon sticks and cardamom pods and let them sizzle for about 10 seconds
2. Add the onions, garlic and ginger. Cook, stirring, for 1 to 2 minutes. Add the lamb and cook, stirring just enough to break up the clumps, for 2 to 3 minutes. Add the garam masala, salt, turmeric, cayenne, coriander, cumin and water. Now Press "Cancel"
3. Now secure the lid on the pot and close the valve. Now Press "Manual" and set the pot at "High" pressure for 10 minutes.
4. After completing the cooking time, allow the pot to sit undisturbed for 10 minutes, then release any remaining pressure. Stir in the peas. Cover and allow to stand until the peas are heated through, about 5 minutes

Poultry Recipes

Delicious Duck Chili

(Prep + Cooking Time: 1 hour and 10 minutes | **Servings:** 4)

Ingredients:
- 1 lb. northern beans, soaked and rinsed
- 1 yellow onion; cut into half
- 1 garlic heat; top trimmed off
- 2 cloves
- 1 bay leaf
- 6 cups water
- Salt to the taste

For the duck:
- 1 lb. duck; ground.
- 15 oz. canned tomatoes and their juices; chopped.
- 4 oz. canned green chilies and their juice
- 1 tsp. brown sugar
- 1 tbsp. vegetable oil
- 1 yellow onion; minced.
- 2 carrots; chopped.
- Salt and black pepper to the taste
- A handful cilantro; chopped.

Directions:
1. Put the beans in your instant pot.
2. Add whole onion, garlic head, cloves, bay leaf, the water and salt to the taste; then stir well. seal the Instant Pot lid and cook at High for 25 minutes
3. Quick release the pressure; carefully open the lid; discard solids and transfer beans to a bowl.
4. Heat up a pan with the oil over medium high heat, add carrots and chopped onion, season with salt and pepper to the taste, stir and cook for 5 minutes
5. Add duck, stir and cook for 5 minutes.
6. Add chilies and tomatoes, bring to a simmer and take off heat.
7. Pour this into your instant pot, seal the Instant Pot lid and cook at High for 5 minutes.
8. Release pressure naturally for 15 minutes; carefully open the lid; add more salt and pepper, beans and brown sugar, stir and divide among plates.
9. Serve with cilantro on top

Chicken and Rice Burrito Bowl

(Prep + Cooking Time: 50 minutes | **Servings:**6)

Ingredients:
- 2 lbs. boneless; skinless chicken breasts (5 or 6 breasts)
- 1 medium red or white onion; chopped.
- 1 (15-oz.) can pinto beans, drained and rinsed
- 3 cups cooked brown rice
- 2 medium avocados, pitted and sliced; for garnish.
- 1 (4-oz.) can chopped or diced green chiles
- 1½ cups low-sodium chicken broth.
- 2 tbsp. extra-virgin olive oil.
- 1 tsp. ground cumin
- ¼ tsp. cayenne pepper or taco seasoning
- Fresh chopped cilantro; for garnish.
- Sliced jalapeño; for garnish.
- Prepared salsa; for garnish. (optional)

Directions:
1. Select *Sauté* and add the olive oil to the inner pot. Once the oil is hot, place the chicken breasts in the pot and brown them for 2 minutes per side
2. Now, press *Cancel* and add the cumin, cayenne pepper, onion, green chiles, and chicken broth. Using a wooden spoon, scrape up any browned bits stuck to the bottom of the pot.
3. Now, Lock the lid. Select, "Manual or Pressure Cook" and set the pressure to *High* and the time to 15 minutes. Make sure the steam release knob is in the sealed position.
4. After completing the cooking cycle, naturally release the pressure for 10 minutes, then quick release any remaining pressure

5. Unlock and remove the lid. Use a slotted spoon to transfer the chicken to a cutting board. Shred the chicken using two forks, and then add it back to the pot. Add the pinto beans and stir the ingredients to combine. Serve hot

Teriyaki Chicken and Rice.

(**Prep + Cooking Time:** 43 minutes | **Servings:** 6)

Ingredients:
- 1½ lbs. boneless; skinless chicken breasts (4 or 5 breasts)
- ¼ cup reduced-sodium soy sauce
- 1¾ cups low-sodium chicken broth.
- 2 carrots, peeled and sliced (about 1 cup)
- 1½ cups white rice; rinsed. (see Cooking Tip)
- 2 garlic cloves; minced.
- 2 tbsp. pure maple syrup
- 1 tbsp. white wine vinegar
- 2 tbsp. extra-virgin olive oil.
- ½ tsp. ground ginger

Directions:
1. Select *Sauté* and add the olive oil to the inner pot. Once the oil is hot, add the garlic and chicken and sauté for 4 minutes, turning the chicken once so it browns on both sides. Use a spoon to transfer the chicken and garlic to a plate
2. Now, press *Cancel* and add the soy sauce. Using a wooden spoon, scrape up any browned bits stuck to the bottom of the pot. Add the broth, maple syrup, ginger, carrots, and rice to the pot. Stir to combine. Place the chicken on top, but don't stir
3. Now, Lock the lid. Select, "Manual or Pressure Cook" and set the pressure to *High* and the time to 8 minutes. Make sure the steam release knob is in the sealed position.
4. After completing the cooking cycle, naturally release the pressure for 10 minutes, then quick release any remaining pressure. Unlock and remove the lid. Stir in the vinegar. Serve hot

Mouthwatering Kung Pao Chicken

(**Prep + Cooking Time:** 48 minutes | **Servings:** 6)

Ingredients:
- 2 lbs. boneless; skinless chicken breasts (5 or 6 breasts); cut into bite-size pieces.
- 1 onion; diced.
- ½ cup water
- ¼ cup chopped roasted peanuts
- 1 cup low-sodium chicken broth.
- 2 red bell peppers; seeded and sliced.
- 2 garlic cloves; minced.
- ¼ cup reduced-sodium soy sauce or tamari
- 1 tbsp. extra-virgin olive oil.
- 2 tbsp. rice vinegar
- 2 tbsp. cornstarch
- 2 tbsp. brown sugar
- ¼ tsp. ground ginger
- ¼ tsp. red pepper flakes

Directions:
1. Take a small bowl, make a slurry by whisking together the cornstarch and water. Set aside
2. Select *Sauté* and add the olive oil to the inner pot. Once hot, add the garlic, onion, and chicken and sauté for 2 minutes, stirring occasionally. Turn the chicken over and let the chicken and vegetables cook for 2 minutes more.
3. Now, press *Cancel* and pour the broth into the pot. Using a wooden spoon, scrape up any browned bits stuck to the bottom of the pot. Add the bell peppers, soy sauce, brown sugar, ginger, and red pepper flakes, and stir to combine
4. Now, Lock the lid. Select, "Manual or Pressure Cook" and set the pressure to *High* and the time to 8 minutes. Make sure the steam release knob is in the sealed position.
5. After completing the cooking cycle, let naturally release the pressure for 10 minutes, then quick release any remaining pressure. Unlock and remove the lid. Using a slotted spoon, transfer the chicken to a plate

6. Select *Sauté*. Once the liquid starts bubbling, whisk the cornstarch slurry and vinegar. Whisk consistently for 2 minutes or until the sauce starts to thicken. Serve immediately with the chopped peanuts sprinkled on top

Braised Duck and Potatoes Recipe

(Prep + Cooking Time: 30 minutes | **Servings:** 4)

Ingredients:
- 1 duck, cut into small chunks
- 4 garlic cloves; minced.
- 4 tbsp. sugar
- 2 green onions; roughly chopped
- 4 tbsp. soy sauce
- 4 tbsp. sherry wine
- 1/4 cup water
- 1 potato; cut into cubes
- 1-inch ginger root; sliced
- A pinch of salt
- Black pepper to the taste

Directions:
1. Set your instant pot on Sauté mode; add duck pieces, stir and brown them for a few minutes
2. Add garlic, ginger, green onions, soy sauce, sugar, wine, a pinch of salt, black pepper and water; then stir well. close the lid; set the pot to Poultry mode and cook for 18 minutes
3. Quick release the pressure, carefully open the lid; add potatoes; then stir well. Seal the Instant Pot lid and cook at High for 5 minutes.
4. Quick release the pressure, divide braised duck among plates and serve

Pepper Chicken Soup

(Prep + Cooking Time: 45 minutes | **Servings:** 4)

Ingredients:
- 1 ½ lbs. boneless; skinless chicken breast, cut into large chunks
- 3 poblano peppers, seeded and chopped
- 1/4 cup chopped fresh cilantro plus more for garnish
- 5 garlic cloves; chopped
- 1/2 cup dried navy beans
- 2 cups hot water
- 2 ½ cups cool water
- 1 cup chopped cauliflower
- 1 cup diced white onions
- 2 ounces cream cheese
- 1 tsp. ground cumin
- 1 tsp. salt or as your liking
- 1 tsp. ground coriander

Directions:
1. Soak the navy beans in the hot water for 1 hour; drain and transfer to the Instant Pot. Add the chicken, cool water, cauliflower, onion, poblanos, cilantro, garlic, salt, coriander and cumin
2. Now secure the lid on the pot and close the valve. Now Press "Manual" and set the pot at "High" pressure for 15 minutes.
3. After completing the cooking time, allow the pot to sit undisturbed for 10 minutes, then release any remaining pressure
4. Using a pair of tongs, remove the chicken from the pot and set aside on a plate. Use an immersion blender to coarsely puree the soup directly in the pot.
5. Now Press "Sauté" on the Instant Pot. When the soup is hot and bubbling, while whisking, add the cream cheese in chunks and whisk until melted and combined.
6. Using two forks, shred the chicken and return it to the pot. Stir until heated through. Now Press "Cancel". Serve garnished with more cilantro

Tuscan Chicken with Mashed Potatoes

(Prep + Cooking Time: 31 minutes | **Servings:** 4)

Ingredients:
- 1 lb. fresh or frozen cauliflower florets
- 1 lb. boneless, skinless chicken breasts
- 1 cup full-fat canned coconut milk
- 3 cloves garlic; minced.
- ¼ cup chopped sun-dried tomatoes
- ½ tsp. dried basil
- ½ tsp. dried oregano
- Fine sea salt and freshly ground black pepper
- Heaping 1 cup baby spinach or chopped kale

Directions:
1. Pour the coconut milk into the Instant Pot and add the cauliflower florets. Place the chicken breasts directly on top of the cauliflower, then sprinkle with ½ teaspoon salt and a few grinds of pepper
2. Now, Lock the lid and Turn the steam release valve to "Sealing" Position. Select *Manual/Pressure* Cook to cook on *High* pressure for 10 minutes.
3. Once the cooking cycle is completed, quickly release the pressure by moving the steam release valve to Venting
4. When the floating valve drops, remove the lid. Use tongs to transfer the chicken to a cutting board to rest. Use oven mitts to lift out the pot and drain the cauliflower, reserving the liquid for the sauce. Pour the drained cauliflower into a separate bowl and set aside.
5. Return the pot to the Instant Pot housing and add the reserved liquid. Press *Cancel* Button, then press Sauté. Add the sun-dried tomatoes, basil, oregano and garlic and simmer, stirring constantly, for about 5 minutes, until the sauce reduces by about one-third
6. Taste and add more salt as needed, then stir in the spinach until it wilts, about 1 minute more. Remove the insert from the pot and set it aside so the sauce can cool and thicken a bit more (though it is still a relatively thin sauce that packs a lot of flavor)
7. Use a fork to mash the cauliflower, then season it with salt and pepper to taste. To serve, slice the chicken and place several slices on a plate with some mash. Top them both with a spoonful of the cream sauce, tomatoes and spinach

Stuffed Chicken Breast

(Prep + Cooking Time: 40 minutes | **Servings:** 2)

Ingredients:
- 2 chicken breasts, skinless and boneless and butterflied
- 16 bacon strips
- 6 asparagus spears
- 1-piece ham; halved and cooked
- 2 cup water
- 4 mozzarella cheese slices
- Salt and black pepper to taste

Directions:
1. In a bowl; mix chicken breasts with salt and 1 cup water, stir, cover and keep in the fridge for 30 minutes
2. Pat dry chicken breasts and place them on a working surface
3. Add 2 slices of mozzarella, 1-piece ham and 3 asparagus pieces on each.
4. Add salt and pepper and roll up each chicken breast
5. Place 8 bacon strips on a working surface, add chicken and wrap it in bacon.
6. Repeat this with the rest of the bacon strips and the other chicken breast.
7. Put rolls in the steamer basket of the pot, add 1 cup water in the pot; cover and cook at High for 10 minutes.
8. Release the pressure quick, pat dry rolls with paper towels and leave them on a plate
9. Set your instant pot on Sauté mode; add chicken rolls and brown them for a few minutes. Divide among plates and serve

Chicken and Brown Rice

(Prep + Cooking Time: 43 minutes | Servings: 4)

Ingredients:
- 1 yellow onion; chopped.
- 8 oz. cremini mushrooms; roughly chopped.
- 2 cloves garlic; minced.
- 1 tbsp. extra-virgin olive oil
- 1 cup long-grain brown rice, rinsed
- 1¼ cups water
- 1 tsp. dried thyme
- 1 tsp. fine sea salt
- 1 lb. boneless, skinless chicken breasts
- Freshly ground black pepper
- 1 cup fresh or frozen peas
- 1 tbsp. freshly squeezed lemon juice
- ¼ cup full-fat canned coconut milk

Directions:
1. Press *Sauté* and add the olive oil to the Instant Pot. Once the oil is hot but not smoking, add the onion, mushrooms and garlic and sauté until softened, about 5 minutes
2. Add the brown rice, water, thyme and ½ teaspoon of the salt and stir well, scraping the bottom of the pot with a wooden spoon or spatula to make sure nothing has stuck.
3. Place the chicken breasts on top of the rice mixture and season with the remaining ½ teaspoon salt and several grinds of pepper. Press *Cancel* Button, then secure the lid and move the steam release valve to Sealing. Select *Manual/Pressure* Cook to cook on *High* pressure for 10 minutes
4. Once the cooking cycle is completed, quickly release the pressure by moving the steam release valve to Venting.
5. When the floating valve drops, remove the lid and use tongs to transfer the chicken to a cutting board to rest for 5 minutes. If using fresh peas, add them now, scattering them over the rice
6. Secure the lid again, making sure the sealing ring is properly placed. Turn the steam release valve to Sealing and select *Manual/Pressure* Cook to cook on *High* pressure for 8 minutes more. While the rice cooks, cut the chicken into bite-sized pieces
7. Once the cooking cycle is completed, let the pressure naturally release for 10 minutes, then move the steam release valve to Venting.
8. When the floating valve drops, remove the lid and stir the chicken into the rice, along with the lemon juice and coconut milk. If using frozen peas, add them now. Taste and adjust the seasoning as needed, then serve immediately

Sesame Honey Chicken

(Prep + Cooking Time: 48 minutes | Servings:6)

Ingredients:
- 2 lbs. boneless; skinless chicken breasts (5 or 6 breasts); cut into bite-size pieces.
- 2 garlic cloves; minced.
- 1 medium yellow onion; diced.
- ½ cup water
- 1 cup low-sodium chicken broth.
- ¼ cup reduced-sodium soy sauce
- ¼ cup honey
- 1 tbsp. extra-virgin olive oil.
- 2 tbsp. cornstarch
- 2 tsp. toasted sesame oil

Directions:
1. Take a small bowl, make a slurry by whisking together the cornstarch and water. Set aside
2. Select *Sauté* and add the olive oil to the inner pot. Once the oil is hot, add the garlic, onion, and chicken and sauté for 2 minutes, stirring occasionally. Turn the chicken over and let it cook for 2 more minutes.
3. Now, press *Cancel* and pour the broth into the pot. Using a wooden spoon, scrape up any browned bits stuck to the bottom of the pot. Add the soy sauce and honey and stir to combine
4. Now, Lock the lid. Select, "Manual or Pressure Cook" and set the pressure to *High* and the time to 8 minutes. Make sure the steam release knob is in the sealed position.

5. After completing the cooking cycle, naturally release the pressure for 10 minutes, then quick release any remaining pressure. Unlock and remove the lid. Using a slotted spoon, transfer the chicken to a plate.
6. Select *Sauté*. Once the liquid starts bubbling, whisk in the cornstarch slurry and sesame oil. Whisk consistently for 2 minutes or until the sauce starts to thicken. Serve hot.

Chicken Fajitas

(**Prep + Cooking Time:** 45 minutes | **Servings:**6)

Ingredients:
- 2 lbs. boneless; skinless chicken breasts (5 or 6 breasts); cut into 1-inch-thick strips
- ½ cup water
- 2 yellow bell peppers; seeded and sliced.
- 2 garlic cloves; minced.
- 2 red bell peppers; seeded and sliced.
- 2 tbsp. extra-virgin olive oil.
- Juice of 2 limes
- 1 medium yellow onion; diced.
- 1 tsp. ground cumin
- 1 tsp. chili powder
- 1 tsp. fine sea salt.
- ½ tsp. freshly ground black pepper.

Directions:
1. Select *Sauté* and add the olive oil to the inner pot. Once the oil is hot, add the chicken strips, bell peppers, garlic, onion, cumin, chili powder, salt, and black pepper; sauté for 2 minutes
2. Now, press *Cancel* and pour in the water. Using a wooden spoon, scrape up any browned bits stuck to the bottom of the pot
3. Now, Lock the lid. Select, "Manual or Pressure Cook" and set the pressure to *High* and the time to 10 minutes. Make sure the steam release knob is in the sealed position.
4. After completing the cooking cycle, naturally release the pressure for 10 minutes, then quick release any remaining pressure. Unlock and remove the lid. Stir in the lime juice. Serve hot

Butter Chicken

(**Prep + Cooking Time:** 45 minutes | **Servings:**6)

Ingredients:
- 2 lbs. boneless; skinless chicken breasts (5 or 6 breasts)
- 1 medium head cauliflower; cut into florets (about 3 cups)
- 1 cup low-sodium chicken broth.
- ½ cup full-fat canned coconut milk
- 2 garlic cloves; minced.
- 1 medium yellow onion; diced.
- 1 (6-oz.) can tomato paste
- 2 tbsp. unsalted butter; cut into small pieces
- 1 tbsp. extra-virgin olive oil.
- 1 tbsp. garam masala
- ¼ tsp. ground ginger
- ½ tsp. fine sea salt.

Directions:
1. Select *Sauté* and add the olive oil to the inner pot. Once the oil is hot, add the garlic, onion, garam masala, and ginger and sauté for 3 minutes, stirring occasionally
2. Now, press *Cancel* and pour the broth into the pot. Using a wooden spoon, scrape up any browned bits stuck to the bottom of the pot. Add the tomato paste, cauliflower, and chicken to the pot, but do not stir. Top the chicken with the butter pieces
3. Now, Lock the lid. Select, "Manual or Pressure Cook" and set the pressure to *High* and the time to 10 minutes. Make sure the steam release knob is in the sealed position.
4. After completing the cooking cycle, naturally release the pressure for 10 minutes, then quick release any remaining pressure.
5. Unlock and remove the lid. Using a slotted spoon, transfer the chicken to a cutting board. Use two forks to shred the chicken, then return it to the pot. Stir in the coconut milk and salt. Serve hot.

Chickpea Chicken Masala

(Prep + Cooking Time: 35 minutes | **Servings:** 4)

Ingredients:
- 3 lb. chicken drumsticks and thighs
- 1 yellow onion; finely chopped
- 2 tbsp. butter
- 1/2 cup chicken stock
- 15 oz. canned tomatoes; crushed.
- 1/4 cup lemon juice
- 15 oz. canned chickpeas; drained
- 4 garlic cloves; minced.
- 1 lb. spinach; chopped.
- 1/2 cup heavy cream
- 1 tbsp. ginger; grated
- 1/2 cup cilantro; chopped.
- 1 ½ tsp. paprika
- 1 tbsp. cumin; ground.
- 1 ½ tsp. coriander; ground.
- 1 tsp. turmeric; ground.
- Salt and black pepper to the taste
- A pinch of cayenne pepper

Directions:
1. Set your instant pot on Sauté mode; add butter and melt it
2. Add ginger, onion, and garlic, stir and cook for 5 minutes.
3. Add paprika, cumin, coriander, cayenne, turmeric, salt, and pepper, stir and cook for 30 seconds.
4. Add tomatoes and spinach; stir and cook for 2 minutes
5. Add half of the cilantro, chicken pieces, and stock; then stir well. seal the instant pot lid and cook at High for 15 minutes
6. Quick release the pressure, carefully open the lid; add heavy cream, chickpeas, lemon juice, more salt, and pepper; then stir well. set the pot on Sauté mode again and simmer for 3 minutes.
7. Sprinkle the rest of the cilantro on top; then stir well. divide among plates and serve.

Simple Chicken Delight

(Prep + Cooking Time: 50 minutes | **Servings:** 4)

Ingredients:
- 6 chicken thighs
- 1 tsp. vegetable oil
- 15 oz. canned tomatoes; chopped.
- 1 yellow onion; chopped.
- 2 tbsp. tomato paste
- 1/2 cup white wine
- 2 cups chicken stock
- 1 ½ lb. potatoes; chopped.
- 1 celery stalk; chopped.
- 1/4 lb. baby carrots; cut into halves
- 1/2 tsp. thyme; dried
- Salt and black pepper to the taste

Directions:
1. Set your instant pot on Sauté mode; add oil and heat it up
2. Add chicken pieces; salt and pepper to the taste and brown them for 4 minutes on each side.
3. Take chicken out of the pot and leave on a plate for now.
4. Add onion, carrots, celery, thyme and tomato paste to the pot, stir and cook for 5 minutes.
5. Add white wine and salt; stir and cook for 3 minutes
6. Add chicken stock, chicken pieces and chopped tomatoes and stir.
7. Place the steamer basket in the pot; add potatoes in it, seal the instant pot lid and cook at High for 30 minutes.
8. Quick release the pressure, take potatoes out of the pot and also take chicken pieces out.
9. Shred chicken meat and return to pot.
10. Also return potatoes; more salt and pepper; then stir well. divide among plates and serve

Garlic Chicken

(Prep + Cooking Time: 50 minutes | **Servings:** 4)

Ingredients:
- 1 lb. boneless; skinless chicken thighs
- 8 garlic cloves; chopped
- 1/4 cup heavy cream
- 1/4 cup water
- 2 tbsp. extra-virgin olive oil
- 2 tbsp. salted butter
- 1 tbsp. minced garlic
- 1 tbsp. Dijon mustard
- 1 tbsp. apple cider vinegar
- 2 tsp. herbes de Provence
- 1 tsp. salt or as your liking
- 1 tsp. black pepper

Directions:
1. In a large bowl, whisk together the mustard, vinegar; minced garlic, herbes de Provence, salt and pepper. Slowly whisk in the olive oil to emulsify and slightly thicken the mixture
2. Add the chicken and turn to coat. Allow the chicken to sit at room temperature for 30 minutes.
3. Now Press "Sauté" on the Instant Pot. When the pot is hot, add the butter. When the butter has melted, add the chicken, leaving as much marinade in the bowl as possible; set the marinade aside.
4. Cook the chicken, turning once, until lightly browned on both sides, 6 to 8 minutes. Transfer the chicken to a plate.
5. Add the chopped garlic to the pot. Cook, stirring continuously, until the garlic is fragrant and slightly softened, about 1 minute. Add the water and reserved marinade and whisk to combine. Return the chicken to the pot. Now Press "Cancel"
6. Now secure the lid on the pot and close the valve. Now Press "Manual" and set the pot at "High" pressure for 5 minutes
7. After completing the cooking time, allow the pot to sit undisturbed for 10 minutes, then release any remaining pressure. Transfer the chicken to a serving platter. Cover lightly with aluminum foil to keep warm.
8. Now Press "Sauté" on the Instant Pot. While stirring continuously, slowly add the cream in a steady stream. Cook, stirring, until the sauce starts to thicken, 5 to 8 minutes. Now Press "Cancel". Pour the sauce over the chicken and serve immediately.

Cheering Chicken Wings

(Prep + Cooking Time: 35 minutes | **Servings:** 6)

Ingredients:
- 12 chicken wings; cut into 24 pieces
- 1 cup yogurt
- 1 tbsp. parsley; finely chopped
- 4 tbsp. hot sauce
- 1 cup water
- 1/4 cup tomato puree
- 1 lb. celery; cut into thin matchsticks
- 1/4 cup honey
- Salt to the taste

Directions:
1. Put 1 cup water into your instant pot.
2. Place chicken wings in the steamer basket of your pot, seal the instant pot lid and cook at High for 19 minutes
3. Meanwhile; in a bowl, mix tomato puree with hot sauce, salt and honey and stir very well
4. Quick release the pressure, add chicken wings to honey mix and toss them to coat.
5. Arrange chicken wings on a lined baking sheet and introduce in preheated broiler for 5 minutes.
6. Arrange celery sticks on a platter and add chicken wings next to it.
7. In a bowl; mix yogurt with parsley, stir well and place next to the platter
8. Serve right away.

Turkey Bolognese with Spaghetti

(Prep + Cooking Time: 48 minutes | **Servings:** 4)

Ingredients:
- One 28-oz. can diced tomatoes
- One 3-lb. spaghetti squash
- 1 lb. ground turkey
- ¼ cup full-fat coconut milk (optional)
- 2 celery stalks, diced
- 2 carrots, diced
- 2 cloves garlic; minced.
- 1 yellow onion; chopped.
- 1 tbsp. aged balsamic vinegar
- 1 tbsp. extra-virgin olive oil
- ½ tsp. dried oregano
- 1 tsp. dried basil
- 1 tsp. pure maple syrup
- Fine sea salt
- Freshly ground black pepper
- Fresh basil; for garnish. (optional)

Directions:
1. Press *Sauté* and add the olive oil, onion, garlic, turkey and 1 teaspoon salt to the Instant Pot. Sauté until the turkey is browned and cooked through, breaking it up with a wooden spoon as you stir, about 8 minutes
2. While the meat is cooking, pour the diced tomatoes with their juices into a blender and blend until smooth. Set aside until the meat is browned.
3. Press *Cancel* Button to stop the cooking cycle. Add the blended tomatoes, the celery, carrots, vinegar, maple syrup, oregano, basil and ½ teaspoon salt and stir well
4. Wash the spaghetti squash and carefully pierce the skin once with a sharp knife to vent. Place the whole squash directly into the sauce, pierced side up.
5. Now, Lock the lid and Turn the steam release valve to "Sealing" Position. Select *Manual/Pressure* Cook to cook on *High* pressure for 15 minutes.
6. Once the cooking cycle is completed, let the pressure naturally release for 10 minutes, then move the steam release valve to Venting to release any remaining pressure
7. When the floating valve drops, remove the lid. Use oven mitts to lift the spaghetti squash out of the pot. Transfer it to a cutting board to cool slightly. Stir the coconut milk into the sauce and season with salt and pepper, to taste.
8. Cut the cooked squash in half crosswise and use a spoon to remove the seeds from the center. Use a fork to scrape out "noodles" from the squash and place them on plates. Spoon the Bolognese sauce on top of the noodles and serve

Italian Chicken

(Prep + Cooking Time: 30 minutes | **Servings:** 6)

Ingredients:
- 2 lb. chicken breasts; skinless and boneless
- 1 tbsp. extra-virgin olive oil
- 3/4 cup marinara sauce
- 2 tbsp. pesto
- 3/4 cup mushrooms; sliced
- 1/2 cup green bell pepper; chopped.
- 1/2 cup red bell pepper; chopped.
- Salt and black pepper to the taste
- 3/4 cup yellow onion; diced
- Cheddar cheese, shredded for serving

Directions:
1. Set your instant pot on Sauté mode; add the oil and heat it up
2. Add onion, red and green bell pepper; salt and pepper to the taste, stir and cook for 4 minutes.
3. Add pesto, marinara sauce and chicken; then stir well. seal the instant pot lid and cook at High for 12 minutes
4. Quick release the pressure; carefully open the lid; remove chicken, place on a cutting board and shred,
5. Discard 2/3 cup cooking liquid, add mushrooms to the pot, set it on Sauté mode again and cook them for 3 minutes.
6. Return chicken; then stir well. divide among plates and serve with shredded cheese on top

Turkey Bolognese.

(Prep + Cooking Time: 60 minutes | **Servings:** 6)

Ingredients:
- 2 lbs. ground turkey
- 1 (28-oz.) can crushed tomatoes
- 1 medium yellow onion; chopped.
- ½ cup water
- ½ cup red wine
- 2 garlic cloves; minced.
- 2 carrots, peeled and diced (about 1 cup)
- 2 tbsp. extra-virgin olive oil.
- 2 tbsp. tomato paste
- 1 tsp. dried oregano

Directions:
1. Select *Sauté* and add the olive oil to the inner pot. Once the oil is hot, add the onion, garlic, carrots, and tomato paste; sauté for 3 minutes or until the vegetables start to soften
2. Pour the wine into the pot. Using a wooden spoon, scrape up any browned bits stuck to the bottom of the pot.
3. Add the ground turkey. Use the wooden spoon to break the meat apart as it cooks, about 3 minutes.
4. Now, press *Cancel* and add the crushed tomatoes, water, and oregano
5. Now, Lock the lid. Select, "Manual or Pressure Cook" and set the pressure to *High* and the time to 10 minutes. Make sure the steam release knob is in the sealed position.
6. After completing the cooking cycle, naturally release the pressure for 10 minutes, then quick release any remaining pressure
7. Unlock and remove the lid. Stir the sauce. If you want to thicken the sauce, select *Sauté* and let the sauce simmer for about 10 minutes. Serve hot

Chicken Curry

(Prep + Cooking Time: 40 minutes | **Servings:** 6)

Ingredients:
- 1 lb. boneless; skinless chicken thighs, cut into 3 pieces each
- 1 large potato; peeled and cut into 1-inch chunks
- 1 Scotch bonnet chile; sliced
- 1 cup chopped yellow onion
- 3 sprigs fresh thyme
- 1 cup water
- 2 tbsp. vegetable oil
- 1 tbsp. minced fresh ginger
- 1 tbsp. minced garlic
- 4 ½ tsp. Jamaican curry powder
- 1 tsp. salt or as your liking
- 1/2 tsp. ground allspice

Directions:
1. Now Press "Sauté" on the Instant Pot. When the pot is hot, add the oil. When the oil is hot, add the ginger and garlic. Cook, stirring continuously, just until fragrant, about 20 seconds
2. Add the onion and cook, stirring, for 1 to 2 minutes. Add the curry powder, chile, thyme, salt and allspice. Stir to combine.
3. If anything is browning or sticking to the bottom of the pot, add ¼ to ⅓ cup water and stir, scraping up the browned bits from the bottom and allowing the water to evaporate. Now Press "Cancel"
4. Add the chicken, potato and the 1 cup water to the pot. Stir to combine.
5. Now secure the lid on the pot and close the valve. Now Press "Manual" and set the pot at "High" pressure for 6 minutes.
6. After completing the cooking time, allow the pot to sit undisturbed for 10 minutes, then release any remaining pressure

Whole Chicken

(**Prep + Cooking Time:** 60 minutes | **Servings:** 10)

Ingredients:
- 1 (4½- to 5-lb.) whole chicken, giblets removed.
- 1 cup water
- 1 tbsp. extra-virgin olive oil.
- ½ tsp. garlic powder
- 1 tsp. dried thyme
- 2 tsp. fine sea salt.

Directions:
1. Place the trivet in the inner pot, then pour in the water. Place the chicken breast-side down on the trivet and drizzle it with the olive oil. Sprinkle the thyme, garlic powder, and salt over the chicken
2. Now, Lock the lid. Select, "Manual or Pressure Cook" and set the pressure to *High* and the time to 30 minutes. Make sure the steam release knob is in the sealed position.
3. After completing the cooking cycle, naturally release the pressure for 10 minutes, then quick release any remaining pressure.
4. Unlock and remove the lid. Using tongs, transfer the chicken to a serving plate. Serve hot

Three Cup Chicken

(**Prep + Cooking Time:** 40 minutes | **Servings:** 6)

Ingredients:
- 2 lbs. boneless; skinless chicken thighs, halved
- 6 dried red chiles
- 1/4 cup soy sauce
- 1/4 cup rice wine
- 1/4 cup toasted sesame oil
- 1/4 cup chopped fresh Thai basil
- 1/4 cup crushed garlic cloves
- 1 tbsp. cornstarch mixed with 1 tbsp. water
- 2 tbsp. julienned fresh ginger
- Salt to taste

Directions:
1. Now Press "Sauté" on the Instant Pot. When the pot is hot, add the sesame oil. When the oil is hot, add the chiles, garlic and ginger
2. Cook, stirring frequently, until the ginger and garlic are just starting to crisp, about 2 minutes. Now Press "Cancel"
3. Add the chicken, soy sauce and rice wine to the pot and season with salt. Stir to combine.
4. Now secure the lid on the pot and close the valve. Now Press "Manual" and set the pot at "High" pressure for 7 minutes
5. After completing the cooking time, allow the pot to stand undisturbed for 10 minutes, then release any remaining pressure.
6. Now Press "Sauté" on the Instant Pot. Add the basil and stir to combine. When the mixture comes to a boil, sprinkle over the xanthan gum and simmer until slightly thickened, 3 to 4 minutes. Now Press "Cancel". Serve

Delicious Chicken in Tomatillo Sauce

(**Prep + Cooking Time:** 35 minutes | **Servings:** 6)

Ingredients:
- 1 lb. chicken thighs; skinless and boneless
- 2 tbsp. extra virgin olive oil
- 5 oz. canned garbanzo beans; drained
- 1 yellow onion; thinly sliced
- 1 garlic clove; crushed.
- 4 oz. canned green chilies; chopped.
- 1 handful cilantro; finely chopped
- 15 oz. rice; already cooked
- 5 oz. tomatoes; chopped.
- 15 oz. cheddar cheese; grated
- 4 oz. black olives; pitted and chopped.
- Salt and black pepper to the taste
- 15 oz. canned tomatillos; chopped.

Directions:
1. Set your instant pot on Sauté mode; add oil and heat it up
2. Add onions, stir and cook for 5 minutes.
3. Add garlic, stir and cook 15 more seconds.
4. Add chicken, chilies, salt, pepper, cilantro, and tomatillos; then stir well. seal the instant pot lid and cook on Poultry mode for 8 minutes
5. Quick release the pressure, carefully open the lid; take the chicken out and shred it.
6. Return chicken to pot; add rice, beans, set the instant pot on Sauté mode again and cook for 1 minute.
7. Add cheese, tomatoes, and olives; then stir well. cook for 2 minutes more; divide among plates and serve

Easy Turkey Chili

(**Prep + Cooking Time:** 20 minutes | **Servings:** 4)

Ingredients:
- 1 lb. turkey meat; ground.
- 15 oz. chickpeas; already cooked
- 1 ½ tsp. cumin
- 5 oz. water
- 1 yellow onion; chopped.
- 1 yellow bell pepper; chopped.
- 3 garlic cloves; chopped.
- 2 ½ tbsp. chili powder
- A pinch of cayenne pepper
- 12 oz. veggies stock
- Salt and black pepper to the taste

Directions:
1. Put turkey meat in your instant pot.
2. Add water; then stir well. seal the Instant Pot lid and cook at High for 5 minutes
3. Quick release the pressure; open the instant pot lid and add chickpeas, bell pepper, onion, garlic, chili powder, cumin, salt, pepper, cayenne and veggie stock.
4. Stir, seal the instant pot lid and cook at High for 5 minutes.
5. Release the pressure naturally for 10 minutes; then release remaining pressure by turning the valve to 'Venting', open the instant pot lid again, stir chili, divide it among plates and serve

Awesome Chicken Adobo

(**Prep + Cooking Time:** 1 hour 10 minutes | **Servings:** 6)

Ingredients:
- 6 bone-in, skin-on chicken thighs
- 3 bay leaves
- 1/2 cup white vinegar
- 1/4 cup soy sauce
- 2 tbsp. vegetable oil
- 2 tbsp. minced garlic
- 1 tbsp. brown sugar
- 1 tsp. whole black peppercorns; crushed
- 1 tsp. red pepper flakes; optional

Directions:
1. In a large bowl, combine the vinegar, soy sauce, oil, garlic, brown sugar, peppercorns, red pepper flakes and bay leaves
2. Stir to combine. Add the chicken thighs and toss well to coat. Allow the chicken to stand at room temperature for 30 minutes.
3. Transfer the chicken and marinade to the Instant Pot. Now secure the lid on the pot and close the valve. Now Press "Manual" and set the pot at "High" pressure for 8 minutes
4. After completing the cooking time, allow the pot to sit undisturbed for 10 minutes, then release any remaining pressure.
5. Meanwhile; preheat the broiler. Line a baking sheet with aluminum foil
6. Transfer the chicken to the prepared baking sheet. Broil until the skin crisps, 3 to 5 minutes.
7. Meanwhile; select "Sauté" on the Instant Pot and simmer the sauce until it has thickened, 3 to 5 minutes. Now Press "Cancel".
8. Transfer the chicken to a platter. Pour the sauce over the chicken and serve

Barbeque Honey Chicken

(Prep + Cooking Time: 35 minutes | **Servings:** 4)

Ingredients:
- 2 lb. chicken wings
- 1/2 cup water
- 1/2 tsp. basil; dried
- 3/4 cup honey BBQ sauce
- 1/2 cup apple juice
- 1 tsp. red pepper; crushed.
- 2 tsp. paprika
- 1/2 cup brown sugar
- Salt and black pepper to the taste
- A pinch of cayenne pepper

Directions:
1. Put chicken wings in your instant pot
2. Add BBQ sauce, apple juice, salt, pepper, red pepper, paprika, basil, sugar, and water.
3. Stir, seal the Instant Pot lid and cook at High for 10 minutes
4. Quick release the pressure, carefully open the lid; transfer chicken to a baking sheet, add sauce all over, introduce in preheated broiler, broil for 7 minutes, flip chicken wings, broil for 7 more minutes, divide among plates and serve

Delicious Chicken Sandwiches

(Prep + Cooking Time: 25 minutes | **Servings:** 8)

Ingredients:
- 20 oz. canned pineapple and its juice; chopped.
- 6 chicken breasts; skinless and boneless
- 1 tsp. soy sauce
- 1 tbsp. cornstarch
- 1/4 cup brown sugar
- 8 hamburger buns
- 12 oz. canned orange juice
- 2 tbsp. lemon juice
- 15 oz. canned peaches and their juice
- 8 grilled pineapple slices; for serving

Directions:
1. In a bowl, mix orange juice with soy sauce, lemon juice, canned pineapples pieces, peaches and sugar and stir well
2. Pour half of this mix in your instant pot; add chicken and pour the rest of the sauce over meat.
3. Cover the pot and cook at High for 12 minutes
4. Quick release the pressure, take the chicken and put on a cutting board
5. Shred meat and leave aside for now.
6. In a bowl; mix cornstarch with 1 tablespoon cooking juice and stir well.
7. Transfer the sauce to a pot, add cornstarch mix and chicken, stir and cook for a few more minutes.
8. Divide this chicken mix on hamburger buns; top with grilled pineapple pieces and serve

Chicken Curry

(Prep + Cooking Time: 30 minutes | **Servings:** 4)

Ingredients:
- 15 oz. chicken breast; chopped.
- 5 oz. canned coconut cream
- 1 tbsp. extra-virgin olive oil
- 1 yellow onion; thinly sliced
- 6 potatoes; cut into halves
- 1 bag chicken curry base
- 1/2 bunch coriander; chopped

Directions:
1. Set your instant pot on Sauté mode; add the oil and heat it up
2. Add chicken; stir and brown for 2 minutes
3. Add onion; stir and cook for 1 minute
4. In a bowl; mix curry base with coconut cream and stir.
5. Pour this over chicken; also add potatoes; then stir well. seal the instant pot lid and cook at High for 15 minutes.

6. Release pressure fast; carefully open the lid; divide curry among plates and serve with chopped coriander on top.

Moroccan Chicken

(**Prep + Cooking Time:** 35 minutes | **Servings:** 4)

Ingredients:
- 6 chicken thighs
- 1 tsp. cloves
- 2 tbsp. extra virgin olive oil
- 10 cardamom pods
- 1/2 tsp. cumin
- 1/2 tsp. ginger
- 1/2 cup parsley; finely chopped
- 1/2 tsp. turmeric
- 1/2 tsp. cinnamon; ground.
- 2 bay leaves
- 1/2 tsp. coriander
- 2 yellow onions; chopped.
- 2 tbsp. tomato paste
- 5 garlic cloves; chopped.
- 1/4 cup cranberries; dried
- Juice of 1 lemon
- 1 cup green olives
- 1 cup chicken stock
- 1 tsp. paprika
- 1/4 cup white wine

Directions:
1. In a bowl; mix bay leaf with cardamom, cloves, coriander, ginger, cumin, cinnamon, turmeric and paprika and stir
2. Set your instant pot on Sauté mode; add the oil and heat up
3. Add chicken thighs; brown for a few minutes and transfer to a plate.
4. Add onion to the pot, stir and cook for 4 minutes
5. Add garlic, stir and cook for 1 minute.
6. Add wine, tomato paste, spices from the bowl, stock and chicken
7. Stir; seal the Instant Pot lid and cook at High for 15 minutes.
8. Quick release the pressure, discard bay leaf, cardamom, and cloves, add olives, cranberries, lemon juice and parsley; then stir well. divide chicken mix among plates and serve

Chicken Salad

(**Prep + Cooking Time:** 60 minutes | **Servings:** 2)

Ingredients:
- 1 chicken breast, skinless and boneless
- 3 tbsp. extra virgin olive oil
- 1 tbsp. mustard
- 3 garlic cloves; minced.
- 1 tbsp. balsamic vinegar
- 1 tbsp. honey
- Mixed salad greens
- A handful cherry tomatoes; cut into halves
- 3 cups water
- Salt and black pepper to the taste

Directions:
1. In a bowl; mix 2 cups water with salt to the taste.
2. Add chicken to this mix, stir and keep in the fridge for 45 minutes.
3. Add 1 cup water to your instant pot, place chicken breast in the steamer basket of the pot, seal the instant pot lid and cook at High for 5 minutes.
4. Release the pressure naturally; leave chicken breast on a plate for 8 minutes and cut into thin strips.
5. In a bowl, mix garlic with salt and pepper to the taste, mustard, honey, vinegar and olive oil and whisk very well.
6. In a salad bowl; mix chicken strips with salad greens and tomatoes.
7. Drizzle the vinaigrette on top and serve.

Delicious Chicken Cacciatore

(Prep + Cooking Time: 52 minutes | **Servings:** 6)

Ingredients:
- 2 lbs. boneless; skinless chicken breasts (5 or 6 breasts)
- ½ cup white wine
- ½ cup low-sodium chicken broth.
- 2 garlic cloves; minced.
- 1 medium yellow onion; diced.
- 2 red bell peppers; seeded and sliced.
- 1 cup button mushrooms; sliced.
- 1 (14-oz.) can crushed tomatoes
- 2 tbsp. extra-virgin olive oil.
- 1 tbsp. balsamic vinegar
- ½ tsp. dried oregano
- ½ tsp. fine sea salt.
- ½ tsp. freshly ground black pepper.

Directions:
1. Select *Sauté* and add the olive oil to the inner pot. Once the oil is hot, add the chicken, garlic, onion, oregano, and salt and sauté for 3 minutes, stirring occasionally. Turn the chicken once and sauté for 3 minutes more, so both sides start to brown
2. Now, press *Cancel* and pour the wine into the pot. Using a wooden spoon, scrape up any browned bits stuck to the bottom of the pot. Add the broth, bell peppers, mushrooms, and crushed tomatoes and stir to combine
3. Now, Lock the lid. Select, "Manual or Pressure Cook" and set the pressure to *High* and the time to 12 minutes. Make sure the steam release knob is in the sealed position.
4. After completing the cooking cycle, naturally release the pressure for 10 minutes, then quick release any remaining pressure. Unlock and remove the lid. Stir in the black pepper and vinegar. Serve hot

Chicken Dish

(Prep + Cooking Time: 45 minutes | **Servings:** 8)

Ingredients:
- 1 whole chicken
- 1 tbsp. cumin powder
- 1 ½ tbsp. lemon zest
- 1 cup chicken stock
- 1 tbsp. thyme leaves
- 1/2 tsp. cinnamon powder
- 2 tsp. garlic powder
- 1 tbsp. coriander powder
- 1 tbsp. extra-virgin olive oil
- Salt and black pepper to the taste

Directions:
1. In a bowl, mix cinnamon with cumin; garlic, coriander, salt, pepper and lemon zest and stir well.
2. Rub chicken with half of the oil, then rub it inside and out with spices mix
3. Set your instant pot on Sauté mode; add the rest of the oil and heat it up.
4. Add chicken and brown it on all sides for 5 minutes
5. Add stock and thyme; then stir well. seal the instant pot lid and cook at High for 25 minutes.
6. Release the pressure naturally and transfer chicken to a platter.
7. Add cooking liquid over it and serve

Chicken Enchilada Casserole

(Prep + Cooking Time: 35 minutes | **Servings:** 4)

Ingredients:
- 2 boneless; skinless chicken breasts
- 1 ½ cups Fire-Roasted Enchilada Sauce
- 4 corn tortillas, cut into 8 pieces each
- 1 cup diced white onions
- 1 cup shredded Mexican cheese blend
- 1 (4.5-ounce) can diced green chiles
- Vegetable oil

Directions:
1. In your Instant Pot, combine the enchilada sauce, chiles and onions. Stir to combine. Add the chicken to the pot
2. Now secure the lid on the pot and close the valve. Now Press "Manual" and set the pot at "High" pressure for 15 minutes. Meanwhile; preheat the oven to 400°F. Grease a 2-quart baking dish with oil
3. After completing the cooking time, quick release the pressure. Remove the chicken from the pot. Using two forks, shred the chicken and return it to the pot. Stir in the tortilla pieces.
4. Transfer the chicken mixture to the prepared baking dish. Top evenly with the cheese. Bake until the cheese melts and is lightly browned and bubbling, about 10 minutes

Balsamic Chicken with Vegetables

(**Prep + Cooking Time:** 50 minutes | **Servings:** 6)

Ingredients:
- 2 lbs. boneless; skinless chicken breasts (5 or 6 breasts)
- ½ lb. zucchini; cut into 1-inch-thick pieces
- ½ lb. small potatoes, halved
- ½ lb. rainbow carrots, peeled and cut into 1-inch-thick pieces
- 2 garlic cloves; minced.
- ½ cup water
- 1 cup low-sodium chicken broth.
- 2 tbsp. balsamic vinegar
- 1 tbsp. unsalted butter
- 1 tbsp. cornstarch
- 2 tbsp. extra-virgin olive oil.
- 1 tsp. dried thyme
- ½ tsp. salt

Directions:
1. Take a small bowl, make a slurry by whisking together the cornstarch and water. Set aside
2. Select *Sauté* and add the olive oil to the inner pot. Once the oil is hot, place the chicken in the pot, along with the garlic, thyme, and salt. *Sauté* the garlic and chicken for 4 minutes, turning the chicken once so it browns on both sides. Using a spoon, transfer the chicken and garlic to a plate.
3. Now, press *Cancel* and add the broth and vinegar. Using a wooden spoon, scrape up any browned bits stuck to the bottom of the pot. Add the carrots, zucchini, and potatoes to the pot. Stir to combine. Place the chicken and garlic on top of the vegetables, but don't stir
4. Now, Lock the lid. Select, "Manual or Pressure Cook" and set the pressure to *High* and the time to 10 minutes. Make sure the steam release knob is in the sealed position.
5. After completing the cooking cycle, naturally release the pressure for 10 minutes, then quick release any remaining pressure.
6. Unlock and remove the lid. Use a slotted spoon to remove the chicken and vegetables to a serving bowl
7. Select *Sauté*. Once the liquid starts bubbling, whisk in the cornstarch slurry and butter until well combined. Whisk consistently for 2 minutes or until the sauce starts to thicken
8. Now, press *Cancel* and return the chicken and vegetables to the pot. Stir to combine. Serve hot

Delicious Chicken with Cumin-Chile Sauce

(**Prep + Cooking Time:** 30 minutes | **Servings:** 8)

Ingredients:
- 2 lbs. boneless; skinless chicken thighs, cut into bite-size pieces
- 1 (5-ounce) can tomato paste
- 1 (14-ounce) can diced tomatoes; undrained
- 1 small white onion; chopped
- 1/4 cup pickled jalapeños, drained
- 3 garlic cloves; minced
- 1 tbsp. salt or as your liking
- 2 tbsp. vegetable oil
- 4 ½ tsp. ground cumin
- 4 ½ tsp. chili powder

Directions:
1. In a small bowl, combine the cumin, chili powder and salt. Place the chicken in a large bowl. Sprinkle the chicken with the spice mixture. Toss well to coat
2. Now Press "Sauté" on the Instant Pot. When the pot is hot, add the oil.

3. When the oil is hot, add the chicken. Cook, stirring, until the chicken is lightly browned, 4 to 5 minutes. Now Press "Cancel"
4. Add the diced tomatoes and their juices, onion, tomato paste, jalapeños and garlic to the pot. Stir to combine.
5. Now secure the lid on the pot and close the valve. Now Press "Manual" and set the pot at "High" pressure for 15 minutes.
6. After completing the cooking time, allow the pot to sit undisturbed for 10 minutes, then release any remaining pressure. Serve with tortillas, sour cream and guacamole

Arroz Con Pollo

(Prep + Cooking Time: 46 minutes | **Servings:** 6)

Ingredients:
- 1 lb. boneless; skinless chicken thighs, cut into bite-size chunks
- 2 tomatoes, quartered
- 1/2 cup coarsely chopped fresh cilantro
- 3 garlic cloves; crushed
- 1/2 jalapeño
- 1 cup basmati rice; rinsed and drained
- 1/2 yellow onion, quartered
- 1 ½ cups water
- 2 tbsp. vegetable oil
- 2 tsp. ground cumin
- 1 tsp. salt or as your liking
- Tomatillo salsa, for serving

Directions:
1. In a blender, combine the onion, tomatoes, cilantro, garlic and jalapeño. Blend until smooth
2. Now Press "Sauté" on the Instant Pot. When the pot is hot, add the oil. When the oil is hot, add the rice and cook, stirring frequently, until the rice is translucent, 3 to 4 minutes. Add the chicken, cumin, and salt. Cook, stirring, for 1 to 2 minutes. Now Press "Cancel"
3. Add the blended vegetables and the water. Stir well to combine.
4. Now secure the lid on the pot and close the valve. Now Press "Manual" and set the pot at "High" pressure for 6 minutes.
5. After completing the cooking time, allow the pot to sit undisturbed for 10 minutes, then release any remaining pressure. Serve with tomatillo salsa, if desired

Potatoes and Chicken

(Prep + Cooking Time: 30 minutes | **Servings:** 4)

Ingredients:
- 2 lb. chicken thighs; skinless and boneless
- 3/4 cup chicken stock
- 1/4 cup lemon juice
- 2 lb. red potatoes; peeled and cut into quarters
- 2 tbsp. extra virgin olive oil
- 3 tbsp. Dijon mustard
- 2 tbsp. Italian seasoning
- Salt and black pepper to the taste

Directions:
1. Set your instant pot on sauté mode; add the oil and heat it up.
2. Add chicken thighs, salt, and pepper, stir and brown for 2 minutes
3. In a bowl; mix stock with mustard, Italian seasoning, and lemon juice and stir well.
4. Pour this over chicken, add potatoes; then stir well. seal the instant pot lid and cook at High for 15 minutes.
5. Quick release the pressure, carefully open the lid; stir chicken, divide among plates and serve

Mushroom Chicken

(Prep + Cooking Time: 45 minutes | **Servings:** 4)

Ingredients:
- 1 lb. boneless; skinless chicken thighs
- 2 cups quartered button mushrooms
- 4 sprigs fresh thyme
- 6 garlic cloves; thickly sliced
- 1 cup sliced yellow onions
- 4 cups baby spinach
- 1/2 cup heavy cream
- 1 tbsp. fresh lemon juice
- 2 tbsp. salted butter
- 2 tbsp. water
- 1 tsp. salt or as your liking
- 1 tsp. black pepper

Directions:
1. Now Press "Sauté" on the Instant Pot. When the pot is hot, add the butter. When the butter has melted, add the garlic
2. Cook, stirring continuously, until garlic is fragrant and slightly softened, about 1 minute.
3. Add the onions and mushrooms and stir to coat. Add the chicken, thyme, water, salt and pepper. Stir to combine. Place the spinach on top of the chicken mixture. Now Press "Cancel"
4. Now secure the lid on the pot and close the valve. Now Press "Manual" and set the pot at "High" pressure for 8 minutes.
5. After completing the cooking time, allow the pot to sit undisturbed for 10 minutes, then release any remaining pressure
6. Transfer the chicken to a serving platter. Cover lightly with aluminum foil to keep warm.
7. Now Press "Sauté" on the Instant Pot. While stirring continuously, slowly add the cream in a steady stream.
8. Cook, stirring, until the mixture starts to thicken, 5 to 8 minutes. Stir in the lemon juice. Now Press "Cancel". Serve the chicken with the mushroom-spinach mixture

Three Cup Chicken

(Prep + Cooking Time: 40 minutes | **Servings:** 6)

Ingredients:
- 2 lbs. boneless; skinless chicken thighs, halved
- 6 dried red chiles
- 1/4 cup soy sauce
- 1/4 cup rice wine
- 1/4 cup toasted sesame oil
- 1/4 cup chopped fresh Thai basil
- 1/4 cup crushed garlic cloves
- 1 tbsp. cornstarch mixed with 1 tbsp. water
- 2 tbsp. julienned fresh ginger
- Salt to taste

Directions:
7. Now Press "Sauté" on the Instant Pot. When the pot is hot, add the sesame oil. When the oil is hot, add the chiles, garlic and ginger
8. Cook, stirring frequently, until the ginger and garlic are just starting to crisp, about 2 minutes. Now Press "Cancel".
9. Add the chicken, soy sauce and rice wine to the pot and season with salt. Stir to combine.
10. Now secure the lid on the pot and close the valve. Now Press "Manual" and set the pot at "High" pressure for 7 minutes
11. After completing the cooking time, allow the pot to stand undisturbed for 10 minutes, then release any remaining pressure
12. Now Press "Sauté" on the Instant Pot. Add the basil and stir to combine. When the mixture comes to a boil, sprinkle over the xanthan gum and simmer until slightly thickened, 3 to 4 minutes. Now Press "Cancel". Serve.

Dolma Casserole

(Prep + Cooking Time: 40 minutes | **Servings:** 4)

Ingredients:
- 1 cup chopped yellow onions
- 1 lb. 85% lean ground beef
- 8 ounces brined grape leaves, drained and chopped
- ⅓ cup fresh lemon juice
- 1/4 cup chopped fresh mint
- 1 cup basmati rice; rinsed and drained
- 1 cup water
- 2 tbsp. extra-virgin olive oil
- 1 tbsp. minced garlic
- 1/4 cup chopped fresh parsley
- 1 tsp. ground allspice
- 1 tsp. salt or as your liking
- 1 tsp. black pepper

Directions:
1. Press "Sauté" on the Instant Pot. When the pot is hot, add the olive oil. When the oil is hot, add the garlic and onions
2. Stir to combine. Add the beef and cook, stirring just enough to break up the clumps, for 2 to 3 minutes (don't worry about it being fully cooked at this point). Add the water, rice, grape leaves, parsley, allspice, salt and pepper. Stir well to combine. Now Press "Cancel"
3. Now secure the lid on the pot and close the valve. Now Press "Manual" and set the pot at "High" pressure for 4 minutes.
4. After completing the cooking time, let the pot sit undisturbed for 10 minutes, then release any remaining pressure. Gently stir in the lemon juice and mint. Serve with tzatziki on the side

Sweet Corn Chicken Soup

(Prep + Cooking Time: 30 minutes | **Servings:** 6)

Ingredients:
- 1 lb. boneless; skinless chicken thighs, cut into bite-size pieces
- 1/4 cup water; optional
- 1/4 cup chopped scallions; Green part
- 3 cups water
- 2 (14-ounce) cans creamed corn
- 2 tbsp. cornstarch; optional
- 1 tbsp. toasted sesame oil
- 1 tbsp. apple cider vinegar
- 1 tbsp. soy sauce
- 1 tsp. salt or as your liking
- 1 tsp. white pepper

Directions:
1. In your Instant Pot, combine the chicken, water, creamed corn, vinegar, soy sauce, salt and white pepper
2. Now secure the lid on the pot and close the valve. Now Press "Manual" and set the pot at "High" pressure for 10 minutes.
3. After completing the cooking time, allow the pot to sit undisturbed for 10 minutes, then release any remaining pressure
4. If you are using cornstarch to thicken the mixture, in a small bowl, stir together the water and cornstarch to make a slurry.
5. Now Press Sauté on the Instant Pot. When the soup boils, stir in the slurry and cook, stirring continuously, until soup is slightly thickened, 2 to 3 minutes. Now Press "Cancel"
6. Stir in the sesame oil. Divide the soup among six serving bowls. Garnish with the scallions and serve

Teriyaki Chicken Delight

(**Prep + Cooking Time:** 25 minutes | **Servings:** 6)

Ingredients:
- 2 lb. chicken breasts; skinless and boneless
- 2/3 cup teriyaki sauce
- 1 tbsp. honey
- 1/2 cup chicken stock
- A handful green onions; chopped.
- Salt and black pepper to the taste

Directions:
1. Set your instant pot on Sauté mode; add teriyaki sauce and honey, stir and simmer for 1 minute
2. Add stock; chicken, salt and pepper; then stir well. seal the instant pot lid and cook at High for 12 minutes
3. Quick release the pressure, take chicken breasts; place them on a cutting board and shred with 2 forks.
4. Remove 1/2 cup of cooking liquid; return shredded chicken to pot; add green onions; then stir well. divide among plates and serve

Garlic Chicken

(**Prep + Cooking Time:** 50 minutes | **Servings:** 4)

Ingredients:
- 1 lb. boneless; skinless chicken thighs
- 8 garlic cloves; chopped
- 1/4 cup heavy cream
- 1/4 cup water
- 2 tbsp. extra-virgin olive oil
- 2 tbsp. salted butter
- 1 tbsp. minced garlic
- 1 tbsp. Dijon mustard
- 1 tbsp. apple cider vinegar
- 2 tsp. herbes de Provence
- 1 tsp. salt or as your liking
- 1 tsp. black pepper

Directions:
9. In a large bowl, whisk together the mustard, vinegar; minced garlic, herbes de Provence, salt and pepper. Slowly whisk in the olive oil to emulsify and slightly thicken the mixture
10. Add the chicken and turn to coat. Allow the chicken to sit at room temperature for 30 minutes.
11. Now Press "Sauté" on the Instant Pot. When the pot is hot, add the butter. When the butter has melted, add the chicken, leaving as much marinade in the bowl as possible; set the marinade aside
12. Cook the chicken, turning once, until lightly browned on both sides, 6 to 8 minutes. Transfer the chicken to a plate
13. Add the chopped garlic to the pot. Cook, stirring continuously, until the garlic is fragrant and slightly softened, about 1 minute. Add the water and reserved marinade and whisk to combine. Return the chicken to the pot. Now Press "Cancel"
14. Now secure the lid on the pot and close the valve. Now Press "Manual" and set the pot at "High" pressure for 5 minutes.
15. After completing the cooking time, allow the pot to sit undisturbed for 10 minutes, then release any remaining pressure. Transfer the chicken to a serving platter. Cover lightly with aluminum foil to keep warm.
16. Now Press "Sauté" on the Instant Pot. While stirring continuously, slowly add the cream in a steady stream. Cook, stirring, until the sauce starts to thicken, 5 to 8 minutes. Now Press "Cancel". Pour the sauce over the chicken and serve immediately

Asian Chicken

(Prep + Cooking Time: 25 minutes | **Servings:** 6)

Ingredients:
- 1 ½ lbs. boneless; skinless chicken thighs, cut into 4 pieces each
- 1/2 cup grated fresh ginger
- 1/4 cup chopped fresh cilantro
- 1 (14.5-ounce) can diced tomatoes; undrained
- 2 tbsp. fresh lemon juice
- 2 tbsp. vegetable oil
- 1 tsp. ground cumin
- 2 tsp. Garam Masala
- 1 tsp. salt or as your liking
- 1/2 to 1 tsp. cayenne pepper
- Fresh ginger, cut into julienne, for serving

Directions:
1. Now Press "Sauté" on the Instant Pot. When the pot is hot, add the oil. When the oil is hot, add the minced ginger. Cook, stirring, until it starts to brown, 2 to 3 minutes
2. Now Press "Cancel". Add the chicken, tomatoes with their juices, cumin, 1 tsp. of the garam masala, the salt and the cayenne. Stir to combine.
3. Now secure the lid on the pot and close the valve. Now Press "Manual" and set the pot at "High" pressure for 5 minutes
4. After completing the cooking time, allow the pot to sit undisturbed for 10 minutes, then release any remaining pressure.
5. Stir in the cilantro, lemon juice, remaining 1 tsp. garam masala and the julienned ginger and serve

Chicken with Rice

(Prep + Cooking Time: 55 minutes | **Servings:** 4)

Ingredients:
For Rice:
- 1 cup water
- 1 cup basmati rice; rinsed and drained
- 1 tbsp. vegetable oil
- 1 tsp. salt or as your liking

For Chicken:
- 1 lb. boneless; skinless chicken thighs
- 4 ounces (½-stick) salted butter, cubed
- 1 (14.5-ounce) can diced tomatoes; undrained
- 1 tbsp. minced garlic
- 1 tbsp. minced fresh ginger
- 2 tsp. Garam Masala
- 1 tsp. ground turmeric
- 1 tsp. paprika
- 1 tsp. salt or as your liking
- 1 tsp. ground cumin
- 1 tsp. cayenne pepper
- 1/2 cup heavy cream
- ½ cup chopped fresh cilantro

Directions:
1. In a heatproof bowl 6-Inch or 7-inch, combine the rice, water, ghee and salt
2. In your Instant Pot, combine the tomatoes and their juices, garlic, ginger, 1 tsp. of the garam masala, the turmeric, paprika, salt, cumin and cayenne.
3. Stir to combine. Add the chicken. Place a tall steamer rack on top of the chicken mixture. Place the bowl of rice on the rack
4. Now secure the lid on the pot and close the valve. Now Press "Manual" and set the pot at "High" pressure for 10 minutes.
5. After completing the cooking time, allow the pot to sit undisturbed for 10 minutes, then release any remaining pressure.
6. Remove the bowl of rice and set aside. Remove the chicken and set aside on a plate.
7. Using an immersion blender, blend the sauce directly in the pot until smooth. Let the sauce cool for 5 minutes
8. Stir in the butter, cream, cilantro and remaining 1 tsp. garam masala. Remove half the sauce, transfer to a storage container and freeze or refrigerate for another use.

9. Break up the chicken into bite-size pieces and add it to the sauce in the pot. Serve the chicken with the hot rice

Lemon Piccata Chicken

(Prep + Cooking Time: 50 minutes | **Servings:** 6)

Ingredients:
- 2 lbs. boneless; skinless chicken breasts (5 or 6 breasts)
- 1½ cups low-sodium chicken broth.
- ⅓ cup capers, drained and rinsed
- ½ cup water
- 2 tbsp. extra-virgin olive oil.
- 2 tbsp. unsalted butter
- 2 tbsp. cornstarch
- Juice of 2 medium lemons
- ¼ tsp. fine sea salt (optional)

Directions:
1. Take a small bowl, make a slurry by whisking together the cornstarch and water. Set aside
2. Select *Sauté* and add the olive oil to the inner pot. Once the oil is hot, place the chicken breasts in the pot and brown them for 2 minutes per side.
3. Now, press *Cancel* and add the broth and capers. Using a wooden spoon, scrape up any browned bits stuck to the bottom of the pot
4. Now, Lock the lid. Select, "Manual or Pressure Cook" and set the pressure to *High* and the time to 10 minutes. Make sure the steam release knob is in the sealed position.
5. After completing the cooking cycle, naturally release the pressure for 10 minutes, then quick release any remaining pressure. Unlock and remove the lid. Use a slotted spoon to remove the chicken to a plate
6. Select *Sauté*. Once the liquid starts bubbling, whisk in the cornstarch slurry and butter. Whisk constantly for 2 minutes or until the sauce starts to thicken
7. Now, press *Cancel* and return the chicken to the pot with the sauce, along with the lemon juice and salt (if using). Serve hot

Creamy Chicken Dish

(Prep + Cooking Time: 30 minutes | **Servings:** 6)

Ingredients:
- 2 lb. chicken breasts; skinless and boneless
- 4 oz. cream cheese
- 1 oz. ranch seasoning
- 2 slices bacon; chopped.
- 1 cup chicken stock
- Green onions; chopped for serving

Directions:
1. Set your instant pot on Sauté mode; add bacon and cook for 4 minutes
2. Add chicken; stock and seasoning; then stir well. seal the instant pot lid and cook at High for 12 minutes.
3. Quick release the pressure; carefully open the lid; transfer chicken to a cutting board and shred it
4. Remove 2/3 cup liquid from the pot, add cream cheese; set the pot to Sauté mode again and cook for 3 minutes.
5. Return chicken to pot; then stir well. add green onions, divide among plates and serve.

Sesame Chicken Recipe

(Prep + Cooking Time: 18 minutes | **Servings:** 4)

Ingredients:
- 2 lb. chicken breasts; skinless; boneless and chopped
- 1/2 cup yellow onion; chopped.
- 1 tbsp. vegetable oil
- 3 tbsp. water
- 2 tsp. sesame oil
- 1/2 cup honey
- 2 tbsp. cornstarch
- 1/4 tsp. red pepper flakes
- 2 green onions; chopped.
- 1 tbsp. sesame seeds; toasted
- 2 garlic cloves; minced.
- 1/2 cup soy sauce
- 1/4 cup ketchup
- Salt and black pepper to the taste

Directions:
1. Set your instant pot on Sauté mode; add the oil and heat it up
2. Add garlic, onion, chicken, salt and pepper, stir and cook for 3 minutes.
3. Add pepper flakes, soy sauce and ketchup; then stir well. seal the instant pot lid and cook at High for 3 minutes
4. Quick release the pressure; carefully open the lid; add sesame oil and honey and stir.
5. In a bowl, mix cornstarch with water and stir well.
6. Add this to the pot, also add green onions and sesame seeds; stir well, divide among plates and serve

Chicken with Rice

(Prep + Cooking Time: 55 minutes | **Servings:** 4)

Ingredients:
For Rice:
- 1 cup water
- 1 cup basmati rice; rinsed and drained
- 1 tbsp. vegetable oil
- 1 tsp. salt or as your liking

For Chicken:
- 1 lb. boneless; skinless chicken thighs
- 4 ounces (½-stick) salted butter, cubed
- 1 (14.5-ounce) can diced tomatoes; undrained
- 1 tbsp. minced garlic
- 1 tbsp. minced fresh ginger
- 2 tsp. Garam Masala
- 1 tsp. ground turmeric
- 1 tsp. paprika
- 1 tsp. salt or as your liking
- 1 tsp. ground cumin
- 1 tsp. cayenne pepper
- 1/2 cup heavy cream
- ½ cup chopped fresh cilantro

Directions:
1. In a heatproof bowl 6-Inch or 7-inch, combine the rice, water, ghee and salt.
2. In your Instant Pot, combine the tomatoes and their juices, garlic, ginger, 1 tsp. of the garam masala, the turmeric, paprika, salt, cumin and cayenne
3. Stir to combine. Add the chicken. Place a tall steamer rack on top of the chicken mixture. Place the bowl of rice on the rack.
4. Now secure the lid on the pot and close the valve. Now Press "Manual" and set the pot at "High" pressure for 10 minutes
5. After completing the cooking time, allow the pot to sit undisturbed for 10 minutes, then release any remaining pressure.
6. Remove the bowl of rice and set aside. Remove the chicken and set aside on a plate.
7. Using an immersion blender, blend the sauce directly in the pot until smooth. Let the sauce cool for 5 minutes
8. Stir in the butter, cream, cilantro and remaining 1 tsp. garam masala. Remove half the sauce, transfer to a storage container and freeze or refrigerate for another use.

9. Break up the chicken into bite-size pieces and add it to the sauce in the pot. Serve the chicken with the hot rice.

Spiced Chicken and Rice Pilaf

(**Prep + Cooking Time:** 30 minutes | **Servings:** 6)

Ingredients:
For Chicken:
- 1 lb. bone-in chicken thighs
- 1 ½ cups water
- 4 whole green cardamom pods
- 6 whole cloves
- 6 whole black peppercorns
- 1/2 cup sliced yellow onions
- 6 garlic cloves
- 3 thin slices fresh ginger
- 1/2 tsp. ground cinnamon
- 1 tsp. salt or as your liking

For Rice:
- 1 tbsp. Ghee
- 1 ½ cups basmati rice; rinsed and drained
- 2 tsp. Garam Masala
- 1 tsp. salt

Directions:
1. Place the onions, garlic, ginger, cinnamon, cardamom, cloves and peppercorns in the center of a double layer of cheesecloth. Bring up the edges to make a bundle and tie tightly with cotton kitchen string
2. In your Instant Pot, combine the chicken, cheesecloth bundle, water and salt. Now secure the lid on the pot and close the valve.
3. Now Press "Manual" and set the pot at "High" pressure for 10 minutes. After completing the cooking time, allow the pot to sit undisturbed for 10 minutes, then release any remaining pressure
4. Remove and discard the cheesecloth bundle. Transfer the chicken to a large plate and remove and discard the skin and bones.
5. Break the meat into large pieces. Measure the liquid in the pot. You'll need 1 ½ cups to cook the rice; if there is less, add water; if there is more, remove enough to make 1 ½ cups
6. Put the rice, garam masala, ghee and salt in the pot. Add the 1 ½ cups liquid and stir to combine; push the rice down to ensure it is covered by the liquid. Lay the chicken meat on top of the rice.
7. Now secure the lid on the pot and close the valve. Now Press "Manual" and set the pot at "High" pressure for 10 minutes. Stir gently before serving

Soups, Stews and Chilis

Chicken Chili Soup

(Prep + Cooking Time: 50 minutes | **Servings:** 4)

Ingredients:
- 1 lb. chicken breast, skinless and boneless
- 30 oz. canned cannellini beans, drained
- 4 garlic cloves; minced.
- 2 tsp. oregano, dried
- 1 tsp. cumin
- 1 white onion; chopped.
- 2 tbsp. olive oil
- 1/2 tsp. red pepper flakes, crushed.
- 3 cups chicken stock
- 1 jalapeno pepper; chopped.
- Salt and black pepper to the taste
- Cilantro; chopped for serving
- Tortilla chips, for serving
- Lime wedges for serving

Directions:
1. Set your instant pot on Sauté mode; add oil and heat it up.
2. Add jalapeno and onion, stir and cook for 3 minutes
3. Add garlic, stir and cook for 1 minute.
4. Add oregano, cumin, pepper flakes, stock, chicken, beans, salt and pepper; then stir well. seal the instant pot lid and cook on Low for 30 minutes.
5. Release the pressure naturally for 15 minutes, then release remaining pressure by turning the valve to 'Venting', carefully open the lid; shred meat with 2 forks, add more salt and pepper, stir and divide into soup bowls
6. Serve with cilantro on top and with tortilla chips and lime wedges on the side

Chicken Noodle Soup.

(Prep + Cooking Time: 55 minutes | **Servings:**6)

Ingredients:
- 2 lbs. boneless; skinless chicken breasts (5 or 6 breasts)
- 1 (16-oz.) package dried spaghetti pasta, broken in half
- 4 cups low-sodium vegetable broth
- 4 carrots, peeled and sliced
- 4 celery stalks; sliced.
- 1 medium yellow onion; chopped.
- 3 garlic cloves; minced.
- 2 bay leaves
- 2 tbsp. extra-virgin olive oil.
- ½ tsp. dried rosemary
- ½ tsp. dried thyme
- 1 tsp. fine sea salt.
- ½ tsp. freshly ground black pepper.

Directions:
1. Select *Sauté* and add the olive oil to the inner pot. Once the oil is hot, add the onion, garlic, carrots, and celery, and cook for about 3 minutes, until the vegetables start to soften
2. Now, press *Cancel* and pour in the broth. Using a wooden spoon, scrape up any browned bits stuck to the bottom of the pot. Add the chicken, rosemary, thyme, salt, pepper, and bay leaves. Stir to combine
3. Now, Lock the lid. Select, "Manual or Pressure Cook" and set the pressure to *High* and the time to 10 minutes. Make sure the steam release knob is in the sealed position.
4. After completing the cooking cycle, naturally release the pressure for 10 minutes, then quick release any remaining pressure
5. Unlock and remove the lid. Remove and discard the bay leaves. Using tongs or a slotted spoon, transfer the chicken to a cutting board. Use two forks to shred the chicken.
6. Select *Sauté*. Bring the soup to a simmer, then stir in the pasta. Let the pasta cook, uncovered, for about 11 minutes or according to the package instructions. Now, press *Cancel* and stir in the shredded chicken. Serve hot.

Tomato Basil Soup

(Prep + Cooking Time: 28 minutes | **Servings:** 5)

Ingredients:
- 3 pounds tomatoes, quartered
- 1/4 cup fresh basil, chopped, plus more for garnishing
- 2 garlic cloves; minced
- 1 large carrot, chopped
- 1 small sweet onion, chopped
- 1 celery stalk, chopped
- 3 cups Vegetable Stock
- 1/4 cup nutritional yeast
- 2 tbsp. vegan butter
- Salt as your liking
- 1/2 to 1 cup nondairy milk
- Freshly ground black pepper

Directions:
1. Select the "Sauté" Low mode on your instant pot. When the display reads "Hot," add the butter to melt. Add the onion and garlic.
2. Sauté for 3 to 4 minutes, stirring frequently. Add the carrot and celery and cook for 1 to 2 minutes more. Continue to stir frequently so nothing sticks.
3. Stir in the stock (now is your chance to reincorporate any veggies stuck to the bottom)
4. Add the tomatoes, basil, yeast and a pinch or two of salt. Stir one last time.
5. Lock the lid and turn the steam release handle to Sealing. Using the Manual function, set the cooker to High Pressure for 5 minutes
6. After completing the cooking time, let the pressure release naturally for 5 to 10 minutes; quick release any remaining pressure.
7. Remove the lid carefully. Using an immersion blender, blend the soup to your preferred consistency.
8. Stir in the milk. Taste and season with salt and pepper, as needed. Garnish with the remaining fresh basil

Veggie Noodle Soup

(Prep + Cooking Time: 20 minutes | **Servings:** 5)

Ingredients:
- 4 celery stalks; chopped into bite-size pieces
- 1 sweet onion; chopped into bite-size pieces
- 1 cup broccoli florets
- 1 tomato; diced
- 2 garlic cloves; minced
- 1 bay leaf
- 2 sweet potatoes, peeled and chopped into bite-size pieces
- 1 cup dried pasta (I prefer a small pasta shape)
- 4 cups Vegetable Stock
- 1 to 1 ½ cups water; or more as needed
- 4 carrots; chopped into bite-size pieces
- 1 tsp. dried oregano
- 1 tsp. dried thyme
- 1 tsp. dried basil
- 2 tsp. salt or as your liking
- Pinch freshly ground black pepper
- Lemon zest, for garnishing; optional
- Chopped fresh parsley, for garnishing; optional
- Crackers; for serving; optional

Directions:
1. In the Instant Pot, combine the celery, carrots, sweet potatoes, onion, broccoli, tomato, garlic, bay leaf; oregano, thyme, basil, salt, pepper, pasta, stock and water, making sure all the good stuff is submerged "you can add more water or stock, if needed"
2. Lock the lid and turn the steam release handle to Sealing. Using the Manual function, set the cooker to High Pressure for 4 minutes.
3. After completing the cooking time, let the pressure release naturally for 5 minutes; quick release any remaining pressure
4. Remove the lid carefully and stir the soup. Remove and discard the bay leaf and enjoy garnished as desired.

Beef Stew

(Prep + Cooking Time: 65 minutes | **Servings:**6)

Ingredients:
- 1 lb. red potatoes; cut into 1-inch chunks
- 2 lbs. beef stew meat; cut into 1-inch cubes
- 3 garlic cloves; minced.
- 1 medium yellow onion; diced.
- 4 carrots, peeled and chopped
- 3 cups low-sodium beef broth
- 4 celery stalks; chopped.
- ¼ cup tomato paste
- 1 cup frozen peas
- 2 tbsp. extra-virgin olive oil.
- 1 tsp. dried thyme
- 1 tsp. dried oregano
- 1 tsp. fine sea salt.
- ½ tsp. freshly ground black pepper.

Directions:
1. Select *Sauté* and add the olive oil. Once the oil is hot, add the beef and sauté for 3 minutes, using a spatula to move the pieces around so they start to brown on all sides
2. Now, press *Cancel* and pour in the broth. Using a wooden spoon, scrape up any browned bits stuck to the bottom of the pot. Add the potatoes, onion, garlic, carrots, celery, tomato paste, salt, pepper, thyme, and oregano, and stir to combine
3. Now, Lock the lid. Select, "Manual or Pressure Cook" and set the pressure to *High* and the time to 30 minutes. Make sure the steam release knob is in the sealed position.
4. After completing the cooking cycle, naturally release the pressure for 10 minutes, then quick release any remaining pressure. Unlock and remove the lid. Stir in the frozen peas. Let the peas warm through, about 5 minutes. Serve hot

Zuppa Toscana Delight

(Prep + Cooking Time: 40 minutes | **Servings:** 8)

Ingredients:
- 1 lb. chicken sausage, ground.
- 6 bacon slices; chopped
- 12 oz. evaporated milk
- 1 cup parmesan, shredded.
- 2 cup spinach; chopped
- 3 potatoes, cubed
- 3 tbsp. cornstarch
- 3 garlic cloves; minced.
- 1 cup yellow onion; chopped.
- 1 tbsp. butter
- 40 oz. chicken stock
- Salt and black pepper to the taste
- A pinch of red pepper flakes

Directions:
1. Set your instant pot on Sauté mode; add bacon; then stir well. cook until it's crispy and transfer to a plate
2. Add sausage to the pot; then stir well. cook until it browns on all sides and also transfer to a plate
3. Add butter to the pot and melt it
4. Add onion, stir and cook for 5 minutes
5. Add garlic, stir and cook for 1 minute
6. Add 1/3 of the stock, salt, pepper and pepper flakes and stir.
7. Place potatoes in the steamer basket of the pot, seal the instant pot lid and cook at High for 4 minutes.
8. Release the pressure naturally for 15 minutes, then release remaining pressure by turning the valve to 'Venting', carefully open the lid and transfer potatoes to a bowl.
9. Add the rest of the stock to the pot, cornstarch mixed with some evaporated milk and the milk, stir and set the pot on Simmer mode.
10. Add parmesan, sausage, bacon, potatoes, spinach, more salt and pepper if needed; then stir well. divide into bowls and serve

Corn Chowder

(Prep + Cooking Time: 15 minutes | **Servings:** 5)

Ingredients:
- 3 large russet potatoes, peeled and cut into large dice
- 1 cup nondairy milk
- 12 ounces frozen sweet corn
- 3 celery stalks, sliced
- 3 ½ cups Vegetable Stock
- 1/2 cup all-purpose flour
- 1 carrot, grated
- 2 garlic cloves; minced
- 1 small sweet onion; diced
- 6 tbsp. vegan butter
- 1 tbsp. olive oil
- 1 tsp. dried thyme
- 1/2 tsp. ground coriander
- 1 tsp. salt or as your liking
- 1/4 tsp. freshly ground black pepper
- Sliced scallion, green and light green parts, for garnishing; optional

Directions:
1. Select the "Sauté" Low mode on your instant pot. When the display reads "Hot," add the oil and heat until it shimmers
2. Add the onion. Cook for 2 to 3 minutes, stirring frequently. Turn off the Instant Pot and add the celery, garlic, thyme, coriander, salt and pepper. Cook for another minute or so.
3. Stir in the potatoes and stock. Lock the lid and turn the steam release handle to Sealing. Using the Manual function, set the cooker to High Pressure for 6 minutes
4. While the chowder cooks, in a small pan over medium-low heat on the stovetop, melt the butter.
5. Whisk in the flour and cook for 3 to 4 minutes. Whisk in the milk, getting rid of any lumps to finish the roux
6. After completing the cooking time, quick release the pressure. Remove the lid carefully and select Sauté Low again. Add the corn and carrot.
7. Stir in the roux and let warm through and thicken. Taste and season with salt and pepper, as desired. Garnish with scallion before serving

Fish Chowder

(Prep + Cooking Time: 30 minutes | **Servings:** 4)

Ingredients:
- 1 lb. haddock fillets
- 3/4 cup bacon; chopped.
- 1 yellow onion; chopped
- 2 celery ribs; chopped.
- 3 cups potatoes, cubed
- 4 cups chicken stock
- 2 tbsp. butter
- 1 tbsp. potato starch
- 2 cups heavy cream
- 1 cup frozen corn
- 1 carrot; chopped
- 2 garlic cloves; chopped
- Salt and white pepper to the taste

Directions:
1. Set your instant pot on Sauté mode; add butter and melt it.
2. Add bacon, stir and cook until it's crispy.
3. Add garlic, celery and onion, stir and cook for 3 minutes.
4. Add salt, pepper, fish, potatoes, corn and stock; then stir well. seal the instant pot lid and cook at High for 5 minutes.
5. Release the pressure naturally, carefully open the lid; add heavy cream mixed with potato starch, stir well, set the pot on Simmer mode and cook everything for 3 minutes
6. Divide into bowls and serve

Peanut Stew

(Prep + Cooking Time: 15 minutes | **Servings:** 5)

Ingredients:
- 1 small onion; cut into large dice
- 2 cups Vegetable Stock
- 3 garlic cloves; minced
- 3 tomatoes; cut into large dice
- 1 sweet potato; cut into large dice
- 1/2 cup creamy all-natural peanut butter; not sweetened
- 1/2 cup chopped roasted peanuts
- 1 small bunch collard green leaves, chopped
- 1 red bell pepper; cut into large dice
- 1 jalapeño pepper; diced
- 2 tbsp. minced peeled fresh ginger
- 1 tbsp. roasted walnut oil
- 1/2 tsp. chili powder
- 1 ½ tsp. ground cumin
- 1/2 tsp. salt or as your liking
- Freshly ground black pepper

Directions:
1. Select the "Sauté" Low mode on your instant pot. When the display reads "Hot," add the oil and heat until it shimmers
2. Add the onion, bell pepper and jalapeño. Cook for 2 to 3 minutes, stirring frequently. Turn off the Instant Pot and add the garlic. Cook for 30 seconds, stirring.
3. Stir in the tomatoes, sweet potato, ginger, cumin, chili powder and salt. Let rest for a few minutes
4. While the stew rests, in a large measuring cup, whisk the peanut butter and 1 cup of stock until smooth. Pour this into the Instant Pot.
5. Use the remaining 1 cup of stock to rinse out the measuring cup, making sure you get as much of the peanut butter as possible
6. Add this to the pot. Lock the lid and turn the steam release handle to Sealing. Using the Manual function, set the cooker to High Pressure for 3 minutes.
7. After completing the cooking time, quick release the pressure
8. Remove the lid carefully and stir in the collard greens, which will wilt in 1 to 2 minutes.
9. Taste and season with salt and pepper, as needed and serve topped with chopped peanuts

Ground Turkey Chili and Sweet Potato

(Prep + Cooking Time: 45 minutes | **Servings:** 8)

Ingredients:
- 2 lbs. ground turkey
- 4 celery stalks; chopped.
- 3 medium sweet potatoes, peeled and cut into 1-inch cubes
- 1 medium red or white onion; diced.
- 3 carrots, peeled and chopped
- 1 red bell pepper, seeded and chopped
- 1 (14. 5-oz.) can diced tomatoes
- 3 cups low-sodium chicken broth.
- 3 garlic cloves; minced.
- 2 tbsp. extra-virgin olive oil.
- ½ tsp. chili powder
- ½ tsp. ground cumin
- Fresh; chopped. cilantro; for garnish. (optional)
- ¼ tsp. fine sea salt (optional)

Directions:
1. Select *Sauté* and add the olive oil to the inner pot. Once the oil is hot, add the ground turkey. Cook for 2 minutes, using a wooden spoon to break up the meat and keep it from sticking to the pot
2. Now, press *Cancel* and add the sweet potatoes, onion, garlic, celery, carrots, bell pepper, tomatoes, and chicken broth to the pot
3. Now, Lock the lid. Select, "Manual or Pressure Cook" and set the pressure to *High* and the time to 10 minutes. Make sure the steam release knob is in the sealed position.
4. After completing the cooking cycle, naturally release the pressure for 10 minutes, then quick release any remaining pressure

5. Unlock and remove the lid. Stir in the cumin, chili powder, and salt (if using). Serve immediately garnished with fresh cilantro

Tomato Soup

(**Prep + Cooking Time:** 60 minutes | **Servings:** 6)

Ingredients:
For the roasted tomatoes:
- 3 lb. cherry tomatoes, cut into halves
- 1/2 tsp. red pepper flakes
- 14 garlic cloves, crushed.
- 2 tbsp. extra virgin olive oil
- Salt and black pepper to the taste

For the soup:
- 1 yellow onion; chopped.
- 2 tbsp. olive oil
- 3 tbsp. tomato paste
- 2 celery ribs; chopped.
- 2 cups chicken stock
- 1 tsp. garlic powder
- 1 tsp. onion powder
- 1 red bell pepper; chopped.
- 1/2 tbsp. basil; dried
- 1/2 tsp. red pepper flakes
- 1 cup heavy cream
- Salt and black pepper to the taste

For serving:
- 1/2 cup parmesan, grated
- Basil leaves; chopped.

Directions:
1. Place tomatoes and garlic in a baking tray, drizzle 2 tablespoon oil, season with salt, pepper and 1/2 tsp. red pepper flakes, toss to coat, introduce in the oven at 425 degrees F and roast for 25 minutes.
2. Take tomatoes out of the oven and leave them aside for now.
3. Set your instant pot on Sauté mode; add 2 tablespoon oil and heat it up
4. Add onion, bell pepper and celery and stir
5. Also add salt, pepper, garlic powder, onion powder, dried basil and 1/2 tsp. pepper flakes, stir and cook for 3 minutes.
6. Add tomato paste, roasted tomatoes and garlic and stir
7. Add stock, close the lid and cook at High for 10 minutes
8. Release the pressure naturally, open the instant pot lid and set it on Sauté mode
9. Add heavy cream and blend everything using an immersion blender
10. Divide in bowls, add basil leaves and cheese on top and serve

Lasagna Soup

(**Prep + Cooking Time:** 25 minutes | **Servings:** 5)

Ingredients:
- 10 lasagna noodles, broken into bite-size pieces
- 1 medium onion; diced
- 1 garlic clove; diced
- 2 tomatoes, chopped
- 6 cups water
- 1 cube vegetable or "not chicken" bouillon
- 1 bay leaf
- ⅔ cup red sauce
- 2 tbsp. olive oil
- 2 tsp. dried oregano
- 1 tsp. dried rosemary
- ½ to ¾ tsp. red pepper flakes
- ½ tsp. salt or as your liking
- Fresh basil, for garnishing; optional
- Freshly ground black pepper
- Shredded vegan mozzarella cheese, for garnishing; optional

Directions:
1. Select the "Sauté" Low mode on your instant pot. When the display reads "Hot," add the oil and heat until it shimmers
2. Add the onion. Sauté for 2 to 3 minutes until softened. Add the garlic and immediately turn off the pressure cooker. Keep stirring as the garlic cooks.

3. Add the oregano, rosemary, red pepper flakes, salt, tomatoes, bouillon cube, bay leaf, noodles, red sauce and water. Stir well to combine
4. You want the noodles to be submerged. Lock the lid and turn the steam release handle to Sealing. Using the Manual function, set the cooker to High Pressure for 4 minutes.
5. After completing the cooking time, turn off the Instant Pot and let the pressure release naturally for 10 minutes; quick release any remaining pressure
6. Remove the lid carefully and remove and discard the bay leaf. Taste and season with salt and pepper, as desired and serve with your favorite toppings.

Taco Chili

(Prep + Cooking Time: 36 minutes | **Servings:** 7)

Ingredients:
- 1 (15-ounce) can diced tomatoes with green chilies, drained
- 1 (15-ounce) can black beans; rinsed and drained
- 1 (16-ounce) can chili beans, undrained
- 1 (8-ounce) package unflavored tempeh; cut into large dice
- 1 small onion; diced
- 1 green bell pepper; diced
- 1 jalapeño pepper; diced
- 2 tbsp. olive oil
- 1/2 tsp. garlic powder
- 1 tsp. ground cumin
- 1 tsp. smoked paprika
- 1/2 tsp. chili powder; or more as needed
- 1 tsp. salt or as your liking
- Chopped scallion, green and light green parts; for garnishing
- Chopped avocado or Cashew Sour Cream; for garnishing
- Shredded vegan cheese; for sprinkling
- Tortilla chips; for serving

Directions:
1. Select the "Sauté" Low mode on your instant pot. When the display reads "Hot," add the oil and heat until it shimmers
2. Add the tempeh and paprika. Cook for 6 to 7 minutes, stirring frequently. The tempeh will break down a bit and that's fine.
3. Add the onion, bell pepper and jalapeño. Sauté for 2 to 3 minutes more; or until soft. Add 1 to 2 tbsp. of water, if things are sticking. Turn off the Instant Pot
4. Stir in the tomatoes and green chilies, black beans, chili beans, cumin, salt, garlic powder and chili powder to taste.
5. Lock the lid and turn the steam release handle to Sealing. Using the Manual function set the cooker to High Pressure for 5 minutes
6. After completing the cooking time, let the pressure release naturally for 10 minutes; quick release any remaining pressure.
7. Remove the lid carefully. If the chili is too thin, select Sauté Low again and cook until the desired consistency is reached. Serve topped as you like

Lentil Minestrone.

(Prep + Cooking Time: 45 minutes | **Servings:** 6)

Ingredients:
- One 28-oz. can diced tomatoes
- 1½ cups chopped carrots (about 3 carrots)
- 1 cup chopped celery (about 3 stalks)
- 1 cup green lentils
- Heaping 1 cup chopped zucchini (about 1 squash)
- 3 cups water
- 3 cloves garlic; minced.
- 1 yellow onion; chopped.
- 1 tbsp. extra-virgin olive oil
- 1 tsp. dried thyme
- 2 tsp. fine sea salt
- 2 tsp. dried basil
- 1 tsp. dried oregano
- Freshly ground black pepper
- Lemon wedges; for serving (optional)

Directions:
1. Press *Sauté* and add the olive oil to the Instant Pot. Once the oil is hot but not smoking, add the onion, carrots and celery and sauté for 5 minutes, until softened
2. Press *Cancel* Button and stir in the garlic while the pot is still hot.
3. Add the zucchini, lentils, tomatoes with their juices, basil, oregano, thyme, water and several grinds of pepper
4. Give the mixture a stir to ensure the lentils are covered in liquid for even cooking. Now, Lock the lid and Turn the steam release valve to "Sealing" Position. Select *Manual/Pressure* Cook and cook on *High* pressure for 5 minutes.
5. Once the cooking cycle is completed, let the pressure naturally release for 10 minutes, then move the steam release valve to Venting to release any remaining pressure
6. When the floating valve drops, remove the lid. Stir in the salt, then taste and adjust the seasonings as needed. Serve immediately, with a squeeze of fresh lemon to brighten the flavors

Corn Potato Chowder

(**Prep + Cooking Time:** 43 minutes | **Servings:** 6)

Ingredients:
- 1½ lbs. red potatoes; cut into 1-inch chunks
- 1 medium yellow onion; diced.
- 1 (16-oz.) bag frozen corn kernels
- 1 cup unsweetened almond milk
- 3 garlic cloves; minced.
- 2 carrots, peeled and sliced
- 4 cups low-sodium vegetable broth
- ½ cup water
- 2 tbsp. cornstarch
- 2 tbsp. extra-virgin olive oil.
- ½ tsp. dried rosemary
- ½ tsp. dried thyme
- 1 tsp. fine sea salt.
- ½ tsp. freshly ground black pepper.

Directions:
1. Take a small bowl, make a cornstarch slurry by whisking together the cornstarch and water. Set aside
2. Select *Sauté* and add the olive oil to the inner pot. Once the oil is hot, add the onion, garlic, and carrots and cook for 3 minutes, until the vegetables start to soften.
3. Now, press *Cancel* and pour in the broth. Using a wooden spoon, scrape up any browned bits stuck to the bottom of the pot. Add the potatoes, corn, rosemary, thyme, salt, and pepper, and stir to combine
4. Now, Lock the lid. Select, "Manual or Pressure Cook" and set the pressure to *High* and the time to 8 minutes. Make sure the steam release knob is in the sealed position.
5. While the chowder is cooking, warm the almond milk on the stovetop or in the microwave. Whisk in the cornstarch slurry
6. After pressure cooking is complete, naturally release the pressure for 10 minutes, and then quick release any remaining pressure. Unlock and remove the lid. Stir in the almond milk mixture. Serve hot

Chicken Noodle Soup

(**Prep + Cooking Time:** 35 minutes | **Servings:** 6)

Ingredients:
- 2 cups chicken, already cooked and shredded.
- 4 carrots, sliced
- 1 yellow onion; chopped
- 1 tbsp. butter
- 6 cups chicken stock
- 1 celery rib; chopped
- Salt and black pepper to the taste
- Egg noodles, already cooked

Directions:
1. Set your instant pot on Sauté mode; add butter and heat it up.
2. Add onion, stir and cook 2 minutes
3. Add celery and carrots, stir and cook 5 minutes
4. Add chicken, stock; then stir well. close the lid and cook at High for 5 minutes

5. Release the pressure naturally for 15 minutes, then release remaining pressure by turning the valve to 'Venting', carefully open the lid; add salt and pepper to the taste and stir
6. Divide noodles into soup bowls, add soup over them and serve.

White Bean and Swiss Chard Stew

(Prep + Cooking Time: 15 minutes | **Servings:** 5)

Ingredients:
- 2 cups cooked great northern beans
- 2 carrots, sliced, with thicker end cut into half-moons
- 1 small bunch Swiss chard leaves, chopped
- 1 celery stalk, sliced
- 1/2 onion; cut into large dice
- 2 or 3 garlic cloves; minced
- 3 tomatoes, chopped
- 1 tbsp. olive oil
- ¼ to ½ tsp. red pepper flakes
- 1/2 tsp. dried rosemary
- 1/2 tsp. dried oregano
- 1/4 tsp. dried basil
- 1/2 tsp. salt or as your liking
- Pinch freshly ground black pepper; or more as needed
- Nutritional yeast, for sprinkling; optional

Directions:
1. Select the "Sauté" Low mode on your instant pot. When the display reads "Hot," add the oil and heat until it shimmers.
2. Add the carrots, celery and onion. Cook for 2 to 3 minutes, stirring occasionally. Add the garlic and cook for 30 seconds more. Turn off the Instant Pot
3. Stir in the tomatoes, red pepper flakes, rosemary; oregano, basil, salt, pepper and beans. Lock the lid and turn the steam release handle to Sealing. Using the Manual function, set the cooker to High Pressure for 4 minutes.
4. After completing the cooking time, quick release the pressure.
5. Remove the lid carefully and stir in the Swiss chard. Let wilt for 2 to 3 minutes
6. Taste and season with salt and pepper, as needed and sprinkle the nutritional yeast over individual servings.

Root and Beef Vegetables Stew

(Prep + Cooking Time: 55 minutes | **Servings:** 4)

Ingredients:
- 1 lb. beef meat, cubed
- 2 tbsp. olive oil
- 4 garlic cloves; minced.
- 2 cups beef stock
- 1 tbsp. tomato paste
- 4 carrots; chopped
- 1/2 cup bourbon
- 1 rutabaga, diced
- A bunch of thyme; chopped
- A bunch of rosemary; chopped
- 1 cup cipollini onions, peeled
- 1 cup peas
- 2 bay leaves
- 2 bacon slices; cooked and crumbled.
- 1/2 cup white flour
- Salt and black pepper to the taste

Directions:
1. Mix flour with salt and pepper and place on a plate
2. Dredge meat in flour mix and leave aside.
3. Set your instant pot on Sauté mode; add oil and heat up
4. Add meat, brown on all sides and transfer to a bowl
5. Add garlic, bourbon, stock, thyme, rutabaga, carrots, tomato paste, rosemary and onions, stir and cook for 2 minutes
6. Return beef to pot, seal the instant pot lid and cook at High for 10 minutes

7. Release the pressure naturally for 15 minutes, then release remaining pressure by turning the valve to 'Venting', carefully open the lid; add bay leaves, bacon, peas, more salt and pepper, stir and cook on Low for 12 minutes.
8. Release the pressure again, carefully open the lid; then stir well. discard bay leaves, divide into bowls and serve

Noodle Soup

(**Prep + Cooking Time:** 37 minutes | **Servings:** 4)

Ingredients:
- 1 lb. zucchini (about 2 medium)
- 1 yellow onion; chopped.
- 3 carrots; peeled and chopped.
- 3 celery stalks; chopped.
- 1 lb. boneless, skinless chicken thighs
- 4 cups (1 quart) low-sodium vegetable broth
- 3 cloves garlic; minced.
- 1 tbsp. extra-virgin olive oil
- 1 tsp. dried thyme, or 2 tsp. fresh thyme
- ½ tsp. dried oregano
- Fine sea salt and freshly ground black pepper
- Chopped fresh flat-leaf parsley; for garnish.

Directions:
1. Press *Sauté* and add the olive oil to the Instant Pot. Once the oil is hot but not smoking, add the onion and sauté until softened, about 3 minutes
2. Add the garlic, thyme and oregano and cook until fragrant, about 1 minute more, then Press *Cancel* Button to stop the cooking cycle.
3. Add the chicken, carrots, celery, 2 teaspoons salt, several grinds of pepper and the broth to the pot. Now, Lock the lid and Turn the steam release valve to "Sealing" Position. Select *Manual/Pressure* Cook to cook on *High* pressure for 12 minutes
4. Meanwhile, use a spiralizer or vegetable peeler to cut noodlelike strips from the zucchini; set the noodles aside.
5. Once the cooking cycle is completed, quickly release the pressure by moving the steam release valve to Venting. When the floating valve drops, remove the lid
6. Use tongs to transfer the cooked chicken to a cutting board, then use two forks to shred the chicken.
7. Add the shredded chicken and zucchini noodles to the pot and stir well. The noodles will soften quickly from the heat. Season with additional salt and pepper, to taste and serve immediately with parsley on top

Cheering Chicken Tortilla Soup

(**Prep + Cooking Time:** 45 minutes | **Servings:**6)

Ingredients:
- 1½ lbs. boneless; skinless chicken breasts (4 or 5 breasts)
- 6 corn tortillas; sliced. into strips
- 1 medium yellow onion; diced.
- 3 garlic cloves; minced.
- 6 cups low-sodium chicken broth.
- 1 (14. 5-oz.) can black beans, drained and rinsed
- 1 (16-oz.) bag frozen corn kernels
- Nonstick cooking spray
- 2 tbsp. extra-virgin olive oil.
- 1 tsp. chili powder
- ½ tsp. ground cumin
- Juice of 1 lime

Directions:
1. Preheat the oven to 350°F. Line a baking sheet with parchment paper and spray it with the cooking spray
2. Spread the tortillas strips on the baking sheet. Bake for 15 minutes, tossing once halfway through to prevent burning. While the tortilla strips are baking, prepare the soup.

3. Select *Sauté* and add the olive oil to the inner pot. Once the oil is hot, add the onion, garlic, chili powder, and cumin, and cook for about 3 minutes or until the onion starts to soften
4. Now, press *Cancel* and pour in the broth. Using a wooden spoon, scrape up any browned bits stuck to the bottom of the pot. Add the chicken, black beans, and corn kernels, but don't stir.
5. Now, Lock the lid. Select, "Manual or Pressure Cook" and set the pressure to *High* and the time to 10 minutes. Make sure the steam release knob is in the sealed position.
6. After completing the cooking cycle, naturally release the pressure for 10 minutes, then quick release any remaining pressure
7. Unlock and remove the lid. Using tongs or a slotted spoon, transfer the chicken to a cutting board. Use two forks to shred the chicken. Return the shredded chicken to the pot. Stir in the lime juice. Serve immediately with the baked tortilla strips on top

Surprising Sweet Potato Stew

(**Prep + Cooking Time:** 40 minutes | **Servings:** 4)

Ingredients:
- 1 sweet potato, cubed
- 1 big onion; chopped.
- 1/2 cup red lentils
- 3 garlic cloves; chopped.
- 1 celery stalk; chopped.
- 2 cups veggie stock
- 1/4 cup raisins
- 2 carrots; chopped
- 1 cup green lentils
- 14 oz. canned tomatoes; chopped.
- Salt and black pepper to the taste

For the spice blend:
- 1/2 tsp. cinnamon
- 1/4 tsp. ginger, grated
- 1 tsp. cumin
- 1 tsp. paprika
- 2 tsp. coriander
- 1 tsp. turmeric
- A pinch of cloves
- A pinch of chili flakes

Directions:
1. Set your instant pot on Sauté mode; add onions and brown them for 2 minutes adding some of the stock from time to time
2. Add garlic, stir and cook for 1 minute
3. Add carrots, raisins, celery, and sweet potatoes, stir and cook for 1 minute.
4. Add red and green lentils, stock, tomatoes, salt, pepper, turmeric, cinnamon, paprika, cumin, coriander, ginger, cloves and chili flakes; then stir well. seal the instant pot lid and cook at High for 15 minutes.
5. Release the pressure naturally for 15 minutes, then release remaining pressure by turning the valve to 'Venting', carefully open the lid; stir stew one more time, add more salt and pepper if needed, ladle into bowls and serve

Beef and Mushroom Stew

(**Prep + Cooking Time:** 45 minutes | **Servings:** 6)

Ingredients:
- 2 lb. beef chuck, cubed
- 1 celery stalk; chopped.
- 1 oz. dried porcini mushrooms; chopped.
- 2 carrots; chopped
- 2 tbsp. butter
- 1/2 cup red wine
- 1 cup beef stock
- 2 tbsp. flour
- 1 tbsp. olive oil
- 1 red onion; chopped
- 1 tsp. rosemary; chopped
- Salt and black pepper to the taste

Directions:
1. Set your instant pot on Sauté mode; add oil and beef, stir and brown for 5 minutes
2. Add onion, celery, rosemary, salt, pepper, wine and stock and stir
3. Add carrots and mushrooms, close the lid and cook at High for 15 minutes.

4. Release the pressure naturally for 15 minutes, then release remaining pressure by turning the valve to 'Venting', open the instant pot lid and set it on Simmer mode
5. Meanwhile, heat up a pan over medium high heat, add butter and melt it
6. Add flour and 6 tablespoon of cooking liquid from the stew and stir well
7. Pour this over stew; then stir well. cook for 5 minutes, divide into bowls and serve

Paprika Lentil Soup

(Prep + Cooking Time: 55 minutes | **Servings:** 6)

Ingredients:
- 1 cup dried brown lentils; rinsed. and picked over
- 2 medium carrots, peeled and chopped
- 4 celery stalks; chopped.
- 1 medium red onion; chopped.
- 2 cups low-sodium vegetable broth
- 1 cup peeled and chopped tomatoes
- 1 tbsp. extra-virgin olive oil.
- 1 tsp. dried thyme
- 1 tsp. dried oregano
- 1 tsp. smoked paprika
- Juice of 2 lemons
- ¼ tsp. fine sea salt (optional)

Directions:
1. Select *Sauté* and add the olive oil to the inner pot. Once the oil is hot, add the lentils, carrots, celery, and onion and sauté for 2 minutes. Add the thyme, oregano, and paprika
2. Now, press *Cancel* and add the broth and tomatoes to the pot.
3. Now, Lock the lid. Select, "Manual or Pressure Cook" and set the pressure to *High* and the time to 15 minutes. Make sure the steam release knob is in the sealed position.
4. After completing the cooking cycle, naturally release the pressure for 10 minutes, then quick release any remaining pressure
5. Unlock and remove the lid. Stir in the salt (if using) and lemon juice. Using an immersion blender, blend the soup to your desired consistency. Serve hot

Classic Cauliflower Soup

(Prep + Cooking Time: 30 minutes | **Servings:** 6)

Ingredients:
- 1 cauliflower head, florets separated and chopped.
- 1 cup cheddar cheese, grated
- 2 tbsp. butter
- 3 cups chicken stock
- 1 small onion; chopped.
- 1 tsp. garlic powder
- 1/2 cup half and half
- 4 oz. cream cheese, cubed
- Salt and black pepper to the taste

Directions:
1. Set your instant pot on Sauté mode; add butter and melt it.
2. Add onion, stir and cook for 3 minutes
3. Add cauliflower, stock, salt, pepper and garlic powder; then stir well. seal the instant pot lid and cook at High for 5 minutes.
4. Release the pressure naturally for 15 minutes, then release remaining pressure by turning the valve to 'Venting', carefully open the lid; blend everything using an immersion blender, add more salt and pepper if needed, cream cheese, grated cheese and half and half.
5. Stir, set the pot on Simmer mode, heat up for 2 minutes, divide into soup bowls and serve

Chicken Meatball Soup Recipe

(Prep + Cooking Time: 40 minutes | **Servings:** 6)

Ingredients:
- 1 ½ lb. chicken breast, ground.
- 2 tbsp. arrowroot powder
- 1/2 tbsp. oregano; dried
- 1/2 tsp. crushed red pepper
- 1 tsp. garlic powder
- 1/2 tbsp. basil; dried
- 1 tsp. onion powder
- 2 tbsp. nutritional yeast
- Salt and black pepper to the taste

For the soup:
- 6 cups chicken stock
- 4 celery stalks; chopped.
- 3 carrots; chopped
- 2 tsp. thyme; dried
- 2 garlic cloves; minced.
- 1/2 tsp. red pepper, crushed.
- 2 yellow onions; chopped.
- 2 eggs, whisked
- 2 tbsp. extra virgin olive oil
- 1 bunch kale; chopped

Directions:
1. Set your instant pot on Sauté mode; add oil and heat it up.
2. Add onions, celery and carrots, stir and cook for 3 minutes
3. Add garlic, salt, pepper, kale, stock, 2 tsp. thyme and 1/2 tsp. red pepper, stir and continue cooking
4. Meanwhile, in a bowl mix chicken meat with arrow powder, salt, pepper, 1/2 tsp. red pepper, garlic powder, onion powder, oregano, basil and yeast and stir well
5. Shape meatballs using your hands and drop them gently into the soup
6. Seal the instant pot lid and cook at High for 15 minutes.
7. Release the pressure naturally for 15 minutes, then release remaining pressure by turning the valve to 'Venting', open the instant pot lid and set it on Sauté mode again
8. Add eggs slowly, stir and cook for 2 minutes.
9. Divide into soup bowls and serve hot.

Chorizo, Kale and Chicken Soup

(Prep + Cooking Time: 30 minutes | **Servings:** 8)

Ingredients:
- 9 oz. chorizo, casings removed
- 4 cups chicken stock
- 4 chicken thighs; chopped.
- 14 oz. garbanzo beans, drained
- 15 oz. canned tomatoes; chopped.
- 4 garlic cloves; minced.
- 2 yellow onions; chopped.
- 2 tbsp. olive oil
- 3 potatoes; chopped
- 2 bay leaves
- 5 oz. baby kale
- Salt and black pepper to the taste

Directions:
1. Set your instant pot on Sauté mode; add oil and heat it up
2. Add chorizo, chicken and onion, stir and cook 5 minutes.
3. Add garlic, stir and cook for 1 minute.
4. Add stock, tomatoes and bay leaves and stir again
5. Also add, kale and potatoes, salt and pepper; then stir well. seal the instant pot lid and cook at High for 4 minutes.
6. Release the pressure naturally for 15 minutes, then release remaining pressure by turning the valve to 'Venting', carefully open the lid; add beans, more salt and pepper if needed; then stir well. divide into bowls and serve.

Cheese and Potato Soup

(**Prep + Cooking Time:** 30 minutes | **Servings:** 6)

Ingredients:
- 6 cups potatoes, cubed
- 1 cup cheddar cheese, shredded.
- 1 cup corn
- 6 bacon slices; cooked and crumbled.
- 2 tbsp. butter
- 3 oz. cream cheese, cubed
- 2 cups half and half
- 1/2 cup yellow onion; chopped
- 28 oz. canned chicken stock
- Salt and black pepper to the taste
- 2 tbsp. parsley; dried
- 1/8 red pepper flakes
- 2 tbsp. cornstarch
- 2 tbsp. water

Directions:
1. Set your instant pot on Sauté mode; add butter and melt it
2. Add onion, stir and cook 5 minutes
3. Add half of the stock, salt, pepper, pepper flakes and parsley and stir
4. Put potatoes in the steamer basket, seal the instant pot lid and cook at High for 4 minutes
5. Release the pressure naturally for 15 minutes, then release remaining pressure by turning the valve to 'Venting', carefully open the lid and transfer potatoes to a bowl.
6. In another bowl, mix cornstarch with water and stir well.
7. Set the pot to Simmer mode, add cornstarch, cream cheese and shredded cheese and stir well.
8. Also add the rest of the stock, corn, bacon, potatoes, half and half.
9. Stir, bring to a simmer, ladle into bowls and serve.

Split Pea Soup.

(**Prep + Cooking Time:** 50 minutes | **Servings:**6)

Ingredients:
- 1 lb. green split peas; rinsed. and drained
- 4 carrots, peeled and sliced
- 1 (6-oz.) ham steak, cubed
- 2 celery stalks; sliced.
- 6 cups low-sodium chicken broth.
- 1 medium yellow onion; chopped.
- 3 garlic cloves; minced.
- 2 tbsp. extra-virgin olive oil.
- ½ tsp. dried thyme
- 1 tsp. dried oregano
- ½ tsp. freshly ground black pepper.
- 1 tsp. fine sea salt.

Directions:
1. Select *Sauté* and add the olive oil to the inner pot. Once the oil is hot, add the onion, garlic, carrots, and celery, and cook for 3 minutes, until the vegetables start to soften
2. Now, press *Cancel* and pour in the broth. Using a wooden spoon, scrape up any browned bits stuck to the bottom of the pot. Add the ham, split peas, oregano, and thyme, and stir to combine
3. Now, Lock the lid. Select, "Manual or Pressure Cook" and set the pressure to *High* and the time to 15 minutes. Make sure the steam release knob is in the sealed position.
4. After completing the cooking cycle, naturally release the pressure for 10 minutes, then quick release any remaining pressure. Unlock and remove the lid. Stir in the salt and pepper. Serve hot

Chicken Soup

(**Prep + Cooking Time:** 40 minutes | **Servings:** 4)

Ingredients:
- 4 chicken breasts, skinless and boneless
- 16 oz. jarred chunky salsa
- 29 oz. canned tomatoes; peeled and chopped.
- 29 oz. canned chicken stock
- 2 tbsp. extra virgin olive oil
- 1 tsp. garlic powder
- 15 oz. frozen corn
- 32 oz. canned black beans, drained
- 1 onion; chopped.
- 1 tbsp. onion powder

- 2 tbsp. parsley; dried
- 1 tbsp. chili powder
- 3 garlic cloves; minced.
- Salt and black pepper to the taste

Directions:
1. Set your instant pot on Sauté mode; add oil and heat it up.
2. Add onion, stir and cook 5 minutes
3. Add garlic, stir and cook for 1 minute more.
4. Add chicken breasts, salsa, tomatoes, stock, salt, pepper, parsley, garlic powder, onion and chili powder; then stir well. seal the instant pot lid and cook at High for 8 minutes.
5. Release the pressure naturally for 15 minutes, then release remaining pressure by turning the valve to 'Venting', carefully open the lid; transfer chicken breasts to a cutting board, shred with 2 forks and return to pot
6. Add beans and corn, set the pot on Simmer mode and cook for 2 - 3 minutes more
7. Divide into soup bowls and serve

Sweet Potato and Turkey Soup

(Prep + Cooking Time: 35 minutes | **Servings:** 4)

Ingredients:
- 1 lb. Italian turkey sausage; chopped
- 1 yellow onion; chopped.
- 5 cups turkey stock
- 2 garlic cloves; minced.
- 1 tsp. red pepper flakes
- 1 tsp. basil; dried
- 1 tsp. oregano; dried
- 2 celery stalks; chopped
- 1 tsp. thyme; dried
- 5 oz. spinach; chopped.
- 2 bay leaves
- 2 carrots; chopped
- 1 big sweet potato, cubed
- Salt and black pepper to the taste

Directions:
1. Set your instant pot on Sauté mode; add sausage, brown it and transfer to a plate
2. Add onion, celery and carrots, stir and cook for 2 minutes
3. Add potato, stir and cook 2 minutes
4. Add stock, garlic, red pepper, salt, pepper, basil, oregano, thyme, spinach and bay leaves,
5. Stir, seal the instant pot lid and cook at High for 4 minutes.
6. Release the pressure naturally for 15 minutes, then release remaining pressure by turning the valve to 'Venting', carefully open the lid; discard bay leaves, divide soup into bowls and serve.

Turkey Stew

(Prep + Cooking Time: 50 minutes | **Servings:** 4)

Ingredients:
- 3 cups turkey meat, already cooked and shredded.
- 1 tbsp. avocado oil
- 1 tbsp. cranberry sauce
- 1 tsp. dried garlic; minced.
- 3 celery stalks; chopped.
- 2 cups potatoes; chopped.
- 15 oz. canned tomatoes; chopped.
- 5 cups turkey stock
- 2 carrots; chopped.
- 1 yellow onion; chopped.
- Salt and black pepper to the taste

Directions:
1. Set your instant pot on Sauté mode; add oil and heat it up
2. Add carrots, celery and onions, stir and cook for 3 minutes
3. Add potatoes, tomatoes, stock, garlic, meat and cranberry sauce; then stir well. seal the instant pot lid and cook on Low for 30 minutes.
4. Release the pressure naturally for 15 minutes, then release remaining pressure by turning the valve to 'Venting', carefully open the lid; add salt and pepper; then stir well. divide into bowls and serve.

Bacon and Broccoli Soup

(**Prep + Cooking Time:** 30 minutes | **Servings:** 6)

Ingredients:
- 4 bacon slices; chopped
- 2 small broccoli heads; chopped.
- 1 tbsp. parmesan, grated
- 1 leek; chopped
- 1 celery rib; chopped
- 1-quart veggie stock
- 1 tsp. olive oil
- 2 cups spinach; chopped
- 4 tbsp. basmati rice
- Salt and black pepper to the taste

Directions:
1. Set your instant pot on Sauté mode; add oil and bacon, cook until it's crispy, transfer to a plate and leave aside
2. Add broccoli, leek, celery, spinach, rice, salt, pepper and veggie stock; then stir well. seal the instant pot lid and cook at High for 6 minutes
3. Release the pressure naturally for 15 minutes, then release remaining pressure by turning the valve to 'Venting', carefully open the lid; add more salt and pepper if needed, add bacon, divide into soup bowls and serve with parmesan on top.

Double Bean Chili

(**Prep + Cooking Time:** 24 minutes | **Servings:** 5)

Ingredients:
- 1 (15-ounce) can black beans, drained and rinsed
- 1 (15-ounce) can kidney beans, drained and rinsed
- 1 (28-ounce) can fire-roasted diced tomatoes, with liquid
- 1 jalapeño pepper, seeded and diced
- 3 garlic cloves; diced
- 1 bell pepper, any color, chopped
- 1 sweet potato, peeled and chopped
- 1/4 cup barbecue sauce
- 3/4 cup water; divided; or more as needed
- 1/2 sweet onion, chopped
- 1 tsp. smoked paprika
- 1 ½ tsp. dried oregano
- 1 tsp. red pepper flakes
- 1 tsp. salt; or more as your liking
- 2 tsp. ground cumin
- 1/2 to 1 tsp. chili powder; or more as needed
- Cashew Sour Cream; for topping; optional
- Chopped avocado; for topping; optional
- Chopped onion; for topping; optional
- Fresh basil; for topping; optional
- Fresh cilantro; for topping; optional
- Crumbled tortilla chips; for topping; optional

Directions:
1. Select the "Sauté" Low mode on your instant pot. When the display reads "Hot," add ¼ cup of water, the onion, jalapeño and garlic. Cook for 2 to 3 minutes, stirring frequently
2. Add the bell pepper and sweet potato. Cook for 2 to 3 minutes more, stirring occasionally and adding water if necessary.
3. Add the salt, cumin, paprika; oregano, red pepper flakes, chili powder, black beans, kidney beans, tomatoes and remaining ½ cup of water
4. Stir well so the spices are mixed in. Lock the lid and turn the steam release handle to Sealing. Using the Manual function, set the cooker to High Pressure for 5 minutes.
5. After completing the cooking time, quick release the pressure
6. Remove the lid carefully and stir in the barbecue sauce. Taste and add salt or more chili powder, as needed, as well as your favorite toppings

Baked Potato Soup

(Prep + Cooking Time: 55 minutes | Servings: 6)

Ingredients:
- 2 lbs. medium russet potatoes (about 6 potatoes)
- 3 scallions, white and light green parts only; chopped.
- ½ cup grated Cheddar cheese
- ¼ cup all-purpose flour
- 4 cups low-fat milk
- ½ cup low-fat Greek yogurt
- 3 bacon slices, cooked and crumbled
- 1 cup water
- 2 tbsp. unsalted butter
- ½ tsp. fine sea salt.
- ¼ tsp. freshly ground black pepper.

Directions:
1. Scrub and rinse the potatoes and pat them dry with a clean cloth. Place the trivet in the inner pot, then pour in the water. Place the potatoes on the trivet
2. Now, Lock the lid. Select, "Manual or Pressure Cook" and set the pressure to *High* and the time to 20 minutes. Make sure the steam release knob is in the sealed position.
3. After completing the cooking cycle, naturally release the pressure for 5 minutes, then quick release any remaining pressure
4. Unlock and remove the lid. Using tongs, transfer the potatoes to a platter. Pour out the water and return the inner pot to the base
5. Select *Sauté* and add the butter. Once the butter is melted, add the flour and whisk to combine. Add the milk, salt, and pepper and continue whisking until there are no lumps.
6. Once the milk starts to simmer, press Cancel. Add the potatoes. Using a potato masher, mash the potatoes into the milk. Serve hot

Double Bean Chili

(Prep + Cooking Time: 24 minutes | Servings: 5)

Ingredients:
- 1 (15-ounce) can black beans, drained and rinsed
- 1 (15-ounce) can kidney beans, drained and rinsed
- 1 (28-ounce) can fire-roasted diced tomatoes, with liquid
- 1 jalapeño pepper, seeded and diced
- 3 garlic cloves; diced
- 1 bell pepper, any color, chopped
- 1 sweet potato, peeled and chopped
- 1/4 cup barbecue sauce
- 3/4 cup water; divided; or more as needed
- 1/2 sweet onion, chopped
- 1 tsp. smoked paprika
- 1 ½ tsp. dried oregano
- 1 tsp. red pepper flakes
- 1 tsp. salt; or more as your liking
- 2 tsp. ground cumin
- 1/2 to 1 tsp. chili powder; or more as needed
- Cashew Sour Cream; for topping; optional
- Chopped avocado; for topping; optional
- Chopped onion; for topping; optional
- Fresh basil; for topping; optional
- Fresh cilantro; for topping; optional
- Crumbled tortilla chips; for topping; optional

Directions:
1. Select the "Sauté" Low mode on your instant pot. When the display reads "Hot," add ¼ cup of water, the onion, jalapeño and garlic. Cook for 2 to 3 minutes, stirring frequently.
2. Add the bell pepper and sweet potato. Cook for 2 to 3 minutes more, stirring occasionally and adding water if necessary
3. Add the salt, cumin, paprika; oregano, red pepper flakes, chili powder, black beans, kidney beans, tomatoes and remaining ½ cup of water.
4. Stir well so the spices are mixed in. Lock the lid and turn the steam release handle to Sealing. Using the Manual function, set the cooker to High Pressure for 5 minutes

5. After completing the cooking time, quick release the pressure
6. Remove the lid carefully and stir in the barbecue sauce. Taste and add salt or more chili powder, as needed, as well as your favorite toppings!

Endive Soup

(**Prep + Cooking Time:** 45 minutes | **Servings:** 4)

Ingredients:
- 6 cups veggie stock
- 1 tbsp. canola oil
- 2 tsp. sesame oil
- 1 tbsp. ginger, grated
- 1 tsp. chili sauce
- 1/2 cup uncooked rice
- 2 scallions; chopped.
- 1 ½ tbsp. soy sauce
- 3 endives, trimmed and roughly chopped
- 3 garlic cloves chopped
- Salt and white pepper to the taste

Directions:
1. Set your instant pot on Sauté mode; add canola and sesame oil and heat it up
2. Add scallions and garlic, stir and cook for 4 minutes.
3. Add chili sauce and ginger, stir and cook for 1 minute
4. Add stock and soy sauce, stir and cook for 2 minutes.
5. Add rice; then stir well. seal the instant pot lid and cook at High for 15 minutes
6. Release the pressure naturally for 15 minutes, then release remaining pressure by turning the valve to 'Venting', carefully open the lid; add salt, pepper and endives; then stir well. seal the instant pot lid and cook at High for 5 minutes.
7. Release the pressure again, carefully open the lid; stir soup, divide into bowls and serve

Lasagna Soup

(**Prep + Cooking Time:** 25 minutes | **Servings:** 5)

Ingredients:
- 10 lasagna noodles, broken into bite-size pieces
- 1 medium onion; diced
- 1 garlic clove; diced
- 2 tomatoes, chopped
- 6 cups water
- 1 cube vegetable or "not chicken" bouillon
- 1 bay leaf
- ⅔ cup red sauce
- 2 tbsp. olive oil
- 2 tsp. dried oregano
- 1 tsp. dried rosemary
- ½ to ¾ tsp. red pepper flakes
- ½ tsp. salt or as your liking
- Fresh basil, for garnishing; optional
- Freshly ground black pepper
- Shredded vegan mozzarella cheese, for garnishing; optional

Directions:
7. Select the "Sauté" Low mode on your instant pot. When the display reads "Hot," add the oil and heat until it shimmers.
8. Add the onion. Sauté for 2 to 3 minutes until softened. Add the garlic and immediately turn off the pressure cooker. Keep stirring as the garlic cooks.
9. Add the oregano, rosemary, red pepper flakes, salt, tomatoes, bouillon cube, bay leaf, noodles, red sauce and water. Stir well to combine
10. You want the noodles to be submerged. Lock the lid and turn the steam release handle to Sealing. Using the Manual function, set the cooker to High Pressure for 4 minutes.
11. After completing the cooking time, turn off the Instant Pot and let the pressure release naturally for 10 minutes; quick release any remaining pressure
12. Remove the lid carefully and remove and discard the bay leaf. Taste and season with salt and pepper, as desired and serve with your favorite toppings!

Delicious Okra Stew

(Prep + Cooking Time: 40 minutes | **Servings:** 4)

Ingredients:
- 1 lb. beef meat, cubed
- 14 oz. frozen okra
- 12 oz. tomato sauce
- 1 yellow onion; chopped.
- 1 garlic clove; minced.
- 1/2 cup parsley; chopped.
- A drizzle of olive oil
- 1 cardamom pod
- 2 cups chicken stock
- Juice of 1/2 lemon
- Salt and black pepper to the taste

For the marinade:
- 1/2 tsp. onion powder
- 1 tbsp. 7- spice mix
- 1/2 tsp. garlic powder
- A pinch of salt

Directions:
1. In a bowl, mix meat with 7-spice mix, a pinch of salt, onion and garlic powder, toss to coat and leave aside for now
2. Set your instant pot on Sauté mode; add some olive oil and heat it up
3. Add onion, stir and cook 2 minutes
4. Add garlic and cardamom, stir and cook for 1 minute
5. Add meat, stir and brown meat for 2 minutes.
6. Add stock, tomato sauce, okra, salt and pepper; then stir well. seal the instant pot lid and cook on Low for 20 minutes.
7. Release the pressure naturally for 15 minutes, then release remaining pressure by turning the valve to 'Venting', carefully open the lid; add more salt and pepper if needed, lemon juice and parsley; then stir well. divide into bowls and serve

Chicken Stew Recipe

(Prep + Cooking Time: 1 hour and 35 minutes | **Servings:** 6)

Ingredients:
- 6 chicken thighs
- 2 cups chicken stock
- 15 oz. canned tomatoes; chopped.
- 1 tsp. vegetable oil
- Salt and black pepper to the taste
- 1 yellow onion; chopped.
- 1/4 lb. baby carrots, sliced
- 1 celery stalk; chopped.
- 3/4 lb. baby carrots
- 1 ½ lb. new potatoes
- 1/2 tsp. thyme, dried
- 2 tbsp. tomato paste
- 1/2 cup white wine

Directions:
1. Set your instant pot on Sauté mode; add oil and heat it up
2. Add chicken, salt and pepper, brown for 4 minutes on each side and transfer to a plate.
3. Add celery, onion, tomato paste, carrots, thyme, salt and pepper, stir and cook for 5 minutes.
4. Add wine; then stir well. bring to a boil and simmer for 3 minutes.
5. Add stock, return chicken, add tomatoes and put potatoes in the steamer basket of your pot
6. Seal the instant pot lid and cook at High for 30 minutes.
7. Release the pressure naturally for 15 minutes, then release remaining pressure by turning the valve to 'Venting', carefully open the lid; take potatoes out of the pot and put them in a bowl
8. Transfer chicken pieces to a cutting board, leave aside to cool down for a few minutes, discard bones, shred meat and return it to the stew.
9. Add more salt and pepper if needed; then stir well. divide into bowls and serve hot

Cheesy Broccoli Soup

(Prep + Cooking Time: 20 minutes | **Servings:** 4)

Ingredients:

- 1 lb. broccoli, cut into florets (about 6 cups)
- 1 small head (8 ounces) cauliflower, cut into florets (about 3 cups)
- 2 carrots; peeled and chopped.
- 1 yellow onion; chopped.
- 1 tbsp. spicy brown mustard
- ¼ cup finely grated Parmesan cheese
- ½ cup almond milk, or any milk of your choice
- ½ cup shredded sharp Cheddar cheese
- 3 cups water
- Fine sea salt
- Freshly ground black pepper

Directions:

1. Combine the onion, carrots, cauliflower, broccoli, mustard, water and 2 teaspoons salt in the Instant Pot
2. Now, Lock the lid and Turn the steam release valve to "Sealing" Position. Select *Manual/Pressure* Cook to cook on *High* pressure for 3 minutes.
3. Once the cooking cycle is completed, immediately move the steam release valve to Venting to quickly release the pressure
4. When the floating valve drops, remove the lid. Use an immersion blender to blend the soup, leaving as much texture as you like.
5. Add the Cheddar, Parmesan and almond milk and stir until combined. Season with salt and pepper to taste, then serve warm

Celery Soup

(Prep + Cooking Time: 35 minutes | **Servings:** 2)

Ingredients:

- 3 potatoes; chopped.
- 1 yellow onion; chopped.
- 1 tbsp. curry powder
- 1 tsp. celery seeds
- 1 tsp. extra virgin olive oil
- 7 celery stalks; chopped.
- 4 cups veggie stock
- Salt and black pepper to the taste
- A handful parsley; chopped for serving

Directions:

1. Set your instant pot on Sauté mode; add oil and heat it up.
2. Add onion, celery seeds and curry powder, stir and cook for 1 minute.
3. Add celery and potatoes, stir and cook for 5 minutes.
4. Add stock, salt, pepper stir, seal the instant pot lid and cook at High for 10 minutes.
5. Release the pressure naturally for 15 minutes, then release remaining pressure by turning the valve to 'Venting', carefully open the lid; blend well using an immersion blender, add parsley; then stir well. divide into soup bowls and serve.

Curried Squash Soup

(Prep + Cooking Time: 40 minutes | **Servings:** 5)

Ingredients:

- 1 (2- to 3-pound) butternut squash, peeled and cubed
- 1 (14-ounce) can lite coconut milk
- 4 cups Vegetable Stock
- 1 onion, chopped
- 2 garlic cloves, chopped
- 1 tbsp. curry powder
- 1 tbsp. olive oil
- 1 tsp. salt or as your liking

Directions:

1. Select the "Sauté" Low mode on your instant pot. When the display reads "Hot," add the oil and heat until it shimmers

2. Add the onion. Cook for 3 to 4 minutes, stirring frequently.
3. Turn off the Instant Pot and add the garlic and curry powder. Cook for 1 minute, stirring. It should start smelling delicious right about now.
4. Add the squash, stock and salt. Lock the lid and turn the steam release handle to Sealing. Using the Manual function, set the cooker to High Pressure for 30 minutes.
5. After completing the cooking time, quick release the pressure
6. Remove the lid carefully. Using an immersion blender, blend the soup until completely smooth.
7. Stir in the coconut milk, saving a little bit for topping when served

Yummy Tomato Soup

(**Prep + Cooking Time:** 40 minutes | **Servings:** 6)

Ingredients:
- 3 (15-oz.) cans diced tomatoes
- 1 medium yellow onion; chopped.
- 3 garlic cloves; minced.
- 4 cups low-sodium chicken broth.
- ¼ cup low-fat plain yogurt
- ½ cup grated Parmesan cheese
- 2 tbsp. extra-virgin olive oil.
- 1 tsp. dried oregano
- ½ tsp. red pepper flakes
- 1 tsp. fine sea salt.
- ½ tsp. freshly ground black pepper.

Directions:
1. Select *Sauté* and add the olive oil to the inner pot. Once the oil is hot, add the onion and garlic and cook for 3 minutes, until they start to soften
2. Now, press *Cancel* and pour in the tomatoes and broth. Using a wooden spoon, scrape up any browned bits stuck to the bottom of the pot. Stir in the oregano, red pepper flakes, salt, and pepper.
3. Now, Lock the lid. Select, "Manual or Pressure Cook" and set the pressure to *High* and the time to 5 minutes. Make sure the steam release knob is in the sealed position.
4. After completing the cooking cycle, naturally release the pressure for 10 minutes, then quick release any remaining pressure
5. Unlock and remove the lid. Using an immersion blender, purée the soup to a smooth consistency. Stir in the yogurt and grated Parmesan cheese. Serve hot

Thai Coconut Curry with Tofu

(**Prep + Cooking Time:** 40 minutes | **Servings:** 6)

Ingredients:
- 1 (13. 5-oz.) can full-fat coconut milk
- 1 medium zucchini; chopped. (about 1 cup)
- 2 red bell peppers; seeded and sliced.
- 3 garlic cloves; minced.
- 1 cup low-sodium vegetable broth
- 10 ounces extra-firm tofu, cubed
- 1 medium yellow onion; chopped.
- 1 tbsp. Thai green curry paste
- 2 tbsp. extra-virgin olive oil.
- ½ tsp. ground ginger
- ½ tsp. fine sea salt.
- Juice of 1 lime

Directions:
1. Select *Sauté* and add the olive oil to the inner pot. Once the oil is hot, add the onion and garlic and cook for about 3 minutes, or until the onion starts to soften
2. Now, press *Cancel* and pour in the broth and coconut milk. Using a wooden spoon, scrape up any browned bits stuck to the bottom of the pot. Add the zucchini, bell peppers, tofu, ginger, and curry paste, and stir to combine.
3. Now, Lock the lid. Select, "Manual or Pressure Cook" and set the pressure to *High* and the time to 5 minutes. Make sure the steam release knob is in the sealed position.
4. After completing the cooking cycle, naturally release the pressure for 10 minutes, then quick release any remaining pressure. Unlock and remove the lid. Stir in the salt and lime juice. Serve hot

Potato Leek Soup

(Prep + Cooking Time: 30 minutes | **Servings:** 4)

Ingredients:
- 1 pound Yukon Gold potatoes, cubed
- 2 large leeks, white and very light green parts only, cleaned well, chopped
- 2 garlic cloves; minced
- ⅔ cup soy milk
- ⅓ cup extra-virgin olive oil
- 4 cups Vegetable Stock
- 1 bay leaf
- 3 tbsp. vegan butter
- 1/2 tsp. salt or as your liking
- Freshly ground white pepper

Directions:
1. Select the "Sauté" Low mode on your instant pot. When the display reads "Hot," add the butter and leeks
2. Cook for about 2 to 3 minutes until soft, stirring occasionally. Add the garlic. Cook for 30 to 45 seconds, stirring frequently, until fragrant.
3. Pour in the stock and add the potatoes, bay leaf and salt. Stir to combine
4. Lock the lid and turn the steam release handle to Sealing. Using the Manual function, set the cooker to High Pressure for 5 minutes.
5. After completing the cooking time, let the pressure release naturally for 15 minutes; quick release any remaining pressure
6. While waiting for the pressure to release, in a blender, combine the soy milk and olive oil. Blend until combined, about 1 minute. This is an easy dairy-free substitute for heavy cream
7. Remove the lid carefully, remove and discard the bay leaf and stir in the "cream."
8. Using an immersion blender, purée the soup until smooth. Taste and season with salt and pepper, as desired

Italian Sausage Stew

(Prep + Cooking Time: 40 minutes | **Servings:** 6)

Ingredients:
- 1 lb. Andouille sausage, crumbled.
- 1 sweet onion; chopped.
- 1 ½ lb. gold potatoes, cubed
- 3/4 lb. collard greens, thinly sliced
- 1 cup chicken stock
- 1/2 lb. cherry tomatoes, cut into halves
- Juice of 1/2 lemon
- Salt and black pepper to the taste

Directions:
1. Set your instant pot on Sauté mode; add sausage, stir and cook for 8 minutes.
2. Add onions and tomatoes, stir and cook 4 minutes more
3. Add potatoes, stock, salt, pepper and collard greens; then stir well. close the lid and cook at High for 10 minutes.
4. Release the pressure naturally for 15 minutes, then release remaining pressure by turning the valve to 'Venting', carefully open the lid; add more salt and pepper and lemon juice; then stir well. divide into bowls and serve

Delicious Beef Stew

(Prep + Cooking Time: 50 minutes | **Servings:** 8)

Ingredients:
- 2 lb. beef stew, cubed
- 1 tbsp. vegetable oil
- 5 carrots; chopped.
- 8 potatoes, cubed
- 1 yellow onion; chopped.
- 2 tsp. cornstarch
- 2 beef bouillon cubes
- Salt and black pepper to the taste
- 2 cups water

Directions:
1. Set your instant pot on Sauté mode; add oil and heat it up
2. Add beef and onion, stir and cook until it browns on all sides.
3. Add carrots, water and bouillon; then stir well. seal the instant pot lid and cook on Medium for 20 minutes.
4. Pour water in a pot, add some salt, bring to a boil over medium high heat, add potatoes, cook for 10 minutes and drain them.
5. Release the pressure naturally for 15 minutes, then release remaining pressure by turning the valve to 'Venting', open the instant pot lid and set it on Simmer mode.
6. Add cornstarch mixed with some water, salt, pepper and potatoes; then stir well. bring to a boil, take off heat and divide stew among plates

Beef Goulash.

(Prep + Cooking Time: 40 minutes | **Servings:**6)

Ingredients:
- 2 lbs. 90% lean ground beef
- 2 cups low-sodium beef broth
- 2 bay leaves
- 1 medium yellow onion; chopped.
- 3 garlic cloves; minced.
- 1 (14. 5-oz.) can diced tomatoes
- 1 (14. 5-oz.) can tomato sauce
- 1 tbsp. extra-virgin olive oil.
- 1 tbsp. balsamic vinegar
- 2 tsp. paprika
- 1 tsp. dried thyme
- Juice of ½ medium lemon
- ½ tsp. freshly ground black pepper.
- 1 tsp. fine sea salt.

Directions:
1. Select *Sauté* and add the olive oil to the inner pot. Once the oil is hot, add the beef, onion, and garlic and sauté for about 3 minutes, stirring occasionally to break up the meat
2. Now, press *Cancel* and pour in the broth. Using a wooden spoon, scrape any browned bits stuck to the bottom of the pot. Stir in the tomato sauce; diced. tomatoes, thyme, paprika, and bay leaves
3. Now, Lock the lid. Select, "Manual or Pressure Cook" and set the pressure to *High* and the time to 10 minutes. Make sure the steam release knob is in the sealed position.
4. After completing the cooking cycle, naturally release the pressure for 5 minutes, then quick release any remaining pressure
5. Unlock and remove the lid. Stir in the lemon juice, salt, pepper, and vinegar. Using tongs, remove and discard the bay leaves. Serve hot

Cheesy Broccoli Soup

(Prep + Cooking Time: 38 minutes | **Servings:**6)

Ingredients:
- 1 lb. fresh or frozen broccoli florets (about 3½ cups)
- 3 cups low-sodium chicken broth.
- 3 cups shredded Cheddar cheese
- 2 cups low-fat milk
- 1 medium yellow onion; chopped.
- 2 garlic cloves; minced.
- 1 tbsp. extra-virgin olive oil.

Directions:
1. Select *Sauté* and add the olive oil to the inner pot. Once the oil is hot, add the onion and garlic and sauté for about 2 minutes
2. Now, press *Cancel* and add the broth. Using a wooden spoon, scrape up any browned bits stuck to the bottom of the pot. Add the broccoli to the pot
3. Now, Lock the lid. Select, "Manual or Pressure Cook" and set the pressure to *High* and the time to 3 minutes (6 minutes if using frozen broccoli). Make sure the steam release knob is in the sealed position.
4. After completing the cooking cycle, naturally release the pressure for 10 minutes, then quick release any remaining pressure.

5. Unlock and remove the lid. Select *Sauté*. Stir in the cheese until melted and combined. Stir in the milk. Let the soup come to a gentle simmer, then press Cancel. Serve hot

Coconut Carrot Soup

Ingredients:
- 1 lb. carrots
- 1 lb. sweet potatoes
- ½ yellow onion; chopped.
- 2 cloves garlic; minced.
- 3½ cups water
- ½ cup full-fat coconut milk
- 1 tbsp. minced fresh ginger (about 1-inch knob)
- 6 tbsp. chopped fresh cilantro
- 1 tbsp. extra-virgin olive oil
- 6 tbsp. hulled pumpkin seeds
- 6 tbsp. dried cranberries
- 2 tsp. curry powder
- 2 tsp. fine sea salt

Directions:
1. Press *Sauté* and add the olive oil to the Instant Pot. Once the oil is hot but not smoking, add the onion and sauté until tender, about 8 minutes, stirring occasionally so it doesn't stick
2. Meanwhile, peel and chop the carrots and sweet potatoes into 1-inch chunks.
3. Once the onion is tender, add the garlic, curry powder and ginger and stir with a wooden spoon or spatula just until fragrant, about 1 minute
4. Add the carrots, sweet potatoes, water and salt and use the spoon to scrape the bottom of the Instant Pot to make sure nothing has stuck.
5. Press *Cancel* Button, then secure the lid and move the steam release valve to Sealing. Select *Manual/Pressure* Cook to cook on *High* pressure for 10 minutes
6. Once the cooking cycle is completed, let the pressure naturally release for 10 minutes before moving the steam release valve to Venting.
7. When the floating valve drops, remove the lid and use an immersion blender to blend the soup directly in the pot until very smooth
8. Stir in the coconut milk and adjust the seasonings to taste. Serve warm with 1 tablespoon each dried cranberries, pumpkin seeds and cilantro sprinkled over each serving

Split Pea Soup

(Prep + Cooking Time: 45 minutes | **Servings:** 5)

Ingredients:
- 2 carrots; diced
- 1 celery stalk; diced
- 1 bay leaf
- 1 cup green split peas
- 2 ½ cups Vegetable Stock
- 1 tbsp. roasted walnut oil
- 1 tsp. dried thyme
- 1 tsp. smoked paprika
- 1 tsp. salt; or as your liking
- 2 garlic cloves; minced
- Freshly ground black pepper

Directions:
1. Select the "Sauté" Low mode on your instant pot. When the display reads "Hot," add the oil and heat until it shimmers
2. Add the carrots, celery, thyme, paprika, bay leaf and salt. Cook for 2 to 3 minutes, stirring frequently, until fragrant. Turn off the Instant Pot and add the garlic.
3. Cook for 30 seconds. Stir in the split peas and stock. Lock the lid and turn the steam release handle to Sealing. Using the Manual function, set the cooker to High Pressure for 18 minutes
4. After completing the cooking time, let the Instant Pot go into Keep Warm mode and let the pressure release naturally for 15 minutes; quick release any remaining pressure.
5. Remove the lid carefully and remove and discard the bay leaf. Taste and season with salt and pepper, as needed

Beef Chili.

(Prep + Cooking Time: 45 minutes | **Servings:**8)

Ingredients:
- 2 lbs. 90% lean ground beef
- 1 (28-oz.) can crushed tomatoes
- 1 (14. 5-oz.) can kidney beans, drained and rinsed
- 4 cups low-sodium beef broth
- 1 medium yellow onion; diced.
- 3 garlic cloves; minced.
- 2 tbsp. extra-virgin olive oil.
- 1 tsp. chili powder
- ½ tsp. ground cumin
- 1 tsp. Worcestershire sauce

Directions:
1. Select *Sauté* and add the olive oil to the inner pot. Once the oil is hot, add the onion, garlic, ground beef, chili powder, and cumin and cook for 3 minutes, until the beef starts to brown
2. Now, press *Cancel* and pour in the broth. Using a wooden spoon, scrape up any browned bits stuck to the bottom of the pot. Add the tomatoes and beans, but don't stir
3. Now, Lock the lid. Select, "Manual or Pressure Cook" and set the pressure to *High* and the time to 10 minutes. Make sure the steam release knob is in the sealed position.
4. After completing the cooking cycle, naturally release the pressure for 10 minutes, then quick release any remaining pressure. Unlock and remove the lid. Stir in the Worcestershire sauce. Serve hot

Beans Chili

(Prep + Cooking Time: 60 minutes | **Servings:** 6)

Ingredients:
- 1 sweet potato, peeled and cut into 1-inch chunks
- One 28-oz. can diced tomatoes
- 2 cups water
- 1 cup dried black beans, soaked for 8 hours
- 1 cup dried red kidney beans, soaked for 8 hours
- 3 carrots; peeled and chopped.
- 3 celery stalks; chopped.
- 4 cloves garlic; minced.
- 1 yellow onion; chopped.
- 1 tbsp. chili powder
- ¼ tsp. cayenne pepper
- 2 tsp. fine sea salt
- 2 tsp. ground cumin
- Chopped fresh cilantro; for garnish. (optional)
- Chopped green onions, tender white and green parts only; for garnish. (optional)
- Freshly ground black pepper

Directions:
1. Drain the soaked beans and rinse well. Combine the beans, onion, carrots, celery, garlic, chili powder, cumin, cayenne, water, tomatoes with their juices, sweet potato and several grinds of black pepper in the Instant Pot
2. Stir well to make sure the beans are submerged in the liquid, then secure the lid and move the steam release valve to Sealing. Select *Manual/Pressure* Cook to cook on *High* pressure for 25 minutes.
3. Once the cooking cycle is completed, let the pressure naturally release for 10 minutes, then move the steam release valve to Venting to release any remaining pressure
4. When the floating valve drops, remove the lid and add the salt. Stir well, using the back of the spoon to mash some of the sweet potatoes against the side of the pot to thicken the chili. Adjust the seasonings to taste and serve immediately with green onions and cilantro on top.

Wild Rice Soup

(Prep + Cooking Time: 50 minutes | **Servings:** 5)

Ingredients:

- 5 carrots, sliced, with thicker end cut into half-moons
- 5 celery stalks, sliced
- 8 ounces baby bella mushrooms, sliced
- 1 small sweet onion; diced
- 4 garlic cloves; minced
- 4 cups Vegetable Stock
- 1 cup wild rice
- 1/2 cup all-purpose flour
- 1 cup nondairy milk
- 2 bay leaves
- 8 tbsp. vegan butter; divided
- 1/2 tsp. paprika
- 1/2 tsp. dried thyme
- 1/2 tsp. salt or as your liking
- Freshly ground black pepper

Directions:

1. Select the "Sauté" Low mode on your instant pot. When the display reads "Hot," add 2 tbsp. of butter to melt
2. Add the carrots, celery, onion, garlic, mushrooms, bay leaves, paprika, thyme and salt. Cook for 2 to 3 minutes, just until fragrant. Turn off the Instant Pot.
3. Stir in the stock and wild rice. Lock the lid and turn the steam release handle to Sealing. Using the Manual function, set the cooker to High Pressure for 35 minutes
4. When there are just a few minutes of cook time remaining, in a small pan over medium-low heat on your stovetop, melt the remaining 6 tbsp. of butter.
5. Whisk in the flour and cook for 3 to 4 minutes. Whisk in the milk, getting rid of any lumps to finish the roux.
6. After completing the cooking time, quick release the pressure. Remove the lid carefully and remove and discard the bay leaves
7. Select Sauté Low again. Stir in the roux and let warm through and thicken. Taste and season with salt and pepper, as needed

Veggie Soup

(Prep + Cooking Time: 25 minutes | **Servings:** 4)

Ingredients:

- 1 cup tomatoes; chopped.
- 1 zucchini; chopped.
- 4 cups veggie stock
- 6 big mushrooms, sliced
- 4 garlic cloves; minced.
- 1 brown onion; chopped
- 1 tbsp. coconut oil
- 1 bay leaf
- 1 tsp. lemon zest
- 1/2 red chili; chopped.
- 2 carrots; chopped.
- 2 celery sticks; chopped.
- 0.3 oz. kale leaves, roughly chopped
- Salt and black pepper to the taste
- A handful dried porcini mushrooms
- A handful parsley; chopped.

Directions:

1. Set your instant pot on Sauté mode; add oil and heat it up
2. Add onion, celery, carrots, salt and pepper, stir and cook for 1 minute
3. Add chili; dried mushrooms, mushrooms, garlic, stir and cook for 2 minutes
4. Add kale leaves, zucchini, tomatoes, bay leaf and stock; then stir well. seal the instant pot lid and cook at High for 10 minutes.
5. Release the pressure naturally for 10 minutes, then release remaining pressure by turning the valve to 'Venting', carefully open the lid; divide soup into bowls, add lemon zest and parsley on top and serve

White Bean, Sausage and Kale Soup

(Prep + Cooking Time: 45 minutes | **Servings:**6)

Ingredients:
- 1 lb. spicy sausage; sliced. into ¾-inch-thick pieces
- 2 (15-oz.) cans white beans, drained and rinsed
- 1 (5-oz.) bag baby kale
- 1 medium yellow onion; diced.
- 3 garlic cloves; minced.
- 4 carrots, peeled and chopped
- 3 celery stalks; sliced.
- 6 cups low-sodium chicken broth.
- 2 tbsp. extra-virgin olive oil.
- Juice of 1 lemon

Directions:
1. Select *Sauté* and add the olive oil. Once the oil is hot, add the onion, garlic, carrots, celery, and sausage, and cook for 3 minutes
2. Now, press *Cancel* and pour in the broth. Using a wooden spoon, scrape up any browned bits stuck to the bottom of the pot. Add the kale and beans and stir to combine.
3. Now, Lock the lid. Select, "Manual or Pressure Cook" and set the pressure to *High* and the time to 10 minutes. Make sure the steam release knob is in the sealed position.
4. After completing the cooking cycle, naturally release the pressure for 10 minutes, then quick release any remaining pressure
5. Unlock and remove the lid. Using an immersion blender, blend the soup about halfway so the beans and vegetables are still chunky. Stir in the lemon juice. Serve hot

Lamb Stew

(Prep + Cooking Time: 50 minutes | **Servings:** 4)

Ingredients:
- 2 lb. lamb shoulder, cubed
- 14 oz. canned tomatoes; chopped.
- 1/4 cup red wine vinegar
- 1 tbsp. garlic; minced.
- 2 yellow onions; chopped.
- 1 tbsp. olive oil
- 2 bay leaves
- 1/3 cup parsley; chopped.
- 2 tbsp. tomato paste
- 1 red bell pepper; chopped.
- 1 green bell pepper; chopped.
- 1 tsp. oregano; dried
- 1 tsp. basil; dried
- Salt and black pepper to the taste

Directions:
1. Set the pot on Sauté mode; add oil and heat it up
2. Add onions and garlic, stir and cook for 2 minutes.
3. Add vinegar, stir and cook for 2 minutes
4. Add lamb, tomatoes, tomato paste, oregano, basil, salt, pepper and bay leaves; then stir well. close the lid and cook at High for 12 minutes.
5. Release the pressure naturally for 15 minutes, then release remaining pressure by turning the valve to 'Venting', carefully open the lid; discard bay leaves, add green and red pepper, more salt and pepper if needed; then stir well. seal the instant pot lid and cook on High for 8 more minutes.
6. Release the pressure again, carefully open the lid, add parsley, stir and divide into bowls.

Chickpeas Stew

(Prep + Cooking Time: 45 minutes | **Servings:** 4)

Ingredients:
- 1 lb. chickpeas, drained
- 1 yellow onion; chopped.
- 1 tsp. oregano; dried
- 2 tbsp. parmesan cheese, grated
- 3 bay leaves
- 2 tbsp. olive oil
- 2 carrots; chopped.
- 1 garlic head, halved
- 22 oz. canned tomatoes; chopped.
- 22 oz. water

- 1/2 tsp. red pepper flakes
- A drizzle of olive oil for serving
- Salt and black pepper to the taste

Directions:
1. Put onion, carrots, garlic, chickpeas, tomatoes, water, oregano, bay leaves, 2 tablespoons olive oil, salt, and pepper in your instant pot.
2. Cover, cook at High for 25 minutes and quick release the pressure
3. Ladle into bowls, add parmesan, pepper flakes and a drizzle of oil on top and serve.

Mushroom and Wild Rice Stew

(Prep + Cooking Time: 60 minutes | **Servings:** 6)

Ingredients:
- 8 oz. cremini mushrooms; roughly chopped.
- ½ cup full-fat coconut milk
- 1 cup wild rice and brown rice blend, or wild rice
- 4 cups water
- 1 yellow onion; chopped.
- 5 carrots; peeled and chopped.
- 5 celery stalks; chopped.
- 3 cloves garlic; minced.
- 1 tsp. dried thyme
- 1 tsp. ground sage
- Lemon wedges; for serving
- Fresh thyme; for garnish.
- Fine sea salt
- Freshly ground black pepper

Directions:
1. Combine the onion, carrots, celery, garlic, mushrooms, thyme, sage, rice, 4 cups of the water and 2 teaspoons salt in the Instant Pot and secure the lid
2. Turn the steam release valve to Sealing and select *Manual/Pressure* Cook to cook on *High* pressure for 25 minutes.
3. Once the cooking cycle is completed, let the pressure naturally release for 10 minutes, then move the steam release valve to Venting to release any remaining pressure. When the floating valve drops, remove the lid. Stir in the coconut milk
4. Season with additional salt and pepper, to taste and serve immediately with a squeeze of fresh lemon to brighten the flavors and a few sprigs of thyme

Broccoli Cream

(Prep + Cooking Time: 30 minutes | **Servings:** 4)

Ingredients:
- 3 carrots; chopped.
- 1 broccoli head, florets separated and chopped.
- 1 potato; chopped
- 1 yellow onion; chopped.
- 1 tbsp. olive oil
- 2 cups chicken stock
- 5 garlic cloves; minced.
- 1 tbsp. chives; chopped.
- 2 tbsp. cream
- Salt and black pepper to the taste
- Cheddar cheese, grated for serving

Directions:
1. Set your instant pot on Sauté mode; add oil and heat it up
2. Add onion and garlic, stir and cook for 2 minutes
3. Add broccoli, carrots, potato, stock, salt and pepper; then stir well. seal the instant pot lid and cook at High for 5 minutes.
4. Release the pressure naturally for 15 minutes, then release remaining pressure by turning the valve to 'Venting', carefully open the lid; set it on Simmer mode, add cream, cheese and chives; then stir well. heat up for 2 minutes, divide into bowls and serve.

Minestrone Soup

(Prep + Cooking Time: 15 minutes | **Servings:** 5)

Ingredients:
- 1 large carrot, sliced, with thicker end cut into half-moons
- 1 zucchini, roughly diced
- 1 (28-ounce) can diced tomatoes
- 1 (16-ounce) can kidney beans, drained and rinsed
- 2 celery stalks, sliced
- 1 sweet onion; diced
- 1 bay leaf
- 1 cup small dried pasta
- 6 cups Vegetable Stock
- 2 to 3 cups fresh baby spinach
- 2 garlic cloves; minced
- 2 tbsp. olive oil
- 1 tsp. dried basil
- 1 tsp. salt; or more as your liking
- 1 tsp. dried oregano
- Freshly ground black pepper

Directions:
1. Select the "Sauté" Low mode on your instant pot. When the display reads "Hot," add the oil, celery, onion and carrot
2. Cook for 2 to 3 minutes, stirring frequently. Add the garlic and cook for another minute or so, stirring frequently.
3. Turn off the Instant Pot and add the oregano, basil, salt and bay leaf. Stir and let sit for 30 seconds to 1 minute
4. Add the zucchini, tomatoes, kidney beans, pasta and stock. Lock the lid and turn the steam release handle to Sealing. Using the Manual function, set the cooker to High Pressure for 4 minutes.
5. After completing the cooking time, quick release the pressure. Remove the lid carefully and remove and discard the bay leaf
6. Stir in the spinach and let it get all nice and wilty. Taste and season with more salt, as needed and pepper. Serve hot

Coconut Sweet Potato Stew

(Prep + Cooking Time: 25 minutes | **Servings:** 5)

Ingredients:
- 2 Roma tomatoes, chopped
- 1 or 2 dashes chili powder
- 1/2 sweet onion; diced
- 2 sweet potatoes, peeled and cubed
- 2 garlic cloves; minced
- 1 (14-ounce) can lite coconut milk, shaken well
- 1 ¼ cups water; or more as needed
- 1 to 2 cups chopped kale
- 2 tbsp. avocado or olive oil
- 1 tsp. paprika
- 1/2 tsp. ground cumin
- 1/2 tsp. dried oregano
- 1 ½ tsp. salt or as your liking
- 1 tsp. ground turmeric

Directions:
1. Select the "Sauté" Low mode on your instant pot. When the display reads "Hot," add the oil and heat until it shimmers
2. Add the onion. Cook for 2 to 3 minutes, stirring frequently. If they start to burn, hit the Cancel button and let the pot cool down a little before turning it back on.
3. Stir in the sweet potatoes, garlic, salt, turmeric, paprika, cumin; oregano and chili powder. Stir, stir, stir and cook for 1 minute or so
4. Add the tomatoes, coconut milk and water and give it one last good stir. Lock the lid and turn the steam release handle to Sealing. Using the Manual function, set the cooker to High Pressure for 5 minutes
5. After completing the cooking time, turn off the Instant Pot. Let the pressure release naturally for 10 minutes; quick release any remaining pressure.
6. Remove the lid carefully and stir in the kale, which will wilt quickly. Add more water if you want a thinner consistency

Simple Fennel Soup

(Prep + Cooking Time: 35 minutes | **Servings:** 3)

Ingredients:
- 1 fennel bulb; chopped
- 1 bay leaf
- 2 tsp. parmesan cheese, grated
- 1 tbsp. extra-virgin olive oil
- 2 cups water
- 1/2 cube vegetable bouillon
- 1 leek; chopped
- Salt and black pepper to the taste

Directions:
1. In your instant pot, mix fennel with leek, bay leaf, vegetable bouillon and water
2. Stir, seal the instant pot lid and cook at High for 15 minutes.
3. Release the pressure naturally for 15 minutes, then release remaining pressure by turning the valve to 'Venting', carefully open the lid; add cheese, oil, salt and pepper; then stir well. divide into bowls and serve.

Corn Soup

(Prep + Cooking Time: 35 minutes | **Servings:** 4)

Ingredients:
- 6 ears of corn, kernels cut off, cobs reserved
- 2 leeks; chopped
- 1 tbsp. chives; chopped
- 1-quart chicken stock
- 2 tbsp. butter
- 2 bay leaves
- 4 tarragon sprigs; chopped.
- A drizzle of extra virgin olive oil
- 2 garlic cloves; minced.
- Salt and black pepper to the taste

Directions:
1. Set your instant pot on Sauté mode; add butter and melt it
2. Add garlic and leeks, stir and cook for 4 minutes
3. Add corn, corn cobs, bay leaves, tarragon and stock to cover everything, close the lid and cook at High for 15 minutes.
4. Release the pressure naturally for 15 minutes, then release remaining pressure by turning the valve to 'Venting', carefully open the lid; discard bay leaves and corn cobs and transfer everything to your blender
5. Pulse well obtain a smooth soup, add the rest of the stock and blend again.
6. Add salt and pepper to the taste, stir well, divide into soup bowls and serve cold with chives and olive oil on top

Easy Carrot Soup

(Prep + Cooking Time: 35 minutes | **Servings:** 4)

Ingredients:
- 1 lb. carrots; chopped.
- 1 tbsp. vegetable oil
- 1 tbsp. butter
- 1 garlic clove; minced.
- 1 small ginger piece, grated
- 1 onion; chopped
- 1/4 tsp. brown sugar
- 2 cups chicken stock
- 1 tbsp. Sriracha
- 14 oz. canned coconut milk
- Salt and black pepper to the taste
- Cilantro leaves; chopped for serving

Directions:
1. Set your instant pot on Sauté mode; add butter and oil and heat them up
2. Add onion, stir and cook for 3 minutes.
3. Add ginger and garlic, stir and cook for 1 minute
4. Add sugar, carrots, salt and pepper, stir and cook 2 minutes more

5. Add sriracha sauce, coconut milk, stock; then stir well. seal the instant pot lid and cook at High for 6 minutes.
6. Release the pressure naturally for 15 minutes, then release remaining pressure by turning the valve to 'Venting', carefully open the lid; blend soup with an immersion blender, add more salt and pepper if needed and divide into soup bowls. Add cilantro on top and serve.

Curried Squash Soup

(**Prep + Cooking Time:** 40 minutes | **Servings:** 5)

Ingredients:
- 1 (2- to 3-pound) butternut squash, peeled and cubed
- 1 (14-ounce) can lite coconut milk
- 4 cups Vegetable Stock
- 1 onion, chopped
- 2 garlic cloves, chopped
- 1 tbsp. curry powder
- 1 tbsp. olive oil
- 1 tsp. salt or as your liking

Directions:
8. Select the "Sauté" Low mode on your instant pot. When the display reads "Hot," add the oil and heat until it shimmers.
9. Add the onion. Cook for 3 to 4 minutes, stirring frequently.
10. Turn off the Instant Pot and add the garlic and curry powder. Cook for 1 minute, stirring. It should start smelling delicious right about now!
11. Add the squash, stock and salt. Lock the lid and turn the steam release handle to Sealing. Using the Manual function, set the cooker to High Pressure for 30 minutes
12. After completing the cooking time, quick release the pressure
13. Remove the lid carefully. Using an immersion blender, blend the soup until completely smooth.
14. Stir in the coconut milk, saving a little bit for topping when served.

White Bean Soup

(**Prep + Cooking Time:** 45 minutes | **Servings:** 5)

Ingredients:
- 1 cup dried great northern white beans; rinsed
- 3 ½ to 4 cups water; or more as needed
- 1 (14-ounce) can lite coconut milk
- 1 cube vegetable or "not chicken" bouillon
- 1 cup frozen sweet corn
- 1 small to medium tomato; diced
- 1/4 cup raw millet
- 1 ½ tsp. smoked paprika; or more as needed
- 1 tsp. salt; or as your liking

Directions:
1. In the Instant Pot, stir together the beans, tomato, millet, bouillon cube, paprika, salt, water and coconut milk
2. Lock the lid and turn the steam release handle to Sealing. Using the Manual function, set the cooker to High Pressure for 32 minutes
3. After completing the cooking time, turn off the Instant Pot "Note: do not let it go into Keep Warm mode" and let the pressure release naturally for 10 minutes; quick release any remaining pressure.
4. Remove the lid carefully and stir in the corn. Taste and adjust the seasonings, as needed

Italian Stew

(Prep + Cooking Time: 28 minutes | **Servings:** 5)

Ingredients:
- 3 Yukon Gold potatoes; chopped into large bite-size pieces
- 2 cups torn kale leaves
- 1 sweet onion; cut into large dice
- 1 carrot, halved lengthwise; cut into half-moons
- 1 celery stalk, sliced
- 1 cup sliced white mushrooms
- 1 small eggplant; cut into large dice
- 3 garlic cloves; minced
- 3 Roma tomatoes; cut into large dice
- 2 leeks, white and very light green parts only, cleaned well, halved lengthwise; cut into half-moons
- 4 cups Vegetable Stock
- 2 tbsp. olive oil
- 1 tsp. dried oregano
- 1/2 tsp. salt or as your liking Freshly ground black pepper
- Fresh basil; for garnishing

Directions:
1. Select the "Sauté" Low mode on your instant pot. When the display reads "Hot," add the oil and heat until it shimmers
2. Add the leeks, onion, carrot, celery, mushrooms and eggplant. Cook for about 2 minutes, stirring occasionally.
3. Add the garlic. Cook for 30 seconds more. Turn off the Instant Pot and add the potatoes, tomatoes, stock; oregano and salt. Lock the lid and turn the steam release handle to Sealing. Using the Manual function, set the cooker to High Pressure for 8 minutes
4. After completing the cooking time, let the pressure release naturally for 10 minutes; quick release any remaining pressure.
5. Remove the lid carefully and stir in the kale. Taste and season with more salt, as needed and pepper
6. If there's too much liquid, select Sauté Low again and cook for a few minutes to evaporate. Serve garnished with basil

Cabbage Head Soup

(Prep + Cooking Time: 30 minutes | **Servings:** 4)

Ingredients:
- 1 cabbage head; chopped
- 12 oz. baby carrots
- 3 celery stalks; chopped.
- 3 tsp. garlic; minced.
- 1/4 cup cilantro; chopped.
- 4 cups chicken stock
- 1/2 onion; chopped
- 1 packet veggie soup mix
- 2 tbsp. olive oil
- 12 oz. soy burger
- Salt and black pepper to the taste

Directions:
1. In your instant pot, mix cabbage with celery, carrots, onion, veggie soup mix, soy burger, stock, olive oil and garlic; then stir well. seal the instant pot lid and cook on High for 5 minutes
2. Release the pressure naturally for 15 minutes, then release remaining pressure by turning the valve to 'Venting', carefully open the lid; add salt, pepper and cilantro, stir again well, divide into soup bowls and serve.

Butternut Squash Soup

(Prep + Cooking Time: 35 minutes | **Servings:** 6)

Ingredients:
- 1 ½ lb. butternut squash, baked, peeled and cubed
- 1/2 cup green onions; chopped.
- 1/8 tsp. red pepper flakes; dried
- 1 cup orzo, already cooked
- 1 cup chicken meat, already cooked and shredded.
- 3 tbsp. butter
- 1 garlic clove; minced.
- 1/2 tsp. Italian seasoning
- 15 oz. canned tomatoes and their juice; chopped.
- 1/8 tsp. nutmeg, grated
- 1 ½ cup half and half
- 1/2 cup carrots; chopped
- 1/2 cup celery; chopped
- 29 oz. canned chicken stock
- Salt and black pepper to the taste
- Some green onions; chopped for serving

Directions:
1. Set your instant pot on Sauté mode; add butter and melt it.
2. Add celery, carrots and onions, stir and cook for 3 minutes
3. Add garlic, stir and cook for 1 minute more
4. Add squash, tomatoes, stock, Italian seasoning, salt, pepper, pepper flakes and nutmeg.
5. Stir, seal the instant pot lid and cook at High for 10 minutes.
6. Release the pressure naturally for 15 minutes, then release remaining pressure by turning the valve to 'Venting', carefully open the lid and puree everything with your immersion blender
7. Set the pot on Simmer mode, add half and half, orzo and chicken, stir and cook for 3 minutes
8. Divide soup into bowls, sprinkle green onions on top and serve

Barley and Beef Soup

(Prep + Cooking Time: 45 minutes | **Servings:** 4)

Ingredients:
- 1 ½ lb. beef stew meat; chopped.
- 10 baby bell mushrooms, cut into quarters
- 3 cups mixed onion, carrots and celery
- 2 bay leaves
- 2/3 cup barley
- 8 garlic cloves; minced.
- 6 cups beef stock
- 2 tbsp. vegetable oil
- 1 cup water
- 1/2 tsp. thyme; dried
- 1 potato; chopped.
- Salt and black pepper to the taste

Directions:
1. Set your instant pot on Sauté mode; add oil and heat it up
2. Add meat, salt and pepper; then stir well. cook for 3 minutes and transfer to a plate
3. Add mushrooms; then stir well. brown them for 2 minutes and transfer to a plate.
4. Add mixed veggies to the pot, stir and cook for 4 minutes
5. Return meat, mushrooms to the pot and stir everything
6. Also add bay leaves, thyme, water, stock, salt and pepper; then stir well. seal the instant pot lid and cook at High for 16 minutes
7. Release the pressure naturally for 15 minutes, then release remaining pressure by turning the valve to 'Venting', carefully open the lid; add potatoes and barley; then stir well. seal the instant pot lid and cook on Low for 1 hour
8. Release the pressure again, stir soup, divide it into bowls and serve.

Veggie Noodle Soup

(Prep + Cooking Time: 20 minutes | **Servings:** 5)

Ingredients:
- 4 celery stalks; chopped into bite-size pieces
- 1 sweet onion; chopped into bite-size pieces
- 1 cup broccoli florets
- 1 tomato; diced
- 2 garlic cloves; minced
- 1 bay leaf
- 2 sweet potatoes, peeled and chopped into bite-size pieces
- 1 cup dried pasta (I prefer a small pasta shape)
- 4 cups Vegetable Stock
- 1 to 1 ½ cups water; or more as needed
- 4 carrots; chopped into bite-size pieces
- 1 tsp. dried oregano
- 1 tsp. dried thyme
- 1 tsp. dried basil
- 2 tsp. salt or as your liking
- Pinch freshly ground black pepper
- Lemon zest, for garnishing; optional
- Chopped fresh parsley, for garnishing; optional
- Crackers; for serving; optional

Directions:
1. In the Instant Pot, combine the celery, carrots, sweet potatoes, onion, broccoli, tomato, garlic, bay leaf; oregano, thyme, basil, salt, pepper, pasta, stock and water, making sure all the good stuff is submerged "you can add more water or stock, if needed".
2. Lock the lid and turn the steam release handle to Sealing. Using the Manual function, set the cooker to High Pressure for 4 minutes
3. After completing the cooking time, let the pressure release naturally for 5 minutes; quick release any remaining pressure
4. Remove the lid carefully and stir the soup. Remove and discard the bay leaf and enjoy garnished as desired!

Spinach Stew

(Prep + Cooking Time: 50 minutes | **Servings:** 4)

Ingredients:
- 6 cups baby spinach
- 1 small yellow onion; chopped.
- 2 tsp. olive oil
- 1 celery stalk; chopped.
- 1 tsp. turmeric
- 2 tsp. cumin
- 4 cups veggie stock
- 1 tsp. thyme
- 1 cup brown lentils, rinsed
- 2 carrots; chopped.
- 4 garlic cloves; minced.
- Salt and black pepper to the taste

Directions:
1. Set your instant pot on Sauté mode; add oil and heat it up
2. Add onions, celery and carrots, stir and cook for 5 minutes.
3. Add garlic, turmeric, cumin, thyme, salt and pepper, stir and cook for 1 minute more
4. Add stock and lentils; then stir well. seal the instant pot lid and cook at High for 12 minutes
5. Release the pressure naturally for 15 minutes, then release remaining pressure by turning the valve to 'Venting', carefully open the lid; add spinach, more salt and pepper; then stir well. divide into bowls and serve

Asian Peanut Stew

(Prep + Cooking Time: 47 minutes | **Servings:** 8)

Ingredients:
- One 15-oz. can diced tomatoes
- 1 yellow onion; chopped.
- 2 cloves garlic; minced.
- 1 sweet potato, peeled and cut into 1-inch chunks
- 2 cups finely chopped kale, stems removed
- ¼ cup red quinoa, rinsed
- 3 to 4 cups water
- ½ cup all-natural peanut butter
- 1 tbsp. extra-virgin olive oil
- 2 tbsp. minced fresh ginger (2-inch knob)
- 2 tsp. fine sea salt
- ½ tsp. red pepper flakes

Directions:
1. Press *Sauté* and add the olive oil to the Instant Pot. Once the oil is hot but not smoking, add the onion and sauté until softened, about 5 minutes
2. Press *Cancel* Button and stir in the garlic and ginger while the pot is still hot.
3. Add the sweet potato, tomatoes with their juices, peanut butter, salt, red pepper flakes, quinoa and 3 cups of the water, without stirring. *The peanut butter will blend in as the soup cooks.
4. Now, Lock the lid and Turn the steam release valve to "Sealing" Position. Select *Manual/Pressure* Cook to cook on *High* pressure for 10 minutes.
5. Once the cooking cycle is completed, let the pressure naturally release for 10 minutes, then move the steam release valve to Venting to release any remaining pressure
6. When the floating valve drops, remove the lid. Stir in the kale, which should wilt quickly.
7. For a thicker stew, press some of the cooked sweet potatoes against the side of the pot and stir them in until you have a creamier texture
8. If you like a thinner soup, add up to 1 cup of the remaining water. Taste and adjust the seasoning as needed and serve warm

Mushroom Cream Soup

(Prep + Cooking Time: 30 minutes | **Servings:** 5)

Ingredients:
- 1 ½ pounds white button mushrooms, sliced
- 1 ¾ cups Vegetable Stock
- 1/2 cup silken tofu
- 1 small sweet onion, chopped
- 2 garlic cloves; minced
- 2 tbsp. vegan butter
- 2 tsp. dried thyme
- 1 tsp. sea salt or as your liking
- Chopped fresh thyme; for garnishing

Directions:
1. Select the "Sauté" Low mode on your instant pot. When the display reads "Hot," add the butter to melt
2. Add the onion. Sauté for 1 to 2 minutes. Add the mushrooms, garlic, dried thyme and salt. Cook for 2 minutes more and then turn off the Instant Pot.
3. Stir in the stock. Lock the lid and turn the steam release handle to Sealing. Using the Manual function, set the cooker to High pressure for 6 minutes
4. While the soup cooks, place the tofu in a food processor or blender and process until smooth. Set aside
5. After completing the cooking time, let the pressure release naturally for 10 minutes; quick release any remaining pressure.
6. Remove the lid carefully. Using an immersion blender, blend the soup until completely creamy. Stir in the tofu, garnish as desired and it's ready.

Classic Lamb Stew

(Prep + Cooking Time: 45 minutes | **Servings:** 6)

Ingredients:
- 3 lb. lamb shoulder, cut into medium chunks
- 2 carrots; chopped.
- 2 big potatoes, roughly chopped
- 2 onions; chopped.
- 2 thyme springs; chopped.
- 1/4 cup parsley; minced.
- 6 oz. dark beer
- 2 cups water
- Salt and black pepper to the taste

Directions:
1. Put onions and lamb in your instant pot
2. Add salt, pepper, potatoes, thyme, water, beer and carrots; then stir well. seal the instant pot lid and cook at High for 15 minutes.
3. Release the pressure naturally for 15 minutes, then release remaining pressure by turning the valve to 'Venting', carefully open the lid; add parsley, more salt and pepper if needed; then stir well. divide into bowls and serve.

White Bean and Swiss Chard Stew

(Prep + Cooking Time: 15 minutes | **Servings:** 5)

Ingredients:
- 2 cups cooked great northern beans
- 2 carrots, sliced, with thicker end cut into half-moons
- 1 small bunch Swiss chard leaves, chopped
- 1 celery stalk, sliced
- 1/2 onion; cut into large dice
- 2 or 3 garlic cloves; minced
- 3 tomatoes, chopped
- 1 tbsp. olive oil
- ¼ to ½ tsp. red pepper flakes
- 1/2 tsp. dried rosemary
- 1/2 tsp. dried oregano
- 1/4 tsp. dried basil
- 1/2 tsp. salt or as your liking
- Pinch freshly ground black pepper; or more as needed
- Nutritional yeast, for sprinkling; optional

Directions:
7. Select the "Sauté" Low mode on your instant pot. When the display reads "Hot," add the oil and heat until it shimmers
8. Add the carrots, celery and onion. Cook for 2 to 3 minutes, stirring occasionally. Add the garlic and cook for 30 seconds more. Turn off the Instant Pot.
9. Stir in the tomatoes, red pepper flakes, rosemary; oregano, basil, salt, pepper and beans. Lock the lid and turn the steam release handle to Sealing. Using the Manual function, set the cooker to High Pressure for 4 minutes
10. After completing the cooking time, quick release the pressure.
11. Remove the lid carefully and stir in the Swiss chard. Let wilt for 2 to 3 minutes
12. Taste and season with salt and pepper, as needed and sprinkle the nutritional yeast over individual servings

Chestnut Soup Recipe

(Prep + Cooking Time: 45 minutes | **Servings:** 4)

Ingredients:
- 1 lb. canned chestnuts, drained and rinsed
- 1 celery stalk; chopped
- 4 tbsp. butter
- 1 potato; chopped
- 1 bay leaf
- 4 cups chicken stock
- 2 tbsp. rum
- 1 yellow onion; chopped
- 1 sage spring; chopped.
- Salt and white pepper to the taste
- A pinch of nutmeg
- Whole cream for serving
- Sage leaves; chopped for serving

Directions:
1. Set your instant pot on Sauté mode; add butter and melt it
2. Add onion, sage, celery, salt and pepper, stir and cook for 5 minutes.
3. Add chestnuts, potato, bay leaf and stock; then stir well. seal the instant pot lid and cook on Low for 20 minutes.
4. Release the pressure naturally for 15 minutes, then release remaining pressure by turning the valve to 'Venting', carefully open the lid; add nutmeg and rum, discard bay leaf and blend soup using an immersion blender
5. Divide soup into bowls, add cream and sage leaves on top and serve.

Black Bean Chipotle Soup

(Prep + Cooking Time: 55 minutes | **Servings:** 8)

Ingredients:
- 1 lb. dried black beans, soaked for 8 hours
- 1 chipotle pepper, canned in adobo sauce; chopped.
- 1 clove garlic; minced.
- 1½ cups chopped carrots (about 3 carrots)
- 1 cup chopped celery (about 3 stalks)
- 1 yellow onion; chopped.
- 3½ cups water
- 2 tsp. fine sea salt
- 2 tsp. ground cumin
- Lime wedges; for serving
- Chopped fresh cilantro and green onion; for garnish.

Directions:
1. Drain the black beans and combine them with the onion, carrots, celery, chipotle pepper, garlic, water and cumin in the Instant Pot
2. Stir well to make sure the beans are submerged in the liquid, then secure the lid and move the steam release valve to Sealing. Select *Manual/Pressure* Cook to cook on *High* pressure for 20 minutes
3. Once the cooking cycle is completed, let the pressure naturally release for 10 minutes. Turn the steam release valve to Venting to release any remaining pressure.
4. When the floating valve drops, remove the lid. Test the beans to make sure they are tender by pressing one against the side of the pot with a fork
5. It should be easily mashed. If they are not done, secure the lid again, making sure the sealing ring is properly seated and cook at *High* pressure for 10 minutes more.
6. Release the pressure naturally for 10 minutes so the soup doesn't sputter out of the steam release valve when you move it to Venting
7. Once you're sure the beans are tender, add the salt, then use an immersion blender to blend the soup, leaving as much texture as you like.
8. Alternatively, transfer 2 cups of the soup to a blender and blend until smooth, then return the blended soup to the pot and stir it in. *If your soup is too thick, add a little more water to thin it out.
9. Taste and adjust the seasonings as needed. For more spice, add some of the canned adobo sauce that was packed with the chipotle peppers, 1 tsp. at a time, to taste
10. Serve immediately with cilantro and green onion on top and a squeeze of lime juice

Ginger Carrot Soup

(**Prep + Cooking Time:** 20 minutes | **Servings:** 3)

Ingredients:
- 1/2 sweet onion, chopped
- 7 carrots, chopped
- 1-inch piece fresh ginger, peeled and chopped
- 1 ¼ cups Vegetable Stock
- 1/2 tsp. salt or as your liking
- 1/2 tsp. sweet paprika
- Freshly ground black pepper
- Cashew Sour Cream, for garnishing; optional
- Fresh herbs, for garnishing; optional

Directions:
1. In the Instant Pot, combine the carrots, ginger, onion, stock, salt and paprika. Season to taste with pepper
2. Lock the lid and turn the steam release handle to Sealing. Using the Manual function, set the cooker to High Pressure for 4 minutes.
3. After completing the cooking time, let the pressure release naturally for 5 minutes; quick release any remaining pressure
4. Remove the lid carefully. Using an immersion blender, blend the soup until completely smooth.
5. Taste and season with more salt and pepper, as needed. Serve with garnishes of choice

Chipotle Sweet Potato Chowder

(**Prep + Cooking Time:** 10 minutes | **Servings:** 5)

Ingredients:
- 2 large sweet potatoes, peeled and diced large
- 1 ½ cups frozen sweet corn
- 1 ¼ cups Vegetable Stock
- 1 (14-ounce) can lite coconut milk
- 2 to 4 canned chipotle peppers in adobo sauce; diced
- 1 red bell pepper; diced
- 1 small onion; diced
- 1 tsp. ground cumin
- 1 tsp. salt or as your liking
- Adobo sauce from the canned peppers, to taste

Directions:
1. In a medium bowl, whisk the stock and coconut milk, ensuring there are no solid bits of coconut milk left
2. Pour into the Instant Pot and add the sweet potatoes, chipotles, bell pepper, onion, cumin and salt.
3. Lock the lid and turn the steam release handle to Sealing. Using the Manual function, set the cooker to High pressure for 2 minutes.
4. After completing the cooking time, let the pressure release naturally for 5 minutes; quick release any remaining pressure
5. Remove the lid carefully and add the frozen corn and adobo sauce, if you want more heat. Let sit for 1 to 2 minutes while the corn warms

Quinoa Butternut Chili

(**Prep + Cooking Time:** 28 minutes | **Servings:** 5)

Ingredients:
- 2 carrots, sliced
- 1 sweet onion; cut into large dice
- 1 red bell pepper; cut into large dice
- 1 jalapeño pepper; diced
- 2 garlic cloves; minced
- 1 butternut squash, peeled and cut into bite-size cubes
- 1 (14-ounce) can diced tomatoes with juice
- 1 cup uncooked quinoa; rinsed
- 2 ½ cups Vegetable Stock
- 1 bay leaf
- 1 to 2 tbsp. olive oil
- 1 tsp. ground cumin

- 1 tbsp. freshly squeezed lemon juice
- 1/2 to 1 tsp. salt; or more as your liking
- 1/2 tsp. sweet paprika
- 1/2 tsp. chili powder; or more to taste
- 1/2 tsp. freshly ground black pepper; or more as needed

Directions:
1. Select the "Sauté" Low mode on your instant pot. When the display reads "Hot," add the oil and heat until it shimmers
2. Add the carrots, onion, bell pepper and jalapeño. Cook for 2 to 3 minutes, stirring. Turn off the Instant Pot and add the garlic, stirring again so it doesn't burn.
3. Add the squash, tomatoes, quinoa, stock, bay leaf, cumin, salt, paprika, chili powder and pepper
4. Lock the lid and turn the steam release handle to Sealing. Using the Manual function, set the cooker to High Pressure for 8 minutes.
5. After completing the cooking time, turn the Instant Pot off and let the pressure release naturally for 10 minutes; quick release any remaining pressure
6. Remove the lid carefully. Remove and discard the bay leaf and stir in the lemon juice.
7. Taste and season with salt and pepper, as needed. If there's too much liquid, select Sauté Low again and cook for 1 to 2 minutes, stirring frequently

Veg Minestrone with Pasta

(**Prep + Cooking Time:** 48 minutes | **Servings:** 6)

Ingredients:
- 2 (15-oz.) cans diced tomatoes
- 1 (6-oz.) can tomato paste
- 2 (15-oz.) cans red kidney beans, drained and rinsed
- 2 cups dried whole-wheat macaroni pasta
- 2 tbsp. extra-virgin olive oil.
- ½ cup grated Parmesan cheese
- 1 medium yellow onion; chopped.
- 3 garlic cloves; minced.
- 4 carrots, peeled and sliced
- 2 celery stalks; sliced.
- 2 bay leaves
- 6 cups low-sodium vegetable broth
- ½ tsp. dried thyme
- 1 tsp. dried oregano
- 1 tsp. fine sea salt.
- ½ tsp. freshly ground black pepper.

Directions:
1. Select *Sauté* and add the olive oil to the inner pot. Once the oil is hot, add the onion, garlic, carrots, and celery; sauté for 3 minutes or until the vegetables start to soften
2. Now, press *Cancel* and pour in the broth. Using a wooden spoon, scrape up any browned bits stuck to the bottom of the pot. Add the oregano, thyme, salt, pepper, and bay leaves, and stir to combine.
3. Add the beans; diced. tomatoes, and tomato paste, but don't stir (this prevents the tomatoes from getting to the bottom of the pot, where they might burn)
4. Now, Lock the lid. Select, "Manual or Pressure Cook" and set the pressure to *High* and the time to 5 minutes. Make sure the steam release knob is in the sealed position.
5. After completing the cooking cycle, naturally release the pressure for 10 minutes, then quick release any remaining pressure. Unlock and remove the lid. Select *Sauté*. Remove and discard the bay leaves.
6. Let the soup come up to a simmer, then stir in the macaroni. Let the pasta cook for 7 minutes. Now, press *Cancel* and stir in the Parmesan cheese. Serve hot

Tomato Soup

(Prep + Cooking Time: 40 minutes | **Servings:** 4)

Ingredients:

- 1 lb. frozen peeled and cubed butternut squash
- One 28-oz. can diced tomatoes
- 1 yellow onion; chopped.
- 1 clove garlic; minced.
- 2 cups water
- ½ cup full-fat coconut milk
- 1 tbsp. extra-virgin olive oil
- 1 tbsp. pure maple syrup (optional)
- 2 tsp. dried basil
- 2 tsp. fine sea salt
- Freshly ground black pepper
- Chopped fresh basil; for garnish. (optional)

Directions:

1. Press *Sauté* and add the olive oil to the Instant Pot. Once the oil is hot but not smoking, add the onion and sauté until softened, about 5 minutes. Press *Cancel* Button and stir in the garlic while the pot is still hot
2. Add the squash, tomatoes with their juices, basil, salt and water to the pot.
3. Now, Lock the lid and Turn the steam release valve to "Sealing" Position. Select *Manual/Pressure* Cook to cook on *High* pressure for 5 minutes
4. Once the cooking cycle is completed, let the pressure naturally release for 10 minutes, then move the steam release valve to Venting.
5. When the floating valve drops, remove the lid. Stir in the coconut milk. Taste the soup and add the maple syrup, if more sweetness is needed
6. Use an immersion blender to blend the soup directly in the pot, or carefully transfer the soup to a blender in batches and blend to your desired texture.
7. Taste and adjust the seasoning as needed, then serve warm with basil on top and a few grinds of black pepper..

Fish and Seafood

Spicy Salmon Dish

(Prep + Cooking Time: 15 minutes | Servings: 4)

Ingredients:
- 4 salmon fillets
- 2 tbsp. assorted chili pepper
- 1 lemon, sliced
- 1 cup water
- Juice of 1 lemon
- Salt and black pepper to the taste

Directions:
1. Place salmon fillets in the steamer basket of your pot, add salt, pepper, lemon juice, lemon slices and chili pepper.
2. Add 1 cup water to the pot, seal the instant pot lid and cook at High for 5 minutes.
3. Quick release the pressure, divide salmon and lemon slices among plates and serve

Coconut Fish Curry.

(Prep + Cooking Time: 40 minutes | Servings: 6)

Ingredients:
- 1½ lbs. mahi mahi fillets (about 4 fillets); cut into 2-inch cubes
- 1 (13. 5-oz.) can full-fat coconut milk
- 2 red bell peppers; seeded and sliced.
- 1 white onion; sliced.
- 2 tbsp. reduced-sodium soy sauce
- 1 tbsp. brown sugar
- 2 tbsp. extra-virgin olive oil.
- 1 tbsp. green curry paste
- ½ tsp. ground ginger
- Juice of 1 lime

Directions:
1. Select *Sauté* and add the olive oil to the inner pot. Once the oil is hot, add the onion, fish, and green curry paste; sauté for about 4 minutes, stirring occasionally, until the fish is browned on all sides
2. Now, press *Cancel* and add the coconut milk, soy sauce, brown sugar, and ginger. Using a wooden spoon, scrape up any browned bits stuck to the bottom of the pot. Add the bell peppers and stir to combine.
3. Now, Lock the lid. Select, "Manual or Pressure Cook" and set the pressure to *High* and the time to 4 minutes. Make sure the steam release knob is in the sealed position.
4. After completing the cooking cycle, naturally release the pressure for 10 minutes, then quick release any remaining pressure. Unlock and remove the lid. Stir in the lime juice. Serve hot

Cajun Dirty Rice

(Prep + Cooking Time: 34 minutes | Servings: 4)

Ingredients:
- 1 lb. 85% lean ground beef
- 1/2 cup diced yellow onion, 1/2 cup diced bell pepper and 1/2 cup diced celery
- 1 cup water
- 1 cup basmati rice; rinsed and drained
- 1 bay leaf
- 2 tbsp. vegetable oil
- 1 tbsp. salt-free Cajun seasoning
- 1 tsp. dried oregano
- 2 tsp. hot sauce
- 1 tsp. salt or as your liking

Directions:
1. Now Press "Sauté" on the Instant Pot. When the pot is hot, add the oil. When the oil is hot, add the mirepoix and ground beef. Cook 2 to 3 minutes, stirring to break up the clumps of meat
2. Add the rice, Cajun seasoning, hot sauce, oregano, salt and bay leaf. Stir well to combine. Now Press "Cancel". Stir in the water

3. Now secure the lid on the pot and close the valve. Now Press "Manual" and set the pot at "High" pressure for 4 minutes.
4. After completing the cooking time, allow the pot to sit undisturbed for 10 minutes, then release any remaining pressure. Stir gently to fluff up the rice, discard the bay leaf and serve

Miso Mackerel

(**Prep + Cooking Time:** 60 minutes | **Servings:** 4)

Ingredients:
- 2 lb. mackerel, cut into big pieces
- 1 cup water
- 1 garlic clove, crushed.
- 2 celery stalks, sliced
- 1/3 cup mirin
- 1/4 cup miso
- 1/3 cup sake
- 1 sweet onion, thinly sliced
- 1 tbsp. rice vinegar
- 1 tsp. Japanese hot mustard
- 1 tsp. sugar
- 1 shallot, sliced
- 1-inch ginger piece; chopped
- Salt to the taste

Directions:
1. Set your instant pot on Sauté mode; add mirin, sake, ginger, garlic and shallot, stir and boil for 2 minutes.
2. Add miso and water and stir.
3. Add mackerel, seal the instant pot lid and cook at High for 45 minutes.
4. Meanwhile, put onion and celery in a bowl and cover with ice water.
5. In another bowl, mix vinegar with salt, sugar and mustard and stir well
6. Release the pressure from the pot naturally for 10 minutes and divide mackerel among plates.
7. Drain onion and celery well and mix with mustard dressing.
8. Divide along mackerel and serve

Mussels and Spicy Sauce

(**Prep + Cooking Time:** 15 minutes | **Servings:** 4)

Ingredients:
- 2 lb. mussels, scrubbed and debearded
- 1/2 tsp. red pepper flakes
- 2 tsp. oregano; dried
- 2 tbsp. extra virgin olive oil
- 14 oz. tomatoes; chopped.
- 2 tsp. garlic; minced.
- 1/2 cup chicken stock
- 1 yellow onion; chopped.

Directions:
1. Set your instant pot on Sauté mode; add oil and heat it up.
2. Add onions, stir and cook for 3 minutes
3. Add pepper flakes and garlic, stir and cook for 1 minute
4. Add stock, oregano and tomatoes and stir well.
5. Add mussels; then stir well. seal the instant pot lid and cook on Low for 2 minutes
6. Quick release the pressure, discard unopened mussels, divide among bowls and serve

Steamed Fish Recipe

(**Prep + Cooking Time:** 20 minutes | **Servings:** 4)

Ingredients:
- 4 white fish fillets
- 1 lb. cherry tomatoes, cut into halves
- A pinch of thyme; dried
- 1 garlic clove; minced.
- A drizzle of olive oil
- 1 cup olives, pitted and chopped.
- 1 cup water
- Salt and black pepper to the taste

Directions:
1. Pour the water in your instant pot.
2. Put fish fillets in the steamer basket of the pot.
3. Add tomatoes and olives on top
4. Also add garlic, thyme, oil, salt and pepper
5. Cover the pot and cook on Low for 10 minutes.
6. Quick release the pressure, carefully open the lid; divide fish, olives and tomatoes mix among plates and serve.

Shrimp with Tomatoes, Spinach

(Prep + Cooking Time: 31 minutes | **Servings:** 4)

Ingredients:
- 1 lb. shrimp (21 to 25 count); peeled and deveined
- 4 cups chopped baby spinach
- 1 ½ cups chopped yellow onions
- 1/4 cup shredded Parmesan cheese
- 1 (14.5-ounce) can diced tomatoes; undrained
- 1/4 cup chopped fresh basil
- 1 tbsp. minced garlic
- 2 tbsp. salted butter
- 1 tsp. dried oregano
- 1/2 tsp. red pepper flakes
- 1 tsp. salt or as your liking
- 1 tsp. black pepper

Directions:
1. Now Press "Sauté" on the Instant Pot. When the pot is hot, add the butter. When the butter has melted, add the garlic and red pepper flakes
2. Cook, stirring, for 1 minute. Add the spinach, shrimp, onions, tomatoes and their juices, oregano, salt and pepper. Stir to combine. Now Press "Cancel"
3. Secure the lid on the pot. Close the pressure release valve. Now Press "Manual" and set the pot at "Low" pressure for 1 minute.
4. After completing the cooking time, quick release the pressure. Allow the mixture to cool for 5 minutes. Stir in the basil. Divide the mixture among four shallow bowls. Top with Parmesan and serve immediately

Tuna and Noodle

(Prep + Cooking Time: 30 minutes | **Servings:** 4)

Ingredients:
- 8 oz. egg noodles
- 1/2 cup red onion; chopped.
- 1 ¼ cups water
- 8 oz. artichoke hearts, drained and chopped.
- 1 tbsp. parsley; chopped.
- 1 tbsp. extra-virgin olive oil
- 14 oz. canned tomatoes; chopped and mixed with oregano, basil and garlic
- 14 oz. canned tuna, drained
- Salt and black pepper to the taste
- Crumbled feta cheese

Directions:
1. Set your instant pot on Sauté mode; add oil and heat it up
2. Add onion, stir and cook for 2 minutes
3. Add tomatoes, noodles, salt, pepper and water, set the pot on Simmer and cook for 10 minutes.
4. Add tuna and artichokes; then stir well. seal the instant pot lid and cook at High for 5 minutes.
5. Quick release the pressure, divide tuna and noodles among plates, sprinkle cheese and parsley on top and serve

Salmon Burger

(**Prep + Cooking Time:** 20 minutes | **Servings:** 4)

Ingredients:
- 1 lb. salmon meat; minced.
- 1 tsp. extra virgin olive oil
- 1/2 cup panko
- 2 tbsp. lemon zest
- Tomatoes slices for serving
- Mustard for serving
- Salt and black pepper to the taste
- Arugula leaves for serving

Directions:
- Put salmon in your food processor and blend it.
- Transfer to a bowl, add panko, salt, pepper and lemon zest and stir well.
- Shape 4 patties and place them on a working surface.
- Set your instant pot on Sauté mode; add oil and heat it up
- Add patties, cook for 3 minutes on each side and divide them on buns.
- Serve with tomatoes, arugula and mustard.

Surprising Shrimp Delight

(**Prep + Cooking Time:** 30 minutes | **Servings:** 4)

Ingredients:
- 18 oz. shrimp, peeled and deveined
- 1/2 tbsp. mustard seeds
- 3 oz. mustard oil
- 1 tsp. turmeric powder
- 2 onions; finely chopped
- 4 oz. curd, beaten
- 2 green chilies, cut into halves lengthwise
- 1-inch ginger; chopped.
- Salt to the taste
- Already cooked rice for serving

Directions:
1. Put mustard seeds in a bowl, add water to cover, leave aside for 10 minutes, drain and grind very well
2. Put shrimp in a bowl, add mustard oil, turmeric, mustard paste, salt, onions, chilies, curd and ginger, toss to coat and leave aside for 10 minutes.
3. Transfer everything to your instant pot, seal the instant pot lid and cook on Low for 10 minutes.
4. Quick release the pressure, divide among plates and serve with boiled rice

Almond Cod.

(**Prep + Cooking Time:** 45 minutes | **Servings:** 4)

Ingredients:
- 8 oz. cod
- 3 tbsp. almond flakes
- 1 tsp. minced garlic
- 3 tbsp. soy sauce
- 1 tbsp. lime zest
- 1/4 cup. fish sauce
- 1/2 cup. almond milk
- 1 tbsp. butter

Directions:
1. Choose the roughly and transfer it to the mixing bowl
2. Add fish sauce and soy sauce. Stir the mixture.
3. Ager this, sprinkle the fish with the lime zest and minced garlic. Stir it.
4. Then add almond milk and leave the fish for 10 minutes to marinate.
5. Then toss the butter in the Instant Pot and melt it.
6. Then add the almond milk cod in the Instant Pot. Close the lid and cook the dish at the "Sauté" mode for 10 minutes
7. When the time is over - open the Instant Pot lid and add almond flakes.
8. Stir the dish gently and cook it for 3 minutes.
9. Then remove the dish from the Instant Pot.
10. Serve it immediately. Enjoy!

Salmon Dish

(Prep + Cooking Time: 25 minutes | **Servings:** 4)

Ingredients:
- 4 salmon fillets
- 4 thyme springs
- 3 tomatoes, sliced
- 1 lemon, sliced
- 1 white onion; chopped.
- 2 cups water
- 3 tbsp. extra virgin olive oil
- 4 parsley springs
- Salt and black pepper to the taste

Directions:
1. Drizzle the oil on a parchment paper
2. Add a layer of tomatoes, salt and pepper.
3. Drizzle some oil again, add fish and season them with salt and pepper
4. Drizzle some more oil, add thyme and parsley springs, onions, lemon slices, salt and pepper
5. Fold and wrap packet, place in the steamer basket of your instant pot
6. Add 2 cups water to the pot, seal the instant pot lid and cook on Low for 15 minutes.
7. Quick release the pressure, carefully open the lid; open packet, divide fish mix among plates and serve.

Tomato Mussels

(Prep + Cooking Time: 15 minutes | **Servings:** 3)

Ingredients:
- 28 oz. canned tomatoes, crushed.
- 2 lb. mussels, cleaned and scrubbed
- 1/4 cup extra virgin olive oil
- 1/4 cup balsamic vinegar
- 1/2 cup white onion; chopped.
- 2 jalapeno peppers; chopped.
- 2 tbsp. red pepper flakes
- 2 garlic cloves; minced.
- 1/4 cup dry white wine
- 1/2 cup basil; chopped.
- Lemon wedges for serving
- Salt to the taste

Directions:
1. Set your instant pot on Sauté mode; add tomatoes, onion, jalapenos, wine, oil, vinegar, garlic and pepper flakes, stir and bring to a boil.
2. Add mussels; then stir well. seal the instant pot lid and cook on Low for 4 minutes.
3. Quick release the pressure, carefully open the lid; discard unopened mussels, add salt and basil; then stir well. divide among bowls and serve with lemon wedges

Shrimp with Herbs and Risotto

(Prep + Cooking Time: 30 minutes | **Servings:** 4)

Ingredients:
- 1 lb. shrimp, peeled and deveined
- 4 tbsp. butter
- 2 garlic cloves; minced.
- 1 ½ cups Arborio rice
- 2 tbsp. dry white wine
- 4 ½ cups chicken stock
- 3/4 cup parmesan, grated
- 1/4 cup tarragon and parsley; chopped
- 1 yellow onion; chopped.
- Salt and black pepper to the taste

Directions:
1. Set your instant pot on Sauté mode; add 2 tablespoon butter and melt.
2. Add garlic and onion, stir and cook for 4 minutes
3. Add rice, stir and cook for 1 minute
4. Add wine, stir and cook 30 seconds more.
5. Add 3 cups stock, salt, and pepper; then stir well. seal the instant pot lid and cook at High for 9 minutes.
6. Quick release the pressure, carefully open the lid; add shrimp, the rest of the stock, set the pot on Sauté mode again and cook for 5 minutes stirring from time to time.
7. Add cheese, the rest of the butter, tarragon and parsley; then stir well. divide among plates and serve.

Poached Salmon Dish

(**Prep + Cooking Time:** 15 minutes | **Servings:** 4)

Ingredients:
- 16 oz. salmon fillet, skin on
- Zest from 1 lemon
- 1/2 cup dry white wine
- 1 tsp. white wine vinegar
- 2 cups chicken stock
- 1/2 tsp. fennel seeds
- 1 bay leaf
- 4 scallions; chopped.
- 3 black peppercorns
- 1/4 cup dill; chopped
- Salt and black pepper to the taste

Directions:
1. Put salmon in the steamer basket of your instant pot and season with salt and pepper.
2. Add stock, scallions, lemon zest, peppercorns, fennel, vinegar, bay leaf, wine, stock and dill to your pot.
3. Cover and cook at High for 5 minutes.
4. Quick release the pressure, carefully open the lid and divide salmon among plates
5. Set the pot on Simmer mode and cook the liquid for a few minutes more
6. Drizzle over salmon and serve

Salmon and Veggies Dish

(**Prep + Cooking Time:** 20 minutes | **Servings:** 2)

Ingredients:
- 2 salmon fillets, skin on
- 1 bay leaf
- 2 cups broccoli florets
- 1 cinnamon stick
- 3 cloves
- 1 tbsp. canola oil
- 1 cup water
- 1 cup baby carrots
- Salt and black pepper to the taste
- Lime wedges for serving

Directions:
1. Pour the water in your instant pot
2. Add bay leaf, cinnamon stick and cloves.
3. Place salmon fillets in the steamer basket of your pot after you've brushed them with canola oil
4. Season with salt and pepper, add broccoli and carrots, seal the instant pot lid and cook at High for 6 minutes
5. Release the pressure naturally for 4 minutes, then release remaining pressure by turning the valve to 'Venting', and carefully open the lid.
6. Divide salmon and veggies among plates.
7. Drizzle the sauce from the pot after you've discarded cinnamon, cloves and bay leaf and serve with lime wedges on the side.

Sesame Honey Salmon

(**Prep + Cooking Time:** 20 minutes | **Servings:** 4)

Ingredients:
- 1 lb. salmon fillet
- 2 cups water
- 1 tbsp. dark soy sauce
- 1 tbsp. toasted sesame oil
- 2 tbsp. sesame seeds
- 1 tbsp. honey
- 2 tsp. minced fresh ginger
- 1 tsp. minced garlic
- 1/2 tsp. red pepper flakes
- Salt and black pepper to taste

Directions:
1. Place the salmon in a 6-inch round heatproof pan. In a small bowl, combine the honey, soy sauce, sesame oil, ginger, garlic and red pepper flakes and season with salt and black pepper. Whisk to combine
2. Pour the mixture over the salmon. Allow the salmon to sit at room temperature for 15 to 30 minutes.

3. Pour the water into the Instant Pot. Place a steamer rack in the pot. Place the pan with the salmon on the rack
4. Now secure the lid on the pot and close the valve. Now Press "Manual" and set the pot at "Low" pressure for 3 minutes.
5. After completing the cooking time, allow the pot to sit undisturbed for 5 minutes, then release any remaining pressure. Sprinkle with the sesame seeds. Serve the salmon immediately

Garlic Shrimp Scampi

(**Prep + Cooking Time:** 32 minutes | **Servings:**8)

Ingredients:
- 2 lbs. fresh or frozen shrimp, peeled and deveined
- ½ cup low-sodium chicken broth.
- ½ cup white wine
- 1 (16-oz.) package dried whole-wheat spaghetti pasta, cooked according to package directions
- 2 garlic cloves; minced.
- 2 tbsp. extra-virgin olive oil.
- 2 tbsp. unsalted butter
- Juice of 1 lemon
- ¼ tsp. freshly ground black pepper.
- ½ tsp. fine sea salt.

Directions:
1. Select *Sauté* and add the olive oil and butter to the inner pot. Once the oil is hot and the butter has melted, add the garlic and sauté for 2 minutes
2. Now, press *Cancel* and add the wine and chicken broth. Using a wooden spoon, scrape up any browned bits stuck to the bottom of the pot. Add the shrimp to the pot. Stir to combine
3. Now, Lock the lid. Select, "Manual or Pressure Cook" and set the pressure to *High* and the time to 2 minutes (4 minutes if using frozen shrimp). Make sure the steam release knob is in the sealed position.
4. After completing the cooking cycle, naturally release the pressure for 5 minutes, then quick release any remaining pressure. Unlock and remove the lid. Stir in the pasta, lemon juice, salt, and pepper. Serve hot

Vegetables and Salmon with Butter Sauce

(**Prep + Cooking Time:** 35 minutes | **Servings:**5)

Ingredients:
- 2 lbs. medium red potatoes; cut into 1-inch chunks
- 5 (4-oz.) frozen salmon fillets
- 4 carrots, peeled and chopped into 1-inch-thick pieces (about 2 cups)
- 1 cup low-sodium vegetable broth
- Juice of 2 lemons
- Freshly ground black pepper.
- 4 tbsp. unsalted butter, melted
- 1 tsp. fine sea salt.
- ½ tsp. garlic powder
- Fresh chopped dill; for garnish. (optional)

Directions:
1. Pour the broth into the inner pot and add the potatoes and carrots. Place the salmon fillets, skin-side down, on top of the vegetables
2. Pour the melted butter over the salmon and sprinkle the salt and garlic powder over the top
3. Now, Lock the lid. Select, "Manual or Pressure Cook" and set the pressure to *High* and the time to 5 minutes. Make sure the steam release knob is in the sealed position.
4. After completing the cooking cycle, naturally release the pressure for 10 minutes, then quick release any remaining pressure. Unlock and remove the lid. Serve immediately garnished with black pepper and dill

Crispy Skin Salmon Fillets.

(Prep + Cooking Time: 20 minutes | **Servings:** 2)

Ingredients:
- 2 salmon fillets, frozen (1-inch thickness)
- 2 tbsp. olive oil
- 1 cup. tap water, running cold
- Salt and pepper, to taste

Directions:
1. Pour 1 cup. water in the Instant Pot.
2. Set the steamer rack and put the salmon fillets in the rack. Lock the lid and close the steamer valve.
3. Press "Manual", set the pressure on "Low", and set the timer for 1 minute
4. When the timer beeps, turn off the pot and quick release the pressure
5. Carefully open the lid. Remove the salmon fillets and pat them dry using paper towels.
6. Over medium-high heat, preheat a skillet.
7. Grease the salmon fillet skins with 1 tablespoon olive oil and generously season with black pepper and salt.
8. When the skillet is very hot, with the skin side down, put the salmon fillet in the skillet.
9. Cook for 1 to 2 minutes until the skins are crispy.
10. Transfer the salmon fillets into serving plates and serve with your favorite side dishes.
11. This dish is great with rice and salad.

Tips: You can use a nonstick skillet to make sure the skin does not stick to the skillet. If you do not like the skin on your salmon, you can remove it after pressure cooking. Increase the cooking time to 2 minutes

Tuna & Pasta Casserole.

(Prep + Cooking Time: 10 minutes | **Servings:** 2)

Ingredients:
- 1 can cream of mushroom soup
- 2 ½ cups. macaroni pasta
- 1/2 tsp. salt
- 1/2 tsp. pepper
- 1 cup. cheddar cheese, shredded.
- 1 cups. frozen peas
- 2 cans tuna
- 3 cups. water

Directions:
1. Mix the soup with the water in the Instant Pot. Except for the cheese, add the rest of the ingredients.
2. Stir to combine. Lock the lid and turn the steam valve to "Sealing". Press "Manual", set the pressure to "High", and set the timer for 4 minutes.
3. When the timer beeps, turn the steam valve to "Venting" to quickly release the pressure. Unlock and open the lid.
4. Sprinkle the cheese on top. Close the lid and let sit for 5 minutes or until the cheese is melted and the sauce is thick

Cheesy Tuna Dish.

(Prep + Cooking Time: 15 minutes | **Servings:** 6)

Ingredients:
- 28 oz. canned cream mushroom soup
- 3 cups. water
- 1 can (5 oz.) tuna, drained
- 1 cup. frozen peas
- 1/4 cup. bread crumbs (optional)
- 16 oz. egg noodles
- 4 oz. cheddar cheese

Directions:
1. Put the noodles in the Instant Pot. Pour in the water to cover the noodles.
2. Add the frozen peas, tuna, and the soup on top of the pasta layer. Cover and lock the lid

3. Press the "Manual" key, set the pressure to "High", and set the timer for 4 minutes. When the Instant Pot timer beeps, press the "Cancel" key and unplug the Instant Pot. Turn the steam valve to quick release the pressure.
4. Unlock and carefully open the lid. Stir in the cheese.
5. If desired, you can pour the pasta mixture in a baking dish, sprinkle the top with bread crumbs, and broil for about 2 to 3 minutes. Serve.

Shrimp Coconut Soup

(Prep + Cooking Time: 21 minutes | **Servings:** 4)

Ingredients:
- 1/2 lb. medium shrimp; peeled (tails left on) and deveined
- 1/4 cup fresh lime juice
- 1 cup canned straw mushrooms; undrained
- 6 thin slices fresh ginger
- 1 (13.5-ounce) can full-fat coconut milk
- Grated zest of 1 lime
- 3 cups chicken broth
- 2 tbsp. fish sauce
- 1 tbsp. minced fresh lemongrass
- 1 tsp. honey
- 1/2 tsp. salt or as your liking
- Chopped fresh cilantro, for garnish
- Lime wedges, for serving

Directions:
1. In your Instant Pot, combine the broth, shrimp, mushrooms and their liquid, half the coconut milk, the ginger, chiles (if using), 1 tbsp. of the fish sauce, the lemongrass, honey and salt
2. Now secure the lid on the pot and close the valve. Now Press "Manual" and set the pot at "Low" pressure for 1 minute.
3. After completing the cooking time, quick release the pressure. Stir in the remaining 1 tbsp. fish sauce, remaining coconut milk, the lime zest and lime juice
4. Divide the soup among four serving bowls. Garnish with cilantro and serve with lime wedges alongside for squeezing

Crab Quiche

(Prep + Cooking Time: 60 minutes | **Servings:** 4)

Ingredients:
- 1 cup half-and-half
- 4 large eggs
- 2 cups water
- 8 ounces imitation crabmeat, real crabmeat
- 1 cup shredded Swiss cheese
- 1 cup chopped scallions
- Vegetable oil
- 1 tsp. smoked paprika
- 1 tsp. herbes de Provence
- 1 tsp. black pepper
- 1 tsp. salt or as your liking

Directions:
1. Grease a 6-inch or 7-inch nonstick springform pan with vegetable oil. Set the pan on a sheet of aluminum foil that is larger than the pan and crimp the foil around the bottom of the pan
2. In a large bowl, whisk together the eggs and half-and-half. Add the cheese, scallions, pepper, paprika, herbes de Provence and salt. Stir with a fork to combine. Add the imitation crabmeat and stir to combine.
3. Pour the egg mixture into the prepared pan. Cover the pan loosely with foil. Pour the water into the Instant Pot. Set a steamer rack in the pot. Place the pan on the steamer rack
4. Now secure the lid on the pot and close the valve. Now Press "Manual" and set the pot at "High" pressure for 25 minutes.
5. After completing the cooking time, allow the pot to sit undisturbed for 10 minutes, then release any remaining pressure. Using silicone oven mitts, very carefully remove the pan from the pot. Using a knife, loosen the sides of the quiche from the pan, then remove the springform ring. Serve warm

Shrimp and Grits

(Prep + Cooking Time: 55 minutes | **Servings:** 6)

Ingredients:
- 1 lb. medium shrimp, peeled and deveined, tails left on
- 2 garlic cloves; minced.
- 1 cup low-sodium chicken broth.
- 2 cups cornmeal grits
- 4 cups water
- 1 tbsp. unsalted butter
- 2 tbsp. extra-virgin olive oil.
- ½ tsp. chili powder
- ½ tsp. fine sea salt.

Directions:
1. Select *Sauté* and add the olive oil to the inner pot. Once the oil is hot, add the shrimp, garlic, and chili powder and sauté for about 5 minutes, stirring occasionally so the shrimp are cooked through on both sides
2. Press Cancel. Using a slotted spoon, transfer the shrimp and garlic to a serving plate. Cover to keep warm.
3. Pour the broth into the pot. Using a wooden spoon, scrape up any browned bits stuck to the bottom of the pot. Add the butter, salt, grits, and water to the pot
4. Now, Lock the lid. Select, "Manual or Pressure Cook" and set the pressure to *High* and the time to 10 minutes. Make sure the steam release knob is in the sealed position.
5. After completing the cooking cycle, naturally release the pressure for 10 minutes, then quick release any remaining pressure. Unlock and remove the lid. Stir the grits.
6. Divide the grits among individual serving plates and top with the shrimp

Steamed Scallion Ginger Fish

(Prep + Cooking Time: 32 minutes | **Servings:** 4)

Ingredients:
For Fish:
- 1 lb. firm white-fleshed fish, such as tilapia, cut into large pieces
- 2 cups water
- 2 tbsp. rice wine

For Sauce:
- 1/4 cup chopped fresh cilantro
- 1/4 cup julienned scallions
- 1 tbsp. Chinese black bean paste
- 3 tbsp. soy sauce
- 1 tsp. minced fresh ginger
- 1 tsp. minced garlic

- 2 tbsp. julienned fresh ginger
- 1 tbsp. peanut oil

Directions:
1. For fish: Place the fish pieces on a rimmed plate. In a small bowl, combine the soy sauce, rice wine, black bean paste; minced ginger and garlic. Whisk to combine. Pour over the fish, turning to coat
2. Allow the fish to stand at room temperature for 20 to 30 minutes. Pour the water into the Instant Pot. Place a steamer basket in the pot. Transfer the fish to the steamer basket, reserving the marinade.
3. Now secure the lid on the pot and close the valve. Now Press "Manual" and set the pot at "Low" pressure for 2 minutes. After completing the cooking time, quick release the pressure. Transfer the fish to a serving platter.
4. Meanwhile; for the sauce: In a small saucepan, heat the peanut oil over medium-high heat. When the oil shimmers, add the julienned ginger and cook, stirring, for 10 seconds
5. Add the scallions and cilantro. Cook, stirring, until the ginger and scallions are just softened, about 2 minutes.
6. Add the reserved marinade and bring to a boil. Boil vigorously for 1 to 2 minutes. Pour the vegetable mixture over the fish and serve immediately

Crispy Salmon Fillet

(Prep + Cooking Time: 15 minutes | **Servings:** 2)

Ingredients:
- 2 salmon fillets, frozen
- 2 tbsp. extra virgin olive oil
- 1 cup water
- Salt and black pepper to the taste

Directions:
1. Pour the water in your instant pot.
2. Place salmon in the steamer basket, seal the instant pot lid and cook on Low for 3 minutes.
3. Quick release the pressure, transfer salmon to paper towels and pat dry them.
4. Heat up a pan with the oil over medium high heat, add salmon fillets skin side down, season with salt and pepper to the taste and cook for 2 minutes.
5. Divide among plates and serve with your favorite salad on the side

Seafood Gumbo.

(Prep + Cooking Time: 35 minutes | **Servings:**6)

Ingredients:
- 1 (14-oz.) can diced tomatoes
- 1 lb. halibut fillets, patted dry and cut into 2-inch cubes
- 1 lb. medium shrimp, peeled and deveined, tails left on
- 1 medium yellow onion; diced.
- 2 garlic cloves; minced.
- 2 celery stalks; diced.
- 2 cups low-sodium chicken broth.
- 2 tbsp. extra-virgin olive oil.
- 2 tsp. paprika
- ½ tsp. cayenne pepper
- 1 tsp. dried oregano
- 1 tsp. dried thyme
- ½ tsp. freshly ground black pepper.
- ½ tsp. fine sea salt.

Directions:
1. Select *Sauté* and add the olive oil to the inner pot. Once the oil is hot, add the onion, garlic, and celery and sauté for 3 minutes, stirring occasionally
2. Now, press *Cancel* and pour the broth and diced tomatoes into the pot. Using a wooden spoon, scrape up any browned bits stuck to the bottom of the pot. Add the halibut, shrimp, cayenne pepper, oregano, thyme, paprika, salt, and pepper. Stir to combine
3. Now, Lock the lid. Select, "Manual or Pressure Cook" and set the pressure to *High* and the time to 5 minutes. Make sure the steam release knob is in the sealed position.
4. After completing the cooking cycle, naturally release the pressure for 5 minutes, then quick release any remaining pressure. Unlock and remove the lid. Stir the gumbo. Serve hot

Simple Clams

(Prep + Cooking Time: 25 minutes | **Servings:** 4)

Ingredients:
- 15 small clams
- 30 mussels, scrubbed and debearded
- 2 tbsp. parsley; chopped.
- 1 tsp. extra virgin olive oil
- 1 yellow onion; chopped.
- 10 oz. beer
- 2 chorizo links, sliced
- 1 lb. baby red potatoes
- Lemon wedges for serving

Directions:
1. Set your instant pot on Sauté mode; add oil and heat it up
2. Add chorizo and onions, stir and cook for 4 minutes.
3. Add clams, mussels, potatoes and beer; then stir well. seal the instant pot lid and cook at High for 10 minutes.
4. Quick release the pressure, carefully open the lid; add parsley; then stir well. divide among bowls and serve with lemon wedges on the side.

Crab Legs and Garlic Butter Sauce.

(Prep + Cooking Time: 15 minutes | **Servings:** 2)

Ingredients:
- 2 lb. frozen or fresh crab legs
- 1 tsp. olive oil
- 1 minced garlic clove
- 1 cup. water
- 1 halved lemon
- 4 tbsp. salted butter

Directions:
1. Pour water in your Instant Pot and lower in the steamer basket. Add the crab legs.
2. Choose the "steam" option adjust time to 3 minutes for fresh, and 4 for frozen. In the meantime, heat the oil in a skillet.
3. Cook garlic for just 1 minute, stirring so it doesn't burn
4. Add the butter and stir to melt. Squeeze the halved lemon in the butter.
5. By now, the crab will be done, so hit "cancel" and quick-release the pressure
6. Serve crabs with the garlic butter on the side

Delicious Shrimp Paella

(Prep + Cooking Time: 15 minutes | **Servings:** 4)

Ingredients:
- 20 shrimps, deveined
- 1 ½ cups water
- 4 garlic cloves; minced.
- 1 cup jasmine rice
- 1/4 cup butter
- 1/4 cup parsley; chopped.
- A pinch of saffron
- A pinch of red pepper, crushed.
- Juice of 1 lemon
- Melted butter for serving
- Salt and black pepper to the taste
- Parsley; chopped for serving
- Hard cheese, grated for serving

Directions:
1. Put shrimp in your instant pot.
2. Add rice, butter, salt, pepper, parsley, red pepper, saffron, lemon juice, water and garlic.
3. Stir, seal the instant pot lid and cook at High for 5 minutes.
4. Quick release the pressure, carefully open the lid; takes shrimps and peel them
5. Return to pot, stir well and divide into bowls
6. Add melted butter, cheese and parsley on top and serve.

Seafood Stew

(Prep + Cooking Time: 43 minutes | **Servings:** 4)

Ingredients:
- 1 cup chopped carrots
- 1 cup chicken broth
- 1 cup diced yellow onions
- 1 cup water
- 1 (14.5-ounce) can fire-roasted diced tomatoes
- 2 bay leaves
- 4 cups mixed seafood, such as white fish chunks; peeled shrimp, bay scallops, shelled mussels and calamari rings
- 1 tbsp. tomato paste
- 2 tbsp. minced garlic
- 1 tbsp. fresh lemon juice
- 2 tsp. fennel seeds, toasted and ground
- 1 tsp. dried oregano
- 1 tsp. red pepper flakes, plus more for garnish
- Salt or as your liking
- Crusty bread, toasted

Directions:
1. In your Instant Pot, combine the tomatoes and their juices, onions, carrots, water, wine, garlic, fennel seeds, tomato paste, oregano, red pepper flakes and bay leaves. Season with salt. Stir to combine

2. Now secure the lid on the pot and close the valve. Now Press "Manual" and set the pot at "High" pressure for 15 minutes
3. After completing the cooking time, allow the pot to sit undisturbed for 10 minutes, then release any remaining pressure. Remove the lid from the Instant Pot. Now Press "Sauté" and bring the soup to a boil.
4. Add the mixed seafood and cook until the fish and shellfish are cooked through, 3 to 4 minutes. Stir in the lemon juice. Now Press "Cancel".
5. Discard the bay leaves. Serve the stew garnished with red pepper flakes, with crusty bread alongside to mop up the delicious, savory broth

Coconut Lime Shrimp

(**Prep + Cooking Time:** 23 minutes | **Servings:** 4)

Ingredients:
- 1 lb. fresh or frozen raw shrimp, peeled and deveined
- 8 oz. sugar snap peas
- ½ cup lightly packed chopped fresh cilantro
- 1 small head cauliflower, cut into florets (about 8 ounces)
- 1 red bell pepper; seeded and chopped.
- 1 cup full-fat coconut milk
- 1 tbsp. Sriracha
- 2 tbsp. freshly squeezed lime juice
- ½ tsp. fine sea salt
- Freshly ground black pepper
- Lime wedges; for serving

Directions:
1. Combine the coconut milk, lime juice, Sriracha, bell pepper, salt and several grinds of pepper in the Instant Pot
2. Arrange a steamer basket over the sauce in the bottom of the pot and place the cauliflower in the basket.
3. Now, Lock the lid and Turn the steam release valve to "Sealing" Position. Select *Manual/Pressure* Cook to cook on *High* pressure for 1 minute
4. Once the cooking cycle is completed, quickly release the pressure by moving the steam release valve to Venting. When the floating valve drops, remove the lid and Press *Cancel* Button to stop the cooking cycle.
5. Use oven mitts to lift the steamer basket of cauliflower out of the pot. Press *Sauté* and add the shrimp and snap peas to the pot.
6. Stir well, simmering the shrimp in the sauce until they are cooked through with a pink exterior, about 3 minutes for fresh and 5 to 6 minutes for frozen
7. Transfer the cooked cauliflower to a large bowl and use a potato masher to break up the florets into ricelike pieces.
8. Add the cilantro to the pot, then ladle the shrimp and vegetables over the cauliflower "rice." Serve with lime wedges on the side

Shrimp and Sausage Boil

(Prep + Cooking Time: 35 minutes | **Servings:** 4)

Ingredients:
- 1/2 lb. shrimp; peeled and deveined
- 4 baby red potatoes, halved
- 4 ears sweet corn, cut into thirds
- 4 shakes hot sauce
- 8 ounces smoked sausage, cut into 4 pieces each
- 1 tbsp. minced garlic
- 1 tbsp. Louisiana-style shrimp and crab boil seasoning
- 6 tbsp. (¾ stick) salted butter
- Juice of ½ lemon
- 1/4 tsp. Old Bay seasoning
- ⅛ tsp. Cajun seasoning
- ⅛ tsp. lemon-pepper seasoning
- Lemon slices

Directions:
1. In your Instant Pot, combine the sausage, corn and potatoes. Add water to cover. Add the shrimp and crab boil seasoning
2. Now secure the lid on the pot and close the valve. Now Press "Manual" and set the pot at "High" pressure for 4 minutes.
3. Meanwhile; in a small saucepan, melt the butter over medium-high heat. Add the garlic and cook, stirring continuously, until fragrant, 1 to 2 minutes.
4. Add the lemon juice, Old Bay, Cajun seasoning, lemon-pepper seasoning and hot sauce. Stir until warmed through; keep warm
5. After completing the cooking time, quick release the pressure. Open the lid carefully and check to ensure the potatoes are cooked. If they are not done, you can boil them for a few minutes using the "Sauté" setting.
6. Gently stir in the shrimp. As soon as the shrimp turn pink, drizzle everything with the spiced garlic-butter sauce. Add the lemon slices to the pot. Stir gently until everything is well coated

Fish with Orange Sauce

(Prep + Cooking Time: 17 minutes | **Servings:** 4)

Ingredients:
- 4 white fish fillets
- 1 cup fish stock
- Juice and zest from 1 orange
- A drizzle of extra virgin olive oil
- A small piece of ginger; chopped.
- 4 spring onions; chopped.
- Salt and black pepper to the taste

Directions:
1. Pat dry fish fillets, season with salt, pepper and rub them with the olive oil
2. Put stock, ginger, orange juice, orange zest and onions in your instant pot.
3. Put fish fillets in the steamer basket, seal the instant pot lid and cook at High for 7 minutes.
4. Quick release the pressure, divide fish among plates and drizzle the orange sauce on top.

Ginger-Soy Salmon with Broccoli

(Prep + Cooking Time: 18 minutes | **Servings:** 4)

Ingredients:
- 1 lb. wild-caught Alaskan salmon, cut into four 4-oz. fillets.
- Fine sea salt and freshly ground black pepper

Soy-Ginger Dressing:
- 1 lb. broccoli, cut into florets
- 1 clove garlic
- 2 tbsp. soy sauce or tamari
- 2 tbsp. raw apple cider vinegar
- 3 tbsp. pure maple syrup
- 6 tbsp. extra-virgin olive oil
- 1 tbsp. minced fresh ginger (about 1-inch knob)
- 1 tsp. toasted sesame oil
- Sesame seeds; for garnish.

Directions:
1. Chopped green onions, tender white and green parts only; for garnish
2. Pour 1 cup water into the Instant Pot and arrange the trivet (Which comes with your instant pot) on the bottom. Place the salmon fillets on the trivet in a single layer, skin side down. Sprinkle them generously with salt and pepper.
3. Now, Lock the lid and Turn the steam release valve to "Sealing" Position. Select *Manual/Pressure* Cook to cook on *High* pressure for 0 minutes (Sure set it to 0 minutes)
4. Once the cooking cycle is completed, immediately move the steam release valve to Venting to quickly release the steam pressure.
5. While the fish is cooking, make the dressing. Combine the olive oil, soy sauce, vinegar, ginger, garlic, maple syrup and sesame oil in a blender and blend until smooth, about 1 minute. Set aside until ready to serve
6. When the floating valve drops, remove the lid and place the broccoli directly on top of the cooked fish. Secure the lid again and move the steam release valve to Sealing
7. Select *Manual/Pressure* Cook to cook on *High* pressure for 0 minutes. Once the cooking cycle is completed, immediately move the steam release valve to Venting to quickly release the steam pressure.
8. When the floating valve drops, remove the lid. Use tongs to transfer the steamed broccoli and salmon to serving plates. Drizzle the dressing over the top and garnish with the sesame seeds and green onions

Vegetable Recipes

Collard Greens Delight

(Prep + Cooking Time: 30 minutes | **Servings:** 4)

Ingredients:
- 1 bunch collard greens, trimmed
- 2 tbsp. extra virgin olive oil
- 2 tbsp. tomato puree
- 1 yellow onion; chopped.
- 3 garlic cloves; minced.
- 1 tbsp. balsamic vinegar
- 1 tsp. sugar
- 1/2 cup chicken stock
- Salt and black pepper to the taste

Directions:
1. In your instant pot, mix stock with oil, garlic, vinegar, onion and tomato puree and stir.
2. Add collard greens after you've rolled them in cigar-shaped bundles
3. Add salt, pepper and sugar, close the lid and cook at High for 20 minutes
4. Quick release the pressure, carefully open the lid; divide collard greens among plates and serve.

Tuscan Stew

(Prep + Cooking Time: 65 minutes | **Servings:** 6)

Ingredients:
- 2 cups stale sourdough bread cubes
- 4 cups vegetable broth
- 1 cup dried cannellini beans
- 1 (14.5-ounce) can fire-roasted diced tomatoes; undrained
- 1/2 cup freshly grated Parmesan cheese
- 1 (12-ounce) package frozen spinach
- 1 small onion; chopped
- 1 cup coarsely chopped carrots
- 1 cup coarsely chopped celery
- 2 tbsp. tomato paste
- 1 tbsp. minced garlic
- 1 tsp. red pepper flakes
- 1 tsp. dried thyme
- 1 tsp. dried rosemary
- 1 tsp. salt or as your liking
- 1 tsp. black pepper

Directions:
1. In your Instant Pot, combine the broth, beans, tomatoes and their juices, spinach, onion, carrots, celery, tomato paste, garlic, red pepper flakes, thyme, salt, black pepper and rosemary. Stir to combine
2. Now secure the lid on the pot and close the valve. Now Press "Manual" and set the pot at "High" pressure for 30 minutes. After completing the cooking time, allow the pot to sit undisturbed for 15 minutes, then release any remaining pressure
3. Now Press "Sauté". Using the back of a spoon, coarsely mash a few of the beans and vegetables to thicken the soup to desired consistency.
4. When the broth is boiling, add the bread cubes and cook the soup for 5 minutes more, or until the bread is completely soft
5. Add water, if needed, to create a relatively thick stew. Now Press "Cancel". Ladle the soup into serving bowls and top with the cheese.

Butternut Mac N Cheese

(Prep + Cooking Time: 20 minutes | **Servings:** 6)

Ingredients:
- 1 cup raw cashews; soaked in water for at least 3 to 4 hours; or overnight, drained and rinsed well
- 4 ½ cups water; divided
- 1 (16-ounce) box pasta
- 1 cup nondairy milk; or more as needed
- 2 cups cooked cubed butternut squash
- ⅓ cup nutritional yeast
- 2 tbsp. freshly squeezed lemon juice
- ⅛ tsp. ground nutmeg
- 1 tsp. Dijon mustard
- 2 tsp. salt or as your liking
- Freshly ground black pepper

Directions:
1. In a high-speed blender or food processor, combine the cashews, squash, nutritional yeast, lemon juice, mustard, salt, nutmeg and 2 cups of water
2. Blend until smooth (the longer you soaked the cashews, the quicker this will be). Pour the cashew mixture into your Instant Pot
3. Pour the remaining 2 ½ cups of water into the blender and swish it around to capture any remaining cashew mixture.
4. Add that to the Instant Pot as well, along with the pasta. Lock the lid and turn the steam release handle to Sealing. Using the Manual function, set the cooker to Low Pressure for 2 minutes
5. After completing the cooking time, turn off the Instant Pot and let the pressure release naturally for 8 minutes; quick release any remaining pressure.
6. Remove the lid carefully and stir in the milk, adding as much as needed to make it nice and creamy. Taste and season with more salt and pepper, as needed

Wrapped Asparagus Canes

(Prep + Cooking Time: 10 minutes | **Servings:** 4)

Ingredients:
- 8 oz. prosciutto slices
- 1 lb. asparagus, trimmed
- 2 cups water
- A pinch of salt

Directions:
1. Wrap asparagus spears in prosciutto slices and place them on the bottom of the steamer basket in your instant pot
2. Add 2 cups water to the pot, add a pinch of salt, close the lid and cook at High for 4 minutes
3. Release the pressure naturally, carefully open the lid; transfer asparagus canes on a platter and serve at room temperature.

Tomato Basil Pasta

(Prep + Cooking Time: 5 minutes | **Servings:** 2)

Ingredients:
- 2 cups dried campanelle or similar pasta
- 12 fresh sweet basil leaves
- 2 tomatoes; cut into large dice
- 1 ¾ cups Vegetable Stock
- 1/2 tsp. salt or as your liking
- 2 pinches red pepper flakes
- 1/2 tsp. dried oregano
- 1/2 tsp. garlic powder
- Freshly ground black pepper

Directions:
1. In the Instant Pot, stir together the pasta, stock and salt. Drop the tomatoes on top "do not stir"
2. Lock the lid and turn the steam release handle to Sealing. Using the Manual function, set the cooker to High Pressure for 2 minutes.
3. After completing the cooking time, quick release the pressure.
4. Remove the lid carefully and stir in the red pepper flakes; oregano and garlic powder

5. If there's more than a few tbsp. of liquid in the bottom, select Sauté Low and cook for 2 to 3 minutes until it evaporates.
6. When ready to serve, chiffonade the basil and stir it in. Taste and season with more salt and pepper, as needed

Polenta and Kale

(Prep + Cooking Time: 45 minutes | Servings: 5)

Ingredients:
- 1 quart Vegetable Stock
- 2 bunches kale, stemmed, leaves chopped
- 4 garlic cloves; minced
- 1 cup polenta
- 1 tbsp. olive oil
- 2 tbsp. nutritional yeast
- 3 tbsp. vegan butter
- 1 tsp. salt as your liking
- Freshly ground black pepper

Directions:
1. Select the "Sauté" Low mode on your instant pot. When the display reads "Hot," add the oil and heat until it shimmers
2. Add the kale, garlic and ½ tsp. of salt. Cook for about 2 minutes, stirring frequently so nothing burns, until the kale is soft and the garlic is fragrant. Note: You can always turn off the Instant Pot if it gets too hot. Transfer the garlicky kale to a bowl and set aside.
3. In the Instant Pot, combine the polenta, stock and remaining ½ tsp. of salt
4. Lock the lid and turn the steam release handle to Sealing. Using the Manual function, set the cooker to High Pressure for 20 minutes.
5. After completing the cooking time, let the pressure release naturally for 15 minutes; quick release any remaining pressure
6. Remove the lid carefully and stir well. Add the nutritional yeast and butter along with any additional salt and pepper. Serve in bowls topped with the kale

Tomatoes and Zucchinis

(Prep + Cooking Time: 22 minutes | Servings: 4)

Ingredients:
- 6 zucchinis, roughly chopped
- 1 cup tomato puree
- 1 lb. cherry tomatoes, cut into halves
- A drizzle of olive oil
- 2 yellow onions; chopped.
- 1 tbsp. vegetable oil
- 2 garlic cloves; minced.
- 1 bunch basil; chopped.
- Salt and black pepper to the taste

Directions:
1. Set your instant pot on Sauté mode; add vegetable oil and heat it up
2. Add onion, stir and cook for 5 minutes
3. Add tomatoes, tomato puree, zucchinis, salt and pepper; then stir well. Seal the Instant Pot lid and cook at High for 5 minutes
4. Quick release the pressure, open the instant pot lid, add garlic and basil, stir and divide among plates.
5. Drizzle some olive oil at the end and serve

Carrots and Turnips

(Prep + Cooking Time: 15 minutes | Servings: 4)

Ingredients:
- 2 turnips, peeled and sliced
- 1 small onion; chopped.
- 1 tsp. lemon juice
- 1 tsp. cumin, ground.
- 3 carrots, sliced
- 1 tbsp. extra-virgin olive oil
- 1 cup water
- Salt and black pepper to the taste

Directions:
1. Set your instant pot on Sauté mode; add oil and heat it up.
2. Add onion, stir and sauté for 2 minutes
3. Add turnips, carrots, cumin and lemon juice, stir and cook for 1 minute
4. Add salt, pepper, and water; then stir well. close the lid and cook at High for 6 minutes.
5. Quick release the pressure, open the instant pot lid, divide turnips and carrots among plates and serve.

Vegetable Stock

(Prep + Cooking Time: 35 minutes | **Servings:** 9)

Ingredients:
- 1 cup mushrooms
- 8 cups water
- 8 whole peppercorns
- 3 celery stalks
- 1 bay leaf
- 3 carrots
- 1 large onion

Directions:
1. In the Instant Pot, combine the celery, carrots, onion, mushrooms, peppercorns, bay leaf and water, making sure the veggies are completely covered by water
2. Lock the lid and turn the steam release handle to Sealing. Using the Manual function, set the cooker to High Pressure for 15 minutes.
3. After completing the cooking time, let the pressure release naturally for 15 minutes; quick release any remaining pressure
4. Remove the lid carefully. Strain the stock through a fine-mesh strainer into a large heatproof container.
5. Use immediately or refrigerate in an airtight container for 3 to 4 days; or keep frozen for up to a year

Maple Glazed Carrots Recipe

(Prep + Cooking Time: 15 minutes | **Servings:** 4)

Ingredients:
- 2 lb. carrots, peeled and sliced on the diagonal
- 1 tbsp. maple syrup
- 1/4 cup raisins
- 1 tbsp. butter
- 1 cup water
- Black pepper to the taste

Directions:
1. Put carrots in your instant pot
2. Add water and raisins, close the lid and cook at High for 4 minutes
3. Quick release the pressure, carefully open the lid; add butter and maple syrup; then stir well. divide carrots among plates and sprinkle black pepper before serving them.

Layered Casserole

(Prep + Cooking Time: 25 minutes | **Servings:** 5)

Ingredients:
- 2 cups mashed sweet potatoes
- 1 ¼ cups Red Hot Enchilada Sauce; or 1 (10-ounce) can; divided
- 1 (15-ounce) can black beans; rinsed and drained
- 1 (10-ounce) can diced tomatoes with green chilies, drained
- 1/2 cup sliced scallion, green and light green parts; divided
- 1/2 cup water
- 1/4 cup frozen sweet corn
- 1 tbsp. freshly squeezed lime juice
- 1 tsp. chili powder
- 1/2 tsp. garlic powder
- 1/2 tsp. onion powder
- 9 taco-size, gluten-free corn tortillas
- Nonstick cooking spray; for preparing the springform pan
- Vegan cheese shreds; for topping; optional
- Sliced avocado; for serving

- Poblano Cheeze Sauce; for serving
- Cashew Sour Cream; for serving

Directions:
1. Lightly coat the bottom and sides of a 7-inch springform pan with nonstick spray and set aside. In a medium bowl, stir together the mashed sweet potatoes, 1 cup of enchilada sauce, the lime juice, chili powder, garlic powder and onion powder
2. In another medium bowl, stir together the black beans, tomatoes and green chilies, ¼ cup of scallion, the corn and 3 tbsp. of enchilada sauce.
3. To build the casserole, spread the remaining 1 tbsp. of enchilada sauce on the bottom of the prepared pan.
4. Add a layer of tortillas, torn as needed to get full coverage. Don't be afraid to overlap. Layer on one-third of the sweet potato mixture
5. Using a slotted spoon, top the sweet potato later with one-third of the black bean mixture. Repeat the tortilla layer, sweet potato layer and black bean layer two more times. Top with the remaining ¼ cup of scallion. If using vegan cheese shreds, add them now.
6. Spray a piece of aluminum foil with nonstick spray and cover the pan tightly.
7. Pour the water into the Instant Pot and place a trivet into the inner pot
8. Set the covered casserole on top of the trivet. Lock the lid and turn the steam release handle to Sealing. Using the Manual function, set the cooker to High Pressure for 8 minutes.
9. After completing the cooking time, let the pressure release naturally for 5 minutes; quick release any remaining pressure
10. Remove the lid carefully and the trivet and casserole from the Instant Pot. Set aside on a heat-resistant surface.
11. Remove the foil and let cool for at least 5 minutes before releasing the sides of the pan. Plate and add desired toppings before serving

Fried Rice

(**Prep + Cooking Time:** 28 minutes | **Servings:** 4)

Ingredients:
- 2 lb. cauliflower, cut into small florets
- 1 red onion; chopped.
- 3 celery stalks; chopped.
- 1 clove garlic; minced.
- ⅓ cup soy sauce or tamari
- 3 carrots; peeled and chopped.
- 1 cup fresh or frozen peas
- 4 eggs
- 1 tbsp. extra-virgin olive oil, plus more as needed
- ½ tsp. fine sea salt
- 1 tsp. sesame oil
- 1 tsp. minced fresh ginger (about ½-inch knob)
- Sesame seeds; for garnish.
- Chopped green onions, tender white and green parts only; for garnish.

Directions:
1. Press *Sauté* and add the olive oil to the Instant Pot. Once the oil is hot but not smoking, add the onion, carrots and celery and sauté until softened, about 4 minutes
2. Stir in the garlic and ginger and sauté just until fragrant, about 1 minute more. Press *Cancel* Button to stop the cooking cycle.
3. Add the cauliflower, soy sauce and salt. Now, Lock the lid and Turn the steam release valve to "Sealing" Position. Select *Manual/Pressure* Cook to cook on *High* pressure for 0 minutes (Sure set it to 0 minutes)
4. Once the cooking cycle is completed, immediately move the steam release valve to Venting to quickly release the steam pressure. This prevents the cauliflower from overcooking.
5. When the floating valve drops, remove the lid and use a potato masher or fork to break up the cauliflower into small rice like pieces
6. Press *Cancel* Button to stop the cooking cycle, then press Sauté. Add the peas and give the rice a stir to combine. The peas will cook quickly.

7. Use a spatula to move the mixture to the edges of the pan, creating a clear space in the center of the pot to scramble the eggs
8. Since there will be some liquid covering the bottom of the pot, crack the eggs into the liquid so you don't have to use additional oil for cooking. Using a spatula, scramble the eggs as they cook until fluffy and cooked through, about 3 minutes.
9. Mix the scrambled eggs into the "fried rice" mixture and stir in the sesame oil. Taste and adjust the seasonings as needed. Serve warm with the green onions and sesame seeds sprinkled over the top

Braised Endives

(Prep + Cooking Time: 17 minutes | **Servings:** 4)

Ingredients:
- 4 endives, trimmed and cut into halves
- 1 tbsp. lemon juice
- 1 tbsp. butter
- Salt and black pepper to the taste

Directions:
1. Set your instant pot on Sauté mode
2. Add butter and melt it
3. Arrange endives in the pot, add salt and pepper and the lemon juice, Seal the Instant Pot lid and cook at High for 7 minutes.
4. Release the pressure naturally, arrange endives on a platter, add cooking juice all over them and serve.

Lentil Swiss Chard Soup

(Prep + Cooking Time: 41 minutes | **Servings:** 4)

Ingredients:
- 1 (12-ounce) package frozen Swiss chard
- 1 cup dry brown lentils; rinsed and drained
- 1 cup diced onions
- 1/2 cup diced celery
- 1/2 cup diced carrot
- 6 cups water
- 1 tbsp. minced garlic
- 1 tbsp. chopped fresh thyme
- 1 tbsp. tomato paste
- 1 tbsp. chicken broth base
- 1 tbsp. red wine vinegar
- 1 tsp. ground cumin
- 1/2 tsp. salt or as your liking
- 1 tsp. black pepper

Directions:
1. In your Instant Pot, combine 4 cups of the water, the Swiss chard, lentils, onions, celery, carrot, garlic, thyme, tomato paste, chicken broth base, cumin, salt and pepper. Stir well to combine
2. Now secure the lid on the pot and close the valve. Now Press "Manual" and set the pot at "High" pressure for 6 minutes.
3. After completing the cooking time, allow the pot to sit undisturbed for 10 minutes, then release any remaining pressure. Add the remaining 2 cups water and the vinegar. Stir well to combine

Sweet & Spicy Cabbage

(Prep + Cooking Time: 18 minutes | **Servings:** 4)

Ingredients:
- 1 cabbage, cut into 8 wedges
- 1/4 cup apple cider vinegar
- 1 ¼ cups apple+2 tsp. water
- 1 tsp. raw sugar
- 2 tsp. cornstarch
- 1/2 tsp. cayenne pepper
- 1/2 tsp. red pepper flakes
- 1 tbsp. sesame seed oil
- 1 carrot, grated

Directions:
1. Set your instant pot on Sauté mode; add oil and heat it up. Add cabbage, stir and cook for 3 minutes.

2. Add carrots, 1 ¼ cups water, sugar, vinegar, cayenne and pepper flakes; then stir well. close the lid and cook at High for 5 minutes
3. Quick release the pressure, carefully open the lid and divide cabbage and carrots mix among plates
4. Add cornstarch mixed with 2 tsp. water to the pot, set the pot on Simmer mode, stir very well and bring to a boil
5. Drizzle over cabbage and serve.

Mushroom Kale Stroganoff

(**Prep + Cooking Time:** 25 minutes | **Servings:** 5)

Ingredients:
- 1 pound baby bella mushrooms, sliced
- 1 cup Cashew Sour Cream
- 3 cups kale leaves; rinsed and torn into bite-size pieces
- 3 cups dried campanelle pasta; or similar shape
- 3 ¼ cups Vegetable Stock
- 1 sweet onion; diced
- 1 bay leaf
- 1 tomato; diced
- 2 garlic cloves; minced
- 1 tbsp. olive oil
- 1 tsp. smoked paprika
- 1/2 tsp. salt or as your liking

Directions:
1. Select the "Sauté" Low mode on your instant pot. When the display reads "Hot," add the oil and heat until it shimmers
2. Add the onion. Sauté for 2 minutes, stirring frequently. Turn off the Instant Pot and add the garlic. Cook for 1 minute, stirring.
3. Add the mushrooms, tomato, paprika, bay leaf and salt. Let sit for 2 to 3 minutes
4. Stir in the pasta and stock. Lock the lid and turn the steam release handle to Sealing. Using the Manual function, set the cooker to High Pressure for 3 minutes.
5. After completing the cooking time, let the pressure release naturally for 5 minutes; quick release any remaining pressure
6. Remove the lid carefully and remove and discard the bay leaf. If there is excess liquid in the pot, select Sauté Low again and cook for 1 to 2 minutes, stirring frequently, to evaporate some of it.
7. Turn off the pot and stir in the sour cream and kale. Let sit for 1 to 2 minutes while the kale wilts. Taste and season with more salt, as needed

Corn Pudding

(**Prep + Cooking Time:** 55 minutes | **Servings:** 8)

Ingredients:
- 1 (4.5-ounce) can chopped mild green chiles
- 1/2 cup whole milk
- 1 (8.5-ounce) package corn muffin mix
- 2 ¼ cups water
- Vegetable oil
- 1 (14-ounce) can creamed corn
- 1/2 tsp. unflavored powdered gelatin
- Poblanos & Corn in Cream

Directions:
1. Generously grease a 6-inch springform pan with oil. In a large bowl, combine the corn muffin mix, creamed corn, chiles, milk, ¼ cup of the water and the gelatin
2. Stir well to combine. Pour the batter into the prepared pan. Cover the top with aluminum foil.
3. Pour the remaining 2 cups water into the Instant Pot. Place a steamer rack in the pot. Set the pan on the rack
4. Now secure the lid on the pot and close the valve. Now Press "Manual" and set the pot at "High" pressure for 25 minutes. After completing the cooking time, allow the pot to sit undisturbed until the pressure has released.
5. Set the pudding on a wire rack to cool to room temperature. Run a knife around the edges to separate the pudding from the sides of the pan.

6. Carefully remove the springform ring. Cut the pudding into wedges. Top with Poblanos & Corn in Cream, if you like

Stuffed Tomatoes Delight

(Prep + Cooking Time: 20 minutes | **Servings:** 4)

Ingredients:
- 4 tomatoes, tops cut off and pulp scooped
- 1 yellow onion; chopped.
- 2 tbsp. celery; chopped.
- 1/2 cup mushrooms; chopped.
- 1 slice of bread, crumbled.
- 1/2 cup water
- 1 cup cottage cheese
- 1 tbsp. butter
- 1/4 tsp. caraway seeds
- 1 tbsp. parsley; chopped.
- Salt and black pepper to the taste

Directions:
1. Chop tomato pulp and put it in a bowl.
2. Heat up a pan with the butter over medium high heat, add onion and celery, stir and cook for 3 minutes.
3. Add tomato pulp and mushrooms, stir and cook for 1 minute more.
4. Add salt, pepper, crumbled bread, cheese, caraway seeds and parsley, stir and cook for 4 minutes more.
5. Fill each tomato with this mix and arrange them in the steamer basket of your instant pot
6. Add the water to the pot, Seal the Instant Pot lid and cook at High for 2 minutes.
7. Quick release the pressure, open the instant pot lid, transfer stuffed potatoes to plates and serve.

Sausages and Cabbage

(Prep + Cooking Time: 15 minutes | **Servings:** 4)

Ingredients:
- 15 oz. canned tomatoes; chopped.
- 1/2 cup yellow onion; chopped.
- 3 tbsp. butter
- 1 lb. sausage links, sliced
- 2 tsp. turmeric
- 1 green cabbage head; chopped.
- Salt and black pepper to the taste

Directions:
1. Set your instant pot on Sauté mode; add sausage slices, stir and cook until they brown.
2. Drain excess grease, add butter, cabbage, tomatoes salt, pepper, onion and turmeric; then stir well. close the lid and cook at High for 2 minutes
3. Quick release the pressure, carefully open the lid; divide cabbage and sausages among plates and serve.

Bacon and Kale

(Prep + Cooking Time: 20 minutes | **Servings:** 4)

Ingredients:
- 6 bacon slices; chopped.
- 10 oz. kale leaves; chopped.
- 1 tbsp. vegetable oil
- 1 tsp. red chili, crushed.
- 1 tsp. liquid smoke
- 1 onion, thinly sliced
- 6 garlic cloves; chopped.
- 1 ½ cups chicken stock
- 1 tbsp. brown sugar
- 2 tbsp. apple cider vinegar
- Salt and black pepper to the taste

Directions:
1. Set your instant pot on Sauté mode; add oil and heat it up. Add bacon, stir and cook for 1 - 2 minutes
2. Add onion, stir and cook for 3 minutes
3. Add garlic, stir and cook for 1 minute
4. Add vinegar, stock, sugar, liquid smoke, red chilies, salt, pepper, kale; then stir well. close the lid and cook at High for 5 minutes
5. Quick release the pressure, carefully open the lid; divide among plates and serve

Tomato and Beet Salad

(Prep + Cooking Time: 60 minutes | Servings: 8)

Ingredients:
- 1-pint mixed cherry tomatoes, cut into halves
- 1 ½ cups water
- 1 cup apple cider vinegar
- 1 cup water
- 2 tsp. pickling juice
- 8 small beets, trimmed
- 1 red onion, sliced
- 2 oz. pecans
- 2 tbsp. extra virgin olive oil
- 2 tbsp. sugar
- 4 oz. goat cheese
- Salt and black pepper to the taste

Directions:
1. Put beets in the steamer basket of your instant pot, add 1 ½ cups water, close the lid and cook at High for 20 minutes
2. Quick release the pressure, open the instant pot lid, transfer beets to a cutting board, leave them to cool down, peel and chop them and put them in a bowl
3. Clean your instant pot, add 1 cup water, vinegar, sugar, pickling juice and salt to the taste; then stir well. close the lid and cook at High for 2 minutes
4. Quick release the pressure, strain liquid into a bowl, add onions, stir and leave aside for 10 minutes.
5. Add tomatoes over beets and onions and stir
6. In a bowl, mix 4 tablespoons of liquid from the onions with 2 tablespoons olive oil, salt and pepper and stir.
7. Add this to beets salad and stir.
8. Also, add goat cheese and pecans, toss to coat and serve.

Cheesy Polenta

(Prep + Cooking Time: 42 minutes | Servings: 6)

Ingredients:
- 1/2 cup shredded Mexican cheese blend
- 1/4 cup half-and-half
- 4 cups chicken broth
- 1 cup polenta (coarse-ground cornmeal)
- 4 tsp. salted butter
- Salt as your liking

Directions:
1. Pour the broth into the Instant Pot. Now Press "Sauté" and bring the broth to a boil. As soon as it starts to boil, slowly whisk in the polenta. Now Press "Cancel"
2. Now secure the lid on the pot and close the valve. Now Press "Manual" and set the pot at "High" pressure for 7 minutes. After completing the cooking time, allow the pot to sit undisturbed until the pressure has released.
3. Whisk the mixture to blend in any unabsorbed water. Whisk in the cheese, half-and-half and butter and season with salt. Allow the polenta to stand for 5 minutes to thicken slightly before serving

Hearts of Palm Soup

(Prep + Cooking Time: 30 minutes | Servings: 4)

Ingredients:
- 1 (14-ounce) can hearts of palm, drained, liquid reserved and coarsely chopped
- ¾ cup heavy cream
- 1/4 cup finely chopped scallions
- 2 ½ cups chicken broth
- 1 cup chopped yellow onion
- 1/2 tsp. freshly grated nutmeg, plus more for garnish
- 1/2 cup shredded Parmesan cheese, plus more for garnish
- 1 tbsp. minced garlic
- 1 tsp. salt or as your liking
- 1 ½ tsp. black pepper

Directions:
1. In your Instant Pot, combine the hearts of palm and their liquid, the broth, onion, garlic, salt and pepper
2. Now secure the lid on the pot and close the valve. Now Press "Manual" and set the pot at "High" pressure for 5 minutes
3. After completing the cooking time, allow the pot to sit undisturbed for 10 minutes, then release any remaining pressure. Using an immersion blender, puree the soup directly in the pot until smooth.
4. Stir in the cream, cheese and nutmeg. Pulse the soup with the immersion blender until everything is well incorporated. Garnish with the chopped scallions and additional nutmeg and cheese and serve

Red Curry Cauliflower

(**Prep + Cooking Time:** 12 minutes | **Servings:** 5)

Ingredients:
- 1 (14-ounce) can full-fat coconut milk
- 1 (14-ounce) can diced tomatoes and liquid
- 1 bell pepper, any color, thinly sliced
- 1 small to medium head cauliflower; cut into bite-size pieces (3 to 4 cups)
- 1/2 to 1 cup water
- 2 tbsp. red curry paste
- 1 tsp. garlic powder
- 1/2 tsp. onion powder
- 1/4 tsp. chili powder
- 1 tsp. salt or as your liking
- 1/2 tsp. ground ginger
- Freshly ground black pepper
- Cooked rice or other grain; for serving; optional

Directions:
1. In the Instant Pot, stir together the coconut milk, water, red curry paste, garlic powder, salt, ginger, onion powder and chili powder
2. Add the bell pepper, cauliflower and tomatoes and stir again. Lock the lid and turn the steam release handle to Sealing. Using the Manual function, set the cooker to High Pressure for 2 minutes.
3. After completing the cooking time, quick release the pressure
4. Remove the lid carefully and give the whole thing a good stir. Taste and season with more salt and pepper, as needed. Serve with rice or another grain (if using)

Roasted Potatoes

(**Prep + Cooking Time:** 30 minutes | **Servings:** 4)

Ingredients:
- 2 lb. baby potatoes
- 5 tbsp. vegetable oil
- 1/2 cup stock
- 1 rosemary spring
- 5 garlic cloves
- Salt and black pepper to the taste

Directions:
1. Set your instant pot on Sauté mode; add oil and heat it up.
2. Add potatoes, rosemary and garlic, stir and brown them for 10 minutes
3. Prick each potato with a knife, add stock, salt and pepper to the pot, Seal the Instant Pot lid and cook at High for 7 minutes
4. Quick release the pressure, open the instant pot lid, divide potatoes among plates and serve

Turnips Dish

(Prep + Cooking Time: 30 minutes | **Servings:** 4)

Ingredients:
- 20 oz. turnips; peeled and chopped.
- 1 tsp. garlic; minced.
- 1 tsp. ginger, grated
- 1 tsp. sugar
- 1 tsp. cumin powder
- 1 tsp. coriander powder
- 2 green chilies; chopped.
- 1/2 tsp. turmeric powder
- 1 cup water
- 2 tbsp. butter
- 2 yellow onions; chopped.
- 2 tomatoes; chopped.
- Salt to the taste
- A handful coriander leaves; chopped.

Directions:
1. Set your instant pot on Sauté mode; add butter and melt it.
2. Add green chilies, garlic and ginger, stir and cook for 1 minute.
3. Add onions, stir and cook 3 minutes
4. Add salt, tomatoes, turmeric, cumin and coriander powder, stir and cook 3 minutes.
5. Add turnips and water; then stir well. Seal the Instant Pot lid and cook on Low for 15 minutes
6. Quick release the pressure, open the instant pot lid, add sugar and coriander; then stir well. divide among plates and serve

Shrimp and Asparagus

(Prep + Cooking Time: 8 minutes | **Servings:** 4)

Ingredients:
- 1 lb. shrimp, peeled and deveined
- 1 cup water
- 1/2 tbsp. Cajun seasoning
- 1 tsp. extra virgin olive oil
- 1 bunch asparagus, trimmed

Directions:
1. Pour the water in your instant pot
2. Put asparagus in the steamer basket of the pot and add shrimp on top.
3. Drizzle olive oil, sprinkle Cajun seasoning; then stir well. close the lid and cook on Low for 2 minutes
4. Release the pressure naturally, transfer asparagus and shrimp to plates and serve

Cabbage Rolls

(Prep + Cooking Time: 32 minutes | **Servings:** 7)

Ingredients:
For Tempeh:
- 1 (8-ounce) package unflavored tempeh, crumbled
- 2 garlic cloves; minced
- 1 bay leaf

For Deconstructed Cabbage Rolls:
- 1 head cabbage, thinly sliced
- 6 ounces tomato paste
- 1 ½ cups Vegetable Stock
- 1 cup basmati rice; rinsed and drained
- 1/4 cup chopped fresh parsley
- 1/2 onion; diced
- 1 tbsp. olive oil
- 2 tsp. vegan Worcestershire sauce
- 2 tsp. Montreal steak seasoning
- 1 cup water
- 1/2 tsp. salt as your liking
- 1/2 tsp. paprika
- 1/4 tsp. freshly ground black pepper
- Pinch cayenne pepper; or more as needed

Directions:
To Make Tempeh:
1. Select the "Sauté" Low mode on your instant pot. When the display reads "Hot," add the oil and heat until it shimmers.
2. Add the tempeh, Montreal steak seasoning, Worcestershire sauce, garlic, bay leaf and onion. Cook for 3 to 4 minutes, stirring frequently. Transfer to a bowl and set aside.

To Make Deconstructed Cabbage Rolls:
1. In the Instant Pot, combine the rice, water and salt. Lock the lid and turn the steam release handle to Sealing
2. Using the Manual function, set the cooker to High Pressure for 8 minutes. After completing the cooking time, let the pressure release naturally for 10 minutes; quick release any remaining pressure
3. Remove the lid carefully and fluff the rice. Add the stock, cabbage, tomato paste, paprika, black pepper and cayenne.
4. Select Sauté Low again and cook for 4 to 5 minutes until the cabbage softens a little. Turn off the Instant Pot, remove and discard the bay leaf and stir in the parsley. Taste and season with more salt and pepper, as needed

Pinto Bean Stew

(Prep + Cooking Time: 2 hours | **Servings:** 8)

Ingredients:
- 1 cup dried pinto beans
- 3 cups cool water
- 1 cup finely chopped onions
- 1 (14.5-ounce) can fire-roasted diced tomatoes; undrained
- 1/2 cup chopped fresh cilantro
- 1/2 green bell pepper, finely chopped
- 4 garlic cloves; minced
- 3 cups hot water
- 2 tsp. ground cumin
- 1 tsp. salt or as your liking

Directions:
1. In a medium bowl, soak the beans in the hot water for 1 hour. Drain. In your Instant Pot, combine the beans, tomatoes and their juices, onions, cilantro, bell pepper, garlic, cumin and salt. Add the cool water
2. Now secure the lid on the pot and close the valve. Now Press "Manual" and set the pot at "High" pressure for 30 minutes.
3. After completing the cooking time, allow the pot to stand undisturbed for 10 minutes, then release any remaining pressure
4. If you'd like, blend with an immersion blender directly in the pot for 10 seconds to mash some of the beans and thicken the broth slightly

Beet and Orange Salad

(Prep + Cooking Time: 20 minutes | **Servings:** 4)

Ingredients:
- 1 ½ lb. beets
- 3 strips orange peel
- 2 tbsp. cider vinegar
- 1/2 cup orange juice
- 2 tsp. orange zest, grated
- 2 tbsp. brown sugar
- 2 scallions; chopped
- 2 tsp. mustard
- 2 cups arugula and mustard greens

Directions:
1. Scrub beets well cut them in halves and put them in a bowl.
2. In your instant pot, mix orange peel strips with vinegar and orange juice and stir
3. Add beets, seal the instant pot lid, cook at High for 7 minutes and release the pressure naturally.
4. Carefully open the lid, take beets and transfer them to a bowl
5. Discard peel strips from the pot, add mustard and sugar and stir well
6. Add scallions and grated orange zest to beets and toss them
7. Add liquid from the pot over beets, toss to coat and serve on plates on top of mixed salad greens.

Instant Steamed Leeks

(**Prep + Cooking Time:** 20 minutes | **Servings:** 4)

Ingredients:
- 4 leeks, washed, roots and ends cut off
- 1 tbsp. butter
- 1/3 cup water
- Salt and black pepper to the taste

Directions:
1. Put leeks in your instant pot, add water and butter, salt and pepper to the taste; then stir well. close the lid and cook at High for 5 minutes
2. Quick release the pressure, open the instant pot lid, set it on Sauté mode and cook leeks for 5 more minutes.
3. Divide among plates and serve

Barbecue Chickpea Tacos

(**Prep + Cooking Time:** 1 hour 20 minutes | **Servings:** 5)

Ingredients:
- 1 cup dried chickpeas; rinsed
- 2 cups pineapple chunks
- 8 taco shells
- ⅓ cup packed light brown sugar
- ⅓ cup soy sauce
- 2 cups plus 3 tbsp. water
- 3 tbsp. cornstarch
- 2 tbsp. hot chili oil
- 3 tbsp. gochujang (Korean hot pepper paste)
- 1/2 tsp. garlic powder
- 1 tsp. sriracha; or more as needed
- 2 tsp. rice wine vinegar
- 1/2 tsp. onion powder

Directions:
1. In the Instant Pot, combine the chickpeas with enough water to cover
2. Lock the lid and turn the steam release handle to Sealing. Using the Manual function, set the cooker to High Pressure for 45 minutes.
3. After completing the cooking time, let the pressure release naturally for 15 minutes; quick release any remaining pressure
4. Remove the lid carefully and pour the contents into a colander to drain. Return the chickpeas to the inner pot.
5. In a small bowl, whisk the cornstarch and 3 tbsp. of water. Set aside. Select the "Sauté" Low mode on your instant pot
6. To the chickpeas, add the gochujang, brown sugar, soy sauce, chili oil, vinegar, onion powder and garlic powder.
7. Cook until it starts to bubble. Stir in the cornstarch slurry. Simmer for 4 to 5 minutes more, stirring frequently, until the sauce thickens and the chickpeas are nice and coated
8. In a medium bowl, stir together the pineapple and sriracha. Taste before adding more sauce. Fill the taco shells with the chickpeas and top with the pineapple

Tomatoes and Okra

(**Prep + Cooking Time:** 25 minutes | **Servings:** 4)

Ingredients:
- 1 ½ lbs. okra, fresh
- 1 (14.5-ounce) can diced tomatoes; undrained
- 1 cup diced onions
- 1/2 cup water
- 2 tbsp. tomato paste
- 1 tbsp. minced garlic
- 1 tbsp. chicken broth
- 1 tbsp. fresh lemon juice
- 2 tbsp. apple cider vinegar
- 1/2 tsp. ground allspice
- 1 tsp. smoked paprika
- 1 tsp. salt or as your liking

Directions:
1. In your Instant Pot, combine ¼ cup of the water, the tomatoes and their juices, onions, vinegar, garlic, broth base, paprika, salt and allspice. Add the okra on top; do not stir
2. Now secure the lid on the pot and close the valve. Now Press "Manual" and set the pot at "High" pressure for 2 minutes. After completing the cooking time, allow the pot to sit undisturbed for 5 minutes, then release any remaining pressure.
3. In a small bowl, dissolve the tomato paste in the remaining ¼ cup water. Gently stir the tomato paste mixture and the lemon juice into the pot

Kimchi Pasta

(**Prep + Cooking Time:** 10 minutes | **Servings:** 5)

Ingredients:
- 8 ounces dried small pasta
- 1 ¼ cups kimchi, with any larger pieces chopped
- 1/2 cup Cashew Sour Cream
- 2⅓ cups Vegetable Stock
- 2 garlic cloves; minced
- 1/2 red onion, sliced
- 1 tsp. salt or as your liking

Directions:
1. In the Instant Pot, combine the pasta, stock, garlic, red onion and salt
2. Lock the lid and turn the steam release handle to Sealing. Using the Manual function, set the cooker to High Pressure for 1 minute.
3. After completing the cooking time, quick release the pressure. Remove the lid carefully. Select the "Sauté" Low mode on your instant pot. Stir in the kimchi. Simmer for 3 to 4 minutes. Stir in the sour cream and serve.

Crunchy Lentil Salad

(**Prep + Cooking Time:** 30 minutes | **Servings:** 6)

Ingredients:
- ½ cup lightly packed chopped fresh flat-leaf parsley
- ¾ cup raisins
- ¾ cup sliced almonds
- 1½ cups green lentils
- 1 red bell pepper
- 1 clove garlic; minced.
- 2 cups water
- ¼ cup minced shallots (2 small shallots)
- 1 English cucumber
- ¼ cup raw apple cider vinegar
- 1 tbsp. spicy brown mustard
- 1 tbsp. pure maple syrup
- 2 tbsp. extra-virgin olive oil
- 1½ tsp. fine sea salt
- Freshly ground black pepper
- Leafy greens, like arugula; for serving

Directions:
1. Combine the lentils and water in the Instant Pot and secure the lid, moving the steam release valve to Sealing. Select *Manual/Pressure* Cook to cook on *High* pressure for 4 minutes
2. Once the cooking cycle is completed, let the pressure naturally release for 10 minutes to fully cook the lentils.
3. While the lentils are cooking, stir together the vinegar, olive oil, salt, several grinds of pepper, the mustard, maple syrup, garlic and shallots in a large bowl to make a dressing. Dice the cucumber (you should have around 2 cups) and add it to the bowl of dressing to marinate. Seed and dice the red bell pepper and add it and the parsley to the bowl of dressing to marinate
4. After 10 minutes have passed, move the steam release valve to Venting to release any remaining pressure. When the floating valve drops, remove the lid.
5. Pour the cooked lentils into a fine-mesh sieve and rinse with cold water to quickly cool them off. Add the cooked lentils to the bowl with the dressing and vegetables and toss well to coat.
6. Stir in the raisins and almonds, then chill in the fridge for 1 hour. Once the salad is chilled, taste and adjust the seasoning as needed. Serve the lentil salad along with the leafy greens

Sweet Potato and Black Bean Tacos

(Prep + Cooking Time: 20 minutes | **Servings:** 5)

Ingredients:
- 1 (15-ounce) can black beans; rinsed and drained
- 1 canned chipotle pepper in adobo sauce; diced
- 1 avocado, peeled, pitted and mashed
- 1/4 cup fresh cilantro, chopped
- 1/2 sweet onion; diced
- 1/2 cup Vegetable Stock
- 1 large sweet potato; diced
- 1 red bell pepper; diced
- 1 garlic clove; minced
- 1 tomato; diced
- 1 tbsp. freshly squeezed lime juice
- 2 tbsp. olive oil
- 2 tsp. adobo sauce from the can
- 2 tsp. chili powder
- 1/2 tsp. ground cumin
- 1/2 tsp. salt as your liking
- Zest of 1 lime
- Corn or flour tortillas; for serving
- Cashew Sour Cream; for serving; optional
- Sliced red cabbage; for serving; optional
- Sliced jalapeño peppers; for serving; optional
- Garden Salsa; for serving; optional

Directions:
1. Select the "Sauté" Low mode on your instant pot. When the display reads "Hot," add the oil and heat until it shimmers
2. Add the onion. Cook for 1 minute, stirring. Add the sweet potato and bell pepper. Cook for 1 minute, stirring so nothing burns. Turn off the Instant Pot and add the garlic. Cook for 30 seconds to 1 minute, stirring.
3. Add the tomato, black beans, chipotle, adobo sauce, chili powder, salt, cumin, stock and lime juice.
4. Lock the lid and turn the steam release handle to Sealing. Using the Manual function, set the cooker to High Pressure for 4 minutes
5. After completing the cooking time, turn off the Instant Pot and let the pressure release naturally for 5 minutes; quick release any remaining pressure.
6. Remove the lid carefully. If there is too much liquid in the inner pot, select Sauté Low again and cook for 1 to 2 minutes, stirring constantly (it gets hot fast!)
7. Stir in the lime zest. Serve in the tortillas, topped with mashed avocado and cilantro and anything else your heart desires

Moo Goo Gai Pan

(Prep + Cooking Time: 1 hour 20 minutes | **Servings:** 4)

Ingredients:

For Marinade:
- 1 garlic clove; minced
- ½-inch piece fresh ginger, peeled and grated

For Stir-Fry:
- 1 (14-ounce) block firm tofu, pressed for least 1 hour, but overnight is best; chopped into bite-size cubes
- 1 (8-ounce) can sliced water chestnuts, drained
- 1 (8-ounce) can bamboo shoots, drained
- 1 tbsp. cornstarch
- ⅓ cup water
- 8 ounces white mushrooms, sliced
- 1 cup sugar snap peas; rinsed, tough ends removed
- 2 tbsp. lite soy sauce
- 1 tbsp. sesame oil
- 2 tbsp. Vegetable Stock
- 1 carrot, sliced into matchsticks
- 1 garlic clove; minced
- 1-inch piece fresh ginger, peeled and grated
- 1 cup Vegetable Stock
- 2 tbsp. soy sauce
- 1 tbsp. sesame oil
- Hot cooked rice or noodles; for serving; optional

Directions:
To Make Marinade:
- In a small bowl, whisk the stock, soy sauce, oil, garlic and ginger. Set aside.

To Make Stir-Fry:
1. In a shallow dish, combine the tofu cubes and marinade. Cover the dish and let sit for at least 30 minutes
2. Select the "Sauté" Low mode on your instant pot. When the display reads "Hot," add the oil and heat until it shimmers.
3. Add the marinated tofu. Cook for 8 to 10 minutes, using tongs to turn the tofu carefully
4. Turn off the Instant Pot and add the mushrooms, snap peas, carrot, garlic, ginger, stock, soy sauce, water chestnuts and bamboo shoots. Using a large spoon, stir well
5. Select the "Sauté" Low mode on your instant pot, again. Cover the pot with a tempered glass lid and simmer for 5 minutes, stirring occasionally.
6. In a small bowl, whisk the cornstarch and water. Add this slurry to the pot. Simmer, uncovered, for 5 minutes more; or until the sauce thickens. Serve over rice or noodles

Parmesan Eggplant Casserole

(**Prep + Cooking Time:** 49 minutes | **Servings:** 6)

Ingredients:
- One 25-oz. jar marinara sauce
- 1 yellow onion; chopped.
- 8 oz. cremini mushrooms; chopped.
- ½ cup shredded fresh mozzarella cheese
- 2 cloves garlic; minced.
- 1 eggplant, cut into 1-inch cubes
- ½ cup water
- 1 cup quinoa, rinsed
- ¼ cup grated Parmesan cheese
- 1 tbsp. extra-virgin olive oil
- ½ tsp. fine sea salt
- Chopped fresh parsley; for garnish.

Directions:
1. Press *Sauté* and add the olive oil to the Instant Pot. Once the oil is hot but not smoking, add the onion and mushrooms and sauté until the onion is softened, about 5 minutes
2. Press *Cancel* Button, then add the garlic, eggplant and salt while the pot is still hot. Stir briefly with a wooden spoon to distribute the salt.
3. Add the water and quinoa, then use the spoon to scrape the bottom of the pot to make sure nothing has stuck. Pour the marinara sauce over the top without stirring
4. Now, Lock the lid and Turn the steam release valve to "Sealing" Position. Select *Manual/Pressure* Cook to cook on *High* pressure for 1 minute.
5. Once the cooking cycle is completed, let the pressure naturally release for 15 minutes, then move the steam release valve to Venting to release any remaining pressure. When the floating valve drops, remove the lid and stir in the Parmesan. Turn on your oven's broiler
6. Transfer the mixture to a 9 by 13-inch casserole dish or a 12-inch oven-safe skillet and smooth the top with a spatula.
7. Sprinkle the mozzarella over the top, place the dish under the broiler and broil until the cheese is bubbly and lightly golden, 2 to 3 minutes. Garnish with the parsley and serve warm

Vegetable Soup

(**Prep + Cooking Time:** 33 minutes | **Servings:** 4)

Ingredients:
- 2 cups cauliflower florets cut into 3-inch pieces
- 1 cup potatoes cut into 2-inch pieces
- 1 large onion; chopped into 2-inch pieces
- 2 cups water
- 1 cup chopped tomatoes
- 1 ½ tsp. Sambhar Spice Mix
- 1 tsp. ground turmeric
- 1 tsp. salt or as your liking

Directions:
1. In your Instant Pot, combine the cauliflower, onion, carrots, tomatoes, spice mix, salt and turmeric. Stir to combine
2. Now secure the lid on the pot and close the valve. Now Press "Manual" and set the pot at "Low" pressure for 3 minutes.
3. After completing the cooking time, allow the pot to sit undisturbed for 10 minutes, then release any remaining pressure. Gradually stir in the water to thin the soup to the desired consistency

Asian Gobi Masala

(**Prep + Cooking Time:** 12 minutes | **Servings:** 5)

Ingredients:
- 1 garlic clove; minced
- 1 head cauliflower, chopped
- 1 white onion; diced
- 1 cup water
- 1 tbsp. ground coriander
- 1 tbsp. olive oil
- 1 tsp. cumin seeds
- 1/2 tsp. garam masala
- 1 tsp. ground cumin
- 1/2 tsp. salt or as your liking
- Hot cooked rice; for serving; optional

Directions:
1. Select the "Sauté" Low mode on your instant pot. When the display reads "Hot," add the oil and heat until it shimmers
2. Add the cumin seeds. Cook for 30 seconds, stirring nearly constantly. Add the onion. Cook for 2 to 3 minutes, still stirring.
3. Turn off the Instant Pot and add the garlic. Cook for about 30 seconds, stirring frequently
4. Add the cauliflower, coriander, cumin, garam masala, salt and water. Lock the lid and turn the steam release handle to Sealing. Using the Manual function, set the cooker to High Pressure for 1 minute.
5. After completing the cooking time, quick release the pressure
6. Remove the lid carefully and serve with hot rice

Thai Farro Salad

(**Prep + Cooking Time:** 34 minutes | **Servings:** 6)

Ingredients:
- 5 green onions, tender white and green parts only
- ¼ cup pure maple syrup
- 1 large carrot
- 1 red bell pepper
- 1 English cucumber
- ½ cup freshly squeezed lime juice
- 1 cup loosely packed chopped fresh cilantro
- 2 cups farro
- 2 cups water
- 2 tbsp. extra-virgin olive oil
- 2 tbsp. soy sauce or tamari
- 1 tsp. fine sea salt

Directions:
1. Combine the farro and water in the Instant Pot and give it a stir. Now, Lock the lid and Turn the steam release valve to "Sealing" Position. Select *Manual/Pressure* Cook to cook on *High* pressure for 10 minutes
2. Once the cooking cycle is completed, let the pressure naturally release for 10 minutes to fully cook the farro.
3. While the farro is cooking, stir together the olive oil, lime juice, salt, soy sauce and maple syrup in a small bowl to make a dressing
4. Seed and chop the red bell pepper, chop the cucumber, peel and shred the carrot and chop the green onions.
5. After 10 minutes have passed, move the steam release valve to Venting to release any remaining pressure.

6. When the floating valve drops, remove the lid. Use oven mitts to lift the stainless-steel insert out of the pot to allow the farro to cool, about 15 minutes
7. Stir the dressing into the cooked farro, along with the bell pepper, cucumber, carrot, green onions and cilantro.
8. Transfer the salad to a large airtight container, or into individual containers for easy packed lunches and chill in the fridge for 2 hours before serving to allow the flavors to fully develop

Barley and Mushroom Risotto

(Prep + Cooking Time: 55 minutes | **Servings:** 4)

Ingredients:
- 1 yellow onion; chopped.
- ¼ cup grated Parmesan cheese, plus more for serving.
- 1 cup pearled barley
- ½ cup dried black-eyed peas, unsoaked
- 2 cups water
- 1 generous handful baby spinach
- 8 oz. cremini mushrooms; chopped.
- 2 cloves garlic; minced.
- 1 tbsp. freshly squeezed lemon juice
- 1 tbsp. extra-virgin olive oil
- 1 tbsp. soy sauce or tamari
- 1 tsp. dried thyme
- 1 tsp. fine sea salt

Directions:
1. Press *Sauté* and add the olive oil to the Instant Pot. Once the oil is hot but not smoking, add the onion and mushrooms and sauté until the onion is softened, about 5 minutes. Press *Cancel* Button and stir in the garlic while the pot is still hot
2. Add the thyme, barley, peas and water and stir well. Now, Lock the lid and Turn the steam release valve to "Sealing" Position. Select *Manual/Pressure* Cook and cook on *High* pressure for 20 minutes.
3. Once the cooking cycle is completed, let the pressure naturally release for 10 minutes, then move the steam release valve to Venting to release any remaining pressure
4. When the floating valve drops, remove the lid. Stir in the salt, soy sauce, spinach, lemon juice and Parmesan until the spinach wilts and the cheese melts. Taste and adjust the seasoning as needed and serve immediately with additional Parmesan on the side

Crispy Potatoes Recipe

(Prep + Cooking Time: 17 minutes | **Servings:** 4)

Ingredients:
- 1 lb. gold potatoes, cubed
- 1/4 cup parsley leaves; chopped.
- 2 tbsp. ghee
- Juice of 1/2 lemon
- 1/2 cup water
- Salt and black pepper to the taste

Directions:
1. Pour the water in your instant pot, add potatoes in the steamer basket, Seal the Instant Pot lid and cook at High for 5 minutes.
2. Release the pressure naturally, open the instant pot lid and set it on Sauté mode
3. Add ghee, lemon juice, parsley, salt and pepper, stir and cook for 2 minutes
4. Transfer to plates and serve.

Asian Coconut Rice and Veggies

(Prep + Cooking Time: 30 minutes | **Servings:** 5)

Ingredients:
- 8 ounces white button mushrooms, sliced
- 1 (14-ounce) can lite coconut milk
- 1 (8-ounce) can sliced water chestnuts, drained
- 1 large carrot, sliced
- 1 small onion; diced
- 1 cup jasmine rice; rinsed and drained
- 1 cup water
- 1 cup chopped bok choy
- 1 cup sugar snap peas; rinsed
- 2 garlic cloves; minced
- 1 tbsp. sesame oil
- 1/2 tsp. ground ginger
- 1 tsp. Chinese five-spice
- 1 tsp. soy sauce
- 1 tsp. salt or as your liking

Directions:
1. In the Instant Pot, combine the rice, water, salt and ginger. Lock the lid and turn the steam release handle to Sealing
2. Using the Manual function, set the cooker to High Pressure for 4 minutes. After completing the cooking time, let the pressure release naturally for 5 minutes; quick release any remaining pressure.
3. Remove the lid carefully and fluff the rice. Transfer to a bowl and set aside.
4. Select the "Sauté" Low mode on your instant pot. When the display reads "Hot," add the oil and heat until it shimmers
5. Add the carrot, onion, bok choy, snap peas, garlic, mushrooms and water chestnuts. Sauté for 2 to 3 minutes.
6. Stir in the coconut milk, five-spice powder, soy sauce and cooked rice. Simmer for 5 to 6 minutes more, stirring occasionally, until the coconut milk is reduced

Mucho Burritos

(Prep + Cooking Time: 20 minutes | **Servings:** 7)

Ingredients:
- 2 canned chipotle peppers in adobo sauce
- 2 cups Cilantro Lime Brown Rice
- ¼ cup Vegetable Stock
- 1 bell pepper, any color, sliced
- 1 small onion, sliced
- 8 burrito-size tortillas
- 2 cups Poblano Cheeze Sauce
- 1 (14-ounce) container firm tofu, pressed for at least 1 hour; or overnight if possible and crumbled
- 1 (16-ounce) can chili beans, drained but not rinsed
- 1 tbsp. roasted walnut oil
- 1/2 tsp. garlic powder
- 1/2 tsp. freshly squeezed lime juice
- 2 tsp. adobo sauce from the can
- 1 tsp. ground cumin
- 1/2 tsp. salt or as your liking
- Pinch freshly ground black pepper
- Garden Salsa; or store-bought salsa of choice; for filling
- Cashew Sour Cream, for filling; optional
- Sliced avocado, for filling; optional

Directions:
1. Select the "Sauté" Low mode on your instant pot. When the display reads "Hot," add the oil and heat until it shimmers
2. Add the tofu crumbles, chipotle peppers, adobo sauce, cumin, salt, garlic powder, lime juice and pepper. Cook for 2 to 3 minutes.
3. Add the bell pepper and onion. Cook for 2 minutes more. If you need additional liquid, add 1 to 2 tbsp. of water
4. Add the stock and simmer, stirring occasionally, for 4 to 5 minutes until the liquid is cooked out. Turn off the Instant Pot
5. To build your burritos, layer the tortillas with rice, tofu mixture, chili beans, salsa, poblano cheeze sauce and other fillings, as desired

Sloppy Janes

(Prep + Cooking Time: 20 minutes | **Servings:** 5)

Ingredients:
- 1 (15-ounce) can vegan refried beans
- 1 (8-ounce) package unflavored tempeh
- 1 (10-ounce) can diced tomatoes with green chilies, with liquid
- 1/4 cup quick cook oats
- 6 buns or rolls; for serving
- 1/2 cup Vegetable Stock
- 2 tbsp. vegan Worcestershire sauce
- 1 tbsp. Dijon mustard
- 1 tbsp. olive oil
- 1 tsp. smoked paprika
- 1/2 tsp. salt or as your liking
- 1/2 tsp. garlic powder
- 2 pinches chili powder
- Freshly ground black pepper
- Vegan cheese; for serving
- Barbecue sauce; for serving
- Sliced onion; for serving
- Sliced bell pepper; for serving
- Pickles; for serving

Directions:
1. Select the "Sauté" Low mode on your instant pot. When the display reads "Hot," add the oil and heat until it shimmers
2. Crumble in the tempeh and add the paprika and salt. Cook for 4 to 5 minutes, stirring occasionally. Turn off the Instant Pot.
3. Add the refried beans, tomatoes and green chilies, stock, Worcestershire sauce, mustard, garlic powder and chili powder and season to taste with pepper
4. Lock the lid and turn the steam release handle to Sealing. Using the Manual function, set the cooker to High Pressure for 2 minutes.
5. After completing the cooking time, quick release the pressure.
6. Remove the lid carefully and stir in the oats. There will likely be too much liquid; if so, select Sauté Medium and cook, uncovered, for 2 to 3 minutes; or until the extra liquid evaporates. Serve on buns, topped as desired

Cauliflower Mac 'n' Cheese

(Prep + Cooking Time: 35 minutes | **Servings:** 8)

Ingredients:
- 1 lb. whole-wheat macaroni
- 1 lb. fresh or frozen cauliflower florets
- 4 oz. extra-sharp Cheddar cheese
- ¼ cup grated Parmesan cheese, or other cheese of your choice, like Gruyère
- 1 tbsp. spicy brown mustard
- 2 tbsp. soy sauce or tamari
- 4 cups water
- 1½ tsp. fine sea salt

Directions:
1. Pour the pasta into the Instant Pot and add the water, soy sauce, mustard and salt. Stir well to combine, then add the cauliflower on top without stirring, making sure that the cauliflower layer completely covers the pasta for even cooking
2. Now, Lock the lid and Turn the steam release valve to "Sealing" Position. Select *Manual/Pressure* Cook to cook on *High* pressure for 3 minutes. While the pot is coming to pressure, shred the Cheddar (you should have about 1 cup).
3. Once the cooking cycle is completed, let the pressure naturally release for 10 minutes, then move the steam release valve to Venting to release any remaining pressure
4. When the floating valve drops, remove the lid and stir the pasta well, using a spatula to break up any pasta that has stuck together or stuck to the bottom of the pot. A little sticking is to be expected, but it will loosen up when you stir.
5. Use the spatula to mash any intact cauliflower florets against the side of the pot to help them dissolve into the pasta sauce. Add the Cheddar and Parmesan and stir well. Adjust the seasonings as needed and serve warm

Falafel Wraps

(Prep + Cooking Time: 35 minutes | Servings: 6)

Ingredients:
- ½ cup chopped fresh flat-leaf parsley
- ½ cup chopped fresh cilantro
- 1 cup green lentils
- 1 yellow onion; chopped.
- ½ cup quinoa, rinsed
- 1¾ cups water
- 2 cloves garlic; minced.
- 1 tbsp. freshly squeezed lemon juice, plus more as needed
- 2 tsp. ground cumin
- ¼ tsp. cayenne pepper (optional)
- 1 tsp. fine sea salt
- ½ tsp. ground coriander

Tahini Dressing:
- 3 to 4 tbsp. water
- 2 cloves garlic; minced.
- ¼ cup tahini
- 3 tbsp. freshly squeezed lemon juice
- ¼ tsp. fine sea salt
- Sliced cucumber, red bell pepper and carrots; for serving
- Freshly ground black pepper
- Romaine or butter lettuce leaves; for serving

Directions:
1. Combine the onion, lentils, quinoa, water, garlic, cumin, coriander and cayenne in the Instant Pot. Now, Lock the lid and Turn the steam release valve to "Sealing" Position. Select *Manual/Pressure* Cook to cook on *High* pressure for 5 minutes
2. While the lentils are cooking, make the dressing. In a bowl, combine the tahini, lemon juice, 3 tablespoons of the water, the garlic, salt and several grinds of black pepper. Add up to 1 tablespoon of the remaining water as needed to thin the dressing. Taste and adjust the seasonings as needed.
3. Once the cooking cycle is completed, let the pressure naturally release for 10 minutes, then move the steam release valve to Venting to release any remaining pressure
4. When the floating valve drops, remove the lid and stir in the salt, parsley, cilantro and lemon juice. Taste and adjust the seasonings as needed, adding more lemon juice to brighten the flavors.
5. Spoon the filling into lettuce leaves and top with the sliced cucumber, bell pepper and carrots. Drizzle the tahini dressing on top and serve

Vegetable Salad

(Prep + Cooking Time: 20 minutes | Servings: 5)

Ingredients:
For Dressing:
- 1/2 cup Vegetable Stock
- 1/2 cup apple cider vinegar
- 2 tsp. Dijon mustard
- 1/2 tsp. garlic powder
- 1 tsp. salt or as your liking

For Salad:
- 1 ½ pounds red potatoes, chopped
- 1/4 cup chopped fresh parsley
- 2 cups Brussels sprouts, ends trimmed
- 1 (8-ounce) package unflavored tempeh; chopped into bite-size pieces
- 1 small red onion, sliced
- 2 bay leaves
- 1 ½ tbsp. olive oil
- 1 ½ tsp. smoked paprika
- 1/2 tsp. salt or as your liking
- 1/4 tsp. garlic powder
- Freshly ground black pepper

Directions:

To Make Dressing:
1. In a medium bowl, whisk the vinegar, stock, mustard, salt and garlic powder until well combined. Set aside.

To Make Salad:
1. Select the "Sauté" Low mode on your instant pot. When the display reads "Hot," add the oil and heat until it shimmers
2. Add the tempeh, paprika, salt and garlic powder. Cook for 5 to 6 minutes, stirring occasionally. Transfer to a bowl and set aside.
3. Now add the potatoes, Brussels sprouts, red onion and bay leaves to the Instant Pot. Pour the dressing over the vegetables
4. Lock the lid and turn the steam release handle to Sealing. Using the Manual function, set the cooker to High Pressure for 4 minutes.
5. After completing the cooking time, quick release the pressure
6. Remove the lid carefully and remove and discard the bay leaves. Stir in the tempeh and parsley.
7. Taste and season with more salt and pepper, as needed. There will be some liquid left in the bottom, which is perfect for spooning over the salad when it's served.
8. If there's too much liquid for your taste, select Sauté Low again and cook for 2 to 3 minutes more

Black Eyed Peas

(Prep + Cooking Time: 55 minutes | **Servings:** 5)

Ingredients:
- 1 cup dried black-eyed peas; rinsed
- 3 ¼ cups Vegetable Stock
- 2 cups cooked brown rice
- 3 cups chopped kale
- 1 cup frozen peas
- 1 red bell pepper; diced
- 2 tomatoes, chopped
- 1 sweet onion; diced
- 1 tbsp. olive oil
- 1/2 tsp. garlic powder
- 1/2 tsp. dried thyme
- 1 tsp. chili powder
- 1 tsp. vegan Worcestershire sauce
- 1/2 tsp. salt or as your liking
- 1/4 tsp. freshly ground black pepper

Directions:
1. Select the "Sauté" Low mode on your instant pot. When the display reads "Hot," add the oil and heat until it shimmers
2. Add the onion and bell pepper. Cook for 2 to 3 minutes, stirring occasionally. Turn off the Instant Pot and add the tomatoes, chili powder, Worcestershire sauce, garlic powder, thyme, salt, pepper, black-eyed peas and stock
3. Lock the lid and turn the steam release handle to Sealing. Using the Manual function, set the cooker to High Pressure for 20 minutes.
4. After completing the cooking time, let the pressure release naturally for about 20 minutes; quick release any remaining pressure
5. Remove the lid carefully and stir in the frozen peas, rice and kale. Give them a minute or two to warm and enjoy

Thai Stir-Fry

(Prep + Cooking Time: 32 minutes | **Servings:** 4)

Ingredients:
- 4 oz. whole-wheat spaghetti
- 1 large carrot, shredded
- 1 red bell pepper; seeded and chopped.
- 2 cups snow peas
- 3 green onions, tender white and green parts only; chopped.
- 4 cups water
- ¼ cup all-natural peanut butter or almond butter

- 1 clove garlic; minced.
- ½ head green or red cabbage, shredded (about 4 cups)
- ¼ cup pure maple syrup
- 5 tbsp. soy sauce or tamari
- 2 tbsp. freshly squeezed lime juice
- 1 tbsp. Sriracha
- 1 tsp. minced fresh ginger (about ½-inch knob)
- Chopped peanuts or almonds; for garnish.
- Chopped fresh cilantro; for garnish.

Directions:
1. Break the spaghetti noodles in half and arrange them in the Instant Pot in a crisscross manner to help avoid clumping. Pour the water over the noodles
2. Now, Lock the lid and Turn the steam release valve to "Sealing" Position. Select *Manual/Pressure* Cook to cook on *High* pressure for 2 minutes.
3. While the noodles are cooking, in a bowl, whisk together the peanut butter, soy sauce, maple syrup, lime juice, Sriracha, ginger and garlic and set aside
4. Once the cooking cycle is completed, let the pressure naturally release for 10 minutes, then move the steam release valve to Venting to release any remaining pressure.
5. When the floating valve drops, Press *Cancel* Button and remove the lid. Drain the noodles through a colander, rinsing them with cold water to remove some starch and stop the cooking process. Rinse and dry the metal insert and return it to the Instant Pot
6. Press *Sauté* and pour the peanut sauce into the pot. Add the cabbage, carrot, bell pepper and snow peas and stir well. Sauté until the vegetables are tender, about 5 minutes.
7. Stir in the drained noodles and the green onions just until everything is heated through. (If the noodles stick together, rinse them again under cold water to unstick them before adding.) Serve the pad thai warm, with the cilantro and peanuts sprinkled over the top

Chickpea Kale Korma

(**Prep + Cooking Time:** 1 hour 20 minutes | **Servings:** 5)

Ingredients:
- 3 garlic cloves, peeled
- 2 Roma tomatoes, quartered
- ½-inch piece fresh ginger, peeled
- 1 (14-ounce) can lite coconut milk
- 1/2 cup cashews, soaked in water overnight, drained and rinsed well
- 1 cup dried chickpeas; rinsed
- 1 to 2 cups water
- 1 tsp. curry powder
- 1/2 tsp. ground cardamom
- 1 tsp. garam masala
- 1/2 tsp. ground cumin
- 1/2 tsp. ground coriander
- 1/2 tsp. ground turmeric
- 1/2 tsp. onion powder
- 1 tsp. salt or as your liking
- 1/4 tsp. freshly ground black pepper
- 1 bunch kale, leaves torn from stems and rinsed
- Hot cooked rice; for serving; optional

Directions:
1. In the Instant Pot, combine the chickpeas and enough water to cover. Lock the lid and turn the steam release handle to Sealing
2. Using the Manual function, set the cooker to High Pressure for 45 minutes. After completing the cooking time, let the pressure release naturally for 15 minutes; quick release any remaining pressure.
3. Remove the lid carefully. Drain the chickpeas and return them to the Instant Pot
4. In a high-speed blender or food processor, combine the cashews, tomatoes, garlic and ginger. Blend until smooth.
5. Add the coconut milk and pulse a few more times to combine. Add this purée to the chickpeas along with the garam masala, curry powder, salt, cumin, coriander, cardamom, turmeric, onion powder, pepper and kale.
6. Select the "Sauté" Low mode on your instant pot. Simmer for 8 to 10 minutes until the kale and beans have absorbed the flavor. Serve with rice, if desired

Walnut Pesto Pasta.

(Prep + Cooking Time: 35 minutes | **Servings:** 6)

Ingredients:

- 8 oz. whole-wheat pasta, like rotini or penne
- ½ cup green lentils
- 1 cup lightly packed arugula
- 2 or 3 cloves garlic; minced.
- ½ cup raw walnut halves
- 4¼ cups water
- 1½ cups cherry tomatoes, halved
- 1 zucchini; chopped.
- One 15-oz. can artichoke hearts, drained and rinsed
- ¼ cup grated Parmesan cheese
- 1 cup lightly packed fresh basil leaves
- 1 tbsp. extra-virgin olive oil
- 2 tbsp. freshly squeezed lemon juice
- 1 tsp. fine sea salt
- Freshly ground black pepper

Directions:

1. Pour 4 cups of the water into the Instant Pot, add the pasta and lentils and stir well to make sure they are submerged in the water for even cooking
2. Now, Lock the lid and Turn the steam release valve to "Sealing" Position. Select *Manual/Pressure* Cook to cook at *High* pressure for 4 minutes.
3. Release the pressure naturally for 10 minutes, then move the steam release valve to Venting to release any remaining pressure
4. While the pasta is cooking, combine the arugula, basil, lemon juice, garlic, walnuts, the remaining ¼ cup water and the salt in the bowl of a food processor or blender and process until a relatively smooth pesto forms.
5. When the floating valve drops, remove the lid and Press *Cancel* Button to stop the cooking cycle. Use oven mitts to remove the pot and drain the cooked pasta and lentils in a fine-mesh sieve.
6. Rinse with cold water to remove some starch and stop the cooking process. Dry the pot with a towel and return it to the Instant Pot housing
7. Press *Sauté* and add the olive oil to the pot. Once the oil is hot but not smoking, add the tomatoes, zucchini and artichoke hearts and stir until softened, about 5 minutes.
8. Stir in the drained pasta and lentils and pesto sauce and toss well to coat. Stir in the Parmesan and several grinds of pepper. Taste and adjust the seasonings as needed, then serve warm

Stuffed Bell Peppers

(Prep + Cooking Time: 30 minutes | **Servings:** 4)

Ingredients:

- 1 lb. turkey meat, ground.
- 5 oz. canned green chilies; chopped.
- 1 cup water
- 1 jalapeno pepper; chopped.
- 2 tsp. chili powder
- 1 tsp. garlic powder
- 1 tsp. cumin, ground.
- 2 green onions; chopped.
- 1 avocado; chopped
- Salt to the taste
- 1/2 cup whole wheat panko
- 4 bell peppers, tops, and seeds discarded
- 4 pepper jack cheese slices
- Crushed tortilla chips
- Pico de gallo

For the chipotle sauce:

- Zest from 1 lime
- Juice from 1 lime
- 1/2 cup sour cream
- 2 tbsp. chipotle in adobo sauce
- 1/8 tsp. garlic powder

Directions:

1. In a bowl, mix sour cream with chipotle in adobo sauce, lime zest and lime juice and garlic powder, stir well and keep in the fridge until you serve it

2. In a bowl, mix turkey meat with green onions, green chilies, bread crumbs, jalapeno, cumin, salt, chili powder and garlic powder, stir very well and stuff your peppers with this mix.
3. Add 1 cup water to your instant pot, add peppers in the steamer basket, close the lid and cook at High for 15 minutes
4. Release the pressure naturally for 10 minutes, then release remaining pressure by turning the valve to 'Venting', transfer bell peppers to a pan, add cheese on top, introduce in preheated broiler and broil until cheese is browned.
5. Divide bell peppers on plates, top with the chipotle sauce you've made earlier and serve

Collard Greens

(Prep + Cooking Time: 20 minutes | **Servings:** 2)

Ingredients:
- 2 cups frozen collard greens
- 1/4 cup chopped yellow onion
- 2 cups water
- 1 tbsp. extra-virgin olive oil
- 1 tsp. paprika
- 1/2 tsp. ground turmeric
- 1 tsp. minced garlic
- 1/2 tsp. salt or as your liking
- 2 tsp. apple cider vinegar

Directions:
1. In a medium bowl, combine the collard greens, onion, garlic, paprika, turmeric and salt. Toss to combine
2. Place on a sheet of aluminum foil. Bring the edges of the foil together and crimp tightly to seal.
3. Pour the water into the Instant Pot. Place a steamer rack in the pot. Place the packet on top of the rack
4. Now secure the lid on the pot and close the valve. Now Press "Manual" and set the pot at "High" pressure for 5 minutes. After completing the cooking time, quick release the pressure.
5. In a medium skillet, heat the olive oil over medium heat until shimmering. Add the steamed vegetables to the pan and cook, stirring, for 2 minutes. Add the vinegar and toss to coat

Corn Chowder

(Prep + Cooking Time: 30 minutes | **Servings:** 4)

Ingredients:
- 4 slices bacon; chopped
- 2 cups diced potatoes; cut into ½-inch cubes
- 1 cup chopped yellow onions
- 3 cups chicken broth
- 1/2 cup heavy cream
- 2 cups corn kernels
- 1 tbsp. minced garlic
- 1/2 tsp. dried thyme
- 1/2 tsp. freshly grated nutmeg
- 1 tsp. salt or as your liking
- 1 tsp. black pepper

Directions:
1. In your Instant Pot, combine the broth, corn, potatoes, onions, bacon, garlic, salt, pepper and thyme. Stir to combine
2. Now secure the lid on the pot and close the valve. Now Press "Manual" and set the pot at "High" pressure for 5 minutes.
3. After completing the cooking time, allow the pot to sit undisturbed for 5 minutes, then release any remaining pressure
4. Using an immersion blender, puree some of the soup to thicken slightly, leaving some chunks of potato and corn intact. Stir in the nutmeg and cream and serve

Sweet Potato Curry

(**Prep + Cooking Time:** 27 minutes | **Servings:** 4)

Ingredients:

- 2 sweet potatoes, cut into 1-inch chunks
- 2 carrots; peeled and chopped.
- 1 yellow onion; chopped.
- ½ cup full-fat coconut milk
- 1 cup chopped kale, stems removed
- 3 cups water
- 1 cup red lentils
- 1 tbsp. curry powder
- 1 tbsp. extra-virgin olive oil
- 1 tbsp. pure maple syrup (optional)
- 1 tsp. ground ginger
- 1½ tsp. fine sea salt
- Freshly ground black pepper
- Chopped fresh cilantro; for garnish.
- Cooked rice, quinoa, or Easy Cauliflower "Rice"; for serving

Directions:

1. Press *Sauté* and add the olive oil to the Instant Pot. Once the oil is hot but not smoking, add the onion, curry powder and ginger and stir just until fragrant, about 1 minute. Press *Cancel* Button to stop the cooking cycle
2. Add the water and use a wooden spoon or spatula to scrape the bottom of the pot, making sure nothing has stuck. Add the sweet potatoes, carrots, lentils, salt and a few grinds of pepper
3. Stir well to ensure the lentils are covered in water, then secure the lid and move the steam release valve to Sealing. Select *Manual/Pressure* Cook to cook on *High* pressure for 1 minute
4. Once the cooking cycle is completed, let the pressure naturally release for 3 minutes, then move the steam release valve to Venting.
5. When the floating valve drops, remove the lid and add the coconut milk and kale. Stir until the kale has wilted, about 2 minutes. Taste and adjust the seasonings as needed, adding the maple syrup if you want a little sweetness. Serve the curry warm over the grain of your choice and garnished with the cilantro

Walnut and Lentil Tacos

(**Prep + Cooking Time:** 33 minutes | **Servings:** 6)

Ingredients:

- One 14-oz. can fire-roasted tomatoes with green chiles
- 1 cup green or brown lentils
- 1 yellow onion; chopped.
- ¾ cup walnut halves
- 1¼ cups water
- 12 taco shells; for serving
- 1 tsp. ground cumin
- 1 tsp. fine sea salt
- 1 tsp. chili powder
- Lettuce, tomatoes, green onions and avocado, or your favorite taco toppings; for serving

Directions:

1. Combine the lentils, water, cumin and chili powder in the Instant Pot. Stir well to ensure the lentils are covered in liquid, then sprinkle the onion and canned tomatoes (along with their juices) over the top, without stirring
2. Now, Lock the lid and Turn the steam release valve to "Sealing" Position. Select *Manual/Pressure* Cook to cook on *High* pressure for 5 minutes
3. While the lentils are cooking, finely chop the walnuts and chop the lettuce, fresh tomatoes, green onions and avocado.
4. Once the cooking cycle is completed, let the pressure naturally release for 10 minutes, then move the steam release valve to Venting to release any remaining pressure
5. When the floating valve drops, remove the lid and use a fork to mash a lentil against the side of the pot to make sure it's tender.
6. If the lentils aren't tender, secure the lid and cook at *High* pressure for 2 minutes more. Release the ressure naturally for 5 minutes before venting and removing the lid

7. Stir in the salt and chopped walnuts. Taste and adjust the seasonings as needed. To serve, spoon the taco "meat" into taco shells and top with lettuce, tomato, green onion and avocado

Greek Style Chickpea Salad.

(Prep + Cooking Time: 47 minutes | **Servings:** 6)

Ingredients:
- 1 cup dried chickpeas, soaked for 8 hours
- 1 red bell pepper, seeded and diced
- ½ cup Kalamata olives, pitted and sliced (optional)
- ½ cup crumbled feta cheese (optional)
- 1 cup cherry tomatoes, quartered
- ½ cup chopped fresh dill
- ½ red onion, diced
- 1 English cucumber, diced
- 3 cups water
- ¼ cup freshly squeezed lemon juice
- 2 cloves garlic; minced.
- 2 tbsp. extra-virgin olive oil
- ½ tsp. fine sea salt
- Freshly ground black pepper

Directions:
1. Drain the soaked chickpeas and add them to the Instant Pot with the water. Now, Lock the lid and Turn the steam release valve to "Sealing" Position. Select *Manual/Pressure* Cook to cook on *High* pressure for 12 minutes
2. While the chickpeas are cooking, stir together the lemon juice, garlic, olive oil, salt and several grinds of black pepper in a large mixing bowl to make a dressing. Add the onion, cucumber, bell pepper, tomatoes, dill and olives and let them marinate in the dressing until the chickpeas are done
3. Once the cooking cycle is completed, let the pressure naturally release for 15 minutes, then move the steam release valve to Venting to release any remaining pressure.
4. When the floating valve drops, remove the lid. Drain and rinse the cooked chickpeas in cold water, then drain again well.
5. Add the chickpeas to the mixing bowl and toss well to coat in the dressing. Add the feta, then taste and adjust the seasonings as needed. Chill the salad in the fridge for 30 minutes before serving to let the flavors meld

Vegetable Bowls.

(Prep + Cooking Time: 65 minutes | **Servings:** 6)

Ingredients:
- 1 lb. sweet potatoes, cut into 1-inch chunks
- 1 lb. brussels sprouts, cleaned and halved
- 2 cups chopped kale
- 1 cup cherry tomatoes, halved
- 1 cucumber; chopped.
- 1 bunch asparagus, cut into 1-inch pieces with woody stems removed (optional)
- ¼ cup freshly squeezed lemon juice
- 2 cloves garlic; minced.
- 1 cup quinoa, rinsed
- 1¼ cups water
- Extra-virgin olive oil, for drizzling
- 6 tbsp. tahini
- 1 tsp. ground cumin
- Fine sea salt and freshly ground black pepper

Directions:
1. Preheat the oven to 400-Degree F. Arrange the sweet potatoes on a large baking sheet and drizzle with olive oil. Toss the potatoes to coat with the oil, then season with salt and pepper and place them in the oven to roast for 25 minutes
2. Once the sweet potatoes are in the oven, arrange the Brussels sprouts and asparagus on a second large baking sheet and drizzle with olive oil.
3. Toss the sprouts and asparagus to coat with the oil, then season with salt and pepper and place them in the oven along with the sweet potatoes
4. Roast until the vegetables are tender and golden, 15 to 20 minutes. (Because the sweet potatoes have a head start, everything should finish cooking at roughly the same time.)

5. While the vegetables are roasting, add the quinoa and 1 cup of the water to the Instant Pot and give it a stir.
6. Now, Lock the lid and Turn the steam release valve to "Sealing" Position. Select *Manual/Pressure* Cook and cook on *High* pressure for 1 minute. Once the cooking cycle is completed, let the pressure naturally release for 15 minutes
7. While the quinoa is cooking, in a small bowl, combine the tahini, lemon juice, garlic, cumin, remaining ¼ cup water, ¼ teaspoon salt and several grinds of pepper. Whisk well (adding more water, 1 tablespoon at a time, as needed to thin).
8. When the screen reads "L0:15", move the steam release valve to Venting to release any remaining pressure. When the floating valve drops, remove the lid and use a fork to fluff the quinoa
9. To serve, fill each bowl with some chopped kale, cooked quinoa, roasted vegetables, cherry tomatoes and cucumber. Drizzle the creamy tahini dressing over the top

Snacks and Appetizers

Shrimp Appetizer

(Prep + Cooking Time: 15 minutes | **Servings:** 4)

Ingredients:
- 1 lb. shrimp, peeled and deveined
- 3/4 cup pineapple juice
- 2 tbsp. coconut aminos
- 3 tbsp. vinegar
- 1 cup chicken stock
- 3 tbsp. stevia

Directions:
1. Put shrimp, pineapple juice, stock, aminos and stevia in your instant pot, stir a bit, seal the instant pot lid and cook on High for 4 minutes.
2. Arrange shrimp on a platter, drizzle cooking juices all over and serve as an appetizer.

Zucchini Rolls Recipe

(Prep + Cooking Time: 18 minutes | **Servings:** 24)

Ingredients:
- 3 zucchinis, thinly sliced
- 2 tbsp. olive oil
- 24 basil leaves
- 2 tbsp. mint; chopped
- 1 ½ cups water
- 1 ⅓ cup ricotta cheese
- Salt and black pepper to the taste
- 1/4 cup basil; chopped
- Tomato sauce for serving

Directions:
1. Set your instant pot on sauté mode; add zucchini slices, drizzle the oil over them, season with salt and pepper, cook for 2 minutes on each side and transfer to a plate.
2. In a bowl, mix ricotta with chopped basil, mint, salt and pepper; then stir well. divide this into zucchini slices and roll them.
3. Add the water to your instant pot, add steamer basket, add zucchini rolls inside, seal the instant pot lid and cook on High for 3 minutes
4. Arrange on a platter and serve with tomato sauce on the side.

Tuna Patties Appetizer

(Prep + Cooking Time: 18 minutes | **Servings:** 12)

Ingredients:
- 15 oz. canned tuna, drained and flaked
- 1/2 cup red onion; chopped.
- 1 tsp. parsley; dried
- 1 tsp. garlic powder
- 1 ½ cups water
- 3 eggs
- 1/2 tsp. dill; chopped
- Salt and black pepper to the taste
- A drizzle of olive oil

Directions:
1. In a bowl, mix tuna with salt, pepper, dill, parsley, onion, garlic powder and eggs, stir and shape medium patties out of this mix.
2. Set your instant pot on sauté mode; add a drizzle of oil, heat it up, add tuna patties, cook them for 2 minutes on each side and transfer to a plate
3. Clean the pot, add the water, add steamer basket, add tuna cakes, close the lid and cook on High for 4 minutes
4. Arrange patties on a platter and serve

Sausage and Shrimp Appetizer

(Prep + Cooking Time: 15 minutes | **Servings:** 4)

Ingredients:
- 1 ½ lb. shrimp, heads removed
- 12 oz. sausage; cooked and chopped.
- 1 tsp. red pepper flakes, crushed.
- 1 tbsp. old bay seasoning
- 16 oz. chicken stock
- 2 sweet onions, cut into wedges
- 8 garlic cloves; minced.
- Salt and black pepper to the taste

Directions:
1. In your instant pot, mix stock with old bay seasoning, pepper flakes, salt, black pepper, onions, garlic, sausage and shrimp; then stir well. seal the instant pot lid and cook on High for 5 minutes.
2. Divide into small bowls and serve as an appetizer.

Spinach Dip Recipe

(Prep + Cooking Time: 30 minutes | **Servings:** 6)

Ingredients:
- 6 bacon slices; cooked and crumbled.
- 1 tbsp. garlic; minced.
- 5 oz. spinach
- 1 ½ cups water
- 1/2 cup coconut cream
- 8 oz. cream cheese, soft
- 1 ½ tbsp. parsley; chopped
- 2.5 oz. parmesan, grated
- 1 tbsp. lemon juice
- A drizzle of olive oil
- Salt and black pepper to the taste

Directions:
1. Set your instant pot on sauté mode; add oil heat it up, add spinach; then stir well. cook for 1 minute and transfer to a bowl.
2. Add cream cheese, garlic, salt, pepper, coconut cream, parsley, bacon, lemon juice and parmesan, stir well and divide this into 6 ramekins.
3. Add the water to your instant pot, add steamer basket, add ramekins inside, seal the instant pot lid and cook on High for 15 minutes
4. Introduce in a preheated broiler for 4 minutes and serve right away

Cauliflower Dip Recipe

(Prep + Cooking Time: 20 minutes | **Servings:** 6)

Ingredients:
- 6 cups cauliflower florets
- 1/2 cup coconut milk
- 7 cups veggie stock
- 2 tbsp. ghee
- 8 garlic cloves; minced.
- Salt and black pepper to the taste

Directions:
1. Set your instant pot on Sauté mode; add ghee, heat it up, add garlic, salt and pepper, stir and cook for 2 minutes.
2. Add stock and cauliflower to the pot, heat up, seal the instant pot lid and cook on High for 7 minutes.
3. Transfer cauliflower and 1 cup stock to your blender, add milk and blend well for a few minutes
4. Transfer to a bowl and serve as a dip for veggies.

Tomatoes Appetizer

(Prep + Cooking Time: 20 minutes | **Servings:** 4)

Ingredients:
- 4 tomatoes, tops cut off and pulp scooped
- 1/2 cup water
- 1 yellow onion; chopped.
- 1 tbsp. ghee
- 2 tbsp. celery; chopped.
- 1/2 cup mushrooms; chopped.
- 1 cup cottage cheese
- 1/4 tsp. caraway seeds
- Salt and black pepper to the taste
- 1 tbsp. parsley; chopped.

Directions:
1. Set your instant pot on sauté mode; add ghee, heat it up, add onion and celery, stir and cook for 3 minutes
2. Add tomato pulp, mushrooms, salt, pepper, cheese, parsley and caraway seeds; then stir well. cook for 3 minutes more and stuff tomatoes with this mix.
3. Add the water to your instant pot, add the steamer basket, and stuffed tomatoes inside, seal the instant pot lid and cook on High for 4 minutes.
4. Arrange tomatoes on a platter and serve as an appetizer.

Spicy Mussels Recipe

(Prep + Cooking Time: 15 minutes | **Servings:** 4)

Ingredients:
- 2 lb. mussels, scrubbed
- 1/2 cup chicken stock
- 1/2 tsp. red pepper flakes
- 2 tbsp. olive oil
- 2 tsp. garlic; minced.
- 2 tsp. oregano; dried
- 1 yellow onion; chopped.
- 14 oz. tomatoes; chopped.

Directions:
1. Set your instant pot on Sauté mode; add oil, heat it up, add onions, stir and sauté for 3 minutes
2. Add pepper flakes, garlic, stock, tomatoes, oregano and mussels; then stir well. seal the instant pot lid and cook on Low for 3 minutes.
3. Divide mussels into small bowls and serve as an appetizer

Shrimp Recipe

(Prep + Cooking Time: 18 minutes | **Servings:** 2)

Ingredients:
- 1/2 lb. big shrimp, peeled and deveined
- 2 tsp. Worcestershire sauce
- 1 tsp. Creole seasoning
- 2 tsp. olive oil
- Juice of 1 lemon
- Salt and black pepper to the taste

Directions:
1. In your instant pot, mix shrimp with Worcestershire sauce, oil, lemon juice, salt, pepper and seasoning; then stir well. seal the instant pot lid and cook on High for 4 minutes.
2. Arrange shrimp on a lined baking sheet, introduce in preheated broiler and broil for 4 minutes more.
3. Arrange on a platter and serve.

Asian Squid Appetizer

(Prep + Cooking Time: 25 minutes | **Servings:** 4)

Ingredients:
- 4 squid, tentacles from 1 squid separated and chopped.
- 1 tbsp. mirin
- 2 tbsp. stevia
- 4 tbsp. coconut aminos
- 1 cup cauliflower rice
- 14 oz. fish stock

Directions:
1. In a bowl, mix chopped tentacles with cauliflower rice, stir well and stuff each squid with the mix.
2. Place squid in your instant pot, add stock, aminos, mirin and stevia; then stir well. seal the instant pot lid and cook on High for 15 minutes.
3. Arrange stuffed squid on a platter and serve as an appetizer

French Endives

(Prep + Cooking Time: 17 minutes | **Servings:** 4)

Ingredients:
- 4 endives, trimmed and halved
- 1 tbsp. ghee
- 1 tbsp. lemon juice
- Salt and black pepper to the taste

Directions:
1. Set your instant pot on Sauté mode; add ghee, heat it up, add endives, season with salt and pepper, drizzle lemon juice, close the lid and cook them on High for 7 minutes.
2. Arrange endives on a platter, drizzle some of the cooking juice over them and serve as an appetizer

Instant Chili Dip

(Prep + Cooking Time: 20 minutes | **Servings:** 8)

Ingredients:
- 5 ancho chilies; dried and chopped.
- 2 garlic cloves; minced.
- 1 ½ cups water
- 2 tbsp. balsamic vinegar
- 1/2 tsp. cumin, ground.
- 1 ½ tsp. stevia
- 1 tbsp. oregano; chopped.
- Salt and black pepper to the taste

Directions:
1. In your instant pot mix water chilies, garlic, salt, pepper, stevia, cumin and oregano; then stir well. seal the instant pot lid and cook on High for 8 minutes.
2. Blend using an immersion blender, add vinegar; then stir well. set the pot on simmer mode and cook your chili dip until it thickens
3. Serve with veggie sticks on the side as a snack.

Black Beans.

(Prep + Cooking Time: 55 minutes | **Servings:**6)

Ingredients:
- 2 bay leaves
- 8 cups water
- 2 cups dried black beans; rinsed. and drained

Directions:
1. Combine the black beans, bay leaves, and water in the inner pot
2. Now, Lock the lid. Select, "Manual or Pressure Cook" and set the pressure to *High* and the time to 25 minutes. Make sure the steam release knob is in the sealed position.
3. After completing the cooking cycle, naturally release the pressure for 10 minutes, then quick release any remaining pressure.
4. Unlock and remove the lid. Drain the beans. Discard the bay leaves. Serve the beans immediately

Sweet Potato Slaw

(Prep + Cooking Time: 24 minutes | Makes: 13 to 15 cups)

Ingredients:
- 3 scallions, green and light green parts, sliced
- 2 cups sliced green cabbage
- 1 cup shredded sweet potato
- 12 to 15 dumpling wrappers
- 1 cup water
- 1/2 sweet onion, sliced
- 1 ½ tbsp. freshly squeezed lime juice
- 1 tbsp. hoisin sauce
- 2 tbsp. lite soy sauce
- 1 ½ tsp. sesame oil
- 1/2 tsp. ground ginger, plus more to taste
- Zest of 1 lime
- Nonstick cooking spray; for preparing the muffin tin

Directions:
1. Preheat the oven to 350°F. Lightly coat a muffin tin with the nonstick spray. Place one wonton wrapper in each well of the prepared tin, pressing down to create a cup shape.
2. Bake for 5 to 6 minutes; or until the cups are crispy and lightly browned. Set aside to cool
3. Pour the water into your Instant Pot. Place the cabbage, sweet potato and onion into a steamer basket and put the basket on a trivet
4. Lock the lid in place. Select Steam and set the cook time for 2 minutes. Because the Steam function doesn't seal the Instant Pot, there's no need to turn the steam release handle to Sealing or release any pressure.
5. While the veggies steam, in a medium bowl, stir together the soy sauce, hoisin sauce, lime juice, oil, lime zest and ginger
6. After completing the cooking time, carefully remove the lid and stir in the veggies, making sure all are coated with the sauce. Taste and add more ginger, if desired.
7. When ready to serve, fill the cups with the slaw and sprinkle the tops with scallion. Enjoy warm or at room temperature.

Tomato Dip Recipe

(Prep + Cooking Time: 25 minutes | **Servings:** 20)

Ingredients:
- 2 lb. tomatoes; peeled and chopped.
- 1 apple, cored and chopped.
- 1 yellow onion; chopped.
- 3 oz. dates chopped
- 3 tsp. whole spice
- 1/2-pint balsamic vinegar
- 4 tbsp. stevia
- Salt to the taste

Directions:
1. Put tomatoes, apple, onion, dates, salt, whole spice and half of the vinegar in your instant pot; then stir well. seal the instant pot lid and cook on High for 10 minutes.
2. Set the pot on simmer mode, add the rest of the vinegar and stevia; then stir well. cook for a few minutes more until it thickens, transfer to bowls and serve as a snack

Mussels and Clams

(Prep + Cooking Time: 23 minutes | **Servings:** 4)

Ingredients:
- 30 mussels, scrubbed
- 2 chorizo links, sliced
- 1 yellow onion; chopped.
- 15 small clams
- 10 oz. veggie stock
- 2 tbsp. parsley; chopped.
- 1 tsp. olive oil
- Lemon wedges for serving

Directions:
1. Set your instant pot on Sauté mode; add oil, heat it up, add onion and chorizo, stir and cook for 3 minutes
2. Add clams, mussels and stock; then stir well. close the lid, cook on High for 10 minutes, add parsley; then stir well. divide into bowls and serve as an appetizer with lemon wedges on the side.

Prosciutto and Asparagus Appetizer

(**Prep + Cooking Time:** 10 minutes | **Servings:** 4)

Ingredients:
- 8 asparagus spears
- 8 oz. prosciutto slices
- 2 cups water
- A pinch of salt

Directions:
1. Wrap asparagus spears in prosciutto slices and place them on a cutting board.
2. Add the water to your instant pot, add a pinch of salt, add steamer basket, place asparagus inside, seal the instant pot lid and cook on High for 4 minutes
3. Arrange asparagus on a platter and serve as an appetizer.

Chili Balls

(**Prep + Cooking Time:** 15 minutes | **Servings:** 3)

Ingredients:
- 3 bacon slices
- 1 cup water
- 3 oz. cream cheese
- 1/4 tsp. onion powder
- 2 jalapeno peppers; chopped.
- 1/2 tsp. parsley; dried
- 1/4 tsp. garlic powder
- Salt and black pepper to the taste

Directions:
1. Set your instant pot on sauté mode; add bacon, cook for a couple of minutes, transfer to paper towels drain grease and crumble it.
2. In a bowl, mix cream cheese with jalapenos, bacon, onion, garlic powder, parsley, salt and pepper, stir well and shape balls out of this mix
3. Clean the pot, add the water, and the steamer basket, add spicy balls inside, seal the instant pot lid and cook on High for 2 minutes.
4. Arrange balls on a platter and serve as an appetizer.

Zucchini Dip Recipe

(**Prep + Cooking Time:** 20 minutes | **Servings:** 4)

Ingredients:
- 2 lb. zucchini; chopped.
- 1 yellow onion; chopped
- 1 tbsp. olive oil
- 2 garlic cloves; minced.
- 1/2 cup water
- 1 bunch basil; chopped.
- Salt and white pepper to the taste

Directions:
1. Set your instant pot on Sauté mode; add oil, heat it up, add onion, stir and sauté for 3 minutes
2. Add zucchini, salt, pepper and water; then stir well. seal the instant pot lid and cook on High for 3 minutes.
3. Add garlic and basil, blend everything using an immersion blender, set the pot on simmer mode and cook your dip for a few more minutes until it thickens.
4. Transfer to a bowl and serve as a tasty snack.

Artichokes

(Prep + Cooking Time: 25 minutes | **Servings:** 4)

Ingredients:
- 4 big artichokes, trimmed
- 2 cups water
- 2 tsp. balsamic vinegar
- Salt and black pepper to the taste
- 2 tbsp. lemon juice
- 1/4 cup olive oil
- 2 garlic cloves; minced.
- 1 tsp. oregano; dried

Directions:
1. Add the water to your instant pot, add the steamer basket, add artichokes inside, seal the instant pot lid and cook on High for 8 minutes.
2. In a bowl, mix lemon juice with vinegar, oil, salt, pepper, garlic and oregano and stir very well.
3. Cut artichokes in halves, add them to lemon and vinegar mix, toss well, place them on preheated grill over medium high heat, cook for 3 minutes on each side, arrange them on a platter and serve as an appetizer.

Tasty Okra Bowls

(Prep + Cooking Time: 25 minutes | **Servings:** 6)

Ingredients:
- 28 oz. canned tomatoes; chopped.
- 1 lb. okra, trimmed
- 6 scallions; chopped.
- 3 green bell peppers; chopped.
- 2 tbsp. olive oil
- 1 tsp. stevia
- Salt and black pepper to the taste

Directions:
1. Set your instant pot on Sauté mode; add oil, heat it up, add scallions and bell peppers, stir and cook for 5 minutes
2. Add okra, salt, pepper, stevia and tomatoes; then stir well. close the lid, cook on High for 10 minutes, divide into small bowls and serve as an appetizer salad.

Squash and Beets Dip

(Prep + Cooking Time: 30 minutes | **Servings:** 8)

Ingredients:
- 4 beets; peeled and chopped.
- 1 butternut squash; peeled and chopped.
- 1 yellow onion; chopped.
- 1 bunch basil; chopped.
- 2 bay leaves
- 8 carrots; chopped.
- 2 tbsp. olive oil
- 5 celery ribs
- 8 garlic cloves; minced.
- 1 cup veggie stock
- 1/4 cup lemon juice
- Salt and black pepper to the taste

Directions:
1. Set your instant pot on Sauté mode; add oil, heat it up, add celery, carrots and onions, stir and cook for 3 minutes.
2. Add beets, squash, garlic, stock, lemon juice, basil, bay leaves, salt and pepper; then stir well. seal the instant pot lid and cook on High for 12 minutes
3. Discard bay leaves, blend dip using an immersion blender, transfer to a bowl and serve as a snack

Delicious Shrimp Appetizer

(Prep + Cooking Time: 30 minutes | Servings: 16)

Ingredients:
- 10 oz. shrimp, cooked, peeled and deveined
- 11 prosciutto slices
- 1/3 cup blackberries, ground.
- 1/3 cup veggie stock.
- 2 tbsp. olive oil
- 1 tbsp. mint; chopped.
- 2 tbsp. erythritol

Directions:
1. Wrap each shrimp in prosciutto slices and drizzle oil over them
2. In your instant pot, mix blackberries with mint, stock and erythritol; then stir well. set on simmer mode and cook for 2 minutes
3. Add steamer basket, and wrapped shrimp, close the lid and cook on High for 2 minutes
4. Arrange wrapped shrimp on a platter, drizzle mint sauce all over and serve.

Beet Hummus

(Prep + Cooking Time: 25 minutes | Servings: 5)

Ingredients:
- 2 beets, leafy greens (if attached) and roots trimmed
- ½-inch piece fresh ginger, peeled
- 1 (15-ounce) can chickpeas, drained, liquid reserved
- 1 cup water
- Juice of 1 lemon
- 1/2 tsp. garlic powder
- 2 tsp. tahini
- 1 tsp. salt or as your liking
- Zest of 1 lemon

Directions:
1. Scrub the beets under cold running water. The skin will be thick and bumpy in parts; just make sure all the dirt is gone. In the Instant Pot, combine the beets and water
2. Lock the lid and turn the steam release handle to Sealing. Using the Manual function, set the cooker to High Pressure for 20 minutes
3. After completing the cooking time, quick release the pressure.
4. Remove the lid carefully. Using tongs, remove the beets and run them under cold water, rubbing vigorously to remove the skins
5. Quarter 1 ½ of the beets and add them to a food processor along with the chickpeas, lemon juice, ginger, tahini, salt and garlic powder. Blend until completely smooth, adding the reserved chickpea liquid, as needed, to get a smooth, creamy texture. Transfer to a serving bowl
6. Dice the remaining ½ beet and sprinkle it over the hummus, followed by the lemon zest.

Stuffed Clams

(Prep + Cooking Time: 14 minutes | Servings: 4)

Ingredients:
- 24 clams, shucked
- 1/4 cup parsley; chopped.
- 1/4 cup parmesan cheese, grated
- 2 cups water
- 3 garlic cloves; minced.
- 1 tsp. oregano; dried
- 1 cup almonds, crushed.
- 4 tbsp. ghee
- Lemon wedges

Directions:
1. In a bowl, mix crushed almonds with parmesan, oregano, parsley, butter and garlic, stir and divide this into exposed clams.
2. Add the water to your instant pot, add steamer basket, add clams inside, seal the instant pot lid and cook on High for 4 minutes

3. Arrange clams on a platter and serve them as an appetizer with lemon wedges on the side.

Creamy Corn

(Prep + Cooking Time: 25 minutes | **Servings:** 5)

Ingredients:
- 20 ounces frozen sweet corn
- 1 cup raw cashews, soaked in water overnight, drained and rinsed well
- 3/4 cup nondairy milk
- 1 cup Vegetable Stock
- 1 tbsp. vegan butter
- 2 tbsp. freshly squeezed lemon juice
- 1 tbsp. sugar
- 1/2 tsp. vegetable oil
- 1/4 tsp. smoked paprika
- 1 tsp. salt or as your liking
- Freshly ground black pepper

Directions:
1. In a blender or food processor, combine the cashews, stock, lemon juice, sugar, salt and oil
2. Blend until smooth. Pour the cashew mixture into the Instant Pot. Add the corn, milk, butter and paprika. Season to taste with salt and pepper.
3. Select Slow Cooker mode and set the cook time for 20 minutes. Cover the cooker with a tempered glass lid
4. After completing the cooking time, carefully remove the lid and stir the creamed corn.
5. If there's too much liquid, select Sauté Normal and cook for 1 to 2 minutes to reduce it be careful of spatter.

Stuffed Mushrooms and Shrimp

(Prep + Cooking Time: 25 minutes | **Servings:** 5)

Ingredients:
- 24 oz. white mushroom caps
- 1 tsp. curry powder
- 4 oz. cream cheese, soft
- 1 cup shrimp, cooked, peeled, deveined and chopped.
- 1/4 cup mayo
- 1 tsp. garlic powder
- 1 small yellow onion; chopped.
- 1/4 cup coconut cream
- 1/2 cup Mexican cheese, shredded.
- 1 ½ cups water
- Salt and black pepper to the taste

Directions:
1. In a bowl, mix mayo with garlic powder, onion, curry powder, cream cheese, cream, Mexican cheese, shrimp, salt and pepper, stir and stuff mushrooms with this mix.
2. Add the water to your instant pot, add steamer basket, add mushrooms inside, close the lid and cook on High for 14 minutes
3. Arrange mushrooms on a platter and serve as an appetizer

Instant Cod Puddings

(Prep + Cooking Time: 30 minutes | **Servings:** 4)

Ingredients:
- 1 lb. cod fillets, skinless, boneless cut into medium pieces
- 2 tbsp. parsley; chopped.
- 4 oz. coconut flour
- 2 tsp. lemon juice
- 2 eggs, whisked
- 2 oz. ghee, melted
- 1/2-pint coconut milk, hot
- 1/2-pint shrimp sauce
- 1/2-pint water
- Salt and black pepper to the taste

Directions:
1. In a bowl, mix fish with flour, lemon juice, shrimp sauce, parsley, eggs, salt and pepper and stir.
2. Add milk and melted ghee, stir well and leave aside for a couple of minutes
3. Divide this mix greased ramekins.

4. Add the water to your instant pot, add the steamer basket, add puddings inside, seal the instant pot lid and cook on High for 15 minutes.
5. Serve the warm.

Artichoke Dip Recipe

(Prep + Cooking Time: 15 minutes | **Servings:** 6)

Ingredients:
- 14 oz. canned artichoke hearts
- 16 oz. parmesan cheese, grated
- 10 oz. spinach, torn
- 1 tsp. onion powder
- 8 oz. cream cheese
- 8 oz. mozzarella cheese, shredded.
- 1/2 cup chicken stock
- 1/2 cup coconut cream
- 1/2 cup mayonnaise
- 3 garlic cloves; minced.

Directions:
1. In your instant pot, mix artichokes with stock, garlic, spinach, cream cheese, coconut cream, onion powder and mayo; then stir well. seal the instant pot lid and cook on High for 5 minutes.
2. Add mozzarella and parmesan, stir well, transfer to a bowl and serve as a snack

Baby Carrots

(Prep + Cooking Time: 5 minutes | **Servings:** 5)

Ingredients:
- 1 (1-pound) bag baby carrots
- 1 cup water
- 3 tbsp. packed light brown sugar
- 3 tbsp. vegan butter
- 1 tsp. salt or as your liking

Directions:
1. Put the carrots in a steamer basket and place the basket into the Instant Pot. Pour in the water.
2. Lock the lid and turn the steam release handle to Sealing. Using the Manual function, set the cooker to High Pressure for 2 minutes
3. After completing the cooking time, quick release the pressure. Remove the lid carefully and add the butter, letting it melt into the carrots for 1 minute or so
4. Add the brown sugar and salt. Stir, stir, stir until the carrots are coated. Taste and add a touch more salt, if you'd like.

Roasted Garlic

(Prep + Cooking Time: 26 minutes | **Servings:** 4)

Ingredients:
- 4 large heads garlic, tops cut off to expose just the top of each clove
- 1 cup water
- Olive oil
- Crusty bread; for serving

Directions:
1. Add the water and a trivet to the Instant Pot. Place the garlic on the trivet, cut-side up.
2. Lock the lid and turn the steam release handle to Sealing. Using the Manual function, set the cooker to High Pressure for 6 minutes
3. After completing the cooking time, turn off the cooker and let the pressure release naturally until the pin drops, about 10 minutes
4. Remove the lid carefully. Using tongs, transfer the garlic to a baking sheet or other heatproof dish.
5. Generously drizzle with olive oil, making sure all the garlic gets oiled! Broil on low for about 5 minutes.
6. Watch so it doesn't burn, but you want it to be golden and caramelized. Remove from the oven and let cool for at least 10 minutes
7. Serve immediately, plated in the skins as is (that's how it's done in restaurants). Your guests can use their butter knives to scoop out the cloves for schmearing.

Simple Baked Potatoes

(**Prep + Cooking Time:** 35 minutes | **Servings:** 4)

Ingredients:
- 4 medium russet potatoes, scrubbed well, pierced on all sides with a fork
- 1 cup water
- Toppings, as desired

Directions:
1. Add the water and a trivet to the Instant Pot. Place the potatoes on the trivet.
2. Lock the lid and turn the steam release handle to Sealing. Using the Manual function, set the cooker to High Pressure for 15 minutes
3. After completing the cooking time, let the Instant Pot go into Keep Warm mode and let the pressure release naturally for 15 minutes; quick release any remaining pressure. Add toppings and ta-da!

Spicy Salsa

(**Prep + Cooking Time:** 13 minutes | **Servings:** 4)

Ingredients:
- 2 avocados, pitted; peeled and chopped.
- 1 red onion; chopped.
- 2 tbsp. lime juice
- 2 tbsp. cumin powder
- 1/2 tomato; chopped.
- 3 jalapeno pepper; chopped.
- Salt and black pepper to the taste

Directions:
1. In your instant pot, mix onion with avocados, peppers, salt, black pepper, cumin, lime juice and tomato; then stir well. seal the instant pot lid and cook on Low for 3 minutes
2. Divide into bowls and serve.

Pumpkin and Cinnamon Muffins

(**Prep + Cooking Time:** 30 minutes | **Servings:** 18)

Ingredients:
- 3/4 cup pumpkin puree
- 1/4 cup coconut flour
- 1/2 cup erythritol
- 1/2 tsp. nutmeg, ground.
- 4 tbsp. ghee
- 2 tbsp. flaxseed meal
- 1/2 tsp. baking powder
- 1/2 tsp. baking soda
- 1 ½ cups water
- one egg
- 1 tsp. cinnamon powder

Directions:
1. In a bowl, mix ghee with pumpkin puree, egg, flaxseed meal, coconut flour, erythritol, baking soda, baking powder, nutmeg and cinnamon, stir well and divide into a greased muffin pan.
2. Add the water to your instant pot, add the steamer basket, add muffin pan inside, close the lid and cook on High for 20 minutes.
3. Arrange muffins on a platter and serve as a snack.

Mushrooms and Mustard Dip

(**Prep + Cooking Time:** 20 minutes | **Servings:** 4)

Ingredients:
- 6 oz. mushrooms; chopped.
- 3 tbsp. olive oil
- 1 thyme sprigs
- 1 garlic clove; minced.
- 4 oz. beef stock
- 1 tbsp. mustard
- 2 tbsp. coconut cream
- 2 tbsp. parsley; finely chopped
- 1 tbsp. balsamic vinegar

Directions:
1. Set your instant pot on Sauté mode; add oil, heat it up, add thyme, mushrooms and garlic, stir and sauté for 4 minutes.
2. Add vinegar and stock; then stir well. close the lid, cook on High for 3 minutes, discard thyme, add mustard, coconut cream and parsley; then stir well. set the pot on simmer mode and cook for 3 minutes more.
3. Divide into bowls and serve as a snack.

Mussels Bowls

(Prep + Cooking Time: 12 minutes | **Servings:** 4)

Ingredients:
- 2 lb. mussels, scrubbed
- 12 oz. veggie stock
- 1 tbsp. olive oil
- 8 oz. spicy sausage; chopped.
- 1 tbsp. sweet paprika
- 1 yellow onion; chopped.

Directions:
1. Set your instant pot on Sauté mode; add oil, heat it up, add onion and sausages, stir and cook for 5 minutes
2. Add stock, paprika and mussels; then stir well. close the lid, cook on Low for 2 minutes, divide into bowls and serve as an appetizer.

Hard Boiled Eggs

(Prep + Cooking Time: 27 minutes | **Servings:**6)

Ingredients:
- 6 eggs
- 1 cup water

Directions:
1. Place the trivet in the inner pot, then pour in the water. Arrange the eggs on the trivet
2. Now, Lock the lid. Select, "Manual or Pressure Cook" and set the pressure to *High* and the time to 7 minutes. Make sure the steam release knob is in the sealed position.
3. After completing the cooking cycle, naturally release the pressure for 5 minutes, then quick release any remaining pressure.
4. Unlock and remove the lid. Using tongs or a serving spoon, transfer the eggs to a bowl and run them under cool tap water to stop the cooking process. Peel the eggs and enjoy

Simple Baked Potatoes

(Prep + Cooking Time: 35 minutes | **Servings:** 4)

Ingredients:
- 4 medium russet potatoes, scrubbed well, pierced on all sides with a fork
- 1 cup water
- Toppings, as desired

Directions:
4. Add the water and a trivet to the Instant Pot. Place the potatoes on the trivet
5. Lock the lid and turn the steam release handle to Sealing. Using the Manual function, set the cooker to High Pressure for 15 minutes.
6. After completing the cooking time, let the Instant Pot go into Keep Warm mode and let the pressure release naturally for 15 minutes; quick release any remaining pressure. Add toppings.

Surprising Oysters

(Prep + Cooking Time: 16 minutes | **Servings:** 3)

Ingredients:
- 6 big oysters, shucked
- 2 tbsp. melted ghee
- 1 ½ cups water
- 1 lemon cut into wedges
- 1 tbsp. parsley
- 3 garlic cloves; minced.
- A pinch of sweet paprika

Directions:
1. Divide ghee, parsley, paprika and garlic in each oyster
2. Add the water to your instant pot, add steamer basket, add oysters, close the lid and cook on High for 6 minutes
3. Arrange oysters on a platter and serve with lemon wedges on the side.

Easy Mango Dip

(Prep + Cooking Time: 23 minutes | **Servings:** 4)

Ingredients:
- 2 mangos; peeled and chopped.
- 1 shallot; chopped.
- 1 ¼ apple cider vinegar
- 1/2 tsp. cinnamon powder
- 2 red hot chilies; chopped.
- 1 tbsp. coconut oil
- 1/4 tsp. cardamom powder
- 2 tbsp. ginger; minced.
- 1/4 cup raisins
- 5 tbsp. stevia
- 1 apple, cored and chopped.

Directions:
1. Set your instant pot on Sauté mode; add oil, heat it up, add shallot and ginger, stir and cook for 3 minutes.
2. Add cinnamon, hot peppers, cardamom, mangos, apple, raisins, stevia and cider; then stir well. seal the instant pot lid and cook on High for 7 minutes.
3. Set the pot on simmer mode, cook your dip for 6 minutes more, transfer to bowls and serve cold as a snack

Crab and Cheese Dip

(Prep + Cooking Time: 30 minutes | **Servings:** 8)

Ingredients:
- 8 bacon strips, sliced
- 8 oz. cream cheese
- 12 oz. crab meat
- 4 garlic cloves; minced.
- 4 green onions; minced.
- 1 cup parmesan cheese, grated
- 2 poblano pepper; chopped.
- 2 tbsp. lemon juice
- 1/2 cup mayonnaise
- 1/2 cup coconut cream
- Salt and black pepper to the taste

Directions:
1. Set your instant pot on sauté mode; add bacon, cook until it's crispy, transfer to paper towels, drain grease and leave aside.
2. In a bowl, mix coconut cream with cream cheese, mayo, half of the parmesan, poblano peppers, garlic, lemon juice, green onions, salt, pepper, crab meat and bacon and stir really well.
3. Clean your instant pot, add crab mix, spread the rest of the parmesan on top, seal the instant pot lid and cook on High for 14 minutes
4. Divide into bowls and serve as a snack

Avocado Dip Recipe

(**Prep + Cooking Time:** 12 minutes | **Servings:** 4)

Ingredients:
- 1/4 cup erythritol powder
- 2 avocados, pitted, peeled and halved
- Juice from 2 limes
- 1/4 tsp. stevia
- 1 cup coconut milk
- 1 cup water
- 1/2 cup cilantro; chopped
- Zest of 2 limes, grated

Directions:
1. Add the water to your instant pot, add the steamer basket, add avocado halves, seal the instant pot lid and cook on High for 2 minutes.
2. Transfer to your blender, add lime juice and cilantro and pulse well
3. Add coconut milk, lime zest, stevia and erythritol powder, pulse again, divide into bowls and serve

Sweet Potatoes

(**Prep + Cooking Time:** 40 minutes | **Servings:**6)

Ingredients:
- 6 medium sweet potatoes
- 1 cup water

Directions:
1. Place a trivet or steaming rack inside the inner pot, then pour in the water. Arrange the sweet potatoes on the rack
2. Now, Lock the lid. Select, "Manual or Pressure Cook" and set the pressure to *High* and the time to 15 minutes. Make sure the steam release knob is in the sealed position.
3. After completing the cooking cycle, naturally release the pressure for 10 minutes, then quick release any remaining pressure.
4. Unlock and remove the lid. Serve the sweet potatoes immediately

Italian Mussels Appetizer

(**Prep + Cooking Time:** 20 minutes | **Servings:** 4)

Ingredients:
- 28 oz. canned tomatoes; chopped.
- 2 jalapeno peppers; chopped
- 1/2 cup white onion; chopped.
- 1/2 cup basil; chopped.
- 1/4 cup balsamic vinegar
- 1/4 cup veggie stock
- 1/4 cup olive oil
- 2 lb. mussels, scrubbed
- 2 tbsp. red pepper flakes, crushed.
- 2 garlic cloves; minced.
- Salt to the taste

Directions:
1. Set your instant pot on Sauté mode; add oil heat it up, add tomatoes, onion, jalapenos, stock, vinegar, garlic and pepper flakes, stir and cook for 5 minutes
2. Add mussels; then stir well. close the lid, cook on Low for 4 minutes, add salt and basil; then stir well. divide everything into small bowls and serve as an appetizer.

Mushroom Dip

(Prep + Cooking Time: 45 minutes | **Servings:** 6)

Ingredients:
- 10 oz. shiitake mushrooms; chopped.
- 10 oz. Portobello mushrooms; chopped.
- 10 oz. cremini mushrooms; chopped.
- 1 tbsp. thyme; chopped
- 1/2 cup coconut cream
- 1 yellow onion; chopped.
- 1/4 cup olive oil
- 1 tbsp. coconut flour
- 1 oz. parmesan cheese, grated
- 1 tbsp. parsley; chopped.
- 3 garlic cloves; minced.
- 1 ¼ cup chicken stock
- Salt and black pepper to the taste

Directions:
1. Set your instant pot on Sauté mode; add oil, heat it up, add onion, salt, pepper, flour, garlic and thyme, stir well and cook for 5 minutes.
2. Add stock, shiitake, cremini and Portobello mushrooms; then stir well. seal the instant pot lid and cook on High for 25 minutes.
3. Add cream, cheese and parsley; then stir well. set the pot on Simmer mode, cook dip for 5 minutes more, transfer to bowls and serve as a dip

Eggplant Spread

(Prep + Cooking Time: 20 minutes | **Servings:** 6)

Ingredients:
- 2 lb. eggplant, peeled and cut into medium chunks
- 3 olives, pitted and sliced
- 1/4 cup olive oil
- 4 garlic cloves; minced.
- 1/2 cup water
- 1/4 cup lemon juice
- 1 bunch thyme; chopped.
- 1 tbsp. sesame seed paste
- Salt and black pepper to the taste

Directions:
1. Set your instant pot on sauté mode; add oil, heat it up, add eggplant pieces, stir and cook for 5 minutes
2. Add garlic, water, salt and pepper; then stir well. close the lid, cook on High for 3 minutes, transfer to a blender, add sesame seed paste, lemon juice and thyme, stir and pulse really well.
3. Transfer to bowls, sprinkle olive slices on top and serve as an appetizer

English Chicken Wings

(Prep + Cooking Time: 27 minutes | **Servings:** 6)

Ingredients:
- 6 lb. chicken wings, cut into halves
- one egg
- 1/2 cup parmesan cheese, grated
- 1/2 tsp. Italian seasoning
- 1 tsp. garlic powder
- 2 tbsp. ghee
- 2 cups water
- Salt and black pepper to the taste
- A pinch of red pepper flakes, crushed.

Directions:
1. Pour the water in your instant pot, add the trivet, add chicken wings, seal the instant pot lid and cook on High for 7 minutes.
2. Meanwhile, in your blender, mix ghee with cheese, egg, salt, pepper, pepper flakes, garlic powder and Italian seasoning and blend very well.
3. Arrange chicken wings on a lined baking sheet, pour cheese sauce over them, introduce in preheated broiler and broil for 5 minutes.
4. Flip and broil for 5 minutes more, arrange them all on a platter and serve.

Lentils

(**Prep + Cooking Time:** 45 minutes | **Servings:**8)

Ingredients:
- 2 cups dried brown or green lentils, picked through and rinsed
- 4 cups water

Directions:
1. Combine the lentils and water in the inner pot
2. Now, Lock the lid. Select, "Manual or Pressure Cook" and set the pressure to *High* and the time to 20 minutes. Make sure the steam release knob is in the sealed position.
3. After completing the cooking cycle, naturally release the pressure for 10 minutes, then quick release any remaining pressure. Unlock and remove the lid. Stir the lentils. Serve hot

Perfect Beets

(**Prep + Cooking Time:** 25 minutes | **Servings:** 5)

Ingredients:
- 6 beets, roughly 6 inches in circumference, roots trimmed
- 1 cup water

Directions:
1. Scrub the beets under cold running water. The skin will be thick and bumpy in parts; just make sure all the dirt is gone.
2. Add the water to your Instant Pot and place a steamer basket inside. Place the beets in the basket in a single layer
3. Seal and lock the lid and turn the steam release handle to Sealing. Using the Manual function, set the cooker to High Pressure for 20 minutes
4. After completing the cooking time, quick release the pressure.
5. Remove the lid carefully. Using tongs, remove the beets
6. I don't peel mine, but if you want to, simply place them in a colander and rub the skins while running them under cold water. Cut them into quarters and season as desired.

Note: If you are cooking larger beets, the rule is 2 to 3 minutes more at High Pressure for every ½-inch increase in circumference.

Perfect Beets

(**Prep + Cooking Time:** 25 minutes | Serves: 5)

Ingredients:
- 6 beets, roughly 6 inches in circumference, roots trimmed
- 1 cup water

Directions:
1. Scrub the beets under cold running water. The skin will be thick and bumpy in parts; just make sure all the dirt is gone
2. Add the water to your Instant Pot and place a steamer basket inside. Place the beets in the basket in a single layer.
3. Seal and lock the lid and turn the steam release handle to Sealing. Using the Manual function, set the cooker to High Pressure for 20 minutes
4. After completing the cooking time, quick release the pressure.
5. Remove the lid carefully. Using tongs, remove the beets
6. I don't peel mine, but if you want to, simply place them in a colander and rub the skins while running them under cold water. Cut them into quarters and season as desired

Note: If you are cooking larger beets, the rule is 2 to 3 minutes more at High Pressure for every ½-inch increase in circumference.

Baby Carrots

(Prep + Cooking Time: 5 minutes | **Servings:** 5)

Ingredients:
- 1 (1-pound) bag baby carrots
- 1 cup water
- 3 tbsp. packed light brown sugar
- 3 tbsp. vegan butter
- 1 tsp. salt or as your liking

Directions:
1. Put the carrots in a steamer basket and place the basket into the Instant Pot. Pour in the water
2. Lock the lid and turn the steam release handle to Sealing. Using the Manual function, set the cooker to High Pressure for 2 minutes
3. After completing the cooking time, quick release the pressure. Remove the lid carefully and add the butter, letting it melt into the carrots for 1 minute or so.
4. Add the brown sugar and salt. Stir, stir, stir until the carrots are coated. Taste and add a touch more salt, if you'd like

Italian Dip

(Prep + Cooking Time: 30 minutes | **Servings:** 4)

Ingredients:
- 4 oz. cream cheese, soft
- 4 black olives, pitted and chopped.
- 2 cups water
- 1/2 cup mozzarella cheese
- 1/4 cup coconut cream
- 1/4 cup mayonnaise
- 1/4 cup parmesan cheese, grated
- 1/2 cup tomato sauce
- 1 tbsp. green bell pepper; chopped.
- 6 pepperoni slices; chopped.
- 1/2 tsp. Italian seasoning
- Salt and black pepper to the taste

Directions:
1. In a bowl, mix cream cheese with mozzarella, coconut cream, mayo, salt and pepper, stir and divide this into 4 ramekins
2. Layer tomato sauce, parmesan cheese, bell pepper, pepperoni, Italian seasoning and black olives on top,
3. Add the water to your instant pot, add the steamer basket, add ramekins inside, seal the instant pot lid and cook on High for 20 minutes.
4. Serve this dip warm with veggie sticks on the side

Sweet Potato Slaw

(Prep + Cooking Time: 24 minutes | **Makes:** 13 to 15 cups)

Ingredients:
- 3 scallions, green and light green parts, sliced
- 2 cups sliced green cabbage
- 1 cup shredded sweet potato
- 12 to 15 dumpling wrappers
- 1 cup water
- 1/2 sweet onion, sliced
- 1 ½ tbsp. freshly squeezed lime juice
- 1 tbsp. hoisin sauce
- 2 tbsp. lite soy sauce
- 1 ½ tsp. sesame oil
- 1/2 tsp. ground ginger, plus more to taste
- Zest of 1 lime
- Nonstick cooking spray; for preparing the muffin tin

Directions:
1. Preheat the oven to 350°F. Lightly coat a muffin tin with the nonstick spray. Place one wonton wrapper in each well of the prepared tin, pressing down to create a cup shape
2. Bake for 5 to 6 minutes; or until the cups are crispy and lightly browned. Set aside to cool.
3. Pour the water into your Instant Pot. Place the cabbage, sweet potato and onion into a steamer basket and put the basket on a trivet

4. Lock the lid in place. Select Steam and set the cook time for 2 minutes. Because the Steam function doesn't seal the Instant Pot, there's no need to turn the steam release handle to Sealing or release any pressure.
5. While the veggies steam, in a medium bowl, stir together the soy sauce, hoisin sauce, lime juice, oil, lime zest and ginger
6. After completing the cooking time, carefully remove the lid and stir in the veggies, making sure all are coated with the sauce. Taste and add more ginger, if desired.
7. When ready to serve, fill the cups with the slaw and sprinkle the tops with scallion. Enjoy warm or at room temperature

Lemon Broccoli

(**Prep + Cooking Time:** 5 minutes | **Servings:** 3)

Ingredients:
- 6 cups chopped broccoli
- 4 garlic cloves, roughly chopped
- 1 cup water
- Juice of 1 lemon
- Zest of 1 lemon
- 1/2 tsp. salt or more as your liking

Directions:
1. In the Instant Pot, combine the water and garlic. Place the broccoli in a steamer basket and put the basket into the inner pot
2. Pour the lemon juice over the broccoli so it runs down into the water.
3. Lock the lid and turn the steam release handle to Sealing. Using the Manual function, set the cooker to High Pressure for 0 minutes
4. After completing the cooking time, quick release the pressure.
5. Remove the lid carefully and remove the broccoli. Sprinkle the salt and lemon zest over the broccoli. Stir well

Beet Hummus

(**Prep + Cooking Time:** 25 minutes | **Servings:** 5)

Ingredients:
- 2 beets, leafy greens (if attached) and roots trimmed
- ½-inch piece fresh ginger, peeled
- 1 (15-ounce) can chickpeas, drained, liquid reserved
- 1 cup water
- Juice of 1 lemon
- 1/2 tsp. garlic powder
- 2 tsp. tahini
- 1 tsp. salt or as your liking
- Zest of 1 lemon

Directions:
1. Scrub the beets under cold running water. The skin will be thick and bumpy in parts; just make sure all the dirt is gone. In the Instant Pot, combine the beets and water
2. Lock the lid and turn the steam release handle to Sealing. Using the Manual function, set the cooker to High Pressure for 20 minutes.
3. After completing the cooking time, quick release the pressure
4. Remove the lid carefully. Using tongs, remove the beets and run them under cold water, rubbing vigorously to remove the skins.
5. Quarter 1 ½ of the beets and add them to a food processor along with the chickpeas, lemon juice, ginger, tahini, salt and garlic powder. Blend until completely smooth, adding the reserved chickpea liquid, as needed, to get a smooth, creamy texture. Transfer to a serving bowl.
6. Dice the remaining ½ beet and sprinkle it over the hummus, followed by the lemon zest

Ginger Lemon Asparagus

(Prep + Cooking Time: 5 minutes | **Servings:** 5)

Ingredients:
- 1 bunch asparagus, tough ends removed, halved if remaining pieces are longer than 4 inches
- 1 cup water
- 2 tbsp. olive oil
- 1 ½ tsp. to 1 tbsp. freshly squeezed lemon juice
- 1/2 tsp. grated peeled fresh ginger
- 1/2 tsp. salt or more as your liking

Directions:
1. Place the asparagus in a steamer basket and put the basket into the Instant Pot. Add the water
2. Lock the lid and turn the steam release handle to Sealing. Using the Manual function, set the cooker to Low Pressure for 0 minutes.
3. After completing the cooking time, quick release the pressure. In a serving bowl, stir together the oil, lemon juice, ½ tsp. of salt and ½ tsp. of ginger
4. Remove the lid carefully and add the asparagus to the bowl. Toss to combine. Taste and add the remaining lemon juice and/or ginger, as needed

Turkey Meatballs

(Prep + Cooking Time: 16 minutes | **Servings:** 16 p)

Ingredients:
- 1 lb. turkey meat, ground.
- one egg
- 1/2 tsp. garlic powder
- 1/2 cup mozzarella cheese, shredded.
- 2 tbsp. olive oil
- 1/4 cup tomato paste
- 2 tbsp. basil; chopped.
- 1/4 cup coconut flour
- 2 tbsp. sun-dried tomatoes; chopped
- Salt and black pepper to the taste

Directions:
1. In a bowl, mix turkey with salt, pepper, egg, flour, garlic powder, sun-dried tomatoes, mozzarella and basil, stir well and shape 12 meatballs out of this mix.
2. Set your instant pot on sauté mode; add oil, heat it up, add meatballs, stir and brown for 2 minutes on each side
3. Add tomato paste over them, toss a bit, seal the instant pot lid and cook on High for 8 minutes.
4. Arrange meatballs on a platter and serve them right away.

Creamy Corn

(Prep + Cooking Time: 25 minutes | **Servings:** 5)

Ingredients:
- 20 ounces frozen sweet corn
- 1 cup raw cashews, soaked in water overnight, drained and rinsed well
- 3/4 cup nondairy milk
- 1 cup Vegetable Stock
- 1 tbsp. vegan butter
- 2 tbsp. freshly squeezed lemon juice
- 1 tbsp. sugar
- 1/2 tsp. vegetable oil
- 1/4 tsp. smoked paprika
- 1 tsp. salt or as your liking
- Freshly ground black pepper

Directions:
1. In a blender or food processor, combine the cashews, stock, lemon juice, sugar, salt and oil.
2. Blend until smooth. Pour the cashew mixture into the Instant Pot. Add the corn, milk, butter and paprika. Season to taste with salt and pepper
3. Select Slow Cooker mode and set the cook time for 20 minutes. Cover the cooker with a tempered glass lid.
4. After completing the cooking time, carefully remove the lid and stir the creamed corn

5. If there's too much liquid, select Sauté Normal and cook for 1 to 2 minutes to reduce it be careful of spatter!

Sesame Noodle Bowls

(Prep + Cooking Time: 40 minutes | **Servings:** 4)

Ingredients:
- ½ head red cabbage, shredded (about 1 pound)
- 1 lb. fresh or frozen raw shrimp, peeled and deveined
- 4 oz. whole-wheat spaghetti, broken in half
- 1 clove garlic; minced.
- 4 cups water
- 1 cup shredded carrot (about 1 large carrot)
- ½ cup chopped green onions, tender white and green parts only (about 3 onions)
- 1 tbsp. sesame oil
- 1 tbsp. extra-virgin olive oil
- 1 tbsp. minced fresh ginger (about 1-inch knob)
- 2 tbsp. freshly squeezed lime juice
- 3 tbsp. soy sauce or tamari
- 2 tbsp. pure maple syrup
- Sesame seeds; for garnish.
- Sriracha (optional)

Directions:
1. Place the spaghetti in the Instant Pot, crisscrossing the noodles as you add them to prevent large clumps of pasta from sticking together
2. Pour the water over the noodles, making sure they are covered for even cooking. Now, Lock the lid and Turn the steam release valve to "Sealing" Position. Select *Manual/Pressure* Cook to cook on *High* pressure for 2 minutes.
3. While the noodles are cooking, in a large bowl, stir together the lime juice, 2 tablespoons of the soy sauce, the maple syrup, sesame oil, ginger and garlic. Add the cabbage, carrot and green onions and toss well to coat
4. Once the cooking cycle is completed, let the pressure naturally release for 10 minutes, then move the steam release valve to Venting to release any remaining pressure. Press *Cancel* Button to stop the cooking cycle.
5. When the floating valve drops, remove the lid and drain the pasta through a colander. Rinse the pasta with cold water to stop the cooking process
6. Dry the pot with a towel, then return the pot to the Instant Pot housing to cook the shrimp. Press *Sauté* and add the olive oil to the Instant Pot
7. Once the oil is hot but not smoking, add the shrimp and the remaining 1 tablespoon soy sauce and sauté until pink and tender, about 4 minutes. *If using frozen shrimp, you'll need to cook it for 2 to 3 minutes more.
8. Add the noodles and cooked shrimp to the bowl and toss well to coat. Taste and adjust the seasoning as needed; add a squeeze of Sriracha if you like spice. Serve with sesame seeds sprinkled over the top.

Roasted Garlic

(Prep + Cooking Time: 26 minutes | **Servings:** 4)

Ingredients:
- 4 large heads garlic, tops cut off to expose just the top of each clove
- 1 cup water
- Olive oil
- Crusty bread; for serving

Directions:
1. Add the water and a trivet to the Instant Pot. Place the garlic on the trivet, cut-side up
2. Lock the lid and turn the steam release handle to Sealing. Using the Manual function, set the cooker to High Pressure for 6 minutes.
3. After completing the cooking time, turn off the cooker and let the pressure release naturally until the pin drops, about 10 minutes

4. Remove the lid carefully. Using tongs, transfer the garlic to a baking sheet or other heatproof dish.
5. Generously drizzle with olive oil, making sure all the garlic gets oiled! Broil on low for about 5 minutes
6. Watch so it doesn't burn, but you want it to be golden and caramelized. Remove from the oven and let cool for at least 10 minutes.
7. Serve immediately, plated in the skins as is (that's how it's done in restaurants). Your guests can use their butter knives to scoop out the cloves for schmearing

Salmon Patties

(Prep + Cooking Time: 17 minutes | **Servings:** 4)

Ingredients:
- 1 lb. salmon meat; minced.
- 1 tsp. olive oil
- one egg, whisked
- 4 tbsp. coconut flour
- 2 tbsp. lemon zest, grated
- Salt and black pepper to the taste
- Arugula leaves for serving

Directions:
1. Put salmon in your food processor, blend it, transfer to a bowl, add salt, pepper, lemon zest, coconut and egg, stir well and shape small patties out of this mix
2. Set your instant pot on sauté mode; add oil, heat it up, add patties and cook them for 3 minutes on each side.
3. Arrange arugula on a platter, add salmon patties on top and serve as an appetizer.

Quinoa

(Prep + Cooking Time: 26 minutes | **Servings:**6)

Ingredients:
- 2 cups water
- 2 cups quinoa; rinsed.

Directions:
1. Combine the quinoa and water in the inner pot
2. Now, Lock the lid. Select, "Manual or Pressure Cook" and set the pressure to *High* and the time to 1 minute. Make sure the steam release knob is in the sealed position.
3. After completing the cooking cycle, naturally release the pressure for 10 minutes, then quick release any remaining pressure.
4. Unlock and remove the lid. Using a fork, fluff the quinoa. Serve the quinoa immediately

Zucchini Appetizer Salad Recipe

(Prep + Cooking Time: 16 minutes | **Servings:** 4)

Ingredients:
- 1 zucchini, roughly sliced
- 1/4 cup tomato sauce
- 1 cup mozzarella, shredded.
- A pinch of cumin, ground.
- A drizzle of olive oil
- Salt and black pepper to the taste

Directions:
1. In your instant pot, mix zucchini with oil, tomato sauce, salt, pepper and cumin, toss a bit, seal the instant pot lid and cook on High for 6 minutes.
2. Divide between appetizer plates and serve right away

Lemon Broccoli

(Prep + Cooking Time: 5 minutes | **Servings:** 3)

Ingredients:
- 6 cups chopped broccoli
- 4 garlic cloves, roughly chopped
- 1 cup water
- Juice of 1 lemon
- Zest of 1 lemon
- 1/2 tsp. salt or more as your liking

Directions:
1. In the Instant Pot, combine the water and garlic. Place the broccoli in a steamer basket and put the basket into the inner pot
2. Pour the lemon juice over the broccoli so it runs down into the water
3. Lock the lid and turn the steam release handle to Sealing. Using the Manual function, set the cooker to High Pressure for 0 minutes.
4. After completing the cooking time, quick release the pressure
5. Remove the lid carefully and remove the broccoli. Sprinkle the salt and lemon zest over the broccoli. Stir well.

Cheeseburger Salad with Sauce

(Prep + Cooking Time: 45 minutes | **Servings:** 6)

Ingredients:
Burger "Meat":
- 1 yellow onion; chopped.
- 1 cup green lentils
- 1¼ cups water
- ½ cup finely chopped raw walnuts
- 1 tbsp. extra-virgin olive oil
- ⅛ tsp. cayenne pepper
- ½ tsp. ground cumin
- 1 tsp. garlic powder
- 1 tsp. paprika
- ¼ tsp. freshly ground black pepper
- 1 tsp. fine sea salt

Special Sauce:
- ½ cup water
- ½ cup raw cashews, soaked for 1 hour
- 2 tbsp. tomato paste
- 2 tbsp. yellow mustard
- 1 tbsp. raw apple cider vinegar
- 2 tbsp. pure maple syrup
- ¾ tsp. fine sea salt
- ½ tsp. onion powder
- Chopped lettuce, tomatoes and green onions; pickle slices; and shredded Cheddar cheese; for serving

Directions:
1. To make the burger "meat," press Sauté and add the olive oil to the Instant Pot
2. Once the oil is hot but not smoking, add the onion and sauté until softened, about 5 minutes. Press *Cancel* Button to stop the cooking cycle.
3. Stir in the garlic powder, paprika, cayenne, cumin and black pepper while the pot is still hot. Add the green lentils and water and stir to make sure the lentils are covered in the liquid for even cooking
4. Now, Lock the lid and Turn the steam release valve to "Sealing" Position. Select *Manual/Pressure* Cook to cook on *High* pressure for 5 minutes.
5. While the lentils are cooking, make the special sauce. Drain and rinse the cashews, then add them to a blender with the water, vinegar, maple syrup, tomato paste, mustard, onion powder and salt. Blend until very smooth and set aside
6. When the cooking cycle on the burger "meat" is complete, let the pressure naturally release for 10 minutes, then move the steam release valve to Venting to release any remaining pressure
7. When the floating valve drops, remove the lid and stir in the salt and chopped walnuts.
8. Fill a bowl with chopped lettuce, the burger "meat," tomatoes, green onions, pickles and cheese. Drizzle plenty of special sauce over the top before serving

Appetizing Cranberry Dip

(Prep + Cooking Time: 15 minutes | **Servings:** 4)

Ingredients:
- 3 tbsp. lemon juice
- 12 oz. cranberries
- 2 ½ tsp. lemon zest, grated
- 4 tbsp. stevia

Directions:
1. In your instant pot, mix lemon juice with stevia, lemon zest and cranberries; then stir well. seal the instant pot lid and cook on High for 2 minutes.
2. Set the pot on simmer mode, stir your dip for a couple more minutes, transfer to a bowl and serve with some biscuits as a snack

Gold Potatoes

(Prep + Cooking Time: 40 minutes | **Servings:**6)

Ingredients:
- 2 lbs. Yukon Gold potatoes
- 1 cup water

Directions:
1. Place the trivet in the inner pot, then pour in the water. Place the potatoes on the trivet
2. Now, Lock the lid. Select, "Manual or Pressure Cook" and set the pressure to *High* and the time to 10 minutes. Make sure the steam release knob is in the sealed position.
3. After completing the cooking cycle, naturally release the pressure for 10 minutes, then quick release any remaining pressure.
4. Unlock and remove the lid. Using tongs, transfer the potatoes to a serving plate or bowl. Serve hot

Broccoli and Carrots

(Prep + Cooking Time: 22 minutes | **Servings:**6)

Ingredients:
- 1 lb. carrots, peeled and cut into 1-inch-long chunks
- 1 cup water
- 1 medium head broccoli; cut into florets (about 2 cups)

Directions:
1. Place the broccoli florets and carrots in a steamer basket
2. Pour the water into the inner pot, then set the steamer basket inside.
3. Now, Lock the lid. Select, "Manual or Pressure Cook" and set the pressure to *High* and the time to 2 minutes. Make sure the steam knob is in the sealed position.
4. After completing the cooking cycle, quick release the pressure. Unlock and remove the lid. Serve hot

Eggroll Bowl

(Prep + Cooking Time: 26 minutes | **Servings:** 4)

Ingredients:
- 1 lb. ground turkey
- ⅓ cup soy sauce or tamari
- 1 small head cabbage, shredded (about 1½ pounds)
- 1 red onion; chopped.
- 3 carrots, peeled and shredded
- 3 celery stalks; chopped.
- 1 tbsp. extra-virgin olive oil
- 1 tsp. toasted sesame oil
- ½ tsp. fine sea salt
- Freshly ground black pepper
- Sesame seeds and chopped green onions, tender white and green parts only; for garnish.

Directions:
1. Press *Sauté* and add the olive oil, onion, turkey and salt to the Instant Pot. Sauté until the turkey is browned and cooked through, breaking it up with a wooden spoon as you stir, about 8 minutes. Press *Cancel* Button to stop the cooking cycle
2. Add the soy sauce, carrots and celery and stir. Add the cabbage on top without stirring. (The cabbage may nearly fill the pot, but it will reduce significantly in size while cooking.)
3. Now, Lock the lid and Turn the steam release valve to "Sealing" Position. Select *Manual/Pressure* Cook to cook on *High* pressure for 0 minutes (Sure set it to 0 minutes). Once the cooking cycle is completed, immediately move the steam release valve to Venting to quickly release the steam pressure (so you don't overcook the vegetables)
4. When the floating valve drops, remove the lid and stir together the vegetables and meat to make sure everything is coated in the soy sauce. Stir in the sesame oil and a few grinds of pepper to taste. Taste and adjust the seasonings as needed.
5. Use tongs to transfer the eggroll filling to bowls. Garnish with the sesame seeds and green onions and serve warm

Side Dishes

Flavored Mashed Sweet Potatoes

(Prep + Cooking Time: 20 minutes | **Servings:** 8)

Ingredients:
- 3 lb. sweet potatoes; peeled and chopped.
- 2 garlic cloves
- 1/4 cup milk
- 1/4 tsp. sage; dried
- 1/2 tsp. rosemary; dried
- 1/2 tsp. thyme dried
- 1/2 cup parmesan, grated
- 2 tbsp. butter
- Salt and black pepper to the taste
- 1/2 tsp. parsley; dried
- 1 ½ cups water

Directions:
1. Put potatoes and garlic in the steamer basket of your instant pot, add 1 ½ cups water in the pot, close the lid and cook at High for 10 minutes.
2. Quick release the pressure, drain water, transfer the potatoes and garlic to a bowl and mash them using your kitchen mixer
3. Add butter, parmesan, milk, salt, pepper, parsley, sage, rosemary and thyme and blend everything well.
4. Divide among plates and serve

Mushroom Risotto

(Prep + Cooking Time: 25 minutes | **Servings:** 4)

Ingredients:
- 2 cups risotto rice
- 4 cups chicken stock
- 4 oz. sherry vinegar
- 2 oz. extra virgin olive oil
- 1 yellow onion; chopped
- 8 oz. mushrooms, sliced
- 4 oz. heavy cream
- 2 tbsp. parmesan cheese, grated
- 1 oz. basil; finely chopped
- 2 garlic cloves, crushed.

Directions:
1. Set your instant pot on Sauté mode; add the oil and heat it up.
2. Add onions, garlic and mushrooms, stir and cook for 3 minutes
3. Add rice, stock and vinegar; then stir well. seal the instant pot lid and cook at High for 10 minutes.
4. Quick release the pressure, open the instant pot lid, add cream and parmesan and stir.
5. Divide among plates, sprinkle basil and serve.

Mashed Sweet Potatoes

(Prep + Cooking Time: 23 minutes | **Servings:** 4)

Ingredients:
- 2 lb. sweet potatoes, peeled and cut into 1-inch chunks
- ½ tsp. fine sea salt
- ½ tsp. minced fresh rosemary
- 1 tsp. minced fresh thyme
- Freshly ground black pepper
- 1 tbsp. extra-virgin olive oil (optional)

Directions:
1. Pour 1 cup water into the Instant Pot and arrange a steamer basket on the bottom. Place the sweet potatoes in the basket, making sure the potatoes don't touch the water
2. Now, Lock the lid and Turn the steam release valve to "Sealing" Position. Select *Manual/Pressure* Cook to cook on *High* pressure for 8 minutes.
3. Once the cooking cycle is completed, quickly release the pressure by moving the steam release valve to Venting

4. When the floating valve drops, remove the lid and Press *Cancel* Button to stop the cooking cycle. Use oven mitts to lift out the steam basket and pour the water out of the pot.
5. Pour the drained sweet potatoes back into the pot and use a potato masher to mash the potatoes. Add the thyme, rosemary, olive oil, salt and several grinds of pepper and stir well to combine. Taste and adjust the seasonings, then serve warm

Up Mashed Potatoes and Gravy

(**Prep + Cooking Time:** 38 minutes | **Servings:** 6)

Ingredients:
- 1 lb. cauliflower, cut into florets
- 2 lb. Yukon gold potatoes
- 4 oz. cremini mushrooms; chopped. (about 1 cup)
- 2 cloves garlic; minced.
- 1 yellow onion; chopped.
- 1 cup water
- 2 tbsp. chopped fresh chives
- 2 tbsp. soy sauce or tamari
- Fine sea salt and freshly ground black pepper
- Cut the potatoes into 1-inch chunks, reserving one cut-up potato for the gravy.

Directions:
1. Combine the onion, mushrooms, the reserved cut-up potato, the garlic, soy sauce, ¼ teaspoon salt, several grinds of black pepper and the water in the Instant Pot
2. Arrange a steamer basket on top of the mushroom mixture and place the cauliflower florets and the remaining potatoes into the basket.
3. Now, Lock the lid and Turn the steam release valve to "Sealing" Position. Select *Manual/Pressure* Cook to cook on *High* pressure for 10 minutes
4. Once the cooking cycle is completed, let the pressure naturally release for 10 minutes, then move the steam release valve to Venting to release any remaining pressure. When the floating valve drops, remove the lid.
5. Use oven mitts to remove the steamer basket and transfer the cauliflower and potatoes to a large bowl
6. Use a potato masher to mash them, then season generously with salt and pepper to taste. *Add a little more water if you want a thinner consistency. Stir in the chives
7. Use an immersion blender to blend the gravy directly in the bottom of the Instant Pot. Alternatively, you can pour the mixture into a blender and blend until smooth. Taste and adjust the seasonings. Serve the mash immediately

Millet Cornbread.

(**Prep + Cooking Time:** 46 minutes | **Servings:** 8)

Ingredients:
- ½ cup pumpkin puree
- 2 eggs, at room temperature
- ¼ cup coconut sugar
- ¼ cup melted coconut oil or butter
- ¾ cup millet flour
- ½ tsp. baking soda
- ½ tsp. fine sea salt

Directions:
1. In a mixing bowl, combine the millet flour, baking soda, salt and coconut sugar and whisk well. Add the pumpkin puree, eggs and melted coconut oil and whisk until a smooth batter forms
2. Grease a 7-inch round pan with olive oil and line the pan with parchment paper for easy removal after baking. Pour the batter into the pan and smooth the top with a spatula
3. Pour 1 cup water into the Instant Pot and arrange the trivet (Which comes with your instant pot) on the bottom.
4. Place the pan on top of the trivet and cover it with an upside-down plate or another piece of parchment to protect the bread from condensation
5. Now, Lock the lid and Turn the steam release valve to "Sealing" Position. Select *Manual/Pressure* Cook to cook at *High* pressure for 30 minutes.

6. Once the cooking cycle is completed, quickly release the pressure by moving the steam release valve to Venting
7. When the floating valve drops, remove the lid. Use oven mitts to lift the trivet and the pan out of the pot. Allow the "cornbread" to cool in the pan for 20 minutes before cutting and serving

Potatoes Side Dish

(Prep + Cooking Time: 16 minutes | **Servings:** 4)

Ingredients:
- 1 lb. new potatoes, peeled and thinly sliced
- 2 garlic cloves; minced.
- 1 cup water
- 1/4 tsp. rosemary; dried
- 1 tbsp. extra-virgin olive oil
- Salt and black pepper to the taste

Directions:
1. Put the potatoes and the water in the steamer basket of your instant pot, close the lid and cook at High for 4 minutes.
2. In a heat proof dish, mix rosemary with oil and garlic, cover and microwave for 1 minute
3. Quick release the pressure, drain potatoes and spread them on a lined baking sheet
4. Add heated oil mix, salt and pepper to the taste, toss to coat, divide among plates and serve as a side dish

Eggplant Dish

(Prep + Cooking Time: 25 minutes | **Servings:** 4)

Ingredients:
- 2 eggplants, cubed
- 1 bunch oregano; chopped
- 2 tbsp. extra virgin olive oil
- 1 garlic clove, crushed.
- 1/2 cup water
- 2 anchovies; chopped
- Salt and black pepper to the taste
- A pinch of hot pepper flakes

Directions:
1. Sprinkle eggplant pieces with salt, place them in a strainer, press them with a plate and then drain them.
2. Set your instant pot on Sauté mode; add the oil and the garlic and heat it up.
3. Add anchovies, oregano and pepper flakes, stir and cook for 5 minutes.
4. Discard the garlic, add eggplants, salt and pepper, toss to coat and cook for 5 minutes.
5. Add the water; then stir well. seal the instant pot lid and cook at High for 3 minutes
6. Quick release the pressure, transfer eggplant mix to plates and serve

Mushrooms & Green Beans Side Dish

(Prep + Cooking Time: 18 minutes | **Servings:** 4)

Ingredients:
- 1 lb. fresh green beans, trimmed
- 8 oz. mushrooms, sliced
- 1 small yellow onion; chopped
- 6 oz. bacon; chopped.
- 1 garlic clove; minced.
- A splash of balsamic vinegar
- Salt and black pepper to the taste

Directions:
1. Put the beans in your instant pot, add water to cover them, seal the instant pot lid and cook at High for 3 minutes
2. Release the pressure naturally, drain beans and leave them aside for now.
3. Set your instant pot on Sauté mode; add bacon and brown it for 1 or 2 minutes stirring often.
4. Add garlic and onion, stir and cook 2 more minutes
5. Add mushrooms, stir and cook until they are soft.
6. Add drained beans, salt, pepper and a splash of vinegar; then stir well. take off heat, divide among plates and serve

Poached Fennel Dish

(Prep + Cooking Time: 10 minutes | **Servings:** 3)

Ingredients:
- 2 big fennel bulbs, sliced
- 2 tbsp. butter
- 1 tbsp. white flour
- 2 cups milk
- A pinch of nutmeg, ground.
- Salt to the taste

Directions:
1. Set your instant pot on Sauté mode; add butter and melt it.
2. Add fennel slices, stir and cook until they brown a bit
3. Add flour, salt, pepper, nutmeg and milk; then stir well. close the lid and cook on Low for 6 minutes
4. Quick release the pressure, transfer fennel to plates and serve.

Artichokes Dish

(Prep + Cooking Time: 35 minutes | **Servings:** 4)

Ingredients:
- 2 medium artichokes, trimmed
- 1 cup water
- 1 lemon wedges
- Salt to the taste

Directions:
1. Rub artichokes with the lemon wedges, place them in the steamer basket of your instant pot, add the water in the pot, close the lid and cook at High for 20 minutes.
2. Release the pressure naturally for 10 minutes, then release remaining pressure by turning the valve to 'Venting', divide artichokes among plates add salt on top and serve them with a dipping sauce and with a steak on the side

Cauliflower Mash Dish

(Prep + Cooking Time: 15 minutes | **Servings:** 4)

Ingredients:
- 1 cauliflower, florets separated
- 1 tbsp. butter
- 1 ½ cups water
- 1/2 tsp. turmeric
- 3 chives; finely chopped
- Salt and black pepper to the taste

Directions:
1. Pour the water in your instant pot, place cauliflower in the steamer basket, seal the instant pot lid and cook at High for 6 minutes.
2. Release the pressure naturally for 2 minutes and then release the rest quick
3. Transfer cauliflower to a bowl and mash it with a potato masher.
4. Add salt, pepper, butter and turmeric; then stir well. transfer to a blender and pulse well.
5. Serve with chives sprinkled on top

Onions & Parsnips

(Prep + Cooking Time: 40 minutes | **Servings:** 4)

Ingredients:
- 1 yellow onion, thinly sliced.
- 1 ½ cups beef stock
- 2 ½ lb. parsnips; chopped.
- 1 thyme spring
- 4 tbsp. pastured lard
- Salt and black pepper to the taste

Directions:
1. Set your instant pot on Sauté mode; add 3 tablespoon lard and heat it up
2. Add parsnips, stir and cook for 15 minutes
3. Add stock and thyme; then stir well. close the lid and cook at High for 3 minutes

4. Quick release the pressure, transfer the parsnips mix to your blender, add salt and pepper to the taste and pulse very well.
5. Set the pot on Sauté mode again, add the rest of the lard and heat it up.
6. Add onion, stir and cook for 10 minutes
7. Transfer blended parsnips to plates, top with sautéed onions and serve.

Black Beans Dish

(Prep + Cooking Time: 15 minutes | **Servings:** 8)

Ingredients:
- 1 cup black beans, soaked overnight, drained and rinsed
- 2 garlic cloves; minced.
- 1 spring epazote
- 1/2 tsp. cumin seeds
- 1-piece kombu seaweed
- 2/3 cup water
- Salt to the taste

Directions:
1. In your instant pot, mix beans with kombu, water, garlic, epazote, and cumin.
2. Stir, seal the instant pot lid and cook at High for 5 minutes
3. Quick release the pressure, discard kombu and epazote, divide beans among plates, season with salt and serve.

Bulgur Pilaf

(Prep + Cooking Time: 38 minutes | **Servings:** 4)

Ingredients:
- ½ cup finely chopped walnuts
- ½ cup golden raisins
- ½ cup finely diced celery
- ¼ cup loosely packed chopped fresh mint
- ¼ cup loosely packed chopped fresh flat-leaf parsley
- 1 cup bulgur
- 1 clove garlic; minced.
- 1¼ cups water
- ½ red onion, diced
- ½ tsp. ground cumin
- ½ tsp. fine sea salt
- 1 tsp. minced fresh ginger (about ½-inch knob)
- ½ tsp. turmeric
- 2 tbsp. freshly squeezed lemon juice
- 1 tbsp. extra-virgin olive oil

Directions:
1. Press *Sauté* and add the olive oil to the Instant Pot. Once the oil is hot but not smoking, add the onion and sauté until softened, about 5 minutes
2. Add the garlic, ginger, turmeric and cumin and stir with a wooden spoon or spatula for 1 minute.
3. Press *Cancel* Button, then add the bulgur, water and salt. Stir well, scraping the bottom of the pot to make sure nothing sticks
4. Now, Lock the lid and Turn the steam release valve to "Sealing" Position. Select *Manual/Pressure* Cook to cook on *High* pressure for 1 minute.
5. Once the cooking cycle is completed, let the pressure naturally release for 15 minutes. Turn the steam release valve to Venting to release any remaining pressure
6. When the floating valve drops, remove the lid and fluff the bulgur with a fork. Stir in the celery, mint, parsley and lemon juice and serve warm topped with the walnuts and raisins

Green Beans

(**Prep + Cooking Time:** 12 minutes | **Servings:** 4)

Ingredients:
- 1 lb. green beans, trimmed and cut into 1-inch pieces
- 2 cloves garlic; minced.
- 1 tbsp. sesame seeds
- 1 tbsp. extra-virgin olive oil
- ¼ tsp. red pepper flakes
- 1½ tsp. toasted sesame oil
- Fine sea salt

Directions:
1. Pour 1 cup water into the Instant Pot and arrange a steamer basket on the bottom. Add the green beans to the basket, making sure the beans don't touch the water
2. Now, Lock the lid and Turn the steam release valve to "Sealing" Position. Select *Manual/Pressure* Cook and cook at *High* pressure for 0 minutes (Sure set it to 0 minutes).
3. When the pot beeps and the screen reads L0:00, quickly release the pressure by moving the steam release valve to Venting
4. When the floating valve drops, remove the lid and Press *Cancel* Button to stop the cooking cycle. Use oven mitts to remove the steamer basket full of beans and set them aside. Drain the water from the pot.
5. Press *Sauté* and add the olive oil to the Instant Pot. Once the oil is hot but not smoking, add the garlic, sesame oil and red pepper flakes
6. Stir briefly, about 30 seconds, then add the steamed green beans and stir well to coat the beans in the fragrant oil, about 30 seconds more. Season with salt to taste and serve warm with a sprinkling of sesame seeds on top

Yummy Not-Fried Pinto Beans

(**Prep + Cooking Time:** 52 minutes | **Servings:** 4)

Ingredients:
- 1 cup dried pinto beans, soaked for 8 hours and drained
- ½ yellow onion; chopped.
- 2 cloves garlic; minced.
- 3 cups water
- ¼ tsp. freshly ground black pepper
- 1 tsp. chili powder
- 1 tsp. ground cumin
- ½ to ¾ tsp. fine sea salt
- Pinch of cayenne pepper (optional)
- Lime wedges; for garnish.
- Chopped fresh cilantro; for garnish.

Directions:
1. Combine the drained beans, water, onion and garlic in the Instant Pot. Stir well, making sure the beans are submerged. Now, Lock the lid and Turn the steam release valve to "Sealing" Position. Select *Manual/Pressure* Cook to cook at *High* pressure for 20 minutes
2. Once the cooking cycle is completed, let the pressure naturally release for 10 minutes, then move the steam release valve to Venting to release any remaining pressure.
3. When the floating valve drops, remove the lid and drain the beans, reserving the liquid. Return the cooked beans to the Instant Pot and stir in ½ cup of the reserved cooking liquid, along with the cumin, chili powder, black pepper, cayenne and ½ teaspoon salt
4. Use a potato masher to mash the cooked beans until smooth, leaving some texture if you like. *You can use an immersion blender for pureed beans, if you prefer.
5. Taste and adjust the seasoning, adding more salt as needed and serve warm with a garnish of cilantro and a squeeze of lime juice

Cauliflower "Rice"

(**Prep + Cooking Time:** 11 minutes | **Servings:** 4)

Ingredients:
- 1 head cauliflower, cut into florets.
- Fine sea salt

Directions:
1. Pour 1 cup water into the Instant Pot and arrange a steamer basket on the bottom. Place the cauliflower florets into the steamer basket, making sure that none of the cauliflower touches the water
2. Now, Lock the lid and Turn the steam release valve to "Sealing" Position. Select *Manual/Pressure* Cook to cook on *High* pressure for 1 minute.
3. Once the cooking cycle is completed, immediately move the steam release valve to Venting to quickly release the steam pressure
4. This ensures the cauliflower doesn't overcook. When the floating valve drops, Press *Cancel* Button and remove the lid.
5. Use oven mitts to lift the steam basket out of the pot and pour out any water from the pot. Add the cooked cauliflower back to the pot
6. Season generously with salt and use a potato masher to break up the cauliflower into a rice.

Potatoes Au Gratin

(**Prep + Cooking Time:** 27 minutes | **Servings:** 6)

Ingredients:
- 6 potatoes, peeled and sliced
- 1/2 cup sour cream
- 1 cup Monterey jack cheese, shredded.
- 2 tbsp. butter
- 1 cup chicken stock
- 1/2 cup yellow onion; chopped.
- Salt and black pepper to the taste

For the topping:
- 3 tbsp. melted butter
- 1 cup bread crumbs

Directions:
1. Set your instant pot on Sauté mode; add butter and melt it
2. Add onion, stir and cook for 5 minutes.
3. Add stock, salt, pepper and put the steamer basket in the pot as well
4. Add potatoes, seal the instant pot lid and cook at High for 5 minutes.
5. In a bowl, mix 3 tablespoon butter with bread crumbs and stir well.
6. Quick release the pressure, take the steamer basket out and transfer potatoes to a baking dish.
7. Pour cream and cheese into instant pot and stir
8. Add potatoes and stir gently.
9. Spread bread crumbs mix all over, introduce in preheated broiler and broil for 7 minutes. Serve right away!

Israeli Couscous Dish

(**Prep + Cooking Time:** 15 minutes | **Servings:** 10)

Ingredients:
- 16 oz. harvest grains blend
- 2 ½ cups chicken stock
- 2 tbsp. butter
- Parsley leaves; chopped for serving
- Salt and black pepper to the taste

Directions:
1. Set your instant pot on Sauté mode; add butter and melt it.
2. Add grains and stock and stir
3. Close the instant pot lid and cook at High for 5 minutes.
4. Quick release the pressure, fluff couscous with a fork, season with salt and pepper to the taste, divide among plates, sprinkle parsley on top and serve.

Herbed Polenta

(Prep + Cooking Time: 20 minutes | **Servings:** 6)

Ingredients:
- 1 cup polenta
- 4 cups veggie stock
- 2 tsp. oregano; finely chopped
- 1/2 cup yellow onion; chopped.
- 1/3 cup sun-dried tomatoes; chopped.
- 3 tbsp. basil; finely chopped
- 1 tsp. rosemary; finely chopped
- 2 tbsp. extra virgin olive oil
- 2 tsp. garlic; minced
- Salt to the taste
- 1 bay leaf
- 2 tbsp. parsley; finely chopped

Directions:
1. Set your instant pot on sauté mode; add the oil and heat it up
2. Add onion, stir and cook for 1 minute
3. Add garlic, stir again and cook for 1 minute
4. Add stock, salt, tomatoes, bay leaf, rosemary, oregano, half of the basil, half of the parsley and polenta
5. Do not stir, seal the instant pot lid, cook at High for 5 minutes and release pressure naturally for 10 minutes.
6. carefully open the lid, discard bay leaf, stir polenta gently, add the rest of the parsley, basil and more salt; then stir well. divide among plates and serve.

Applesauce

(Prep + Cooking Time: 35 minutes | Makes 6 Cups)

Ingredients:
- 3 lb. apples (Fuji or McIntosh), peeled and sliced
- ½ cup water
- ½ tsp. ground cinnamon.

Directions:
1. Add the apples, cinnamon and water to the Instant Pot and secure the lid. Turn the steam release valve to Sealing and select *Manual/Pressure* Cook to cook on *High* pressure for 10 minutes
2. Release the pressure naturally for 10 minutes, then move the steam release valve to Venting. When the floating valve drops, remove the lid.
3. Use a potato masher or immersion blender to puree the apples to the consistency of your choice. Serve the applesauce warm, or transfer it to an airtight container and chill in the fridge until ready to serve

Fava Bean Sauté

(Prep + Cooking Time: 18 minutes | **Servings:** 4)

Ingredients:
- 3 lb. fava beans, shelled
- 1/2 cup white wine
- 3 parsley springs; chopped.
- 4 oz. bacon; chopped.
- 3/4 cup water
- 1 tsp. extra virgin olive oil
- Salt and black pepper to the taste

Directions:
1. Set your instant pot on Sauté mode; add the oil and heat up.
2. Add bacon, stir and cook until it browns.
3. Add wine, stir and cook for 2 minutes
4. Add water and fava beans; then stir well. close the lid and cook at High for 7 minutes
5. Quick release the pressure, transfer beans to plates, add parsley, salt and pepper, stir and serve.

Mashed Squash

(**Prep + Cooking Time:** 30 minutes | **Servings:** 4)

Ingredients:
- 2 Acorn squash, cut into halves and seeded
- 1/4 tsp. baking soda
- 2 tbsp. butter
- 1/2 cup water
- 1/2 tsp. nutmeg, grated
- 2 tbsp. brown sugar
- Salt and black pepper to the taste

Directions:
1. Sprinkle squash halves with salt, pepper and baking soda and place them in the steamer basket of your instant pot
2. Add 1/2 cup water to the pot, close the lid and cook at High for 20 minutes.
3. Quick release the pressure, take squash and leave aside on a plate to cool down
4. Scrape flesh from the squash and put in a bowl.
5. Add salt, pepper to the taste, butter, sugar and nutmeg and mash everything with a potato mashes. Stir well and serve.

Mashed Turnips Dish

(**Prep + Cooking Time:** 15 minutes | **Servings:** 4)

Ingredients:
- 4 turnips; peeled and chopped.
- 1 yellow onion; chopped.
- 1/4 cup sour cream
- 1/2 cup chicken stock
- Salt and black pepper to the taste

Directions:
1. In your instant pot, mix turnips with stock and onion
2. Stir, close the lid and cook at High for 5 minutes.
3. Release the pressure naturally, drain turnips and transfer them to a bowl.
4. Puree them using your mixer and add salt, pepper to the taste and sour cream
5. Blend again and serve right away.

Special Side Dish

(**Prep + Cooking Time:** 30 minutes | **Servings:** 4)

Ingredients:
- 1 bread loaf, cubed and toasted
- 1 cup celery; chopped.
- ½ cup butter
- 1 ¼ cup turkey stock
- 1 yellow onion; chopped.
- 1 tsp. sage
- 1 tsp. poultry seasoning
- 1 ½ cups water
- Salt and black pepper to the taste

Directions:
1. Set your instant pot on Sauté mode; add butter and melt it.
2. Add stock, onion, celery, salt, pepper, sage and poultry seasoning and stir well
3. Add bread cubes, stir and cook for 1 minute
4. Transfer this to a Bundt pan and close the lid it with tin foil
5. Clean your instant pot, add the water and place the pan in the steamer basket, seal the instant pot lid and cook at High for 15 minutes.
6. Quick release the pressure, take out the pan, introduce it in the oven at 350 degrees F and bake for 5 minutes. Serve hot.

Brussels Sprouts Dish

(**Prep + Cooking Time:** 15 minutes | **Servings:** 8)

Ingredients:
- 2 lb. Brussels sprouts
- 2 tbsp. maple syrup
- 1 tsp. orange zest, grated
- 1/4 cup orange juice
- 1 tbsp. buttery spread
- Salt and black pepper to the taste

Directions:
1. In your instant pot, mix Brussels sprouts with orange juice, orange zest, buttery spread, maple syrup, salt and pepper to the taste; then stir well. close the lid and cook at High for 4 minutes.
2. Release the pressure naturally, transfer sprouts mix to plates and serve them.

Potato Casserole

(**Prep + Cooking Time:** 25 minutes | **Servings:** 4)

Ingredients:
- 3 lb. sweet potatoes, scrubbed
- 2 tbsp. coconut flour
- 1 tsp. cinnamon
- 1/4 tsp. allspice
- 1/3 cup palm sugar
- 1/2 tsp. nutmeg, ground.
- 1 cup water
- 1/4 cup coconut milk
- Salt to the taste

For the topping:
- 1/2 cup almond flour
- 1/4 cup pecans, soaked, drained and ground.
- 1/4 cup shredded coconut
- 1 tbsp. chia seeds
- 1/2 cup walnuts, soaked, drained and ground.
- 1/4 cup palm sugar
- 1 tsp. cinnamon, ground.
- 5 tbsp. salted butter
- A pinch of salt

Directions:
1. Prick potatoes with a fork, place them in the steamer basket of your instant pot, add 1 cup water to the pot, close the lid and cook at High for 20 minutes.
2. Meanwhile, in a bowl, mix almond flour with pecans, walnuts, 1/4 cup coconut, 1/4 cup palm sugar, chia seeds, 1 tsp. cinnamon, a pinch of salt and the butter and stir everything.
3. Release the pressure naturally from the pot, take potatoes and peel them and add 1/2 cup water to the pot.
4. Chop potatoes and place them in a baking dish
5. Add crumble mix you've made, stir everything, spread evenly in the dish, place in the steamer basket, seal the instant pot lid again and cook at High for 10 minutes.
6. Quick release the pressure, take the dish out of the pot, leave it to cool down, cut and serve as a side dish.

Quinoa Pilaf

(**Prep + Cooking Time:** 12 minutes | **Servings:** 4)

Ingredients:
- 2 cups quinoa
- 2 garlic cloves; minced.
- 3 cups water
- 2 tsp. turmeric
- 1 handful parsley; chopped.
- 2 tsp. cumin, ground.
- 2 tbsp. extra virgin olive oil
- Salt to the taste

Directions:
1. Set your instant pot on Sauté mode; add oil and heat it up.
2. Add garlic, stir and cook for 30 seconds.
3. Add water, quinoa, cumin, turmeric and salt; then stir well. close the lid and cook at High for 1 minute
4. Release the pressure naturally for 10 minutes, then release remaining pressure by turning the valve to 'Venting', fluff quinoa with a fork, transfer to plates, season with more salt if needed, sprinkle parsley on top and serve as a side dish.

Easy Veggies Dish

(Prep + Cooking Time: 16 minutes | Servings: 4)

Ingredients:
- 2 yellow bell peppers, thinly sliced
- 1 green bell pepper, thinly sliced
- 2 tomatoes; chopped
- 2 garlic cloves; minced.
- 1 red onion, thinly sliced
- 2 red bell peppers, thinly sliced
- 1 bunch parsley; finely chopped
- A drizzle of extra virgin olive oil
- Salt and black pepper to the taste

Directions:
1. Set your instant pot on Sauté mode; add a drizzle of oil and heat it up
2. Add onions, stir and cook for 3 minutes
3. Add red, yellow and green peppers, stir and cook for 5 minutes.
4. Add tomatoes, salt and pepper; then stir well. close the lid and cook at High for 6 minutes
5. Quick release the pressure, open the instant pot lid, transfer peppers and tomatoes to a bowl, add more salt and pepper if needed; chopped garlic, parsley and a drizzle of oil.
6. Toss to coat and serve as a side dish.

Pumpkin Risotto

(Prep + Cooking Time: 15 minutes | Servings: 4)

Ingredients:
- 6 oz. pumpkin puree
- 2 oz. extra virgin olive oil
- 1 small yellow onion; chopped.
- 1/2 tsp. nutmeg
- 1 tsp. thyme; chopped.
- 1/2 tsp. ginger, grated
- 4 oz. heavy cream
- 1/2 tsp. cinnamon
- 1/2 tsp. allspice
- 2 garlic cloves; minced.
- 12 oz. risotto rice
- 4 cups chicken stock

Directions:
1. Set your instant pot on Sauté mode; add oil and heat it up
2. Add onion and garlic, stir and cook for 1 - 2 minutes
3. Also add risotto, chicken stock, pumpkin puree, thyme, nutmeg, cinnamon, ginger and allspice and stir.
4. Close the instant pot lid and cook at High for 10 minutes.
5. Quick release the pressure, add cream, stir very well and serve as a side dish.

Hummus

(Prep + Cooking Time: 1 hour 30 minutes | Makes 2½ Cups)

Ingredients:
- ¼ cup tahini
- 1 cup dried chickpeas (not soaked)
- 2 cloves garlic; minced.
- 3½ cups water
- 2 tbsp. freshly squeezed lemon juice
- 1 tsp. ground cumin
- 1 tsp. fine sea salt
- Freshly ground black pepper

Directions:
1. Place the dried chickpeas in the Instant Pot and add 3 cups of the water. Now, Lock the lid and Turn the steam release valve to "Sealing" Position. Select *Manual/Pressure* Cook to cook on *High* pressure for 50 minutes
2. Release the pressure naturally for 20 minutes, then move the steam release valve to Venting. When the floating valve drops, remove the lid and drain the cooked chickpeas in a colander.
3. To blend the hummus, you can either return the cooked chickpeas to the Instant Pot and use an immersion blender, or add the chickpeas to a food processor or blender

4. Add the tahini, the remaining ½ cup water, the lemon juice, garlic, salt, cumin and several grinds of black pepper and blend until smooth. Adjust the seasonings to your taste. Serve the hummus right away

Vegetable Medley

(Prep + Cooking Time: 12 minutes | **Servings:** 4)

Ingredients:
- 1 lb. assorted non-starchy vegetables, such as cauliflower, carrots and green beans
- 1 clove garlic; minced.
- 2 tbsp. extra-virgin olive oil
- Chopped fresh parsley; for garnish.
- Fine sea salt and freshly ground black pepper

Directions:
1. Pour 1 cup water into the Instant Pot and arrange a steamer basket on the bottom. Place the vegetables in the steamer basket, making sure the vegetables aren't touching the water
2. Now, Lock the lid and Turn the steam release valve to "Sealing" Position. Select *Manual/Pressure* Cook to cook on *High* pressure for 0 minutes (Sure set it to 0 minutes)
3. When the pot beeps and the screen reads L0:00, immediately move the steam release valve to Venting to quickly release the steam pressure.
4. When the floating valve drops, remove the lid and Press *Cancel* Button to stop the cooking cycle. The vegetables should be tender, but with some tooth to them
5. Use oven mitts to remove the steamer basket full of vegetables, drain the water from the pot, then dry the pot and return it to the Instant Pot housing
6. Press *Sauté* and add the olive oil to the Instant Pot. Once the oil is hot but not smoking, add in the garlic and stir briefly, just until fragrant, about 30 seconds.
7. Add the steamed vegetables to the pot and stir well to coat them in the garlic-infused olive oil, about 30 seconds more. Season generously with salt and pepper, then serve warm with parsley on top

Green Beans Dish

(Prep + Cooking Time: 15 minutes | **Servings:** 4)

Ingredients:
- 1 lb. green beans, trimmed
- 1 tsp. extra virgin olive oil
- 2 cups tomatoes; chopped.
- 1 basil spring
- 1 tbsp. extra-virgin olive oil
- 1 garlic clove crushed.
- Salt to the taste

Directions:
1. Set your instant pot on Sauté mode; add 1 tablespoon oil and heat it up
2. Add garlic, stir and cook for 1 minute.
3. Add tomatoes, stir and cook for 1minute.
4. Place green beans in the steamer basket and introduce it in the pot
5. Add salt to the taste, seal the instant pot lid and cook at High for 5 minutes
6. Quick release the pressure, transfer green beans from the basket into the pot and toss to coat
7. Transfer to plates, sprinkle with basil and drizzle 1 tsp. oil over them.

Easy Glazed Carrots

(Prep + Cooking Time: 15 minutes | **Servings:** 4)

Ingredients:
- 1 lb. baby carrots
- 1/2 cup water
- 1 tsp. thyme; dried
- 1 tsp. dill; dried
- 1/2 cup honey
- 2 tbsp. butter
- Salt to the taste

Directions:
1. Pour the water in your instant pot, place carrots in the steamer basket, close the lid and cook at High for 3 minutes.
2. Quick release the pressure, drain carrots and put them in a bowl.
3. Set your instant pot on Sauté mode; add butter and melt it
4. Add dill, thyme, honey and salt and stir well
5. Add carrots, toss to coat, cook for 1 minute, transfer them to plates and serve hot as a side dish.

Bok Choy Dish

(Prep + Cooking Time: 20 minutes | **Servings:** 4)

Ingredients:
- 5 bok choy bunches, end cut off
- 5 cups water
- 2 garlic cloves; minced.
- 1 tsp. ginger, grated
- 1 tbsp. coconut oil
- Salt to the taste

Directions:
1. Put bok choy in your instant pot, add the water, seal the instant pot lid and cook at High for 7 minutes
2. Quick release the pressure, drain bok choy, chop it and put them in a bowl.
3. Heat up a pan with the oil over medium heat, add bok choy, stir and cook for 3 minutes.
4. Add more salt to the taste, garlic and ginger, stir and cook for 2 more minutes
5. Divide among plates and serve with your favorite meat.

Parmesan Spaghetti Squash

(Prep + Cooking Time: 20 minutes | **Servings:** 4)

Ingredients:
- One 3-lb. spaghetti squash
- 3 cloves garlic; minced.
- ¼ cup grated Parmesan cheese
- 1 tbsp. extra-virgin olive oil
- 1 tsp. fine sea salt
- Freshly ground black pepper
- Chopped fresh flat-leaf parsley; for garnish.

Directions:
1. Pour 1 cup water into the Instant Pot and arrange the trivet (Which comes with your instant pot) on the bottom
2. Cut the spaghetti squash in half crosswise (for longer spaghetti strands) and use a spoon to scoop out and discard the seeds. Place the two cut halves on the Instant Pot trivet (they may have to face each other to fit in the pot as if the squash were still whole) and secure the lid
3. Turn the steam release valve to Sealing and select *Manual/Pressure* Cook to cook on *High* pressure for 7 minutes.
4. Once the cooking cycle is completed, immediately move the steam release valve to Venting to quickly release any remaining steam pressure. When the floating valve drops, remove the lid and Press *Cancel* Button to stop the cooking cycle
5. Use oven mitts to transfer the squash halves to a cutting board. Remove the trivet and drain the water from the pot, then dry the pot and return it to the Instant Pot housing.
6. Press *Sauté* and add the olive oil to the pot. Once the oil is hot but not smoking, add the garlic and stir just until fragrant, about 30 seconds

7. Hold one half of the spaghetti squash with an oven mitt and use a fork to scrape the cooked squash out of the shell directly into the pot.
8. Repeat with the other squash half, then stir in the salt and several grinds of pepper. Stir in the Parmesan cheese. Taste and adjust the seasonings as needed, then serve warm with a sprinkling of parsley

Rice Recipes

Steamed Eggs with Rice

(Prep + Cooking Time: 15 minutes | **Servings:** 2)

Ingredients:
- 2 eggs
- 1 ⅓ cup water
- 2 scallions; finely chopped
- Salt and black pepper to the taste
- A pinch of sesame seeds
- A pinch of garlic powder
- Hot rice for serving

Directions:
1. In a bowl, mix the eggs with 1/3 cup water and whisk well.
2. Strain this into a heat proof dish
3. Add salt, pepper to the taste, sesame seeds, garlic powder and scallions and whisk very well.
4. Put 1 cup water in your instant pot, place the dish in the steamer basket, seal the instant pot lid and cook at High for 5 minutes
5. Quick release the pressure, open the instant pot lid, divide the rice among plates and add eggs mix on the side.

Rice & Beef Soup

(Prep + Cooking Time: 25 minutes | **Servings:** 6)

Ingredients:
- 1 lb. beef meat, ground.
- 3 garlic cloves; minced.
- 1 yellow onion; chopped
- 15 oz. canned garbanzo beans, rinsed.
- 1 potato, cubed
- 1/2 cup frozen peas
- 14 oz. canned tomatoes, crushed.
- 1/2 cup white rice
- 12 oz. spicy V8 juice
- 2 carrots, thinly sliced
- 1 tbsp. vegetable oil
- 1 celery rib; chopped
- 28 oz. canned beef stock
- Salt and black pepper to the taste

Directions:
8. Set your instant pot on Sauté mode; add beef; then stir well. cook until it browns and transfer to a plate
9. Add the oil to your pot and heat it up.
10. Add celery and onion, stir and cook for 5 minutes
11. Add garlic, stir and cook for 1 minute more.
12. Add V8 juice, stock, tomatoes, rice, beans, carrots, potatoes, beef, salt and pepper; then stir well. close the lid and cook at High for 5 minutes
13. Quick release the pressure, remove the instant pot lid and set it on Simmer mode
14. Add more salt and pepper if needed and peas; then stir well. bring to a simmer, transfer to bowls and serve hot.

Chipotle Rice.

(Prep + Cooking Time: 35 minutes | **Servings:** 4)

Ingredients:
- 2 cups. brown rice, rinsed
- 1 ½ tbsp. olive oil
- 1 tsp. salt
- 1/2 cup. chopped cilantro
- 2 ¾ cups. water, hot
- 1 lime, juiced
- 4 small bay leaves

Directions:
1. In a 6-quarts Instant Pot place rice, then add bay leaves and water.
2. Plug in and switch on the pot, select RICE option and secure pot with lid. Then position pressure indicator and let cook on default time.
3. When the timer beeps, switch off the Instant Pot and let pressure release naturally for 10 minutes and then do quick pressure release.
4. Carefully open the lid, add salt, oil, lime juice and cilantro and mix until combined. Serve warm and enjoy!

Wild Rice & Farro Pilaf

(Prep + Cooking Time: 45 minutes | **Servings:** 12)

Ingredients:
- 1 ½ cups whole grain faro
- 1 tbsp. parsley and sage; finely chopped
- 1/2 cup hazelnuts, toasted and chopped.
- 3/4 cup wild rice
- 1 shallot; finely chopped
- 1 tsp. garlic; minced.
- 6 cups chicken stock
- 3/4 cup cherries; dried
- Some chopped chives for serving
- A drizzle of extra virgin olive oil
- Salt and black pepper to the taste

Directions:
1. Set your instant pot on Sauté mode; add a drizzle of oil and heat it up.
2. Add onion and garlic, stir and cook for 2 - 3 minutes.
3. Add farro, rice, salt, pepper, stock and 1 tablespoon mixed sage and parsley; then stir well. seal the instant pot lid and cook on High for 25 minutes.
4. Meanwhile, put cherries in a pot, add hot water to cover, leave aside for 10 minutes and drain them
5. Release the pressure naturally for 5 minutes, then release remaining pressure by turning the valve to 'Venting', now open the instant pot lid, drain excess liquid, add hazelnuts and cherries, stir gently, divide among plates and garnish with chopped chives

Kale and Wild Rice Salad

(Prep + Cooking Time: 43 minutes | **Servings:** 4)

Ingredients:
- 1 cup wild rice, or wild and brown rice blend
- 1¼ cups water
- 5 green onions, tender white and green parts only
- ¼ cup freshly squeezed lemon juice, plus more as needed
- 1 clove garlic; minced.
- 1 small bunch kale
- 1 cup cherry tomatoes
- 1 red bell pepper
- ½ cup crumbled feta cheese
- 2 tbsp. extra-virgin olive oil
- ¼ tsp. freshly ground black pepper
- 2 tsp. pure maple syrup
- ½ tsp. fine sea salt

Directions:
1. Add the wild rice and water to the Instant Pot. Now, Lock the lid and Turn the steam release valve to "Sealing" Position. Select *Manual/Pressure* Cook and cook on *High* pressure for 22 minutes

2. While the rice is cooking, in a large bowl, whisk together the olive oil, lemon juice, garlic, salt, pepper and maple syrup to make a dressing and set aside.
3. Remove the ribs from the kale and finely chop the leaves (you should have about 2 cups); add the kale to the bowl
4. Chop the green onions (about 1 cup) and cut the tomatoes into quarters, adding both to the bowl as you work. Seed and chop the red bell pepper and add it to the bowl. Toss the vegetables to coat well in the dressing.
5. Once the cooking cycle is completed, let the pressure naturally release for 10 minutes, then move the steam release valve to Venting to release any remaining pressure
6. When the floating valve drops, remove the lid. Give the rice a stir and add it to the bowl of dressed vegetables. (If you haven't finished chopping the vegetables, you can finish as the rice cools.) Toss well to coat, then chill the bowl in the fridge for 30 minutes.
7. Just before serving, stir in the feta and taste and adjust the seasonings as needed, adding an extra squeeze of lemon juice to brighten the flavors

Coconut Sweet Rice.

(Prep + Cooking Time: 25 minutes | **Servings:** 4)

Ingredients:
- 1 cup. Thai sweet rice
- 1/2 can Full-Fat: coconut milk
- 1 ½ cups. water
- 2 tbsp. sugar Dash of salt

Directions:
1. Mix rice and water in your Instant Pot
2. Select "Manual" and cook for just 3 minutes on "High" pressure
3. When time is up, hit "Cancel" and wait 10 minutes for a natural release
4. In the meanwhile, heat coconut milk, sugar, and salt in a saucepan.
5. When the sugar has melted, remove from the heat.
6. When the cooker has released its pressure, mix the coconut milk mixture into your rice and stir
7. Put the lid back on and let it rest 5 - 10 minutes, without returning it to pressure. Serve and enjoy!

Pink Rice

(Prep + Cooking Time: 15 minutes | **Servings:** 8)

Ingredients:
- 2 cups pink rice
- 2 ½ cups water
- 1 tsp. salt

Directions:
1. Put the rice in your instant pot
2. Add the water and salt; then stir everything well. close the lid and cook at High for 5 minutes
3. Release the pressure naturally for 10 minutes, then release remaining pressure by turning the valve to 'Venting', open the instant pot lid, fluff rice with a fork, divide among plates and serve

Instant Brown Rice.

(Prep + Cooking Time: 30 minutes | **Servings:** 6)

Ingredients:
- 2 cups. brown rice
- 2 ½ cups. any kind vegetable broth or water
- 1/2 tsp. of sea salt

Directions:
1. Put the rice into the Instant Pot
2. Pour in the broth or water and salt. Close and lock the lid. Press the "Manual" and set the timer to 22 minutes pressure cooking.

3. When the timer beeps, Release the pressure naturally for 10 minutes, then release remaining pressure by turning the valve to 'Venting'
4. Carefully open the lid and Serve hot.

Mix-Fruit Wild Rice.

(**Prep + Cooking Time:** 50 minutes | **Servings:** 6)

Ingredients:
- 2 peeled and chopped small apples
- 1 chopped pear
- 1 tbsp. maple syrup
- 1/2 cup. slivered almonds
- 2 tbsp. apple juice
- 1 tsp. veggie oil
- 1 tsp. cinnamon
- 1/2 tsp. ground nutmeg
- 3 ½ cups. water
- 1 ½ cups. wild rice
- 1 cup. dried, mixed fruit
- Salt and pepper to taste

Directions:
1. Pour water into your Instant Pot along the rice
2. Close and seal the lid. Select "Manual" and cook for 30 minutes on "High" pressure.
3. While that cooks, soak the dried fruit in just enough apple juice to cover everything.
4. After 30 minutes, drain the fruit. By now, the rice should be done, so hit "Cancel" and wait for the pressure to come down on its own. Drain the rice and move rice to a bowl
5. Turn your instant pot to "Sauté" and add veggie oil. Cook the apples, pears, and almonds for about 2 minutes.
6. Pour in 2 tablespoon apple juice and keep cooking for a few minutes more
7. Add syrup, the cooked rice, soaked fruit, and seasonings. Keep stirring for 2 to 3 minutes. Serve.

Grain Rice Millet Blend.

(**Prep + Cooking Time:** 15 minutes | **Servings:** 8)

Ingredients:
- 2 cups. jasmine rice OR long-grain white rice
- 1/2 tsp. sea salt (optional)
- 3 ¼ cups. water
- 1/2 cup. millet

Directions:
1. Put all the ingredients in the Instant Pot and stir
2. Cover and lock the lid.
3. Press the RICE button and let the pot do all the cooking, about 10 minutes

Wild Rice and Chicken Soup

(**Prep + Cooking Time:** 25 minutes | **Servings:** 6)

Ingredients:
- 2 chicken breasts, skinless and boneless and chopped.
- 1 cup yellow onion; chopped.
- 28 oz. chicken stock
- 4 oz. cream cheese, cubed.
- 6 oz. wild rice
- 2 tbsp. butter
- 1 cup celery; chopped.
- 1 cup milk
- 1 cup half and half
- 1 tbsp. parsley; dried
- 2 tbsp. cornstarch mixed with 2 tbsp. water
- 1 cup carrots; chopped.
- A pinch of red pepper flakes
- Salt and black pepper to the taste

Directions:
1. Set your instant pot on Sauté mode; add butter and melt it
2. Add carrot, onion and celery, stir and cook for 5 minutes.

3. Add rice, chicken, stock, parsley, salt and pepper; then stir well. close the lid and cook at High for 5 minutes.
4. Quick release the pressure, carefully open the lid; add cornstarch mixed with water, stir and set the pot on Simmer mode.
5. Add cheese, milk and half and half; then stir well. heat up, transfer to bowls and serve.

Mexican Basmati Rice.

(Prep + Cooking Time: 30 minutes | **Servings:** 6)

Ingredients:
- 2 cups. rice, long-grain, such as Lundberg Farms Brown Basmati.
- 1/2 cup. tomato paste
- 2 tsp. salt
- 1/2 white onion; chopped.
- 3 cloves garlic; minced
- 1 small jalapeño, optional
- 2 cups. water

Directions:
1. Set the Instant Pot to normal "Sauté". Heat the olive oil.
2. Add the garlic, onion, rice, and salt. Sauté for about 3 - 4 minutes or until fragrant
3. Mix the tomato paste with the water until well combined. Pour into the pot. Add the whole jalapeno pepper.
4. Press "Cancel". Close and lock the lid. Press "Pressure", set to "High", and the timer for 3 minutes is using white rice or for 22 minutes if using brown rice
5. When the timer beeps, release the pressure naturally for about 15 minutes. Turn the steam valve to "Venting". Carefully open the lid
6. Using a fork, fluff the rice and serve hot

Chickpea & Rice Stew.

(Prep + Cooking Time: 35 minutes | **Servings:** 6)

Ingredients:
- 3 medium-sized onions, peeled and sliced.
- 6 oz. brown basmati rice, rinsed
- 30 oz. cooked chickpeas
- 8 fluid-ounce orange juice
- 1 tbsp. olive oil
- 4 cups. vegetable broth
- 4 oz. chopped cilantro
- 1 lb. sweet potato, peeled and diced.
- 1/4 tsp. salt
- 1/4 tsp. ground black pepper
- 2 tsp. ground cumin
- 2 tsp. ground coriander

Directions:
1. Plug in and switch on a 6-quarts Instant Pot, select "Sauté" option, add oil and onion and let cook for 10 - 12 minutes or until browned.
2. Stir in coriander and cumin and continue cooking for 15 seconds or until fragrant.
3. Add remaining ingredients into the pot except for black pepper and cilantro and stir until just mixed
4. Press "Cancel" and secure pot with lid. Then position pressure indicator, select "Manual" option and adjust cooking time on timer pad to 5 minutes and let cook on "High" pressure
5. Instant Pot will take 10 minutes to build pressure before cooking timer starts.
6. When the timer beeps, switch off the Instant Pot and let pressure release naturally for 10 minutes and then do quick pressure release.
7. Then remove the instant pot lid and stir in pepper until mixed
8. Garnish with cilantro and serve

Mexican Rice

(Prep + Cooking Time: 15 minutes | **Servings:** 8)

Ingredients:
- 1 cup long grain rice
- 1/2 cup cilantro; chopped
- 1/2 avocado, pitted; peeled and chopped.
- 1/4 cup green hot sauce
- 1 ¼ cups veggie stock
- Salt and black pepper to the taste

Directions:
1. Put the rice in your instant pot, add stock; then stir well. close the lid and cook at High for 4 minutes
2. Release the pressure naturally for 10 minutes, then release remaining pressure by turning the valve to 'Venting', open the instant pot lid, fluff it with a fork and transfer to a bowl
3. Meanwhile, in your food processor, mix avocado with hot sauce and cilantro and blend well.
4. Pour this over rice, stir well, add salt and pepper to the taste, stir again, divide among plates and serve

Salmon and Rice

(Prep + Cooking Time: 10 minutes | **Servings:** 2)

Ingredients:
- 2 wild salmon fillets, frozen
- 1/2 cup jasmine rice
- 1/4 cup vegetable soup mix; dried
- 1 cup chicken stock
- 1 tbsp. butter
- A pinch of saffron
- Salt and black pepper to the taste

Directions:
1. In your instant pot, mix stock with rice, soup mix, butter and saffron and stir.
2. Season salmon with salt and pepper, place in the steamer basket of your pot, close the lid and cook on High for 5 minutes.
3. Quick release the pressure, divide salmon among plates, add rice mix on the side and serve.

Mexican Brown Rice Casserole.

(Prep + Cooking Time: 35 minutes | **Servings:** 4)

Ingredients:
- 2 cups. uncooked brown rice
- 5 cups. water
- 1 cup. soaked black beans
- 6 oz. tomato paste
- 2 tsp. chili powder
- 2 tsp. onion powder
- 1 tsp. garlic
- 1 tsp. salt

Directions:
1. A few hours before dinner, put your dry beans in a bowl with enough water to cover them.
2. Soak on the countertop for at least two hours and drain.
3. Put everything in your Instant Pot. Close and seal the pressure cooker. Select "Manual" and then cook on "High" pressure for 28 minutes.
4. When time is up, hit "Cancel" and quick-release
5. Taste and season more if necessary

Pumpkin Rice Pudding

(Prep + Cooking Time: 1 hour | **Servings:** 6)

Ingredients:
- 1 cup pumpkin puree
- 1/2 cup maple syrup
- 1 tsp. pumpkin spice mix
- 1 cup brown rice
- 1 cinnamon stick
- 1/2 cup water
- 1 tsp. vanilla extract
- 3 cups cashew milk
- 1/2 cup dates; chopped
- A pinch of salt

Directions:
1. Put the rice in your instant pot, add boiling water to cover, leave aside for 10 minutes and drain
2. Pour the water in milk in your instant pot, add rice, cinnamon stick, dates and salt; then stir well. close the lid and cook at High for 20 minutes.
3. Quick release the pressure, carefully open the lid; add maple syrup, pumpkin pie spice and pumpkin puree; then stir well. set the pot on Simmer mode and cook for 5 minutes.
4. Discard cinnamon stick, add vanilla; then stir well. transfer pudding to bowls, leave aside for 30 minutes to cool down and serve

Cauliflower & Pineapple Rice

(**Prep + Cooking Time:** 30 minutes | **Servings:** 6)

Ingredients:
- 2 cups rice
- 2 tsp. extra virgin olive oil
- 1 cauliflower, florets separated and chopped.
- 1/2 pineapple; peeled and chopped.
- 4 cups water
- Salt and black pepper to the taste

Directions:
1. In your instant pot, mix rice with pineapple, cauliflower, water, oil, salt and pepper; then stir well. close the lid and cook for 20 minutes on Low.
2. Release the pressure naturally for 10 minutes, then release remaining pressure by turning the valve to 'Venting', open the instant pot lid, fluff with a fork, add more salt and pepper to the taste, divide among plates and serve.

Artichokes Rice and Side Dish

(**Prep + Cooking Time:** 30 minutes | **Servings:** 4)

Ingredients:
- 15 oz. canned artichoke hearts chopped
- 5 oz. Arborio rice
- 16 oz. cream cheese
- 1 tbsp. extra-virgin olive oil
- 1 tbsp. grated parmesan cheese
- 1 tbsp. white wine
- 6 oz. graham cracker crumbs
- 1 ¼ cups water
- 1 ½ tbsp. thyme chopped
- 2 garlic cloves crushed.
- 1 ¼ cups chicken broth
- Salt and black pepper to the taste

Directions:
1. Set your instant pot on Sauté mode; add the oil, heat up, add rice and cook for 2 minutes.
2. Add garlic, stir and cook for 1 minute
3. Transfer this to a heat proof dish.
4. Add stock, crumbs, salt, pepper and wine, stir and cover the with tin foil.
5. Place the dish in the steamer basket of the pot, add water, close the lid and cook at High for 8 minutes
6. Quick release the pressure, take the dish out, uncover, add cream cheese, parmesan, artichoke hearts, and thyme.
7. Mix well and serve while it's hot!

Easy Risotto.

(Prep + Cooking Time: 25 minutes | **Servings:** 6)

Ingredients:
- 28 oz. chicken stock
- 12 oz. Arborio rice
- 1 ½ tbsp. olive oil
- 3 tbsp. Romano or Parmesan cheese
- 1 finely chopped medium onion
- Salt and pepper to taste

Directions:
1. Press sauté button and Heat the oil in your instant pot
2. Add onion and Sauté until soft and nearly translucent
3. Add the rice and chicken stock.
4. Close the lid and select the RICE function. Set a timer for 15 minutes
5. Wait for the cycle to end and for the pressure to naturally drop
6. Open the lid and stir in a little bit of black pepper
7. Add the Romano or Parmesan cheese.
8. Serve warm and enjoy!

Veggie Rice Acorn Squash.

(Prep + Cooking Time: 20 minutes | **Servings:** 4)

Ingredients:
- 3 ¾ cups. veggie stock
- 2 medium-sized, halved acorn squash
- 1/2 cup. quinoa
- 1/2 cup. vegan cheese
- 2 minced garlic cloves
- 1 tbsp. Earth Balance spread
- 1 cup. white rice
- 1 tsp. chopped rosemary
- 1 tsp. chopped thyme
- 1 tsp. chopped sage
- 1 cup. diced onion

Directions:
1. Turn your Instant Pot to "Sauté" and melt the Earth Balance. Add onion and salt, and cook for 2 minutes.
2. Toss in the garlic and cook for another minute or so. Add rice, quinoa, herbs, and pour in the broth. Stir.
3. Put your de-seeded squash halves with the cut-side UP in a steamer basket
4. Put the trivet in the cooker, and place the basket on top. Close and seal the lid.
5. Hit "Manual" and cook for 6 minutes on "High" pressure
6. When the timer beeps, carefully quick-release the pressure after hitting "Cancel"
7. Take out the steamer basket and drain any liquid that's hanging around in the squash.
8. Add vegan cheese to the pot and stir. Wait 5 minutes or so for the stuffing to thicken
9. Fill the squash and sprinkle on some extra cheese. Serve!

Black Beans and Rice.

(Prep + Cooking Time: 35 minutes | **Servings:** 4)

Ingredients:
- 1 cup. onion, diced
- 2 cups. brown rice
- 2 cups. dry black beans
- 4 cloves garlic, crushed and then minced.
- 9 cups. water
- 1 tsp. salt
- 1 to 2 limes, optional
- Avocado, optional

Directions:
1. Put garlic and onion in your Instant Pot
2. Add the black beans and the brown rice. Pour in the water and sprinkle the salt. Close the lid. Press "Manual" and set the time to 28 minutes.
3. When the timer is up, press "Cancel" or unplug the pot. Let the pressure release naturally. You can let it sit for 20 minutes

4. Scoop into a serving bowl and squeeze a lime wedge over the bowl
5. Serve with a couple of avocado slices for garnishing.

Cajun Rice

(**Prep + Cooking Time:** 34 minutes | **Servings:** 4)

Ingredients:
- 1 lb. 85% lean ground beef
- 1/2 cup diced yellow onion, 1/2 cup diced bell pepper and 1/2 cup diced celery
- 1 cup water
- 1 cup basmati rice; rinsed and drained
- 1 bay leaf
- 2 tbsp. vegetable oil
- 1 tbsp. salt-free Cajun seasoning
- 1 tsp. dried oregano
- 2 tsp. hot sauce
- 1 tsp. salt or as your liking

Directions:
5. Now Press "Sauté" on the Instant Pot. When the pot is hot, add the oil. When the oil is hot, add the mirepoix and ground beef. Cook 2 to 3 minutes, stirring to break up the clumps of meat.
6. Add the rice, Cajun seasoning, hot sauce, oregano, salt and bay leaf. Stir well to combine. Now Press "Cancel". Stir in the water
7. Now secure the lid on the pot and close the valve. Now Press "Manual" and set the pot at "High" pressure for 4 minutes
8. After completing the cooking time, allow the pot to sit undisturbed for 10 minutes, then release any remaining pressure. Stir gently to fluff up the rice, discard the bay leaf and serve.

Green Rice.

(**Prep + Cooking Time:** 50 minutes | **Servings:** 6)

Ingredients:
- 2 cups. rice basmati.
- 1 cup. dill
- 3 oz. butter
- 1 tbsp. salt
- 4 cups. beef broth
- 1 cup. spinach
- 1 tsp. olive oil
- 1 tsp. dried oregano
- 1 tbsp. minced garlic

Directions:
1. Pour the olive oil in the Instant Pot. Add rice, butter, and minced garlic
2. "Sauté" the mixture for 5 minutes. Stir it frequently
3. After this, add beef broth.
4. Wash the spinach and dill carefully. Chop the greens
5. Transfer the chopped greens in the blender and blend them well
6. Then add the blended greens in the rice mixture
7. Add butter, salt, and dried oregano
8. Mix up the mixture carefully with the help of the wooden spoon. After this, close the lid and set the Instant Pot mode RICE
9. Cook the dish for 20 minutes.
10. When the time is over - release the remaining pressure and transfer the green rice in the serving bowl.

Fried Basmati Rice.

(**Prep + Cooking Time:** 15 minutes | **Servings:** 4)

Ingredients:
- 1 cup. basmati rice, uncooked
- 1/2 cups. peas, frozen OR your preferred vegetable
- 1/4 cup. soy sauce
- 1 ½ cups. chicken stock
- 1 tbsp. butter (or oil)
- 1 medium onion, diced
- 2 cloves garlic; minced.
- one egg

Directions:
1. Heat the Instant Pot to more "Sauté" mode. Put the oil in the pot
2. Add the garlic and the onion. Sauté for 1 minute.
3. Add the egg, scramble with the garlic mix for about 1 to 2 minutes
4. Add the rice, stock, and soy sauce in the pot. Press "Cancel". Close and lock the lid. Press RICE and set the time for 10 minutes
5. When the timer beeps, quick release the pressure. Carefully open the lid. Stir in the frozen peas or veggies.
6. Let sit until the peas/ veggies are warmed through.

French Butter Rice.

(Prep + Cooking Time: 30 minutes | **Servings:** 4)

Ingredients:
- 1 ¼ cups. vegetable stock
- 2 cups. brown rice
- 1 stick (1/2 cup) butter
- 1 ¼ cups. French Onion soup

Directions:
1. Put all of the ingredients in the Instant Pot. Stir to incorporate.
2. Close and lock the lid. Press "Manual". Set to "High" pressure and the time for 22 minutes
3. When the timer beeps, let the pressure release naturally.
4. Serve warm. If desired, garnish with parsley

Rice Pudding

(Prep + Cooking Time: 20 minutes | **Servings:** 6)

Ingredients:
- 7 oz. long grain rice
- 1 tbsp. butter
- 4 oz. water
- 16 oz. milk
- 3 oz. sugar
- one egg
- 1 tbsp. cream
- 1 tsp. vanilla
- A pinch of salt
- Cinnamon to the taste

Directions:
1. Put the butter in your instant pot, set it on Sauté mode; melt it, add rice and stir.
2. Add water and milk and stir again
3. Add salt and sugar, stir again, close the lid and cook at High for 8 minutes.
4. Meanwhile, in a bowl, mix cream with vanilla and eggs and stir well
5. Quick release the pressure, carefully open the lid; and pour some of the liquid from the pot over egg mixture and stir very well.
6. Pour this into the pot and whisk well
7. Seal the instant pot lid, cook at High for 10 minutes, release pressure, open the instant pot lid, pour pudding into bowls, sprinkle cinnamon on top and serve

Lentil & Rice.

(Prep + Cooking Time: 55 minutes | **Servings:** 4)

Ingredients:
For the sauté:
- 2 cloves garlic; minced.
- 1/2 cup. onion; chopped.
- 1 tbsp. oil, OR dry sauté (or add a little water/vegetable broth)

For the porridge:
- 1 ½ cups. brown rice
- 2-inch sprig fresh rosemary
- 1 cup. brown lentils
- 1 tbsp. dried marjoram (or thyme)
- 3 ½ cups. water

- 1 cup. rutabaga, peeled and diced, OR potato OR turnip
- Salt and pepper, to taste

Directions:
1. Press the "Sauté" key of the Instant Pot and select the Normal option.
2. Put the oil/ broth in the pot and, if using oil, heat. When the oil is hot, add the onion and sauté for 5 minutes or until transparent
3. Add the garlic and sauté for 1 minute
4. Add the lentils, brown rice, rutabaga, marjoram, rosemary, and pour in the water into the pot and stir to combine. Press the "Cancel" key to stop the sauté function
5. Press the "Manual" key, set the pressure to "High", and set the timer for 23 minutes
6. When the Instant Pot timer beeps, press the "Cancel" key. Let the pressure release naturally for 10 - 15 minutes or until the valve drops. Release remaining pressure. Unlock and carefully open the lid
7. Taste and, if needed, season with pepper and salt to taste.
8. If needed, add more ground rosemary and more marjoram.

Dolma Casserole

(Prep + Cooking Time: 40 minutes | **Servings:** 4)

Ingredients:
- 1 cup chopped yellow onions
- 1 lb. 85% lean ground beef
- 8 ounces brined grape leaves, drained and chopped
- ⅓ cup fresh lemon juice
- 1/4 cup chopped fresh mint
- 1 cup basmati rice; rinsed and drained
- 1 cup water
- 2 tbsp. extra-virgin olive oil
- 1 tbsp. minced garlic
- 1/4 cup chopped fresh parsley
- 1 tsp. ground allspice
- 1 tsp. salt or as your liking
- 1 tsp. black pepper

Directions:
1. Press "Sauté" on the Instant Pot. When the pot is hot, add the olive oil. When the oil is hot, add the garlic and onions.
2. Stir to combine. Add the beef and cook, stirring just enough to break up the clumps, for 2 to 3 minutes (don't worry about it being fully cooked at this point). Add the water, rice, grape leaves, parsley, allspice, salt and pepper. Stir well to combine. Now Press "Cancel"
3. Now secure the lid on the pot and close the valve. Now Press "Manual" and set the pot at "High" pressure for 4 minutes
4. After completing the cooking time, let the pot sit undisturbed for 10 minutes, then release any remaining pressure. Gently stir in the lemon juice and mint. Serve with tzatziki on the side.

Ground Beef and Rice

(Prep + Cooking Time: minutes | **Servings:** 6)

Ingredients:
- 1 lb. 85% lean ground beef
- 5 cardamom pods,
- 2 cups water
- 1 cup basmati rice; rinsed and drained
- 1 cup sliced yellow onions
- 1/2 cup pine nuts
- 1/2 cup chopped fresh cilantro
- 1 tbsp. minced garlic
- 2 tbsp. vegetable oil
- 1 tsp. ground cinnamon
- 1/2 tsp. freshly grated nutmeg
- 1 ½ tsp. ground allspice
- 1 tsp. salt or as your liking
- 1 tsp. black pepper
- Tzatziki, for serving; optional

Directions:
1. Press "Sauté" on the Instant Pot. When the pot is hot, add the oil. When the oil is hot, add the pine nuts. Cook, stirring, for 1 to 2 minutes.

2. Add the onions and garlic and stir to combine. Add the ground beef and cook, stirring just enough to break up the clumps of meat, for 2 to 3 minutes.
3. Add the rice, cardamom, allspice, cinnamon, nutmeg, salt and pepper. Stir well to combine. Stir in the water. Now Press "Cancel"
4. Now secure the lid on the pot and close the valve. Now Press "Manual" and set the pot at "High" pressure for 4 minutes
5. After completing the cooking time, allow the pot to sit undisturbed for 10 minutes, then release any remaining pressure.
6. Stir gently to fluff up the rice. Sprinkle with the chopped fresh herbs. Serve hot, with a side of tzatziki if you like.

Pineapple Rice.

(Prep + Cooking Time: 12 minutes | Servings: 4)

Ingredients:
- 8 oz. crushed pineapple
- 1 cup. brown rice
- 1/4 cup. pineapple juice
- 1 tbsp. butter

Directions:
1. Put everything in your instant pot pressure cooker and seal the lid
2. Hit "Manual" and adjust time to 7 minutes
3. When time is up, wait 1 to 2 minutes before quick-releasing.
4. Stir and serve!

Rice and Peas

(Prep + Cooking Time: 20 minutes | Servings: 6)

Ingredients:
- 1 cup canned kidney beans, drained and rinsed
- 1/2 cup full-fat coconut milk
- 1 cup jasmine rice; rinsed and drained
- 3 sprigs fresh thyme
- 1 cup water
- 1 Scotch bonnet chile
- 1 tbsp. melted Ghee, vegetable oil
- 1 tsp. salt or as your liking
- 1/2 tsp. ground allspice

Directions:
1. In your Instant Pot, combine the rice, water, whole chile, thyme, salt and allspice. Stir to combine. Add the ghee and stir to combine. Gently add the kidney beans on the top of the rice; do not stir.
2. Now secure the lid on the pot and close the valve. Now Press "Manual" and set the pot at "High" pressure for 4 minutes
3. After completing the cooking time, allow the pot to sit undisturbed for 10 minutes, then release any remaining pressure
4. Stir in the coconut milk. Place the lid back on the pot and allow to stand for about 10 minutes for the coconut milk to be absorbed. Remove the thyme sprigs and the chile and serve.

Rice & Veggies Dish

(Prep + Cooking Time: 20 minutes | Servings: 4)

Ingredients:
- 2 cups basmati rice
- 3 garlic cloves; minced.
- 2 tbsp. butter
- 1 cinnamon stick
- 1 tbsp. cumin seeds
- 2 bay leaves
- 3 whole cloves
- 1/2 tsp. ginger, grated
- 1 cup mixed frozen carrots, peas, corn, green beans
- 2 cups water
- 1/2 tsp. green chili; minced.

- 5 black peppercorns
- 2 whole cardamoms
- 1 tbsp. sugar
- Salt to the taste

Directions:
1. Pour the water in your instant pot.
2. Add rice, mixed frozen veggies, green chili, grated ginger, garlic cloves, cinnamon stick, whole cloves and butter
3. Also add cumin seeds, bay leaves, cardamoms, black peppercorns, salt and sugar.
4. Stir, close the lid and cook at High for 15 minutes.
5. Quick release the pressure, divide among plates and serve with your favorite steaks

Arroz Con Pollo

(Prep + Cooking Time: 46 minutes | Servings: 6)

Ingredients:
- 1 lb. boneless; skinless chicken thighs, cut into bite-size chunks
- 2 tomatoes, quartered
- 1/2 cup coarsely chopped fresh cilantro
- 3 garlic cloves; crushed
- 1/2 jalapeño
- 1 cup basmati rice; rinsed and drained
- 1/2 yellow onion, quartered
- 1 ½ cups water
- 2 tbsp. vegetable oil
- 2 tsp. ground cumin
- 1 tsp. salt or as your liking
- Tomatillo salsa, for serving

Directions:
1. In a blender, combine the onion, tomatoes, cilantro, garlic and jalapeño. Blend until smooth.
2. Now Press "Sauté" on the Instant Pot. When the pot is hot, add the oil. When the oil is hot, add the rice and cook, stirring frequently, until the rice is translucent, 3 to 4 minutes. Add the chicken, cumin, and salt. Cook, stirring, for 1 to 2 minutes. Now Press "Cancel"
3. Add the blended vegetables and the water. Stir well to combine.
4. Now secure the lid on the pot and close the valve. Now Press "Manual" and set the pot at "High" pressure for 6 minutes
5. After completing the cooking time, allow the pot to sit undisturbed for 10 minutes, then release any remaining pressure. Serve with tomatillo salsa, if desired.

Rice and Chicken

(Prep + Cooking Time: 50 minutes | Servings: 2)

Ingredients:
- 3 chicken quarters cut into small pieces
- 2 carrots, cut into chunks
- 1 yellow onion, sliced
- 1 tsp. cumin, ground
- 1 tbsp. soy sauce
- 1 tbsp. peanut oil
- 2 potatoes, cut into quarters
- 1 shallot, sliced
- 1 ½ tbsp. cornstarch mixed with 2 tbsp. water
- 1 ½ tsp. turmeric powder
- 1 green bell pepper; chopped
- 7 oz. coconut milk
- 2 bay leaves
- 3 garlic cloves; minced.
- Salt and black pepper to the taste

For the marinade:
- 1 ½ cups water
- 1 ½ cups rice
- 1 tbsp. white wine
- 1 tbsp. soy sauce
- 1/2 tsp. sugar
- A pinch of white pepper

Directions:
1. In a bowl, mix chicken with sugar, white pepper, 1 tablespoon soy sauce and 1 tablespoon white wine, stir and keep in the fridge for 20 minutes.
2. Set your instant pot on Sauté mode; add peanut oil and heat it up

3. Add onion and shallot, stir and cook for 3 minutes
4. Add garlic, salt, and pepper, stir and cook for 2 minutes more.
5. Add chicken, stir and brown for 2 minutes
6. Add turmeric and cumin, stir and cook for 1 minute.
7. Add bay leaves, carrots, potatoes, bell pepper, coconut milk and 1 tablespoon soy sauce
8. Stir everything, place steamer basket in the pot, place the rice in a bowl and the basket
9. Add 1 ½ cups water in the bowl, seal the instant pot lid and cook at High for 4 minutes.
10. Release the pressure naturally, take the rice out of the pot and divide among plates, add cornstarch to pot and stir
11. Add chicken next to rice and serve.

Mix Rice Medley.

(**Prep + Cooking Time:** 35 minutes | **Servings:** 4)

Ingredients:
- 3/8 to 1/2 tsp. sea salt, optional
- 3/4 cup. (or more) short grain brown rice.
- 2 to 4 tbsp. red, wild or black rice
- 1 tbsp. water
- 1 ½ cups. water

Directions:
1. Put as much as 2 to 4 tablespoons of red, wild, or black rice or use all three kinds in 1-cup measuring cup.
2. Add brown rice to make 1 cup. total of rice. Put the rice in a strainer and wash. Put the rice in the Instant Pot
3. Add 1 ½ cup. plus 1 tablespoon water in the pot. If desired, add salt.
4. Stir and then check the sides of the pot to make sure the rice is pushed down into the water. Close and lock the lid. Press MULTIGRAIN and set the time to 23 minutes.
5. When the timer beeps, let the pressure release naturally for 5 minutes, then turn the steam valve and release the pressure slowly
6. If you have time, let the pressure release naturally for 15 minutes. Stir and serve.

Delicious Rice Pudding

(**Prep + Cooking Time:** 45 minutes | **Servings:** 4)

Ingredients:
- 2 cups black rice, washed and rinsed
- 6 ½ cups water
- 3/4 cup sugar
- 5 cardamom pods, crushed.
- 3 cloves
- 1/2 cup coconut, grated
- Chopped mango for serving
- 2 cinnamon sticks
- A pinch of salt

Directions:
1. Put the rice in your instant pot, add a pinch of salt and the water and stir
2. In a cheesecloth bag, mix cardamom with cinnamon and cloves and tie it.
3. Place this in the pot with the rice, close the lid and cook on Low for 35 minutes
4. Release the pressure naturally, open the instant pot lid, stir the rice, add coconut and set your pot to sauté mode
5. Cook for 10 minutes, discard spices bag, transfer to breakfast bowls and serve with chopped mango on top.

Rice Bowl

(Prep + Cooking Time: 12 minutes | **Servings:** 4)

Ingredients:
- 1 cup brown rice
- 1 cup coconut milk
- 2 cups water
- 1/2 cup maple syrup
- 1/2 cup coconut chips
- 1/4 cup raisins
- 1/4 cup almonds
- A pinch of cinnamon powder
- A pinch of salt

Directions:
1. Put the rice in a pot, add the water, place on stove over medium high heat, cook according to instructions, drain and transfer it to your instant pot.
2. Add milk, coconut chips, almonds, raisins, salt, cinnamon and maple syrup, stir well, seal the instant pot lid and cook at High for 5 minutes
3. Quick release the pressure, transfer rice to breakfast bowls and serve right away.

Simple White Rice.

(Prep + Cooking Time: 15 minutes | **Servings:** 4)

Ingredients:
- 1 cup. white basmati rice
- 1 cup. water

Directions:
1. Put the rice in a colander. Rinse until the water is clear
2. Transfer into the Instant Pot and then add the water.
3. Set the pot to "Manual", set the pressure to "Low", and the timer to 8 minutes.
4. When the timer beeps, quick release the pressure.
5. Fluff the rice using a fork and serve

Lentils and Rice

(Prep + Cooking Time: 45 minutes | **Servings:** 6)

Ingredients:
- 1 cup basmati rice; rinsed and drained
- 2 cups thinly sliced yellow onions
- 1/3 cup brown lentils
- 2 cups water
- 2 tbsp. Ghee
- 1/2 tsp. ground cumin
- 1/2 tsp. ground coriander
- Salt to taste

Directions:
1. Place the lentils in a small bowl. Cover with hot water and let soak while you get everything else going.
2. Now Press "Sauté" on the Instant Pot. When the pot is hot, add the ghee. When the ghee has melted, add the onions.
3. Season with a little salt and cook, stirring, until the onions begin to crisp around the edges but are not burned, 5 to 10 minutes. Remove half the onions from the pot and reserve for garnish. Now Press "Cancel".
4. Drain the lentils. Add the lentils, water, rice, cumin and coriander to the pot and season with salt. Stir well to combine
5. Now secure the lid on the pot and close the valve. Now Press "Manual" and set the pot at "High" pressure for 6 minutes. After completing the cooking time, allow the pot to sit undisturbed for 10 minutes, then release any remaining pressure
6. Very gently stir and place the lid halfway on the pot. Let the rice and lentils rest for 5 to 10 minutes. Transfer the rice and lentils to a serving dish. Sprinkle with the reserved onions and serve.

Sauce Recipes

Guava Sauce Recipe

(Prep + Cooking Time: 30 minutes | **Servings:** 6)

Ingredients:
- 1 can guava shells and syrup
- 2 onions; chopped.
- 2 garlic cloves; chopped.
- 1/2 tsp. nutmeg
- 2 bird chilies; chopped.
- 1-inch ginger piece; minced.
- 1/4 cup vegetable oil
- Juice from 2 lemons

Directions:
1. Put guava shells and syrup in your blender, pulse well and leave aside.
2. Set your instant pot on Sauté mode; add oil and heat it up
3. Add onion and garlic, stir and cook for 4 minutes
4. Add guava mix, ginger, lemon juice, chilies and nutmeg; then stir well. seal the instant pot lid and cook on High for 15 minutes.
5. Quick release the pressure, open the instant pot lid and serve sauce with fish

Carrot Sauce Recipe

(Prep + Cooking Time: 25 minutes | **Servings:** 6)

Ingredients:
- 2 cups carrot juice
- 4 tbsp. butter
- 1 tbsp. mixed chervil, chives and tarragon
- Salt and black pepper to the taste
- A pinch of cayenne pepper
- A pinch of cinnamon

Directions:
1. Put carrot juice in your instant pot, set the pot on Simmer mode and bring to a boil.
2. Add butter, salt, pepper, cayenne and cinnamon; then stir well. seal the instant pot lid and cook at High for 5 minutes.
3. Quick release the pressure, carefully open the lid; add mixed herbs, stir and serve

Pineapple Sauce

(Prep + Cooking Time: 13 minutes | **Servings:** 4)

Ingredients:
- 3 cups pineapple tidbits
- 3 tbsp. rum
- 1 tsp. cinnamon
- 1 tsp. ginger
- 1 tsp. allspice
- 1 tsp. nutmeg
- 3 tbsp. butter
- 4 tbsp. brown sugar

Directions:
1. Set your instant pot on sauté mode; add butter and melt it.
2. Add sugar, pineapple tidbits, rum, allspice, nutmeg, cinnamon and ginger; then stir well. seal the instant pot lid and cook at High for 3 minutes.
3. Quick release the pressure, carefully open the lid; stir sauce one more time and serve.

Garden Salsa

(Prep + Cooking Time: 20 minutes | **Makes:** 7 Cups)

Ingredients:
- 8 large tomatoes, roughly chopped
- 6 garlic cloves, finely diced
- 1/4 cup tomato paste
- 2 jalapeño peppers, seeded and diced
- 1 bell pepper, any color; diced
- 1 small red onion; diced
- 1 small yellow onion; diced
- 1 tbsp. ground cumin

- 2 tbsp. freshly squeezed lime juice
- 1/2 tsp. baking soda
- 1/2 tsp. freshly ground black pepper
- 4 tsp. salt or as your liking
- Chopped fresh cilantro leaves, to taste

Directions:
1. In the Instant Pot, stir together the tomatoes, garlic, jalapeños, bell pepper, red onion, yellow onion, cumin, salt, pepper and baking soda
2. Lock the lid and turn the steam release handle to Sealing. Using the Manual function, set the cooker to High Pressure for 5 minutes
3. After completing the cooking time, let the pressure release naturally for 10 minutes; quick release any remaining pressure.
4. Remove the lid carefully and stir in the tomato paste, lime juice and cilantro. Let cool completely before serving

Mushroom Gravy

(Prep + Cooking Time: 40 minutes | Servings: 5)

Ingredients:
- 8 ounces baby bella mushrooms; diced
- 1 ¼ cups Vegetable Stock
- 1/4 cup red wine
- 1/2 small sweet onion; diced
- 2 garlic cloves; minced
- 1 tbsp. cornstarch
- 2 tbsp. vegan Worcestershire sauce
- 1 tbsp. olive oil
- 1 tsp. Montreal chicken seasoning
- 1 tsp. Dijon mustard
- 1 tsp. rubbed sage

Directions:
1. Select the "Sauté" Low mode on your instant pot. When the display reads "Hot," add the oil and heat until it shimmers
2. Add the mushrooms and onion. Sauté for 2 to 3 minutes, stirring frequently. Turn off the Instant Pot and add the garlic. Cook, stirring so it doesn't burn, for 30 seconds more.
3. Add the Worcestershire sauce, mustard, sage, Montreal chicken seasoning, ¾ cup of stock and the red wine.
4. Lock the lid and turn the steam release handle to Sealing. Using the Manual function, set the cooker to High Pressure for 20 minutes
5. After completing the cooking time, let the pressure release naturally for 10 minutes; quick release any remaining pressure.
6. In a small bowl, whisk the remaining ½ cup of stock and cornstarch.
7. Remove the lid carefully and stir this slurry into the gravy. Select Sauté Low again and simmer the gravy for 2 to 3 minutes until thickened.

Orange Sauce

(Prep + Cooking Time: 17 minutes | Servings: 6)

Ingredients:
- 1 cup orange juice
- 1/4 cup white wine vinegar
- 2 tbsp. agave nectar
- 1/4 cup veggie stock
- 2 tbsp. cornstarch
- 1 tsp. ginger paste
- 2 tbsp. tomato paste
- 3 tbsp. sugar
- 1 tsp. sesame oil
- 1 tsp. chili sauce
- 2 tbsp. soy sauce
- 1 tsp. garlic; finely chopped

Directions:
1. Set your instant pot on Sauté mode; add oil and heat it up
2. Add garlic and ginger paste, stir and cook for 2 minutes.
3. Add tomato paste, sugar, orange juice, vinegar, agave nectar, soy and chili sauce; then stir well. seal the instant pot lid and cook at High for 3 minutes more.

4. Quick release the pressure, carefully open the lid; add stock and cornstarch; then stir well. seal the instant pot lid again and cook at High for 4 minutes
5. Release pressure again and serve your sauce

Poblano Sauce

(Prep + Cooking Time: 20 minutes | Makes: 3 Cups)

Ingredients:
- 2 poblano peppers, roasted
- 1 medium sweet potato, peeled and chopped
- 1 cup raw cashews, soaked in water overnight, drained and rinsed well
- 1 cup unsweetened nondairy milk
- 1 cup water
- 1/4 cup nutritional yeast
- 1 tbsp. apple cider vinegar
- 2 tsp. salt or as your liking
- 1/4 tsp. garlic powder
- Pinch freshly ground black pepper
- Chili powder, to taste; optional

Directions:
1. In the Instant Pot, combine the sweet potato and water. Lock the lid and turn the steam release handle to Sealing
2. Using the Manual function, set the cooker to High Pressure for 5 minutes.
3. After completing the cooking time, quick release the pressure. Remove the lid carefully and drain the water from the pot
4. In a high-speed blender or food processor, combine the cashews, milk, nutritional yeast, vinegar, salt, garlic powder and pepper.
5. Blend until completely smooth. Add the sweet potatoes and blend again. Finally, add the poblanos and pulse just until there are green specks throughout
6. Pour the blended mixture back into the Instant Pot. Using a rubber spatula, make sure you get as much as possible.
7. Select Sauté Low. When the sauce is hot, turn off the Instant Pot. Taste and adjust the seasonings. If you want more heat, add chili powder to taste

Cashew Sour Cream

(Prep + Cooking Time: 5 minutes | **Servings:** 5)

Ingredients:
- 1/4 cup nondairy milk; or more as needed
- 1 cup raw cashews, soaked in water overnight, drained and rinsed well
- Juice of 1 lemon; or more as needed
- 1 ½ tsp. apple cider vinegar
- 1/2 tsp. salt or as your liking

Directions:
1. In a blender, combine the cashews, lemon juice, milk, vinegar and salt. Blend until completely smooth
2. Taste and add more salt or lemon juice as desired.
3. If you want a thinner cream, add a little more milk. Keep refrigerated in an airtight container for 4 to 6 days

Apple sauce

(Prep + Cooking Time: 18 minutes | **Servings:** 4)

Ingredients:
- 8 apples, cored and chopped.
- 1 tsp. cinnamon powder
- 2 drops cinnamon oil
- 1 cup water

Directions:
1. Put apples in your instant pot, add the water, close the lid and cook at High for 8 minutes
2. Quick release the pressure, carefully open the lid; add oil and cinnamon and puree using an immersion blender. serve cold.

Tomato Sauce

(Prep + Cooking Time: 25 minutes | **Servings:** 20)

Ingredients:
- 2 lb. tomatoes; peeled and chopped.
- 1 apple, cored and chopped.
- 3 tsp. whole spice
- 1/2 lb. brown sugar
- 1/2-pint vinegar
- 1 yellow onion; chopped.
- 6 oz. sultanas; chopped.
- 3 oz. dates chopped
- Salt to the taste

Directions:
1. Put tomatoes in your instant pot
2. Add apple, onion, sultanas, dates, salt, whole spice and half of the vinegar; then stir well. seal the instant pot lid and cook at High for 10 minutes.
3. Quick release the pressure, carefully open the lid; set it on Simmer mode, add the rest of the vinegar and sugar, stir and simmer until sugar dissolves
4. Transfer to jars and serve when needed

Red Enchilada Sauce

(Prep + Cooking Time: 20 minutes | Makes: 3 Cups)

Ingredients:
- 2 canned chipotle peppers in adobo sauce
- 2 tomatoes, chopped
- 6 garlic cloves, peeled
- 1/2 red onion, chopped
- 1/2 cup Vegetable Stock
- 2 poblano peppers, chopped
- 8 ounces tomato paste
- 1 tbsp. adobo sauce from the can
- 1 tsp. chili powder; or more as needed
- 1 tsp. apple cider vinegar
- 1/2 tsp. smoked paprika
- 1 tsp. ground cumin
- 1 tsp. salt or as your liking

Directions:
1. In the Instant Pot, combine the garlic, poblanos, tomatoes, chipotles, red onion, stock, adobo sauce, chili powder, cumin, salt, vinegar and paprika. Stir well
2. Spoon the tomato paste on top, without mixing it in. Lock the lid and turn the steam release handle to Sealing. Using the Manual function, set the cooker to High Pressure for 10 minutes.
3. After completing the cooking time, turn off the Instant Pot and let the pressure release naturally until the pin drops
4. Remove the lid carefully. Using an immersion blender. There may still be a few small intact pieces of basil—I like it that way

Ginger and Orange Sauce

(Prep + Cooking Time: 12 minutes | **Servings:** 4)

Ingredients:
- 1-inch ginger piece; chopped
- 1 tbsp. olive oil
- 1 cup fish stock
- 4 spring onions; chopped.
- Salt and black pepper to the taste
- Zest and juice from 1 orange

Directions:
1. In your instant pot, mix fish stock with salt, pepper, olive oil, spring onions, ginger, orange juice and zest and stir well

2. Seal the instant pot lid and cook at High for 7 minutes.
3. Quick release the pressure, open the instant pot lid and serve your sauce

Mushroom Gravy

(Prep + Cooking Time: 40 minutes | **Servings:** 5)

Ingredients:
- 8 ounces baby bella mushrooms; diced
- 1 ¼ cups Vegetable Stock
- 1/4 cup red wine
- 1/2 small sweet onion; diced
- 2 garlic cloves; minced
- 1 tbsp. cornstarch
- 2 tbsp. vegan Worcestershire sauce
- 1 tbsp. olive oil
- 1 tsp. Montreal chicken seasoning
- 1 tsp. Dijon mustard
- 1 tsp. rubbed sage

Directions:
8. Select the "Sauté" Low mode on your instant pot. When the display reads "Hot," add the oil and heat until it shimmers
9. Add the mushrooms and onion. Sauté for 2 to 3 minutes, stirring frequently. Turn off the Instant Pot and add the garlic. Cook, stirring so it doesn't burn, for 30 seconds more
10. Add the Worcestershire sauce, mustard, sage, Montreal chicken seasoning, ¾ cup of stock and the red wine.
11. Lock the lid and turn the steam release handle to Sealing. Using the Manual function, set the cooker to High Pressure for 20 minutes
12. After completing the cooking time, let the pressure release naturally for 10 minutes; quick release any remaining pressure.
13. In a small bowl, whisk the remaining ½ cup of stock and cornstarch.
14. Remove the lid carefully and stir this slurry into the gravy. Select Sauté Low again and simmer the gravy for 2 to 3 minutes until thickened

Leeks Sauce Recipe

(Prep + Cooking Time: 12 minutes | **Servings:** 8)

Ingredients:
- 2 leeks, thinly sliced
- 2 tbsp. butter
- 1 cup whipping cream
- 3 tbsp. lemon juice
- Salt and pepper to the taste

Directions:
1. Set your instant pot on Sauté mode; add butter and melt it.
2. Add leeks, stir and cook for 2 minutes.
3. Add lemon juice; then stir well. seal the instant pot lid and cook at High for 3 minutes
4. Quick release the pressure, carefully open the lid; transfer sauce to your blender, add whipping cream and blend everything.
5. Return sauce to the pot, set on Simmer mode, add salt and pepper to the taste, stir and cook for 2 minutes.
6. Serve with fish

Basil Red Sauce

(Prep + Cooking Time: 45 minutes | **Makes:** 4 Cups)

Ingredients:
- 2 medium tomatoes, quartered
- 4 ounces tomato paste
- 2 garlic cloves, peeled
- 3 cups butternut squash, peeled and cubed
- ¼ to ½ cup water; if necessary
- 1/2 cup fresh sweet basil leaves, torn
- 1 bay leaf
- Pinch red pepper flakes

- 2 tbsp. fresh Italian parsley leaves
- 1/4 tsp. baking soda
- 1 tsp. salt or as your liking
- 1/2 tsp. freshly ground black pepper

Directions:
1. In the Instant Pot, combine the squash, tomatoes, garlic and water (if using). Top with the tomato paste, bay leaf, salt, pepper, baking soda and red pepper flakes
2. There is no need to stir. Lock the lid and turn the steam release handle to Sealing. Using the Manual function, set the cooker to High Pressure for 20 minutes.
3. After completing the cooking time, let the pressure release naturally for 10 to 15 minutes; quick release any remaining pressure
4. Remove the lid carefully, Let the sauce cool for a few minutes. Discard the bay leaf and add the basil and parsley. Using an immersion blender, blend the sauce until smooth

Mustard Sauce Recipe

(Prep + Cooking Time: 18 minutes | **Servings:** 4)

Ingredients:
- 6 oz. mushrooms; chopped.
- 3.5 oz. beef stock
- 3.5 oz. dry sherry
- 1 thyme spring
- 1 garlic clove; minced.
- 2 tbsp. parsley; finely chopped
- 3 tbsp. olive oil
- 1 tbsp. balsamic vinegar
- 1 tbsp. mustard
- 2 tbsp. crème fraiche

Directions:
1. Set your instant pot on Sauté mode; add oil and heat it up.
2. Add garlic, thyme and mushrooms, stir and cook for 5 minutes.
3. Add sherry, vinegar and stock; then stir well. seal the instant pot lid and cook at High for 3 minutes.
4. Quick release the pressure, carefully open the lid; discard thyme, add crème fraiche, mustard, and parsley; then stir well. set the pot on Simmer mode and cook the sauce for 3 minutes
5. Serve right away

Garlic Red Sauce

(Prep + Cooking Time: 40 minutes | Makes: 2 ½ Cups)

Ingredients:
- 1 pound tomatoes, quartered
- 4 ounces tomato paste
- 1 small sweet onion, peeled and quartered
- 1/2 cup water; or more as needed
- ⅓ cup strong hearty wine
- 5 garlic cloves; or to taste, peeled
- 1 ½ tsp. dried oregano
- 1/4 tsp. baking soda
- 1 tsp. dried basil
- 1 tsp. salt or as your liking
- Pinch red pepper flakes

Directions:
1. Drop the tomatoes and onion into the Instant Pot. Add the wine, water and tomato paste. Cover the veggies with the garlic; oregano, basil, salt, baking soda and red pepper flakes
2. There is no need to stir; it's better to have everything mostly on top of the tomatoes than at the bottom of the pot
3. Lock the lid and turn the steam release handle to Sealing. Using the Manual function, set the cooker to High Pressure for 20 minutes.
4. After completing the cooking time, turn off the Instant Pot and let the pressure release naturally for 15 minutes; quick release any remaining pressure.
5. Remove the lid carefully. Using an immersion blender, create the red sauce of your dreams. Add a bit more water (or wine!) if you need to thin it

Peach Sauce Recipe

(Prep + Cooking Time: 8 minutes | **Servings:** 6)

Ingredients:
- 10 oz. peaches, stoned and chopped.
- 2 tbsp. cornstarch
- 3 tbsp. sugar
- 1/2 cup water
- 1/8 tsp. almond extract
- 1/8 tsp. nutmeg, ground.
- 1/8 tsp. cinnamon
- A pinch of salt

Directions:
1. In your instant pot, mix peaches with nutmeg, cornstarch, sugar, cinnamon and salt; then stir well. seal the instant pot lid and cook at High for 3 minutes.
2. Quick release the pressure, carefully open the lid; add almond extract, stir and serve sauce.

Plum Sauce Recipe

(Prep + Cooking Time: 25 minutes | **Servings:** 20)

Ingredients:
- 3 lb. plumps, pitted and chopped.
- 2 apples, cored and chopped.
- 4 tbsp. ginger, ground.
- 1 ½ tbsp. salt
- 2 onions; chopped.
- 4 tbsp. cinnamon
- 4 tbsp. allspice
- 1-pint vinegar
- 3/4 lb. sugar

Directions:
1. Put plumps, apples, and onions in your instant pot
2. Add ginger, cinnamon, allspice, salt and almost all the vinegar; then stir well. seal the instant pot lid and cook at High for 10 minutes.
3. Quick release the pressure, carefully open the lid; set it on Simmer mode, add the rest of the vinegar and the sugar, stir and cook until sugar dissolves.

Sriracha Sauce

(Prep + Cooking Time: 25 minutes | **Servings:** 6)

Ingredients:
- 4 oz. red chilies, seeded and chopped.
- 3 tbsp. palm sugar
- 3 oz. bird's eye chilies
- 12 garlic cloves; minced.
- 5 oz. distilled vinegar
- 5 oz. water

Directions:
1. In your instant pot, mix water with palm sugar and stir
2. Add all chilies and garlic; then stir well. seal the instant pot lid and cook at High for 7 minutes
3. Quick release the pressure, carefully open the lid; blend sauce using an immersion blender, add vinegar; then stir well. set the pot on Simmer mode and cook the sauce for 10 minutes
4. Serve when needed

Cranberry Sauce

(Prep + Cooking Time: 25 minutes | **Servings:** 4)

Ingredients:
- 12 oz. cranberries
- 1/4 cup orange juice
- 2 ½ tsp. orange zest
- 2 tbsp. maple syrup
- A pinch of salt
- 1 cup sugar

Directions:
1. In your instant pot, mix orange juice with maple syrup and stir well
2. Add orange zest and almost all cranberries; then stir well. seal the instant pot lid and cook at High for 2 minutes
3. Quick release the pressure, open the instant pot lid and set it on Sauté mode.
4. Add the rest of the cranberries, a pinch of salt and the sugar, stir and cook until sugar dissolves. Serve cold.

Beans, Legumes & Grains

Cracked Wheat and Jaggery

(**Prep + Cooking Time:** 22 minutes | **Servings:** 2)

Ingredients:
- 2 cups cracked wheat
- 2 cups jaggery
- 3 cloves
- 1 cup milk
- 1 tsp. fennel seeds
- 2 ½ cups clarified butter
- 3 cups water
- A pinch of salt
- A few almonds; chopped.

Directions:
1. Set your instant pot on Sauté mode; add butter and heat it up
2. Add cracked wheat, stir and cook for 5 minutes
3. Add cloves and fennel seeds, stir and cook for 2 minutes
4. Add jaggery, a pinch of salt, milk and water; then stir well. close the lid and cook at High for 10 minutes.
5. Quick release the pressure, open the instant pot lid, divide into bowls and serve with chopped almonds on top

Cold Quinoa Salad with Pecans and Fruit

(**Prep + Cooking Time:** 25 minutes | **Servings:** 5)

Ingredients:
- 1/2 cup fresh cilantro, chopped
- 1 cup pecans, chopped
- 1/2 bunch scallions, green and light green parts, sliced
- 2 celery stalks, halved lengthwise and chopped
- 2 apples, unpeeled; cut into large dice
- 1 cup quinoa; rinsed
- 1 cup dried cranberries, white raisins and regular raisins
- 1 cup water
- 2 tbsp. freshly squeezed lemon juice
- 1 tbsp. white rice vinegar
- 2 tbsp. avocado oil; or walnut oil
- 1 tsp. chili powder
- 1/4 tsp. salt; or more as your liking
- Pinch freshly ground black pepper

Directions:
1. In the Instant Pot, combine the quinoa, water and salt and stir
2. Lock the lid and turn the steam release handle to Sealing. Using the Manual function, set the cooker to High Pressure for 8 minutes.
3. After completing the cooking time, let the pressure release naturally for 10 minutes; quick release any remaining pressure
4. Remove the lid carefully and transfer the quinoa to a large bowl. Refrigerate for 5 minutes to cool.
5. In a small resealable container, combine the apples, lemon juice and vinegar. Cover and shake lightly to coat the apples, then refrigerate
6. Remove the cooled quinoa from the refrigerator and stir in the scallions, celery, cranberry-raisin mix, chili powder and oil.
7. Taste and season with more salt and pepper, as needed. Stir the apples and whatever lemon-vinegar juice is in the container into the salad. Add the cilantro and pecans immediately before serving

Cranberry Beans Mix

(Prep + Cooking Time: 25 minutes | **Servings:** 6)

Ingredients:
- 1 ½ cups cranberry beans; soaked for 8 hours and drained
- 8 cups kale; chopped.
- 4 oz. shiitake mushrooms; chopped.
- 4-inch kombu piece; sliced
- 4 bacon slices; chopped
- 1/2 tsp. garlic powder
- 1 tsp. extra virgin olive oil
- Salt and black pepper to the taste

Directions:
1. Put beans in your instant pot, add 2 inches' water, salt, pepper, kombu, close the lid and cook at High for 8 minutes.
2. Release the pressure open the instant pot lid, transfer beans and cooking liquid to a pot and leave aside for now
3. Set your pot on Sauté mode; add oil and heat it up
4. Add garlic powder, bacon, mushrooms, salt, pepper and 3/4 cup cooking liquid from the pot, stir well and cook for 1 minute.
5. Seal the instant pot lid; cook at High for 3 minutes and Quick release the pressure.
6. Add beans and kale, stir and divide into bowls

Chickpeas Curry

(Prep + Cooking Time: 30 minutes | **Servings:** 6)

Ingredients:
- 28 oz. canned tomatoes; chopped.
- 3 potatoes; cubed
- 3 cups chickpeas; already cooked; drained and rinsed
- 1 yellow onion; finely chopped
- 2 tsp. garam masala
- 2 tsp. coriander; ground.
- 2 tsp. turmeric; ground.
- 4 tsp. cumin seeds
- 1/2 cup water
- 8 tsp. olive oil
- 4 tsp. garlic; minced.
- Salt and black pepper to the taste
- Basmati rice; already cooked for serving
- Some cilantro; chopped for serving

Directions:
1. Set your instant pot on Sauté mode; add oil and heat it up.
2. Add cumin seeds; stir and cook for 30 seconds
3. Add onion; stir and cook for 5 minutes
4. Add garlic, garam masala, coriander, turmeric, tomatoes, potatoes, chickpeas, water, salt and pepper; then stir well. close the lid and cook at High for 15 minutes.
5. Quick release the pressure; open the instant pot lid, divide chickpeas curry on plates and serve with rice on the side and cilantro on top

Kidney Beans Curry Recipe

(Prep + Cooking Time: 1 hour and 10 minutes | **Servings:** 8)

Ingredients:
- 2 cups red kidney beans, soaked for 8 hours and drained
- 1-inch piece ginger; chopped
- 1 tsp. turmeric; ground.
- 2 tbsp. vegetable oil
- 2 tsp. ghee
- 2 red chili peppers; dried and crushed.
- Salt and black pepper to the taste
- 6 cloves
- 1 tsp. cumin; ground.
- 1 tsp. coriander; ground.
- 1 yellow onion; chopped.
- 2 cups water
- 1 tsp. sugar
- 1 tsp. red pepper; ground.

- 2 tsp. garam masala
- 4 garlic cloves; chopped.
- 1 tsp. cumin seeds
- 2 tomatoes chopped
- 1/4 cup cilantro; chopped.

Directions:
1. Grind ginger, garlic and onion using a mortar and pestle and transfer paste to a bowl.
2. Set your instant pot on Sauté mode; add ghee and oil and heat it up.
3. Add red chili pepper, cloves and cumin seeds, stir and fry for 3 minutes
4. Add onion paste, stir and cook for 3 more minutes
5. Add coriander, cumin and turmeric, stir and cook for 30 seconds.
6. Add tomatoes, stir and cook 5 minutes.
7. Add beans, 2 cups water, salt, pepper and sugar; then stir well. close the lid and cook at High for 40 minutes.
8. Switch instant pot to Low and cook for 10 minutes more.
9. Quick release the pressure, open the instant pot lid; add red pepper, garam masala and cilantro; then stir well. divide among plates and serve

Garlic and Chickpeas

(**Prep + Cooking Time:** 45 minutes | **Servings:** 4)

Ingredients:
- 2 cups chickpeas, rinsed
- 2 tomatoes; chopped.
- 2 small cucumbers; chopped
- 2 bay leaves
- 4 garlic cloves
- Water
- 1 tsp. olive oil
- Salt and black pepper to the taste

Directions:
1. Put chickpeas in your instant pot
2. Add water, garlic and bay leaves; then stir well. close the lid and cook at High for 35 minutes.
3. Release the pressure naturally for 10 minutes, then release remaining pressure by turning the valve to 'Venting', carefully open the lid; drain water and put chickpeas and garlic in a bowl
4. Add cucumber, tomatoes, salt, pepper and oil, toss to coat and serve

Mexican Cranberry Beans

(**Prep + Cooking Time:** 30 minutes | **Servings:** 6)

Ingredients:
- 1 lb. cranberry beans, soaked for 8 hours and drained
- 1 yellow onion; chopped.
- 1 ½ tsp. cumin
- 1/3 cup cilantro; chopped.
- 3 ¼ cups water
- 4 garlic cloves; minced.
- 1 tbsp. chili powder
- 1 tsp. oregano; dried
- Salt and black pepper to the taste
- Cooked rice for serving

Directions:
1. Put beans in your instant pot; add the water, garlic and onion, close the lid and cook at High for 20 minutes.
2. Quick release the pressure, open the instant pot lid; add cumin, cilantro, oregano, chili powder, salt and pepper; stir well, mash a bit using a potato mashes, divide among plates on top of rice and serve

Creamy White Beans

(Prep + Cooking Time: 45 minutes | **Servings:** 8)

Ingredients:
- 1 lb. white beans
- 1 yellow onion; chopped.
- 1 green bell pepper; chopped.
- 5 cups water
- 2 celery ribs; chopped.
- 2 bay leaves
- 1 tsp. oregano
- 1 tsp. thyme
- 1 tbsp. soy sauce
- 1 tbsp. Tabasco sauce
- 4 garlic cloves; minced.
- Salt and white pepper to the taste

Directions:
1. Put beans and water in your instant pot
2. Add onion; celery, garlic, bell pepper, oregano, thyme, salt, white pepper and soy sauce; then stir well. close the lid and cook at High for 15 minutes
3. Release the pressure naturally for 15 minutes, carefully open the lid and set it on Simmer mode
4. Add more salt and pepper to the taste and Tabasco sauce; stir and cook for 20 minutes.
5. Divide into bowls and serve.

Classic Cranberry Bean Chili

(Prep + Cooking Time: 50 minutes | **Servings:** 8)

Ingredients:
- 1 lb. cranberry beans, soaked in water for 7 hours and drained
- 14 oz. canned tomatoes and green chilies; chopped.
- 5 cups water
- 1 ½ tsp. cumin; ground.
- 2 tbsp. tomato paste
- 1 tsp. chili powder
- 1/2 tsp. ancho chili powder
- 1/4 cup millet
- 1/2 cup bulgur
- 1 tsp. garlic; minced.
- 1/2 tsp. liquid smoke
- 1 tsp. oregano; dried
- Salt and black pepper to the taste
- Hot sauce for serving
- Pickled jalapenos for serving

Directions:
1. Put beans and 3 cups water in your instant pot, close the lid and cook at High for 25 minutes
2. Quick release the pressure, add the rest of the water, tomatoes and chilies, millet, bulgur, cumin, tomato paste, chili powder, garlic, liquid smoke, oregano, ancho chili powder, salt and pepper; then stir well. close the lid and cook on High for 10 minutes more
3. Release the pressure again, carefully open the lid; divide into bowls and serve with hot sauce on top and pickled jalapenos on the side.

Black Eyed Peas with Peanuts

(Prep + Cooking Time: 45 minutes | **Servings:** 6)

Ingredients:
- 1 cup dried black-eyed peas
- 1 cup chopped yellow onions
- 1 cup drained canned diced tomatoes
- 2 ½ cups water
- 1/2 cup peanut butter
- 2 cups frozen Swiss chard
- 1 tsp. salt or as your liking
- 1 tsp. black pepper

Directions:
1. In your Instant Pot, combine the water, Swiss chard, onions, tomatoes, black-eyed peas, salt and pepper. Stir to combine
2. Add the peanut butter to the top of the mixture; do not stir in. Be sure that everything, including the peanut butter, is submerged under the liquid. (This is to prevent the peanut butter from sticking to the pot and burning.)

3. Now secure the lid on the pot and close the valve. Now Press "Manual" and set the pot at "High" pressure for 15 minutes
4. After completing the cooking time, allow the pot to sit undisturbed for 10 minutes, then release any remaining pressure. Stir thoroughly before serving

Red Beans and Rice

(Prep + Cooking Time: 1 hour 15 minutes | **Servings:** 5)

Ingredients:
- 5 cups cooked white rice
- 2 celery stalks, sliced
- 5 garlic cloves; minced
- 2 cups dried red beans
- 4 cups Vegetable Stock
- 2 bay leaves
- 1 red onion; diced
- 1 bell pepper, any color; diced
- 1 tbsp. olive oil
- 2 tsp. Cajun seasoning
- 1/2 tsp. dried oregano
- 1/2 tsp. dried parsley
- Salt as your liking
- Freshly ground black pepper
- Chopped fresh parsley; for garnishing
- Hot sauce; for serving

Directions:
1. Select the "Sauté" Low mode on your instant pot. When the display reads "Hot," add the oil and heat until it shimmers
2. Add the red onion, bell pepper and celery. Cook for 3 to 4 minutes, stirring frequently.
3. Turn off the Instant Pot and add the garlic, bay leaves, Cajun seasoning; oregano and dried parsley. Continue to cook for 1 minute more, stirring
4. Stir in the beans and stock. Lock the lid and turn the steam release handle to Sealing. Using the Manual function, set the cooker to High Pressure for 40 minutes.
5. After completing the cooking time, let the pressure release naturally for about 25 minutes; or until the pin drops
6. Remove the lid carefully and remove and discard the bay leaves.
7. Taste and season with salt and pepper, as needed. Serve with rice and top with parsley and hot sauce

Cheesy Barley Dish

(Prep + Cooking Time: 35 minutes | **Servings:** 4)

Ingredients:
- 1 ½ cups pearl barley, rinsed
- 1 tbsp. extra-virgin olive oil
- 1 tbsp. butter
- 1/3 cup mushrooms; chopped.
- 4 cups veggie stock
- 2 ¼ cups water
- 1 white onion; chopped.
- 3 tbsp. parsley; chopped.
- 1 cup parmesan cheese; grated
- 1 garlic clove; minced.
- 1 celery stalk; chopped.
- Salt and black pepper to the taste

Directions:
1. Set your instant pot on Sauté mode; add oil and butter and heat them up
2. Add onion and garlic; stir and cook for 4 minutes.
3. Add celery and barley and toss to coat
4. Add mushrooms, water, stock, salt and pepper; then stir well. close the lid and cook at High for 18 minutes.
5. Quick release the pressure, open the instant pot lid; add cheese and parsley and more salt and pepper if needed, stir for 2 minutes; divide into bowls and serve

Green Chile and Baked Beans

(Prep + Cooking Time: 1 hour 25 minutes | **Servings:** 5)

Ingredients:
- 1 pound dried navy beans, soaked in water overnight; rinsed and drained
- 1/4 cup maple syrup
- 1 ½ cups diced roasted green chiles
- 1/4 cup blackstrap molasses
- 1/4 cup packed light brown sugar
- 1 small sweet onion; cut into large dice
- 3 garlic cloves; minced
- 2 tbsp. ketchup
- 1 tbsp. vegan Worcestershire sauce
- 1 tbsp. olive oil
- 1 tsp. salt or as your liking
- 1 tsp. apple cider vinegar

Directions:
1. In a small bowl, whisk the molasses, maple syrup, brown sugar, ketchup and Worcestershire sauce. Set aside
2. Select the "Sauté" Low mode on your instant pot. When the display reads "Hot," add the oil and heat until it shimmers.
3. Add the onion and garlic. Turn off the Instant Pot and sauté the veggies for 1 to 2 minutes, stirring frequently. Add the salt, beans and molasses mix, stirring well
4. Lock the lid and turn the steam release handle to Sealing. Using the Manual function, set the cooker to High Pressure for 35 minutes
5. After completing the cooking time, let the pressure release naturally for 20 minutes; or until the pin drops.
6. Remove the lid carefully and stir. Select Sauté Medium. Stir in the green chiles and simmer the beans for 5 to 10 minutes; or until the sauce thickens. Stir in the vinegar and serve

Asian Lentils Recipe

(Prep + Cooking Time: 30 minutes | **Servings:** 4)

Ingredients:
- 1 cup red lentils
- 1/4 tsp. red pepper flakes
- 1 yellow onion; chopped.
- 2 tsp. cumin
- 1/4 tsp. coriander
- 1/4 tsp. garlic powder
- 3 tsp. butter
- 1 tsp. extra virgin olive oil
- 1/4 tsp. turmeric
- 1/4 tsp. Aleppo pepper
- Salt and black pepper to the taste
- 3 cups chicken stock

Directions:
1. Set your instant pot on Sauté mode; add butter and oil and heat up
2. Add onions; stir and cook for 4 minutes
3. Add cumin, coriander, garlic powder, turmeric, Aleppo pepper and pepper flakes, stir and cook for 2 minutes.
4. Add lentils and stock; then stir well. close the lid and cook at High for 15 minutes
5. Quick release the pressure, carefully open the lid; divide into bowls and serve

Kidney Beans Dish

(Prep + Cooking Time: 35 minutes | **Servings:** 8)

Ingredients:
- 1 lb. red kidney beans, soaked for 8 hours and drained
- 8 oz. smoked Cajun Tasso; chopped.
- 1 celery rib; chopped.
- 2 tbsp. garlic; minced.
- 1 green bell pepper; chopped.
- 2 tsp. thyme; dried
- 4 green onions; chopped.
- 2 yellow onions; chopped.
- 3 tbsp. extra virgin olive oil
- 2 bay leaves
- Cajun seasoning to the taste
- Hot sauce to the taste

Directions:
1. Set your instant pot on Sauté mode; add oil and heat it up
2. Add Tasso; then stir well. cook for 5 minutes and transfer to a bowl
3. Add onions and Cajun seasoning to the pot; stir and cook for 10 minutes
4. Add garlic, stir and cook 5 minutes.
5. Add bell pepper and celery; stir and cook 5 minutes.
6. Add beans, water to cover everything, bay leaves, thyme, close the lid and cook at High for 15 minutes.
7. Quick release the pressure, open the instant pot lid, add Tasso and leave aside for 5 minutes
8. Divide beans and Tasso mix on plates, garnish with green onions and serve with hot sauce to the taste.

Pea and Parmesan Risotto

(Prep + Cooking Time: 35 minutes | **Servings:** 6)

Ingredients:
- 1 (16-oz.) bag frozen green peas
- 1 cup grated Parmesan cheese
- 1 medium yellow onion; diced.
- 2 garlic cloves; minced.
- 4 cups low-sodium vegetable broth
- 2 cups short-grain Arborio white rice
- 2 tbsp. extra-virgin olive oil.

Directions:
1. Select *Sauté* and add the olive oil to the inner pot. Once the oil is hot, add the onion and garlic and cook for 3 minutes or until they start to soften
2. Now, press *Cancel* and pour in the broth. Using a wooden spoon, scrape up any browned bits stuck to the bottom of the pot. Add the rice and peas and stir to combine
3. Now, Lock the lid. Select, "Manual or Pressure Cook" and set the pressure to *High* and the time to 5 minutes. Make sure the steam release knob is in the sealed position.
4. After completing the cooking cycle, naturally release the pressure for 5 minutes, then quick release any remaining pressure. Unlock and remove the lid. Stir in the Parmesan cheese. Serve hot

Cabbage & Navy Beans

(Prep + Cooking Time: 50 minutes | **Servings:** 8)

Ingredients:
- 1 ½ cups navy beans; soaked for 8 hours and drained
- 6 bacon slices; chopped.
- 1 cabbage head; chopped.
- 3 tbsp. white wine vinegar
- 1/4 tsp. cloves
- 1 yellow onion; chopped.
- 3 tbsp. honey
- 1 bay leaf
- 3 cups chicken stock
- Salt and black pepper to the taste

Directions:
1. Set your instant pot on Sauté mode; add bacon, stir and brown it for 4 minutes.
2. Add onions, stir and cook for 4 minutes
3. Add stock, beans, clove and bay leaf; then stir well. close the lid and cook at High for 35 minutes.
4. Quick release the pressure, carefully open the lid; add vinegar, honey and cabbage; then stir well. close the lid and cook at High for 12 minutes more
5. Release pressure again, carefully open the lid; add salt and pepper; then stir well. divide into bowls and serve.

Red Lentils with Turmeric

(Prep + Cooking Time: 25 minutes | **Servings:** 4)

Ingredients:
- ⅓ cup split red lentils
- 2⅓ cups water
- 2 tbsp. chopped yellow onion
- 1/2 tsp. ground turmeric
- 2 tsp. Niter Kibbeh
- 1/2 tsp. paprika
- 1 tsp. minced fresh ginger
- 1 tsp. minced garlic

Directions:
1. In a heatproof bowl that fits inside the Instant Pot, combine the lentils, ⅓ cup of the water, the onion, ginger, garlic, turmeric and paprika
2. Pour the remaining 2 cups water into the Instant Pot. Place a steamer rack in the pot. Place the bowl of lentils on the rack.
3. Now secure the lid on the pot and close the valve. Now Press "Manual" and set the pot at "High" pressure for 5 minutes. After completing the cooking time, quick release the pressure
4. In a small saucepan, melt the niter kibbeh over medium heat. Add the lentils and a little bit of water. Stir to combine. Bring the mixture to a simmer and cook until slightly thickened, 4 to 5 minutes

Tasty Mashed Sweet Potatoes

(Prep + Cooking Time: 38 minutes | **Servings:**10)

Ingredients:
- 5 medium sweet potatoes, peeled and cut into 1-inch pieces
- 1 tbsp. pure maple syrup
- 2 tbsp. unsalted butter
- 1 cup water
- 2 tsp. fine sea salt.
- 1 tsp. ground cinnamon

Directions:
1. Place the sweet potatoes in the inner pot. Add the water and cinnamon
2. Now, Lock the lid. Select, "Manual or Pressure Cook" and set the pressure to *High* and the time to 8 minutes. Make sure the steam release knob is in the sealed position.
3. After completing the cooking cycle, naturally release the pressure for 10 minutes, then quick release any remaining pressure
4. Unlock and remove the lid. Using a potato masher, mash the sweet potatoes with the remaining liquid in the pot. Once mashed, add the butter, maple syrup, and salt. Stir to combine. Serve hot

Veg Quinoa Tabbouleh.

(Prep + Cooking Time: 40 minutes | **Servings:**6)

Ingredients:
- 2 cups quinoa; rinsed.
- 4 scallions, white and light green parts only; chopped.
- ¼ cup chopped fresh flat-leaf parsley
- ⅓ cup pine nuts, toasted
- 3½ cups water
- 2 tbsp. chopped fresh mint
- 1 tbsp. extra-virgin olive oil.
- Juice of 1 lemon
- 1 English cucumber, peeled and diced
- 2 medium tomatoes; diced.

Directions:
1. Combine the quinoa, water, olive oil, and lemon juice in the inner pot
2. Now, Lock the lid. Select, "Manual or Pressure Cook" and set the pressure to *High* and the time to 20 minutes. Make sure the steam release knob is in the sealed position.
3. After completing the cooking cycle, quick release the pressure.
4. Unlock and remove the lid. Using a fork, fluff the quinoa, then stir in the cucumber, tomatoes, scallions, parsley, mint, and pine nuts. Serve hot

Delicious Frijoles

(Prep + Cooking Time: 1 hour 45 minutes | **Servings:** 4)

Ingredients:
- 1 cup finely chopped white onions
- 1/2 cup finely chopped fresh cilantro
- 1/2 cup finely chopped green bell pepper
- 1 cup dried pinto beans
- 3 cups cool water
- 4 garlic cloves; minced
- 1 (14.5-ounce) can fire-roasted diced tomatoes; undrained
- 6 slices bacon; chopped
- 1 ½ tsp. ground cumin
- 1 ½ tsp. salt or as your liking

Directions:
1. Place the pinto beans in a medium bowl. Cover with hot water. Soak for 1-hour drain. Place the pinto beans in the Instant Pot. Add the cool water, tomatoes and their juices, onions, cilantro, bell pepper, bacon, garlic, cumin and salt
2. Now secure the lid on the pot and close the valve. Now Press "Manual" and set the pot at "High" pressure for 30 minutes
3. After completing the cooking time, allow the pot to sit undisturbed for 10 minutes, then release any remaining pressure. If you like, use an immersion blender to puree some of the beans to thicken the broth.

Spicy Lentils

(Prep + Cooking Time: 34 minutes | **Servings:** 5)

Ingredients:
- 2 Roma tomatoes; diced
- 2 cups Vegetable Stock
- 1 cup green; rinsed and drained
- 1 cup well chopped kale
- 1 small onion; diced
- 1 or 2 garlic cloves, finely diced
- 1 bell pepper, any color; diced
- 1 tbsp. olive oil
- 1 tsp. smoked paprika
- 1 tsp. chili powder
- 1 tsp. ground cumin
- 1 tsp. salt; or more as your liking
- Freshly ground black pepper

Directions:
1. Select the "Sauté" Low mode on your instant pot. When the display reads "Hot," add the oil and heat until it shimmers
2. Add the onion. Sauté for 1 to 2 minutes and then turn off the Instant Pot. Add the garlic. Cook for about 30 seconds, stirring (don't let it burn).
3. Add the bell pepper, tomatoes, stock, lentils, salt, cumin, chili powder and paprika
4. Lock the lid and turn the steam release handle to Sealing. Using the Manual function, set the cooker to High Pressure for 15 minutes.
5. After completing the cooking time, let the Instant Pot go into Keep Warm mode and let the pressure release naturally for 10 minutes; quick release any remaining pressure.
6. Remove the lid carefully and stir in the kale, which will wilt after 1 to 2 minutes. Taste and season with salt and pepper, as needed

Bacon Butter Beans

(Prep + Cooking Time: 1 hour and 10 minutes | **Servings:** 8)

Ingredients:
- 1 lb. butter beans, soaked for 8 hours and drained
- 1/2 tsp. cumin; ground.
- 1 garlic clove; minced.
- 12 oz. beer
- 1 lb. bacon; chopped.
- 1 jalapeno pepper; chopped.
- 4 cups water
- Salt and black pepper to the taste

Directions:
1. Set your instant pot on Sauté mode; add bacon and brown it for 10 minutes
2. Transfer bacon to paper towels, drain grease, put in a bowl and leave aside.
3. Add the water, cumin and beer to your pot and stir
4. Add beans; then stir well. close the lid and cook at High for 30 minutes.
5. Quick release the pressure, open the instant pot lid, add garlic, bacon, jalapeno, salt and pepper; then stir well. close the lid again and cook at High for 3 minutes more.
6. Release pressure again, carefully open the lid; transfer to bowls and serve

Basmati Rice

(**Prep + Cooking Time:** 23 minutes | **Servings:** 6)

Ingredients:
- 3 cups water
- 2 cups white basmati rice; rinsed.

Directions:
1. Combine the rice and water in the inner pot.
2. Now, Lock the lid. Select, "Manual or Pressure Cook" and set the pressure to *High* and the time to 8 minutes. Make sure the steam release knob is in the sealed position.
3. After completing the cooking cycle, quick release the pressure. Unlock and remove the lid. Serve the rice immediately

Cold Quinoa Salad with Pecans and Fruit

(**Prep + Cooking Time:** 25 minutes | **Servings:** 5)

Ingredients:
- 1/2 cup fresh cilantro, chopped
- 1 cup pecans, chopped
- 1/2 bunch scallions, green and light green parts, sliced
- 2 celery stalks, halved lengthwise and chopped
- 2 apples, unpeeled; cut into large dice
- 1 cup quinoa; rinsed
- 1 cup dried cranberries, white raisins and regular raisins
- 1 cup water
- 2 tbsp. freshly squeezed lemon juice
- 1 tbsp. white rice vinegar
- 2 tbsp. avocado oil; or walnut oil
- 1 tsp. chili powder
- 1/4 tsp. salt; or more as your liking
- Pinch freshly ground black pepper

Directions:
1. In the Instant Pot, combine the quinoa, water and salt and stir.
2. Lock the lid and turn the steam release handle to Sealing. Using the Manual function, set the cooker to High Pressure for 8 minutes
3. After completing the cooking time, let the pressure release naturally for 10 minutes; quick release any remaining pressure.
4. Remove the lid carefully and transfer the quinoa to a large bowl. Refrigerate for 5 minutes to cool.
5. In a small re-sealable container, combine the apples, lemon juice and vinegar. Cover and shake lightly to coat the apples, then refrigerate
6. Remove the cooled quinoa from the refrigerator and stir in the scallions, celery, cranberry-raisin mix, chili powder and oil
7. Taste and season with more salt and pepper, as needed. Stir the apples and whatever lemon-vinegar juice is in the container into the salad. Add the cilantro and pecans immediately before serving.

Marrow Beans & Lemon Dish

(Prep + Cooking Time: 55 minutes | **Servings:** 4)

Ingredients:
- 2 cups marrow beans, soaked for 8 hours and drained
- 1 tbsp. rosemary; chopped.
- 4 garlic cloves; minced.
- 1 carrot; chopped
- 4 cups water
- 1 bay leaf
- 2 tbsp. lemon juice
- 1 cup yellow onion; chopped.
- 1 tbsp. extra-virgin olive oil
- Salt and black pepper to the taste
- Already cooked quinoa for serving

Directions:
1. Set your instant pot on Sauté mode; add oil and heat it up.
2. Add onion; carrot, garlic and rosemary, stir and cook for 3 minutes
3. Add water, bay leaf, beans and some salt; then stir well. close the lid and cook at High for 45 minutes.
4. Release the pressure naturally, open the instant pot lid, discard bay leaf, add salt and pepper to the taste and lemon juice; stir well and divide into bowls over already cooked quinoa

Lentils and Tomato Sauce

(Prep + Cooking Time: 30 minutes | **Servings:** 4)

Ingredients:
- 1 ½ cups lentils
- 1 yellow onion; chopped.
- 1 celery stalk; chopped.
- 1 ½ cups tomatoes; chopped.
- 1 tbsp. olive oil
- 1 green bell pepper; chopped.
- 1 tsp. curry powder
- 2 cups water
- Salt and black pepper to the taste

Directions:
1. Set your instant pot on Sauté mode; add the oil and heat it up.
2. Add celery, bell pepper, onion and tomatoes, stir and cook for 4 minutes
3. Add curry, salt, pepper, lentils and water; then stir well. close the lid and cook at High for 15 minutes
4. Quick release the pressure, open the instant pot lid; divide lentils among bowls and serve

Green Chile Chickpeas

(Prep + Cooking Time: 1 hour 15 minutes | **Servings:** 5)

Ingredients:
- 2 cups dried chickpeas; rinsed
- 1 small tomato; diced
- 6 cups water
- 1 cup diced roasted green chiles or from a can
- 2 tsp. freshly squeezed lemon juice
- 1 tsp. ground cumin
- 1/2 tsp. chili powder; or more as your liking
- 1/2 tsp. onion powder
- 1/4 tsp. dried oregano
- 1/2 tsp. garlic powder
- 1/2 tsp. red pepper flakes
- 1/2 tsp. smoked paprika
- 1/4 tsp. freshly ground black pepper
- 1 tsp. salt or as your liking

Directions:
1. In the Instant Pot, combine the chickpeas and water
2. Lock the lid and turn the steam release handle to Sealing. Using the Manual function, set the cooker to High Pressure for 45 minutes.
3. After completing the cooking time, let the pressure release naturally for 20 minutes; quick release any remaining pressure
4. Remove the lid carefully and drain the chickpeas, reserving 1 to 2 tbsp. of the cooking water. Return the chickpeas to the Instant Pot.

5. Stir in the tomato, green chiles, lemon juice, cumin, chili powder, salt, garlic powder, red pepper flakes, paprika, onion powder; oregano and black pepper. If they're too dry, add the reserved cooking water.
6. Select the "Sauté" Low mode on your instant pot and cook for 3 to 4 minutes. You may need to turn the Instant Pot off if anything starts to burn at the bottom
7. Put the lid back on and turn on the Keep Warm function. Let the chickpeas sit in all that goodness for 5 minutes, then they're ready

Re-fried Pinto Beans

(**Prep + Cooking Time:** 1 hour | **Servings:** 7)

Ingredients:
- 1 pound dried pinto beans; rinsed
- 2 quarts Vegetable Stock
- 1 onion, quartered
- 3 garlic cloves, peeled
- 1 tbsp. freshly squeezed lime juice
- 1 tbsp. olive oil
- 1 tbsp. salt or as your liking
- 1/2 tsp. chili powder
- 1 tsp. ground cumin
- 1 tsp. dried Mexican oregano
- 1/4 tsp. freshly ground black pepper

Directions:
1. In the Instant Pot, combine the oil, onion, garlic, beans, stock, cumin; oregano, chili powder and pepper
2. Lock the lid and turn the steam release handle to Sealing. Using the Manual function, set the cooker to High Pressure for 38 minutes.
3. After completing the cooking time, let the pressure release naturally for about 20 minutes; or until the pin drops
4. Remove the lid carefully and use a ladle to remove most of the remaining liquid, saving it.
5. Using an immersion blender, blend the beans until smooth, adding the cooking water back in as needed. Stir in the lime juice and salt

Mediterranean Lentils

(**Prep + Cooking Time:** 40 minutes | **Servings:** 3)

Ingredients:
- 1 cup brown or green lentils
- 1 tomato; diced
- 2 ½ cups Vegetable Stock
- 1 bay leaf
- 1 small sweet or yellow onion; diced
- 1 garlic clove; diced
- 1 tbsp. olive oil
- 1 tsp. dried oregano
- 1/2 tsp. ground cumin
- 1/2 tsp. dried parsley
- 1/2 tsp. salt or as your liking
- 1/4 tsp. freshly ground black pepper; or more as needed

Directions:
1. Select the "Sauté" Low mode on your instant pot. When the display reads "Hot," add the oil and heat until it shimmers
2. Add the onion. Cook for 3 to 4 minutes until soft. Turn off the Instant Pot and add the garlic; oregano, cumin, parsley, salt and pepper. Cook until fragrant, about 1 minute.
3. Stir in the tomato, lentils, stock and bay leaf. Lock the lid and turn the steam release handle to Sealing.
4. Using the Manual function, set the cooker to High Pressure for 18 minutes
5. After completing the cooking time, let the pressure release naturally for 10 minutes; quick release any remaining pressure.
6. Remove the lid carefully and remove and discard the bay leaf
7. Taste and season with more salt and pepper, as needed. If there's too much liquid remaining, select Sauté Medium or High and cook until it evaporate

Butternut Lentils

(Prep + Cooking Time: 30 minutes | **Servings:** 5)

Ingredients:
- 3 cups butternut squash, peeled and cubed
- 1 ¾ cups water; or Vegetable Stock,
- 1/2 onion; diced
- 1 cup red lentils; rinsed
- 1 tbsp. olive oil
- 1 garlic clove; minced
- 1 tsp. smoked paprika
- 1/2 tsp. salt or as your liking
- 1/2 tsp. ground cumin
- Pinch chili powder

Directions:
1. Select the "Sauté" Low mode on your instant pot. When the display reads "Hot," add the oil and heat until it shimmers
2. Add the onion. Cook for 2 to 3 minutes, stirring frequently. Turn off the Instant Pot and add the garlic. Cook for 30 seconds, stirring
3. Stir in the squash, water, lentils, paprika, salt, cumin and chili powder.
4. Lock the lid and turn the steam release handle to Sealing. Using the Manual function, set the cooker to High Pressure for 10 minutes
5. After completing the cooking time, let the pressure release naturally for 10 minutes; quick release any remaining pressure.
6. Remove the lid carefully and stir. The lentils and butternut will break down quickly, no need to mash. Just stir and, when they're smooth, taste and adjust the seasonings, as needed

Veggie Risotto

(Prep + Cooking Time: 16 minutes | **Servings:** 5)

Ingredients:
- 1 cup Arborio rice; rinsed and drained
- 1 bunch asparagus tips; cut into 1-inch pieces
- 2 ¾ cups Vegetable Stock
- 2 cups fresh baby spinach
- 1 cup sugar snap peas; rinsed, tough ends removed
- 1/2 sweet onion; diced
- 1 garlic clove; minced
- 2 tbsp. vegan butter
- 2 tbsp. olive oil
- 1 tsp. dried thyme
- 1/2 tsp. salt; or as your liking
- 1/4 tsp. freshly ground black pepper
- Pinch red pepper flakes
- Juice of 1/2 lemon

Directions:
1. Select the "Sauté" Low mode on your instant pot. When the display reads "Hot," add the oil and heat until it shimmers
2. Add the onion. Cook for about 2 minutes, stirring frequently. Turn off the Instant Pot and stir in the garlic and asparagus, cooking for 30 seconds.
3. Add the stock, rice, peas, thyme, salt, black pepper and red pepper flakes, stirring well
4. Lock the lid and turn the steam release handle to Sealing. Using the Manual function, set the cooker to High Pressure for 8 minutes.
5. After completing the cooking time, quick release the pressure
6. Remove the lid carefully and stir in the butter, lemon juice and spinach, being gentle so as not to tear the snap peas. Taste and season with more salt, as needed.

Black Eyed Peas with Peanuts

(Prep + Cooking Time: 45 minutes | **Servings:** 6)

Ingredients:
- 1 cup dried black-eyed peas
- 1 cup chopped yellow onions
- 1 cup drained canned diced tomatoes
- 2 ½ cups water
- 1/2 cup peanut butter
- 2 cups frozen Swiss chard
- 1 tsp. salt or as your liking
- 1 tsp. black pepper

Directions:
5. In your Instant Pot, combine the water, Swiss chard, onions, tomatoes, black-eyed peas, salt and pepper. Stir to combine.
6. Add the peanut butter to the top of the mixture; do not stir in. Be sure that everything, including the peanut butter, is submerged under the liquid. (This is to prevent the peanut butter from sticking to the pot and burning)
7. Now secure the lid on the pot and close the valve. Now Press "Manual" and set the pot at "High" pressure for 15 minutes
8. After completing the cooking time, allow the pot to sit undisturbed for 10 minutes, then release any remaining pressure. Stir thoroughly before serving.

Asian Rice

(Prep + Cooking Time: 22 minutes | **Servings:** 5)

Ingredients:
- 2 cups basmati rice; rinsed well, drained and dried
- 2 ½ cups water
- 1 tbsp. chili oil
- 1/2 tsp. ground cardamom
- 2 tsp. cumin seeds
- 1 tsp. salt as your liking

Directions:
1. Select the "Sauté" Low mode on your instant pot. When the display reads "Hot," add the oil and heat until it shimmers
2. Add the cumin seeds and cardamom. Cook until fragrant, stirring frequently. Add the salt, rice and water and stir well
3. Lock the lid and turn the steam release handle to Sealing. Using the Manual function, set the cooker to High Pressure for 6 minutes.
4. After completing the cooking time, let the pressure release naturally for 10 minutes; quick release any remaining pressure. Remove the lid carefully and fluff the rice

Lentils and Rice

(Prep + Cooking Time: 45 minutes | **Servings:** 6)

Ingredients:
- 1 cup basmati rice; rinsed and drained
- 2 cups thinly sliced yellow onions
- ⅓ cup brown lentils
- 2 cups water
- 2 tbsp. Ghee
- 1/2 tsp. ground cumin
- 1/2 tsp. ground coriander
- Salt to taste

Directions:
1. Place the lentils in a small bowl. Cover with hot water and let soak while you get everything else going
2. Now Press "Sauté" on the Instant Pot. When the pot is hot, add the ghee. When the ghee has melted, add the onions

3. Season with a little salt and cook, stirring, until the onions begin to crisp around the edges but are not burned, 5 to 10 minutes. Remove half the onions from the pot and reserve for garnish. Now Press "Cancel".
4. Drain the lentils. Add the lentils, water, rice, cumin and coriander to the pot and season with salt. Stir well to combine
5. Now secure the lid on the pot and close the valve. Now Press "Manual" and set the pot at "High" pressure for 6 minutes. After completing the cooking time, allow the pot to sit undisturbed for 10 minutes, then release any remaining pressure.
6. Very gently stir and place the lid halfway on the pot. Let the rice and lentils rest for 5 to 10 minutes. Transfer the rice and lentils to a serving dish. Sprinkle with the reserved onions and serve

Orange & Bulgur Salad

(**Prep + Cooking Time:** 25 minutes | **Servings:** 4)

Ingredients:
- 1 cup bulgur; rinsed
- 1 tbsp. soy sauce
- 2/3 cup scallions; chopped.
- 2 tsp. brown sugar
- Zest from 1 orange
- Juice from 2 oranges
- 1/2 cups water
- 1/3 cup almonds; chopped.
- 2 garlic cloves; minced.
- 2 tsp. canola oil
- 2 tbsp. ginger; grated
- Salt to the taste

Directions:
1. Set your instant pot on Sauté mode; add oil and heat it up
2. Add ginger and garlic; stir and cook for 1 minutes.
3. Add bulgur; sugar, water, and orange juice; then stir well. close the lid and cook at High for 5 minutes.
4. Release the pressure naturally, remove the instant pot lid and leave bulgur aside for now.
5. Heat up a pan over medium heat, add almonds, stir them for 3 minutes
6. Add orange zest, salt, soy sauce and scallions; stir and cook for 1 minute
7. Add this to bulgur mix; stir with a fork, transfer to a bowl and serve.

Spanish Style Rice

(**Prep + Cooking Time:** 38 minutes | **Servings:**8)

Ingredients:
- 2 cups long-grain white rice; rinsed.
- 3 cups low-sodium vegetable broth
- 1 red bell pepper, seeded and chopped
- 1 medium yellow onion; diced.
- 2 tbsp. extra-virgin olive oil.
- 2 tbsp. tomato paste
- ½ tsp. fine sea salt.
- ½ tsp. chili powder

Directions:
1. Select *Sauté* and add the olive oil to the inner pot. Once the oil is hot, add the onion and bell pepper and sauté for 2 minutes. Add the chili powder, salt, and tomato paste. Using a wooden spoon, scrape up any browned bits stuck to the bottom of the pot
2. Press Cancel. Add the rice and broth to the pot. Stir to combine
3. Now, Lock the lid. Select, "Manual or Pressure Cook" and set the pressure to *High* and the time to 8 minutes. Make sure the steam release knob is in the sealed position.
4. After completing the cooking cycle, naturally release the pressure for 10 minutes, then quick release any remaining pressure. Unlock and remove the lid. Serve hot

Instant Wheat Berry Salad

(Prep + Cooking Time: 45 minutes | **Servings:** 6)

Ingredients:
- 1 ½ cups wheat berries
- 1 tbsp. extra-virgin olive oil

For the salad:
- 1/2 cup Kalamata olives; pitted and chopped.
- 1 handful basil leaves; chopped.
- 1 handful parsley leaves; chopped.
- 1 tbsp. balsamic vinegar
- 4 cups water
- Salt and black pepper to the taste

- 1 tbsp. olive oil
- 2 green onions; chopped.
- 2 oz. feta cheese; crumbled.
- 1 cup cherry tomatoes, cut into halves

Directions:
1. Set your instant pot on Sauté mode; add 1 tablespoon oil and heat it up.
2. Add wheat berries; stir and cook for 5 minutes
3. Add water, salt and pepper to the taste, close the lid and cook on High for 30 minutes.
4. Release the pressure naturally for 10 minutes, then release remaining pressure by turning the valve to 'Venting', open the instant pot lid, drain wheat berries and put them in a salad bowl
5. Add salt and pepper, 1 tablespoon oil, balsamic vinegar, tomatoes, green onions, olives, cheese, basil and parsley, toss to coat and serve right away

Healthy Barley Salad

(Prep + Cooking Time: 30 minutes | **Servings:** 4)

Ingredients:
- 1 cup hulled barley, rinsed
- 3/4 cup jarred spinach pesto
- 1 green apple; chopped.
- 2 ½ cups water
- 1/4 cup celery; chopped.
- Salt and white pepper to the taste

Directions:
1. Put barley, water, salt and pepper in your instant pot; then stir well. close the lid and cook at High for 20 minutes
2. Quick release the pressure, carefully open the lid; strain barley and put in a bowl
3. Add celery, apple, spinach pesto and more salt and pepper, toss to coat and serve right away.

Rice and Peas

(Prep + Cooking Time: 20 minutes | **Servings:** 6)

Ingredients:
- 1 cup canned kidney beans, drained and rinsed
- 1/2 cup full-fat coconut milk
- 1 cup jasmine rice; rinsed and drained
- 3 sprigs fresh thyme
- 1 cup water
- 1 Scotch bonnet chile
- 1 tbsp. melted Ghee, vegetable oil
- 1 tsp. salt or as your liking
- 1/2 tsp. ground allspice

Directions:
1. In your Instant Pot, combine the rice, water, whole chile, thyme, salt and allspice. Stir to combine. Add the ghee and stir to combine. Gently add the kidney beans on the top of the rice; do not stir
2. Now secure the lid on the pot and close the valve. Now Press "Manual" and set the pot at "High" pressure for 4 minutes.
3. After completing the cooking time, allow the pot to sit undisturbed for 10 minutes, then release any remaining pressure.
4. Stir in the coconut milk. Place the lid back on the pot and allow to stand for about 10 minutes for the coconut milk to be absorbed. Remove the thyme sprigs and the chile and serve

Sticky Mango Brown Rice

(Prep + Cooking Time: 52 minutes | **Servings:** 8)

Ingredients:
- 2 cups long-grain brown rice (see Cooking Tip)
- 2 cups frozen mango chunks
- 1 (13. 5-oz.) can light coconut milk
- 2 tbsp. brown sugar
- 1 cup water
- ½ tsp. ground cinnamon
- ¼ tsp. ground cardamom

Directions:
1. Place the rice, coconut milk, water, cardamom, cinnamon, and mango in the inner pot. Stir to combine
2. Now, Lock the lid. Select, "Manual or Pressure Cook" and set the pressure to *High* and the time to 22 minutes. Make sure the steam release knob is in the sealed position.
3. After completing the cooking cycle, naturally release the pressure for 10 minutes, then quick release any remaining pressure. Unlock and remove the lid. Stir in the brown sugar. Serve hot.

Coconut Jasmine Rice

(Prep + Cooking Time: 20 minutes | **Servings:** 5)

Ingredients:
- 1 (14-ounce) can lite coconut milk
- 2 cups jasmine rice; rinsed and drained
- 1/2 cup water
- 1/2 tsp. sea salt or as your liking

Directions:
1. In the Instant Pot, combine the rice, coconut milk, water and salt
2. Lock the lid and turn the steam release handle to Sealing. Using the Manual function, set the cooker to High Pressure for 4 minutes
3. After completing the cooking time, let the pressure release naturally for 10 minutes; quick release any remaining pressure.
4. Remove the lid carefully and fluff the rice. Taste and season with more salt, as needed

Chinese Fried Rice

(Prep + Cooking Time: 22 minutes | **Servings:** 5)

Ingredients:
- 1 small onion; diced
- 1 ¾ cups jasmine rice; rinsed and drained
- 1/4 cup lite soy sauce
- 1 ¾ cups water
- 2 cups frozen mixed vegetable; peas, carrots, corn
- 1 tbsp. sesame oil
- 3/4 tsp. garlic powder
- 3/4 tsp. ground ginger

Directions:
1. Select the "Sauté" Low mode on your instant pot. When the display reads "Hot," add the oil and heat until it shimmers
2. Add the onion. Cook for 1 minute, stirring frequently. Turn off the Instant Pot and add the rice, ginger, garlic powder, soy sauce and water.
3. Lock the lid and turn the steam release handle to Sealing. Using the Manual function, set the cooker to High Pressure for 5 minutes
4. After completing the cooking time, turn off the Instant Pot and let the pressure release naturally for 10 minutes; quick release any remaining pressure.
5. Remove the lid carefully and stir in the frozen vegetables
6. Rest the lid back on "no need to lock it" and select the Keep Warm function. Let the veggies warm for 3 to 4 minutes before serving

Black Beans

(Prep + Cooking Time: 1 hour 5 minutes | **Servings:** 7)

Ingredients:
- 2 cups dried black beans; rinsed but not soaked
- 4 garlic cloves; diced
- 1 small onion; diced
- 3 cups Vegetable Stock
- 1/4 cup fresh cilantro leaves, chopped
- 1 cup diced roasted green chiles
- 2 tbsp. freshly squeezed lime juice
- 1 to 2 tbsp. olive oil
- 1 tbsp. ground cumin
- 1 tsp. dried oregano
- 1 tsp. chili powder
- 1 tsp. salt; or more as your liking

Directions:
1. Select the "Sauté" Low mode on your instant pot. When the display reads "Hot," add the oil and onion. Sauté for 1 to 2 minutes, turning off the Instant Pot after about 1 minute
2. Add the garlic. Sauté for 30 seconds. Stir in the cumin; oregano and chili powder and cook for another 30 seconds or so until the spices "bloom".
3. Add the green chiles, stock and black beans, stirring well. Lock the lid and turn the steam release handle to Sealing
4. Using the Manual function, set the cooker to High Pressure for 35 minutes.
5. After completing the cooking time, let the pressure release naturally for 20 minutes; or until the pin drops
6. Remove the lid carefully and stir. Add the salt, lime juice and cilantro. Stir again and serve.

Hummus

(Prep + Cooking Time: 1 hour 45 minutes | **Servings:** 8)

Ingredients:
- 1/2 cup dried chickpeas
- 4 garlic cloves
- 2 tbsp. tahini
- Juice of 1 lemon
- Salt to taste

Directions:
1. Place the chickpeas in a medium bowl and cover with hot water. Soak for 1 hour; drain. Place the chickpeas in the Instant Pot with enough water to cover and a little salt
2. Now secure the lid on the pot and close the valve. Now Press "Manual" and set the pot at "High" pressure for 20 minutes
3. After completing the cooking time, allow the pot to sit undisturbed until the pressure has released. Drain the chickpeas, reserving about ½ cup of the water
4. In a food processor, combine the chickpeas, the reserved ½ water, the garlic, tahini, lemon juice and salt to taste. Process until smooth. Transfer the hummus to a serving bowl.

Veg Lo Mein

(Prep + Cooking Time: 33 minutes | **Servings:** 8)

Ingredients:
- 1 (16-oz.) package dried spaghetti pasta
- 1 (12-oz.) bag frozen stir-fry vegetables
- 4 cups low-sodium vegetable broth
- ¼ cup reduced-sodium soy sauce
- 2 garlic cloves; minced.
- 1 tbsp. extra-virgin olive oil.
- 2 tbsp. brown sugar
- 2 tbsp. rice vinegar
- ½ tsp. ground ginger

Directions:
1. Select *Sauté* and add the olive oil to the inner pot. Once the oil is hot, add the garlic and sauté for about 3 minutes, stirring occasionally

2. Press Cancel. Using a wooden spoon, scrape up any browned bits stuck to the bottom of the pot. Add the soy sauce, rice vinegar, ginger, brown sugar, and broth to the pot. Stir to combine.
3. Break the spaghetti noodles in half and place them in the pot. Using a wooden spoon or spatula, push the noodles down and make sure they are covered with the liquid
4. Place the frozen stir-fry vegetables on top of the noodle mixture, but don't stir
5. Now, Lock the lid. Select, "Manual or Pressure Cook" and set the pressure to *High* and the time to 8 minutes. Make sure the steam release knob is in the sealed position.
6. After completing the cooking cycle, quick release the pressure. Unlock and remove the lid. Serve hot

Yummy Cauliflower Faux Mashed Potatoes

(Prep + Cooking Time: 23 minutes | **Servings:**6)

Ingredients:
- 1 large head cauliflower; cut into florets (about 4 cups)
- 2½ cups water
- 2 tbsp. unsalted butter
- ½ tsp. fine sea salt.

Directions:
1. Set a steamer basket in the inner pot. Pour in the water, then place the cauliflower florets in the steamer basket
2. Now, Lock the lid. Select, "Manual or Pressure Cook" and set the pressure to *High* and the time to 3 minutes. Make sure the steam release knob is in the sealed position.
3. After completing the cooking cycle, quick release the pressure. Unlock and remove the lid. Using a serving spoon or ladle, transfer the cauliflower to a large bowl.
4. Add the butter and salt, and use a potato masher or spatula to mash the cauliflower and mix everything together. Serve hot

Mexican Style Refried Beans

(Prep + Cooking Time: 70 minutes | **Servings:**6)

Ingredients:
- 2 cups dried pinto beans; rinsed. and drained
- 1 jalapeño pepper, seeded and diced
- 4 cups low-sodium vegetable broth
- 3 cups water
- 1 medium yellow onion; diced.
- 2 garlic cloves; minced.
- ½ tsp. chili powder
- 1 tsp. fine sea salt.
- 1 tsp. ground cumin
- 2 tsp. extra-virgin olive oil.
- 1 tsp. dried oregano

Directions:
1. Select *Sauté* and add the olive oil to the inner pot. Once the oil is hot, add the onion, garlic, and jalapeño. *Sauté* for 3 minutes, stirring occasionally
2. Now, press *Cancel* and pour the broth into the pot. Using a wooden spoon, scrape up any browned bits stuck to the bottom of the pot. Add the water, beans, cumin, oregano, and chili powder and stir to combine
3. Now, Lock the lid. Select, "Manual or Pressure Cook" and set the pressure to *High* and the time to 30 minutes. Make sure the steam release knob is in the sealed position.
4. After completing the cooking cycle, naturally release the pressure for 15 minutes, then quick release any remaining pressure. Unlock and remove the lid. Stir in the salt. Using an immersion blender, purée the beans. Serve hot

Mushroom and Leek Risotto

(Prep + Cooking Time: 20 minutes | **Servings:** 5)

Ingredients:
- 12 ounces baby bella mushrooms, sliced
- 1 leek, white and lightest green parts only, halved and sliced
- 2 garlic cloves; minced
- 1 cup Arborio rice; rinsed and drained
- 2 ¾ cups Vegetable Stock
- 4 tbsp. vegan butter; divided
- 1 tsp. dried thyme
- 1/2 tsp. salt; or as your liking
- Juice of 1/2 lemon
- Freshly ground black pepper
- Chopped fresh parsley; for garnishing

Directions:
1. Select the "Sauté" Low mode on your instant pot. When the display reads "Hot," add 2 tbsp. of butter to melt.
2. Add the leek and mushrooms. Sauté for about 2 minutes, stirring frequently
3. Add the garlic. Cook for about 30 seconds, stirring, turn off the Instant Pot if it starts to burn. Add the rice and toast it for 1 minute. Turn off the Instant Pot
4. Stir in the stock, thyme and salt. Lock the lid and turn the steam release handle to Sealing. Using the Manual function, set the cooker to High Pressure for 8 minutes
5. After completing the cooking time, quick release the pressure.
6. Remove the lid carefully and stir in the lemon juice and remaining 2 tbsp. of vegan butter. Taste and season with more salt and pepper, as needed. Garnish with fresh parsley

Veggie Risotto

(Prep + Cooking Time: 16 minutes | **Servings:** 5)

Ingredients:
- 1 cup Arborio rice; rinsed and drained
- 1 bunch asparagus tips; cut into 1-inch pieces
- 2 ¾ cups Vegetable Stock
- 2 cups fresh baby spinach
- 1 cup sugar snap peas; rinsed, tough ends removed
- 1/2 sweet onion; diced
- 1 garlic clove; minced
- 2 tbsp. vegan butter
- 2 tbsp. olive oil
- 1 tsp. dried thyme
- 1/2 tsp. salt; or as your liking
- 1/4 tsp. freshly ground black pepper
- Pinch red pepper flakes
- Juice of 1/2 lemon

Directions:
7. Select the "Sauté" Low mode on your instant pot. When the display reads "Hot," add the oil and heat until it shimmers
8. Add the onion. Cook for about 2 minutes, stirring frequently. Turn off the Instant Pot and stir in the garlic and asparagus, cooking for 30 seconds.
9. Add the stock, rice, peas, thyme, salt, black pepper and red pepper flakes, stirring well.
10. Lock the lid and turn the steam release handle to Sealing. Using the Manual function, set the cooker to High Pressure for 8 minutes
11. After completing the cooking time, quick release the pressure.
12. Remove the lid carefully and stir in the butter, lemon juice and spinach, being gentle so as not to tear the snap peas. Taste and season with more salt, as needed

Cilantro Lime Brown Rice

(Prep + Cooking Time: 34 minutes | **Servings:** 5)

Ingredients:
- 2 cups brown rice; rinsed and drained
- ⅓ cup fresh cilantro, chopped
- 2 ½ cups water
- Juice of 1 lime
- Zest of 1 lime
- Dash ground cumin
- Salt as your liking

Directions:
1. In the Instant Pot, combine the rice and water
2. Lock the lid and turn the steam release handle to Sealing. Using the Manual function, set the cooker to High Pressure for 22 minutes.
3. After completing the cooking time, let the pressure release naturally for 10 minutes while the Instant Pot goes into Keep Warm mode; quick release any remaining pressure
4. Remove the lid carefully and stir in the cilantro, lime juice and zest and cumin. Season to taste with salt

Mung Beans

(Prep + Cooking Time: 27 minutes | **Servings:** 4)

Ingredients:
- 3/4 cup mung beans, soaked for 15 minutes and drained
- 28 oz. canned tomatoes; crushed.
- 1/2 cup brown rice; soaked for 15 minutes and drained
- 1 small red onion; chopped.
- 1/2 tsp. cumin seeds
- 1 tsp. coriander; ground.
- 1 tsp. turmeric
- 1/2 tsp. garam masala
- 1/2 tsp. coconut oil
- 1 tsp. lemon juice
- 4 cups water
- 5 garlic cloves; minced.
- 1-inch ginger piece; chopped
- A pinch of cayenne
- Salt and black pepper to the taste

Directions:
1. In your food processor, mix tomatoes with onions, ginger, garlic, coriander, turmeric, cayenne, salt, pepper and garam masala and blend well
2. Set your instant pot on Sauté mode; add oil and heat up.
3. Add cumin seeds; stir and fry for 2 minutes.
4. Add tomatoes mix; stir and cook for 15 minutes
5. Add beans; rice, water, salt, pepper and lemon juice; then stir well. close the instant pot lid and cook at High for 15 minutes.
6. Release the pressure naturally for 10 minutes, then release remaining pressure by turning the valve to 'Venting', open the instant pot lid; stir again, divide into bowls and serve

Black Bean Soup

(Prep + Cooking Time: 1 hour 25 minutes | **Servings:** 4)

Ingredients:
- 1/2 cup chopped scallions, for garnish
- 4 slices bacon, diced
- 1 green bell pepper; chopped
- 1 jalapeño; chopped
- 4 garlic cloves; minced
- 1/2 bunch fresh cilantro, finely chopped
- 1 yellow onion, diced
- 1 cup dried black beans
- 3 cups chicken broth
- 2 bay leaves
- 1 tsp. dried thyme
- 2 tsp. dried oregano
- 2 tsp. ground cumin
- 2 tsp. salt or as your liking

Directions:
1. In your Instant Pot, combine the beans, broth, bacon, onion, bell pepper, jalapeño, garlic, cilantro, salt, oregano, thyme, cumin and bay leaves. Stir well to combine
2. Now secure the lid on the pot and close the valve. Now Press "Manual" and set the pot at "High" pressure for 45 minutes.
3. After completing the cooking time, allow the pot to sit undisturbed for 10 minutes, then release any remaining pressure.
4. Using an immersion blender, puree some of the soup to thicken it while leaving some beans intact. Garnish with the scallions and serve

Sour and Sweet Brussels Sprouts.

(Prep + Cooking Time: 28 minutes | **Servings:**6)

Ingredients:
- 1 lb. Brussels sprouts, trimmed and halved
- 2 garlic cloves; minced.
- ⅔ cup freshly squeezed orange juice
- 1 tbsp. brown sugar
- 1 tbsp. apple cider vinegar
- 1 tbsp. extra-virgin olive oil.
- 3 tbsp. unsalted sliced almonds
- 2 tbsp. reduced-sodium soy sauce
- 1 tsp. Dijon mustard

Directions:
1. To make the sauce, place the garlic, orange juice, soy sauce, brown sugar, vinegar, and mustard in a medium bowl. Whisk to combine
2. Select *Sauté* and add the oil to the inner pot. Once the oil is hot, add the Brussels sprouts and sauté for 3 minutes, stirring occasionally.
3. Press Cancel. Pour the sauce into the pot. Stir to coat the Brussels sprouts in the sauce
4. Now, Lock the lid. Select, "Manual or Pressure Cook" and set the pressure to *High* and the time to 3 minutes (for firmer sprouts, set the time for 2 minutes). Make sure the steam release knob is in the sealed position.
5. After completing the cooking cycle, quick release the pressure. Unlock and remove the lid. Using a spoon, transfer the Brussels sprouts and sauce to a serving plate. Sprinkle with the sliced almonds. Serve hot

Chickpea Basil Salad

(Prep + Cooking Time: 1 hour 10 minutes | **Servings:** 3)

Ingredients:
- 1 cup dried chickpeas; rinsed
- 1 cup fresh basil leaves; chopped or sliced
- 1 ½ cups grape tomatoes, halved
- water, enough to cover the chickpeas by 3 to 4 inches
- 3 tbsp. balsamic vinegar
- 1/2 tsp. garlic powder
- 1/2 tsp. salt; or more as your liking

Directions:
1. In the Instant Pot, combine the chickpeas and water. Lock the lid and turn the steam release handle to Sealing. Using the Manual function, set the cooker to High Pressure for 45 minutes
2. After completing the cooking time, let the pressure release naturally for 20 minutes; quick release any remaining pressure.
3. Remove the lid carefully and drain the chickpeas. Refrigerate to cool (unless you want to serve this warm, which is good, too)
4. While the chickpeas cool, in a large bowl, stir together the basil, tomatoes, vinegar, garlic powder and salt. Add the beans, stir to combine and serve.

Beans with Bacon and Mushrooms

(Prep + Cooking Time: 30 minutes | **Servings:**6)

Ingredients:
- 1 lb. fresh or frozen green beans, trimmed
- 8 ounces button mushrooms; sliced.
- 4 bacon slices; chopped.
- 1 cup low-sodium vegetable broth
- 1 garlic clove; minced.
- 1 tbsp. balsamic vinegar
- Juice of ½ medium lemon

Directions:
1. Select *Sauté* and let the pot heat up for about 2 minutes. Add the bacon, garlic, and mushrooms and sauté for about 6 minutes, until the bacon starts to brown
2. Press Cancel. Add the broth. Using a wooden spoon, scrape up any browned bits stuck to the bottom of the pot. Add the green beans to the pot
3. Now, Lock the lid. Select, "Manual or Pressure Cook" and set the pressure to *High* and the time to 2 minutes (4 minutes if using frozen green beans). Make sure the steam release knob is in the sealed position.
4. After completing the cooking cycle, quick release the pressure. Unlock and remove the lid. Stir in the lemon juice and balsamic vinegar. Serve hot

Hummus

(Prep + Cooking Time: 1 hour 45 minutes | **Servings:** 8)

Ingredients:
- 1/2 cup dried chickpeas
- 4 garlic cloves
- 2 tbsp. tahini
- Juice of 1 lemon
- Salt to taste

Directions:
5. Place the chickpeas in a medium bowl and cover with hot water. Soak for 1 hour; drain. Place the chickpeas in the Instant Pot with enough water to cover and a little salt
6. Now secure the lid on the pot and close the valve. Now Press "Manual" and set the pot at "High" pressure for 20 minutes
7. After completing the cooking time, allow the pot to sit undisturbed until the pressure has released. Drain the chickpeas, reserving about ½ cup of the water.
8. In a food processor, combine the chickpeas, the reserved ½ water, the garlic, tahini, lemon juice and salt to taste. Process until smooth. Transfer the hummus to a serving bowl

Noodles with Tofu

(Prep + Cooking Time: 31 minutes | **Servings:**8)

Ingredients:
- 1 (16-oz.) package dried whole-wheat spaghetti pasta
- 10 ounces extra-firm tofu, cubed
- 3 garlic cloves; minced.
- ⅓ cup reduced-sodium soy sauce
- 2 red bell peppers, seeded and thinly sliced
- 4 cups water
- ¼ cup unsalted cashews; chopped.
- 2 tbsp. brown sugar
- 2 tbsp. extra-virgin olive oil.
- 3 tbsp. apple cider vinegar

Directions:
1. Select *Sauté* and add the olive oil to the inner pot. Once the oil is hot, add the garlic and tofu and sauté for 2 minutes
2. Press Cancel. Using a wooden spoon, scrape up any browned bits stuck to the bottom of the pot. Add the soy sauce, vinegar, water, and brown sugar to the pot. Stir to combine.
3. Break the spaghetti noodles in half and place them on top of the mixture-do not stir
4. Now, Lock the lid. Select, "Manual or Pressure Cook" and set the pressure to *High* and the time to 6 minutes.
5. Make sure the steam release knob is in the sealed position.
6. After completing the cooking cycle, quick release the pressure. Unlock and remove the lid. Stir in the bell peppers and cashews. Serve hot.

Brown Rice

(Prep + Cooking Time: 48 minutes | Servings: 8)

Ingredients:
- 2½ cups water
- 2 cups long-grain brown rice; rinsed.

Directions:
1. Combine the brown rice and water in the inner pot
2. Now, Lock the lid. Select, "Manual or Pressure Cook" and set the pressure to *High* and the time to 22 minutes. Make sure the steam release knob is in the sealed position.
3. After completing the cooking cycle, naturally release the pressure for 10 minutes, then quick release any remaining pressure. Unlock and remove the lid. Serve the rice immediately

Texas Roma Caviar

(Prep + Cooking Time: 25 minutes | Servings: 8)

Ingredients:
- 1 cup diced yellow onions
- 1 cup dried black-eyed peas
- 1/2 cup extra-virgin olive oil
- 2 Roma (plum) tomatoes; chopped
- 1/2 cup chopped fresh cilantro
- 2 cups water
- 3 tbsp. apple cider vinegar
- 1 tbsp. minced jalapeño
- 2 tbsp. fresh lemon juice
- 1 tsp. ground cumin
- 2 tsp. salt or as your liking

Directions:
1. In your Instant Pot, combine the water and black-eyed peas. Now secure the lid on the pot and close the valve. Now Press "Manual" and set pot at "High" pressure for 10 minutes
2. After completing the cooking time, allow the pot to sit undisturbed until the pressure has released. Drain any excess water. Allow the peas to cool slightly
3. Meanwhile; in a large bowl, whisk together the olive oil, vinegar, cumin, lemon juice, salt and ancho chile powder (if using). Add the black-eyed peas, onions, tomatoes, cilantro and jalapeño to the bowl. Stir gently to combine.
4. Taste and adjust the lemon juice, vinegar and salt as needed. (Resist the urge to oversalt at this point, as the salad will get saltier as it sits.) Allow the salad to rest for 1 hour before serving

Mushroom & Barley Risotto

(Prep + Cooking Time: 40 minutes | Servings: 4)

Ingredients:
- 1.5 oz. dried mushrooms
- 2 cups yellow onions; chopped
- 1/3 cup dry sherry
- 1 cup pearl barley
- 1 tsp. fennel seeds
- 1 ½ cups water
- 1 tbsp. olive oil
- 2 tbsp. black barley
- 3 cups chicken stock
- Salt and black pepper to the taste
- 1/4 cup parmesan; grated

Directions:
1. Set your instant pot on Sauté mode; add oil and heat it up.
2. Add fennel and onions, stir and cook for 4 minutes
3. Add barley and black barley, sherry, mushrooms, stock, water, salt and pepper and stir well.
4. Close the instant pot lid, cook at High for 18 minutes; Quick release the pressure, open the instant pot lid and set it on Simmer mode
5. Add more salt and pepper of needed, stir and cook for 5 more minutes.
6. Divide into bowls; add parmesan on top and serve

Classic Chili Lime Black Beans

(Prep + Cooking Time: 50 minutes | **Servings:** 4)

Ingredients:
- 2 cups black beans, soaked for 8 hours and drained
- 4 garlic cloves; minced.
- 3 cups water
- 1 tsp. smoked paprika
- 2 tsp. red palm oil
- 1 tbsp. chili powder
- 1 yellow onion; chopped.
- Salt to the taste
- Juice from 1 lime

Directions:
1. Set your instant pot on Sauté mode; add oil and heat it up
2. Add garlic and onion, stir and cook for 2 minutes
3. Add beans, chili powder, paprika, salt and water; then stir well. close the lid and cook on High for 40 minutes.
4. Release the pressure naturally, open the instant pot lid, add lime juice and more salt; then stir well. divide into bowls and serve

Rice with Corn and Peas

(Prep + Cooking Time: 40 minutes | **Servings:**6)

Ingredients:
- 1 medium yellow onion; diced.
- 2¼ cups low-sodium vegetable broth
- 2 cups white basmati rice; rinsed.
- 1 cup frozen corn kernels
- 1 cup frozen peas
- 2 garlic cloves; minced.
- 1 tbsp. extra-virgin olive oil.
- ½ tsp. freshly ground black pepper.
- ½ tsp. ground turmeric
- ½ tsp. fine sea salt.

Directions:
1. Select *Sauté* and add the olive oil to the inner pot. Once the oil is hot, add the garlic, onion, turmeric, salt, and pepper and sauté for 3 minutes, stirring occasionally
2. Now, press *Cancel* and pour the broth into the pot. Using a wooden spoon, scrape up any browned bits stuck to the bottom of the pot. Add the rice, peas, and corn and stir to combine
3. Now, Lock the lid. Select, "Manual or Pressure Cook" and set the pressure to *High* and the time to 4 minutes. Make sure the steam release knob is in the sealed position.
4. After completing the cooking cycle, naturally release the pressure for 10 minutes, then quick release any remaining pressure. Unlock and remove the lid. Serve hot

Pasta & Cranberry Beans

(Prep + Cooking Time: 30 minutes | **Servings:** 8)

Ingredients:
- 26 oz. canned tomatoes; chopped.
- 3 tsp. basil; dried
- 1/2 tsp. smoked paprika
- 2 tsp. oregano; dried
- 2 cups dried cranberry beans; soaked for 8 hours and drained.
- 7 garlic cloves; minced.
- 6 cups water
- 2 celery ribs; chopped.
- 1 yellow onion; chopped.
- 2 cups small pasta
- 3 tbsp. nutritional yeast
- 1 tsp. rosemary; chopped.
- 1/4 tsp. red pepper flakes
- Salt and black pepper to the taste
- 10 oz. kale leaves

Directions:
1. Set your instant pot on Sauté mode; add onion, celery, garlic, pepper flakes, rosemary and a pinch of salt, stir and brown for 2 minutes
2. Add tomatoes, basil, oregano and paprika, stir and cook for 1 minute
3. Add beans; 6 cups water, close the lid and cook at High for 10 minutes

4. Quick release the pressure; open the instant pot lid, add pasta, yeast, kale, salt and pepper, stir and set the pot on Sauté mode again
5. Cook for 5 minutes more, divide into bowls and serve.

Lentils Tacos

(Prep + Cooking Time: 25 minutes | Servings: 4)

Ingredients:
- 2 cups brown lentils
- 4 cups water
- 1 tsp. salt
- 1 tsp. garlic powder
- 4 oz. tomato sauce
- 1/2 tsp. cumin
- 1 tsp. chili powder
- 1 tsp. onion powder
- Taco shells for serving

Directions:
1. In your instant pot, mix lentils with water, tomato sauce, cumin, garlic powder, chili powder and onion powder; then stir well. close the lid and cook at High for 15 minutes
2. Quick release the pressure, open the instant pot lid; divide lentils mix into taco shells and serve.

Curried White Bean Broccoli Salad

(Prep + Cooking Time: 52 minutes | Servings: 6)

Ingredients:
- 1 cup dried navy beans, soaked for 8 hours
- 5 green onions, tender white and green parts only
- 1 large carrot
- 2 cups water
- 1 head broccoli
- Small handful of fresh cilantro
- ½ cup sliced almonds (optional)
- ½ cup dried cranberries (optional)

Curried Tahini Dressing:
- 1 clove garlic; minced.
- ¼ cup tahini
- ¼ cup freshly squeezed lemon juice
- 2 tbsp. pure maple syrup
- 2 tsp. curry powder
- 1 tsp. minced fresh ginger (about ½-inch knob)
- 1 tsp. fine sea salt
- Freshly ground black pepper

Directions:
1. Drain the soaked navy beans and add them to the Instant Pot with the water. Now, Lock the lid and Turn the steam release valve to "Sealing" Position. Select *Manual/Pressure* Cook to cook on *High* pressure for 25 minutes
2. Once the cooking cycle is completed, let the pressure naturally release for 10 minutes, then move the steam release valve to Venting to release any remaining pressure.
3. While the beans are cooking, finely chop the broccoli (you should have around 4 cups) and shred the carrot (about 1 cup), adding them to a large mixing bowl as you work. Chop the green onions (about 1 cup) and cilantro (about ½ cup), but leave them on the cutting board for now
4. To make the dressing, in a separate small bowl, combine the tahini, lemon juice, maple syrup, garlic, curry powder, ginger, salt and several grinds of black pepper. Whisk well to combine, then add water, 1 tablespoon at a time and whisk until the dressing is creamy and easy to pour.
5. When the floating valve on the Instant Pot drops, remove the lid. Use a fork to mash a bean against the side of the pot to be sure it is tender
6. If the beans don't mash easily, secure the lid (be sure the sealing ring is properly seated in the lid) and cook at *High* pressure for 5 minutes more. Release the pressure naturally for 10 minutes so no foam spurts from the vent, then test the beans for tenderness again.
7. When ready, drain the beans and add them to the bowl with the broccoli and carrots. Stir well and let the beans cool for 15 minutes; the heat from the beans will soften the broccoli slightly

8. Once cool, stir in the green onions, cilantro, cranberries and almonds and pour the dressing over the top. Toss well to coat evenly. Serve right away

Delicious Frijoles

(Prep + Cooking Time: 1 hour 45 minutes | **Servings:** 4)

Ingredients:
- 1 cup finely chopped white onions
- 1/2 cup finely chopped fresh cilantro
- 1/2 cup finely chopped green bell pepper
- 1 cup dried pinto beans
- 3 cups cool water
- 4 garlic cloves; minced
- 1 (14.5-ounce) can fire-roasted diced tomatoes; undrained
- 6 slices bacon; chopped
- 1 ½ tsp. ground cumin
- 1 ½ tsp. salt or as your liking

Directions:
4. Place the pinto beans in a medium bowl. Cover with hot water. Soak for 1 hour drain. Place the pinto beans in the Instant Pot. Add the cool water, tomatoes and their juices, onions, cilantro, bell pepper, bacon, garlic, cumin and salt
5. Now secure the lid on the pot and close the valve. Now Press "Manual" and set the pot at "High" pressure for 30 minutes.
6. After completing the cooking time, allow the pot to sit undisturbed for 10 minutes, then release any remaining pressure. If you like, use an immersion blender to puree some of the beans to thicken the broth

Pepper Lemon Quinoa

(Prep + Cooking Time: 20 minutes | **Servings:** 5)

Ingredients:
- 1 ½ cups quinoa; rinsed
- 1 ½ cups water
- 1 tbsp. vegan butter
- 1/4 tsp. garlic powder
- 1/4 tsp. dried basil
- 1 tsp. salt; or more as your liking
- 1/2 tsp. freshly ground black pepper
- Juice of 1 lemon
- Zest of 1 lemon

Directions:
1. In the Instant Pot, combine the quinoa, water, salt, pepper, garlic powder and basil
2. Lock the lid and turn the steam release handle to Sealing. Using the Manual function, set the cooker to High Pressure for 8 minutes.
3. After completing the cooking time, let the pressure release naturally for 10 minutes; quick release any remaining pressure
4. Remove the lid carefully and stir in the butter, lemon juice and zest. Taste and season with more salt and pepper, as needed

Veggies Rice Pilaf

(Prep + Cooking Time: 28 minutes | **Servings:** 5)

Ingredients:
- 1/2 cup frozen peas
- 1/2 cup sliced almonds
- 1/2 sweet onion, chopped
- 1 carrot, halved lengthwise and sliced
- 1 celery stalk, sliced
- 1 cup basmati rice; rinsed and drained
- 1 cup Vegetable Stock
- 1 cup broccoli florets
- 1/2 cup sliced white mushrooms
- 2 garlic cloves; minced
- 1 tbsp. olive oil; or avocado oil
- Salt as your liking
- Freshly ground black pepper

Directions:
1. Select the "Sauté" Low mode on your instant pot. When the display reads "Hot," add the oil and heat until it shimmers
2. Add the onion, carrot, celery, broccoli and mushrooms. Sauté for 2 to 3 minutes, stirring frequently. Add the garlic and turn off the Instant Pot. Sauté the garlic for 30 seconds, stirring frequently.
3. Stir in the rice and stock and season to taste with salt and pepper
4. Lock the lid and turn the steam release handle to Sealing. Using the Manual function, set the cooker to High Pressure for 3 minutes.
5. After completing the cooking time, let the pressure release naturally for 15 minutes; quick release any remaining pressure.
6. Remove the lid carefully and stir in the frozen peas. Replace the cover (no need to seal it) and let sit for a few minutes. When ready to serve, stir in the almonds

Yogurt Recipes

Pumpkin Spice Yogurt.

(Prep + Cooking Time: 20 minutes | **Servings:** 4)

Ingredients:
- 2 cans full cream milk
- 4 capsules high-quality probiotic
- 2 tbsp. gelatin powder
- 1 tsp. vanilla paste
- 1 tbsp. raw honey
- 1 tbsp. pumpkin spice

Directions:
1. Pour the milk in instant pot
2. Lock the lid and select the yogurt button; then press the adjust button till the display states boil
3. When the Instant Pot beeps; turn off the pot, remove the lid and take out the metal bowl
4. Using a candy thermometer measure the temperature of the milk till it reaches 115 C.
5. Once the milk is cooled below 115 C; empty the contents of probiotic capsules in the milk
6. Return the metal bowl to the pot; close the lid and seal it and press the yogurt button again.
7. Use the (+) button to adjust the time to 14hours. When the Instant pot beeps; taste the yogurt to make sure it is tart
8. Transfer the yogurt to the blender or food processor, sprinkle gelatin powder and add remaining ingredients.
9. Blending the yogurt in a food blender until smooth
10. Pour the yogurt into glasses or bowls and refrigerate the same for 2 - 3 hours

Raspberry Yogurt.

(Prep + Cooking Time: 20 minutes | **Servings:** 6)

Ingredients:
- 1 cup raspberry puree
- 4 capsules high-quality probiotic
- 2 tbsp. gelatin powder
- 1 tsp. vanilla paste
- 1 tbsp. raw honey
- 2 cans full cream milk

Directions:
1. Pour the milk in instant pot
2. Lock the lid and select the yogurt button; then press the adjust button till the display states boil
3. When the Instant Pot beeps; turn off the pot, remove the lid and take out the metal bowl.
4. Using a candy thermometer measure the temperature of the milk till it reaches 115 C.
5. Once the milk is cooled below 115 C; empty the contents of probiotic capsules in the milk.
6. Return the metal bowl to the pot; close the lid and seal it and press the yogurt button again.
7. Use the (+) button to adjust the time to 14hours. When the Instant pot beeps; taste the yogurt to make sure it is tart.
8. Transfer the yogurt to the blender or food processor, sprinkle gelatin powder and add remaining ingredients.
9. Blending the yogurt in a food blender until smooth.
10. Pour the yogurt into glasses or bowls and refrigerate the same for 2 - 3 hours

White Chocolate Yogurt.

(Prep + Cooking Time: 20 minutes | **Servings:** 4)

Ingredients:
- 1 cup melted white chocolate
- 2 tbsp. gelatin powder
- 1 tbsp. raw honey
- 2 cans full cream milk
- 4 capsules high-quality probiotic
- 1 tsp. vanilla paste

Directions:
1. Pour the milk in instant pot
2. Lock the lid and select the yogurt button; then press the adjust button till the display states boil.
3. When the Instant Pot beeps; turn off the pot, remove the lid and take out the metal bowl
4. Using a candy thermometer measure the temperature of the milk till it reaches 115 C
5. Once the milk is cooled below 115 C; empty the contents of probiotic capsules in the milk
6. Return the metal bowl to the pot; close the lid and seal it and press the yogurt button again
7. Use the (+) button to adjust the time to 14hours. When the Instant pot beeps; taste the yogurt to make sure it is tart
8. Transfer the yogurt to the blender or food processor, sprinkle gelatin powder and add remaining ingredients, including white chocolate.
9. Blending the yogurt in a food blender until smooth
10. Pour the yogurt into glasses or bowls and refrigerate the same for 2 - 3 hours

Vanilla Yogurt.

(**Prep + Cooking Time:** 20 minutes | **Servings:** 4)

Ingredients:
- 4 capsules high-quality probiotic
- 2 cans full cream milk
- 3 tsp. vanilla paste
- 2 tbsp. gelatin powder
- 1 tbsp. raw honey

Directions:
1. Pour the milk in instant pot.
2. Lock the lid and select the yogurt button; then press the adjust button till the display states boil.
3. When the Instant Pot beeps; turn off the pot, remove the lid and take out the metal bowl
4. Using a candy thermometer measure the temperature of the milk till it reaches 115 C
5. Once the milk is cooled below 115 C; empty the contents of probiotic capsules in the milk
6. Return the metal bowl to the pot; close the lid and seal it and press the yogurt button again
7. Use the (+) button to adjust the time to 14hours. When the Instant pot beeps; taste the yogurt to make sure it is tart.
8. Transfer the yogurt to the blender or food processor, sprinkle gelatin powder and add remaining ingredients.
9. Blending the yogurt in a food blender until smooth
10. Pour the yogurt into glasses or bowls and refrigerate the same for 2 - 3 hours.

Kiwi Yogurt.

(**Prep + Cooking Time:** 20 minutes | **Servings:** 4)

Ingredients:
- 4 capsules high-quality probiotic
- 1 tsp. vanilla paste
- 3/4 cup kiwi puree
- 2 tbsp. gelatin powder
- 1 tbsp. raw honey
- 2 cans full cream milk

Directions:
1. Pour the milk in instant pot.
2. Lock the lid and select the yogurt button; then press the adjust button till the display states boil
3. When the Instant Pot beeps; turn off the pot, remove the lid and take out the metal bowl.
4. Using a candy thermometer measure the temperature of the milk till it reaches 115 C
5. Once the milk is cooled below 115 C; empty the contents of probiotic capsules in the milk
6. Return the metal bowl to the pot; close the lid and seal it and press the yogurt button again
7. Use the (+) button to adjust the time to 14hours. When the Instant pot beeps; taste the yogurt to make sure it is tart
8. Transfer the yogurt to the blender or food processor, sprinkle gelatin powder and add remaining ingredients.

9. Blending the yogurt in a food blender until smooth
10. Pour the yogurt into glasses or bowls and refrigerate the same for 2 - 3 hours.

Chocolate Yogurt.

(Prep + Cooking Time: 20 minutes | **Servings:** 4)

Ingredients:
- 4 capsules high-quality probiotic
- 2 tbsp. cocoa powder
- 1 cup melted dark chocolate
- 1 tbsp. raw honey
- 2 tbsp. gelatin powder
- 2 cans full cream milk
- 1 tsp. vanilla paste

Directions:
1. Pour the milk in instant pot. Add cocoa powder.
2. Lock the lid and select the yogurt button; then press the adjust button until the display states boil
3. When the Instant Pot beeps; turn off the pot, remove the lid and take out the metal bowl
4. Using a candy thermometer measure the temperature of the milk till it reaches 115 C.
5. Once the milk is cooled below 115 C; empty the contents of probiotic capsules in the milk
6. Return the metal bowl to the pot; close the lid and seal it and press the yogurt button again.
7. Use the (+) button to adjust the time to 14hours. When the Instant pot beeps; taste the yogurt to make sure it is tart
8. Transfer the yogurt to the blender or food processor, sprinkle gelatin powder and add remaining ingredients.
9. Blending the yogurt in a food blender until smooth.
10. Pour the yogurt into glasses or bowls and refrigerate the same for 2 - 3 hours

Blueberry Oats Yogurt.

(Prep + Cooking Time: 20 minutes | **Servings:** 6)

Ingredients:
- 4 capsules high-quality probiotic
- 2 cans full cream milk
- 1/2 cup roasted oats
- 2 tbsp. gelatin powder
- 1 tbsp. raw honey
- 1 tsp. vanilla paste
- 1 cup blueberry puree or pulp

Directions:
1. Pour the milk in instant pot.
2. Lock the lid and select the yogurt button; then press the adjust button till the display states boil
3. When the Instant Pot beeps; turn off the pot, remove the lid and take out the metal bowl
4. Using a candy thermometer measure the temperature of the milk till it reaches 115 C
5. Once the milk is cooled below 115 C; empty the contents of probiotic capsules in the milk
6. Return the metal bowl to the pot; close the lid and seal it and press the yogurt button again.
7. Use the (+) button to adjust the time to 14hours. When the Instant pot beeps; taste the yogurt to make sure it is tart.
8. Transfer the yogurt to the blender or food processor, sprinkle gelatin powder and add remaining ingredients.
9. Blending the yogurt in a food blender until smooth
10. Pour the yogurt into glasses or bowls and refrigerate the same for 2 - 3 hours

Slow Cooked Fruity Yogurt.

(**Prep + Cooking Time:** 12 hours | **Servings:** 4)

Ingredients:
- 5 ⅔ cups. milk; organic, reduced fat or whole
- 4 tbsp. yogurt culture; plain; divided
- 4 tbsp. dry milk powder; non-fat; divided
- 1 ½ cup. water; for the pot
- 4 tbsp. sugar; all natural; divided
- 2 cups. fresh fruit; chopped

Equipment:
- 4 wide mouth pint jars

Directions:
1. Pour the water into the Instant Pot and then put a rack or a grate in the pot.
2. Pour 1 and 1/3 cup. Milk into each jar and the cover the jar loosely with their lids. Put the jars onto the rack/ grate
3. Set the Instant Pot to Pressure Cycle and set the timer to 2 minutes; this will heat the milk and kill any pathogens that might be in the milk.
4. When the cycle is done; turn the steam valve to quick release the pressure
5. Open the pot lid and with a jar lifter, remove the jars from the pot. Put the jars into cool water and carefully remove the jar lids.
6. Once the milk is below 100F; add 1 tbsp. yogurt culture, 1 tbsp. dry milk powder; and 1 tbsp. sugar into each jar; stir until well mixed.
7. Carefully add about 1/2 cup. of fresh fruits into each jar; do not over fill them and leave at least 1/ 8-inch clear from the top each jar. Return the jar lids back
8. Check and make sure that there is still 1 ½ cup. of water in the bottom of the Instant Pot
9. Put the jars back onto the rack/ grate. Press the yogurt cycle and set the timer for 8 - 12 hours.
10. When the cycle is complete; put the jars in the refrigerator; this will cool them down and stop the cooking process

Tips: Making the yogurt in jars enables you to make plain or different flavored yogurt at the same time

Cinnamon Yogurt.

(**Prep + Cooking Time:** 20 minutes | **Servings:** 6)

Ingredients:
- 2 cans full cream milk
- 1 tsp. vanilla paste
- 2 tbsp. gelatin powder
- 4 capsules high-quality probiotic
- 1 tbsp. raw honey
- 2 tsp. Ceylon cinnamon

Directions:
1. Pour the milk in instant pot.
2. Lock the lid and select the yogurt button; then press the adjust button till the display states boil.
3. When the Instant Pot beeps; turn off the pot, remove the lid and take out the metal bowl.
4. Using a candy thermometer measure the temperature of the milk till it reaches 115 C
5. Once the milk is cooled below 115 C; empty the contents of probiotic capsules in the milk.
6. Return the metal bowl to the pot; close the lid and seal it and press the yogurt button again.
7. Use the (+) button to adjust the time to 14hours. When the Instant pot beeps; taste the yogurt to make sure it is tart.
8. Transfer the yogurt to the blender or food processor, sprinkle gelatin powder and add remaining ingredients.
9. Blending the yogurt in a food blender until smooth
10. Pour the yogurt into glasses or bowls and refrigerate the same for 2 - 3 hours

Mango Yogurt.

(Prep + Cooking Time: 30 minutes | **Servings:** 4)

Ingredients:
- 2 cans full cream milk
- 2 tbsp. gelatine
- 1 tsp. vanilla extract
- 4 capsules high-quality probiotic
- 1 tbsp. raw honey
- 1 cup mango puree or pulp

Directions:
1. Pour the milk in instant pot
2. Lock the lid and select the yogurt button; then press the adjust button till the display states boil.
3. When the Instant Pot beeps; turn off the pot, remove the lid and take out the metal bowl
4. Using a candy thermometer measure the temperature of the milk till it reaches 115 C.
5. Once the milk is cooled below 115 C; empty the contents of probiotic capsules in the milk
6. Stir in mango puree as well
7. Return the metal bowl to the pot, close the lid and seal it and press the yogurt button again
8. Use the (+) button to adjust the time to 14hours. When the Instant pot beeps; taste the yogurt to make sure it is tart
9. Transfer the yogurt to the blender or food processor, sprinkle gelatin powder, add honey and vanilla extract
10. Blending the yogurt until smooth.
11. Pour the yogurt into glasses or bowls and refrigerate the same for 2 - 3 hours.

Vegan Soy Yogurt.

(Prep + Cooking Time: 12 hours | **Servings:** 4)

Ingredients:
- 1 packet vegan yogurt culture
- 1-quart soy milk (use only made soybeans and water; no vitamins or sugar added)
- Sweetener; if desired

Directions:
1. Pour the soymilk into a wide mouth; 1-quart Mason jar with lid or into multiple heatproof containers with a lids.
2. Add the vegan yogurt culture. Close the lid and shake to mix. Remove the lid from the jar; you don't need it at this point.
3. Put the Mason jar directly into the Instant Pot container. Close and lock the Instant Pot lid. You can leave the steam valve to "Sealing" or "Releasing"; it won't affect the cooking. Press the YOGURT button and the timer to 12 hours.
4. When the timer beeps at the end of the cooking cycle, carefully remove the Mason jar from the pot, cover with its lid and refrigerate for at least 6 hours
5. Sweeten and/ or flavor, if desired. This will keep for up to 6 days in the refrigerator.

Tips: This thick, creamy, unsweetened, tart soy yogurt can be used as a sour cream substitute or in recipes. You can enjoy it topped with pears and cinnamons; with bananas, shredded coconut and pecans, with jam or sweetened with coconut sugar. You can also strain it overnight to make yogurt cheese

Passionfruit Yogurt.

(Prep + Cooking Time: 20 minutes | **Servings:** 4)

Ingredients:
- 4 capsules high-quality probiotic
- 2 cans full cream milk
- 2 tbsp. gelatin powder
- 1 ½ cups passionfruit pulp
- 1 tbsp. raw honey
- 1 tsp. vanilla paste

Directions:
1. Pour the milk in instant pot
2. Lock the lid and select the yogurt button; then press the adjust button till the display states boil
3. When the Instant Pot beeps; turn off the pot, remove the lid and take out the metal bowl
4. Using a candy thermometer measure the temperature of the milk till it reaches 115 C
5. Once the milk is cooled below 115 C; empty the contents of probiotic capsules in the milk.
6. Return the metal bowl to the pot; close the lid and seal it and press the yogurt button again
7. Use the (+) button to adjust the time to 14hours. When the Instant pot beeps; taste the yogurt to make sure it is tart.
8. Transfer the yogurt to the blender or food processor, sprinkle gelatin powder and add remaining ingredients, including pulp.
9. Blending the yogurt in a food blender until smooth
10. Pour the yogurt into glasses or bowls and refrigerate the same for 2 - 3 hours

Strawberry Yogurt.

(Prep + Cooking Time: 20 minutes | **Servings:** 4)

Ingredients:
- 1 cup strawberry puree
- 4 capsules high-quality probiotic
- 1 tbsp. raw honey
- 1 tsp. vanilla paste
- 2 tbsp. gelatin powder
- 2 cans full cream milk

Directions:
1. Pour the milk in instant pot.
2. Lock the lid and select the yogurt button; then press the adjust button till the display states boil.
3. When the Instant Pot beeps; turn off the pot, remove the lid and take out the metal bowl
4. Using a candy thermometer measure the temperature of the milk till it reaches 115 C.
5. Once the milk is cooled below 115 C; empty the contents of probiotic capsules in the milk
6. Return the metal bowl to the pot; close the lid and seal it and press the yogurt button again
7. Use the (+) button to adjust the time to 14hours. When the Instant pot beeps; taste the yogurt to make sure it is tart.
8. Transfer the yogurt to the blender or food processor, sprinkle gelatin powder and add remaining ingredients.
9. Blending the yogurt in a food blender until smooth
10. Pour the yogurt into glasses or bowls and refrigerate the same for 2 - 3 hours

Desserts

Chocolate Lava Cake Recipe

(Prep + Cooking Time: 15 minutes | **Servings:** 3)

Ingredients:
- 1 tbsp. cocoa powder
- 1/2 tsp. baking powder
- 1/2 tsp. orange zest
- 4 tbsp. milk
- 4 tbsp. flour
- one egg
- 4 tbsp. sugar
- 2 tbsp. olive oil
- A pinch of salt
- 1 cup water

Directions:
1. In a bowl, mix the egg with sugar, oil, milk, flour, salt, cocoa powder, baking powder and orange zest and stir very well.
2. Pour this into greased ramekins and place them in the steamer basket of your instant pot.
3. Add 1 cup water to the pot, seal the instant pot lid and cook at High for 6 minutes.
4. Quick release the pressure, carefully open the lid; take lava cakes out and serve them after they cool down a bit.

Instant pot Banana Cake

(Prep + Cooking Time: 60 minutes | **Servings:** 5)

Ingredients:
- 3 bananas, peeled and mashed
- 1 cup water
- 1 ½ cups sugar
- 1 tsp. cinnamon
- 1 stick butter, soft
- 1 tsp. nutmeg
- 2 cups flour
- 2 tsp. baking powder
- A pinch of salt
- 2 eggs

Directions:
1. In a bowl, mix eggs with butter and sugar and stir very well
2. Add salt, baking powder, cinnamon and nutmeg and stir well again.
3. Add bananas and flour and stir again.
4. Grease a spring form pan with some butter, pour the batter in it and cover the pan with a paper towel and tin foil.
5. Add 1 cup water to your instant pot, place the pan in the pot, seal the instant pot lid and cook at High for 55 minutes
6. Quick release the pressure, remove the pot, leave banana breakfast cake to cool down, cut and serve it.

Carrot Cake Recipe

(Prep + Cooking Time: 40 minutes | **Servings:** 6)

Ingredients:
- 1/3 cup carrots, grated
- 1/2 cup sugar
- 1/4 cup pineapple juice
- 4 tbsp. coconut oil, melted
- 1/2 tsp. baking soda
- 1/2 tsp. cinnamon powder
- 3/4 tsp. baking powder
- 1/4 tsp. nutmeg, ground.
- 1/2 tsp. allspice
- 1/3 cup pecans, toasted and chopped.
- 1/3 cup coconut flakes
- one egg
- 5 oz. flour
- A pinch of salt
- 3 tbsp. yogurt
- 2 cups water
- Cooking spray

Directions:
1. In a bowl, mix flour with baking soda and powder, salt, allspice, cinnamon and nutmeg and stir.
2. In another bowl, mix egg with yogurt, sugar, pineapple juice, oil, carrots, pecans and coconut flakes and stir well.
3. Combine the two mixtures and stir very well everything.
4. Pour this into a spring form greased with some cooking spray, add 2 cups water in your instant pot and place the form into the steamer basket.
5. Cover the instant pot and cook at High for 32 minutes.
6. Release pressure for 10 minutes, remove cake from the pot, leave it to cool down, then cut and serve it

Chocolate Cheese cake

(Prep + Cooking Time: 2 hours | **Servings:** 12)

Ingredients:
For the crust:
- 1 ½ cups chocolate cookie crumbs
- 4 tbsp. melted butter

For the filling:
- 24 oz. cream cheese, soft
- 2 tbsp. cornstarch
- 4 oz. bittersweet chocolate
- 4 oz. white chocolate
- 4 oz. milk chocolate
- 1 cup water
- 1/2 cup Greek yogurt
- 1 cup sugar
- 3 eggs
- 1 tbsp. vanilla extract
- Cooking spray

Directions:
1. In a bowl mix cookie crumbs with butter and stir well.
2. Spray a spring form pan with some cooking oil, line with parchment paper, press crumbs and butter mix on the bottom and keep in the freezer for now.
3. In a bowl, mix cream cheese with cornstarch and sugar and stir using your mixer.
4. Add eggs, yogurt, and vanilla, stir again to combine everything and divide into 3 bowls.
5. Put milk chocolate in a heatproof bowl and heat up in the microwave for 30 seconds
6. Add this into one of the bowls with the batter you've made earlier and stir well
7. Put dark and white chocolate in 2 heatproof bowls and heat them up in the microwave for 30 seconds.
8. Add these to the other 2 bowls with cheesecake batter, stir and introduce them all in the fridge for 30 minutes
9. Take bowls out of the fridge and layer your cheesecake
10. Pour the dark chocolate batter in the center of the crust.
11. Add white chocolate batter on top and spread evenly and end with milk chocolate batter
12. Put the pan in the steamer basket of your pot, add 1 cup water in the pot, seal the instant pot lid and cook at High for 45 minutes
13. Release pressure for 10 minutes, take the cake out of the pot, leave aside to cool down and serve.

Crème Brule

(Prep + Cooking Time: 1 hour 15 minutes | **Servings:** 6)

Ingredients:
- 2 cups fresh cream
- 2 cups water
- 5 tbsp. white sugar
- 1 tsp. cinnamon powder
- 6 egg yolks
- 4 tbsp. raw sugar
- Zest from 1 orange
- A pinch of nutmeg for serving

Directions:
1. In a pan, mix cream with cinnamon and orange zest, stir and bring to a boil over medium high heat.
2. Take the pan off heat and leave it aside for 30 minutes.

3. In a bowl, mix egg yolks with white sugar and whisk well. Add this to cooled cream and whisk well again.
4. Strain this mix and then divide it into ramekins
5. Cover with foil, place them in the steamer basket of your instant pot, add 2 cups water to the pot, seal the instant pot lid and cook on Low for 10 minutes.
6. Release the pressure naturally, carefully open the lid; take ramekins out and leave them aside for 30 minutes.
7. Sprinkle nutmeg and raw sugar on top of each and melt this with a culinary torch. Serve right away.

Mix Berries Compote

(**Prep + Cooking Time:** 15 minutes | **Servings:** 8)

Ingredients:
- 1 cup blueberries
- 2 tbsp. lemon juice
- 3/4 cup sugar
- 1 tbsp. cornstarch
- 1 tbsp. water
- 2 cups strawberries, sliced

Directions:
1. In your instant pot, mix blueberries with lemon juice and sugar; then stir well.
2. Seal the instant pot lid and cook at High for 3 minutes.
3. Release pressure naturally for 10 minutes and carefully open the lid
4. In a bowl, mix cornstarch with water, stir well and add to the pot.
5. Stir, set the pot on Sauté mode and cook compote for 2 minutes more
6. Divide into jars and keep in the fridge until you serve it.

Poached Pears with Caramel Sauce

(**Prep + Cooking Time:** 12 minutes | **Servings:** 4)

Ingredients:
- 1 whole vanilla bean, split and scraped
- 4 Bosc pears, ripe but not soft
- 1 batch Easy Caramel Sauce, warmed
- 1 lemon, halved
- 2 cups sugar
- 3 cups water
- 2 cups white wine
- 1 cinnamon stick

Directions:
1. Select the "Sauté" Low mode on your instant pot. When the display reads "Hot," add the water, white wine, sugar, vanilla bean and seeds and cinnamon stick, stirring well
2. Cook for 1 to 2 minutes; or until the sugar dissolves completely. Cancel Sauté and select Keep Warm.
3. Gently peel the pears. If presentation is important, keep the stems intact. Rub the pears with the lemon halves to prevent browning and add the pears to the Instant Pot.
4. Lock the lid and turn the steam release handle to Sealing. Using the Manual function, set the cooker to High Pressure for 3 minutes
5. After completing the cooking time, quick release the pressure. Remove the lid carefully and remove the pears. Set aside to cool
6. Save the sauce and pour it over the pears once cooled. Serve, warm or at room temperature, topped with caramel sauce.

Pumpkin Chocolate Cake Recipe

(Prep + Cooking Time: 55 minutes | **Servings:** 12)

Ingredients:
- 3/4 tsp. pumpkin pie spice
- 3/4 cup white flour
- 3/4 cup whole wheat flour
- 1/2 tsp. vanilla extract
- 2/3 cup chocolate chips
- 1 tsp. baking soda
- one egg
- 3/4 cup sugar
- 1/2 tsp. baking powder
- 1/2 cup Greek yogurt
- 1 banana, mashed
- 2 tbsp. canola oil
- 8 oz. canned pumpkin puree
- 1-quart water
- Cooking spray
- A pinch of salt

Directions:
1. In a bowl, mix white flour with whole wheat flour, salt, baking soda and powder and pumpkin spice and stir.
2. In another bowl, mix sugar with oil, banana, yogurt, pumpkin puree, vanilla and egg and stir using a mixer.
3. Combine the 2 mixtures, add chocolate chips and mix everything.
4. Pour this into a greased Bundt pan, cover pan with paper towels and foil and place in the steamer basket of your instant pot.
5. Add 1-quart water to the pot, seal the instant pot lid and cook at High for 35 minutes.
6. Release the pressure naturally for 10 minutes, then release remaining pressure by turning the valve to 'Venting', carefully open the lid; leave the cake to cool down, before cutting and serving it.

Instant Pot Key Lime Pie

(Prep + Cooking Time: 25 minutes | **Servings:** 6)

Ingredients:
For the crust:
- 5 graham crackers, crumbled.
- 3 tbsp. butter, melted
- 1 tbsp. sugar

For the filling:
- 4 egg yolks
- 1/2 cup key lime juice
- 1/3 cup sour cream
- 14 oz. canned condensed milk
- 2 tbsp. key lime zest, grated
- Cooking spray
- 1 cup water

Directions:
1. In a bowl, whisk egg yolks very well
2. Add milk gradually and stir again well.
3. Add lime juice, sour cream and lime zest and stir again
4. In a bowl, whisk butter with crackers and sugar, stir well and spread on the bottom of a spring form greased with some cooking spray.
5. Cover pan with some tin foil and place it in the steamer basket of your instant pot.
6. Add 1 cup water to the pot, seal the instant pot lid and cook at High for 15 minutes.
7. Release the pressure naturally for 10 minutes, then release remaining pressure by turning the valve to 'Venting', carefully open the lid; take pie out, leave aside to cool down and keep in the fridge for 4 hours before slicing and serving it.

Bourbon Apple Crisp

(**Prep + Cooking Time:** 25 minutes | **Servings:** 4)

Ingredients:
- 5 apples, peeled and cut into thick slices
- 1/4 cup all-purpose flour
- 3/4 cup old-fashioned oats
- 1/4 cup bourbon
- 1/2 cup packed light brown sugar
- 1/4 cup water
- 4 tbsp. vegan butter
- 2 tbsp. maple syrup
- 2 tbsp. ground cinnamon
- 1/2 tsp. ground nutmeg
- Salt as your liking

Directions:
1. In the Instant Pot, stir together the apples, maple syrup, cinnamon, nutmeg and pinch of salt. Cover the apples with the water and bourbon
2. In a medium microwave-safe bowl, microwave the butter until just barely melted. Add the oats, flour, brown sugar and ½ tsp. of salt. Stir to combine
3. Spoon the oat mixture over the apples, getting as much coverage as possible. Lock the lid and turn the steam release handle to Sealing.
4. Using the Manual function, set the cooker to High Pressure for 8 minutes
5. After completing the cooking time, let the pressure release naturally for 10 to 12 minutes; quick release any remaining pressure. Turn off the Instant Pot.
6. Remove the lid carefully and let the crisp rest for a few minutes to thicken before serving

Brown Rice Pudding.

(**Prep + Cooking Time:** 47 minutes | **Servings:** 6)

Ingredients:
- One 15-oz. can full-fat coconut milk
- ⅓ cup maple syrup
- 1 cup long-grain brown rice, like jasmine or basmati, rinsed
- 2 cups water
- ½ tsp. ground cinnamon., plus more for serving.
- ½ tsp. pure vanilla extract
- Pinch of fine sea salt

Directions:
1. Combine the rice and water in the bottom of the Instant Pot and secure the lid, moving the steam release valve to Sealing. Select *Manual/Pressure* Cook to cook on *High* pressure for 22 minutes
2. When the cooking cycle has completed, allow the pressure to naturally release for 10 minutes before moving the steam release valve to Venting. Carefully remove the lid.
3. Stir the rice, making sure that it's tender, then add in the coconut milk, maple syrup, vanilla, cinnamon and salt. Stir well to combine and adjust any seasoning to taste
4. Use an immersion blender directly in the pot to briefly pulse the pudding until your desired texture has been reached. The more you blend, the creamier it will be. Serve warm, with extra cinnamon on top

Berry Jam Recipe

(**Prep + Cooking Time:** 50 minutes | **Servings:** 12)

Ingredients:
- 1 lb. cranberries
- 2 lb. sugar
- 1 lb. strawberries
- 1/2 lb. blueberries
- Zest from 1 lemon
- 2 tbsp. water
- 3.5 oz. black currant
- A pinch of salt

Directions:
1. In your instant pot, mix strawberries with cranberries, blueberries, currants, lemon zest and sugar.
2. Stir and leave aside for 1 hour.
3. Add salt and water, set the pot on Simmer mode and bring to a boil

4. Seal the instant pot lid, cook on Low for 10 minutes and release pressure for 10 minutes
5. Carefully open the lid, set it on Simmer mode again, bring to a boil and simmer for 4 minutes. Divide into jars and keep in the fridge until you need it.

Ruby Pears Delight

(**Prep + Cooking Time:** 20 minutes | **Servings:** 4)

Ingredients:
- 4 pears
- 26 oz. grape juice
- 11 oz. currant jelly
- 4 garlic cloves
- Juice and zest of 1 lemon
- 4 peppercorns
- 2 rosemary springs
- 1/2 vanilla bean

Directions:
1. Pour the jelly and grape juice in your instant pot and mix with lemon zest and juice
2. Dip each pear in this mix, wrap them in tin foil and arrange them in the steamer basket of your pot
3. Add garlic cloves, peppercorns, rosemary and vanilla bean to the juice mixture,
4. close the lid and cook at High for 10 minutes.
5. Quick release the pressure, carefully open the lid; take the pears out, unwrap them, arrange them on plates and serve cold with cooking juice on top.

Apple Crumble

(**Prep + Cooking Time:** 40 minutes | **Servings:** 6)

Ingredients:
- 5 large apples (about 2 pounds), cut into 1-inch chunks
- ¾ cup quick-cooking oats
- ½ cup coconut sugar
- ⅓ cup water
- ¼ cup melted coconut oil or butter
- 3 tbsp. 100 percent white whole-wheat flour
- 2 tsp. ground cinnamon
- ¼ tsp. fine sea salt

Directions:
1. Add the apples and the water to the Instant Pot and stir well to be sure the apples cover the bottom of the pot in an even layer
2. In a separate bowl, combine the flour, oats, coconut sugar, cinnamon and salt and stir well. Add the melted coconut oil and stir until thoroughly mixed.
3. Spoon the oat crumble over the apples as a topping. Now, Lock the lid and Turn the steam release valve to "Sealing" Position. Select *Manual/Pressure* Cook to cook on *High* pressure for 8 minutes
4. Once the cooking cycle is completed, let the pressure naturally release for 10 minutes, then move the steam release valve to Venting to release any remaining pressure. When the floating valve drops, remove the lid.
5. Use oven mitts to remove the insert from the Instant Pot and let the crumble cool for 10 minutes before serving warm

Caramel Sauce

(**Prep + Cooking Time:** 1 hour 10 minutes | **Servings:** 5)

Ingredients:
- 1 cup water
- 1 (11-ounce) can sweetened condensed coconut milk
- 1 tsp. coarse sea salt; optional

Directions:
1. Peel the label off the can and place the can on a trivet and into your Instant Pot. Pour in the water
2. Lock the lid and turn the steam release handle to Sealing. Using the Manual function, set the cooker to High Pressure for 45 minutes.

3. After completing the cooking time, let the pressure release naturally for about 20 minutes; or until the pin drops
4. Remove the lid carefully. Wearing oven mitts, carefully remove the can and trivet. Set aside until cool enough to handle.
5. Once cooled, open the can and pour the caramel sauce into a glass jar for storage. If separation occurs, whisk for 1 minute or so. For a salted caramel, stir in the sea salt

Ginger-Coconut Pudding

(Prep + Cooking Time: 21 minutes | Servings: 4)

Ingredients:
- 1 large sweet potato (about 1 pound), peeled and cut into 1-inch pieces.
- 6 tbsp. pure maple syrup , plus more as needed.
- ½ cup full-fat canned coconut milk.
- 1 tsp. grated fresh ginger (about ½-inch knob), plus more as needed

Directions:
1. Pour 1 cup water into the Instant Pot and arrange a steamer basket on the bottom. Place the sweet potato pieces in the steamer basket and secure the lid, moving the steam release valve to Sealing
2. Select *Manual/Pressure* Cook to cook on *High* pressure for 10 minutes. Once the cooking cycle is completed, immediately move the steam release valve to Venting to quickly release the steam pressure. When the floating valve drops, remove the lid.
3. Use oven mitts to lift the steamer basket out of the pot and transfer the cooked potatoes to a large bowl. Add the coconut milk, maple syrup and ginger
4. Use an immersion blender or potato masher to puree the potatoes into a smooth pudding. Taste and adjust the flavor, adding more ginger or maple syrup as needed. Serve the pudding right away, or chill it in the fridge

Delicious Cobbler Recipe

(Prep + Cooking Time: 22 minutes | Servings: 4)

Ingredients:
- 3 apples, cored and cut into chunks
- 1 tsp. cinnamon
- 1 ½ cup hot water
- 1/4 cup date syrup
- 2 pears, cored and cut into chunks
- 1 cup steel cut oats
- ice cream for serving

Directions:
1. Put apples and pears in your instant pot and mix with hot water, date syrup, oats and cinnamon
2. Stir, seal the instant pot lid and cook at High for 12 minutes.
3. Release pressure naturally, transfer cobbler to bowls and serve it with ice cream on top.

Vanilla Applesauce

(Prep + Cooking Time: 25 minutes | Servings: 7)

Ingredients:
- 3 pounds apples, cored and quartered, no need to peel
- ⅓ cup water
- 1 tsp. ground cinnamon; or more as needed
- 1 tsp. freshly squeezed lemon juice
- 1 tsp. vanilla extract
- 1/2 tsp. salt or as your liking

Directions:
1. In the Instant Pot, combine the apples, water, vanilla, cinnamon, lemon juice and salt
2. Lock the lid and turn the steam release handle to Sealing. Using the Manual function, set the cooker to High Pressure for 5 minutes.

3. After completing the cooking time, let the pressure release naturally for 10 minutes; quick release any remaining pressure
4. Remove the lid carefully. Using an immersion blender, blend the applesauce until smooth. Taste and add more cinnamon, as desired

Pears Jam Recipe

(Prep + Cooking Time: 15 minutes | **Servings:** 12)

Ingredients:
- 8 pears, cored and cut into quarters
- 2 apples, peeled, cored and cut into quarters
- 1/4 cup apple juice
- 1 tsp. cinnamon, ground.

Directions:
1. In your instant pot, mix pears with apples, cinnamon and apple juice; then stir well. seal the instant pot lid and cook at High for 4 minutes.
2. Release the pressure naturally, carefully open the lid;
3. blend using an immersion blender, divide jam into jars and keep in a cold place until you serve it

Sticky Rice and Fruit

(Prep + Cooking Time: 31 minutes | **Servings:** 4)

Ingredients:
- 1 cup full-fat coconut milk
- 1/4 cup sugar
- 1 cup sweet rice; rinsed and drained
- 2 ¼ cups water; divided
- 1/2 tsp. salt or as your liking
- Sliced fresh fruit; for serving

Directions:
1. In a small saucepan over low heat, make the coconut sauce by combining the coconut milk, sugar and salt
2. Cook for 2 to 3 minutes, stirring frequently, don't let it boil-until the sugar dissolves. Remove from the heat.
3. Pour 1 cup of water into the Instant Pot and place a trivet into the inner pot. In a medium glass or stainless steel bowl, combine the remaining 1 ¼ cups water and the rice, ensuring the rice is completely covered.
4. Place the bowl atop the trivet. Lock the lid and turn the steam release handle to Sealing. Using the Manual function, set the cooker to High Pressure for 14 minutes
5. After completing the cooking time, let the pressure release naturally for 10 to 12 minutes; quick release any remaining pressure.
6. Remove the lid carefully and add half the coconut sauce. Cover the cooker and let sit for at least 5 minutes so the rice absorbs the liquid. Top each serving with fruit and additional coconut sauce

Delicious Brownies

(Prep + Cooking Time: 45 minutes | Makes 16)

Ingredients:
- ¾ cup almond butter
- 1 egg
- ⅓ cup raw cacao powder
- ¾ cup coconut sugar
- ½ tsp. baking soda
- ½ tsp. pure vanilla extract
- ¼ tsp. fine sea salt
- ½ cup dark chocolate chips (optional)

Directions:
1. Line a 7-inch round pan with parchment paper. Take a large bowl, combine the almond butter, coconut sugar, cacao powder, egg, salt, baking soda and vanilla and stir well to create a thick batter
2. Transfer the batter to the prepared pan and use your hands to press it evenly into the pan. Sprinkle with the chocolate chips and gently press them into the batter.

3. Pour 1 cup water into the Instant Pot and arrange the trivet (Which comes with your instant pot) on the bottom. Place the pan on top of the trivet and cover it with an upside-down plate or another piece of parchment to protect the brownies from condensation
4. Now, Lock the lid and Turn the steam release valve to "Sealing" Position. Select *Manual/Pressure* Cook to cook on *High* pressure for 15 minutes.
5. Once the cooking cycle is completed, let the pressure naturally release for 10 minutes, then move the steam release valve to Venting to release any remaining pressure. When the floating valve drops, remove the lid.
6. Use oven mitts to lift the trivet and the pan out of the pot. Let the brownies cool completely in the pan before cutting and serving

Stuffed Peaches

(**Prep + Cooking Time:** 15 minutes | **Servings:** 6)

Ingredients:
- 6 peaches, insides removed
- 2 tbsp. coconut butter
- 1 tsp. almond extract
- 1/4 cup coconut flour
- 1/2 tsp. cinnamon powder
- 1/4 cup maple syrup
- 1 cup water
- A pinch of salt

Directions:
1. In a bowl, mix flour with salt, syrup, butter, cinnamon and half of the almond extract and stir well.
2. Fill peaches with this mix, place them in the steamer basket of your instant pot, add the water and the rest of the almond extract to the pot, seal the instant pot lid and cook at High for 4 minutes.
3. Release pressure naturally, divide stuffed peaches on servings plates and serve warm

Pina Colada Pudding

(**Prep + Cooking Time:** 15 minutes | **Servings:** 8)

Ingredients:
- 8 oz. canned pineapple tidbits, drained and halved
- 14 oz. canned coconut milk
- 1 tbsp. coconut oil
- 2 eggs
- 1/2 tsp. vanilla extract
- 1/2 cup milk
- 1/2 cup sugar
- 1 ½ cups water
- 1 cup Arborio rice
- A pinch of salt

Directions:
1. In your instant pot, mix oil, water, rice and salt; then stir well. seal the instant pot lid and cook at High for 3 minutes.
2. Release the pressure naturally for 10 minutes, then release remaining pressure by turning the valve to 'Venting', carefully open the lid; add sugar and coconut milk and stir well.
3. In a bowl, mix eggs with milk and vanilla, stir and pour over rice.
4. Stir, set the pot on Sauté mode and bring to a boil
5. Add pineapple tidbits; then stir well. divide into dessert bowls and serve

Delicious Apple Cake

(**Prep + Cooking Time:** 30 minutes | **Servings:** 8)

Ingredients:
- 1 apple, sliced
- 1 cup white flour
- 2 tsp. baking powder
- 1 tbsp. lemon juice
- 1/4 cup raw sugar
- 1/8 tsp. cinnamon powder
- one egg
- 1 tsp. vanilla extract
- 3 tbsp. olive oil
- 1 apple; chopped.

- 2 cup water
- 1 cup ricotta cheese
- 1 tsp. baking soda

Directions:
1. Put chopped and sliced apple in a bowl, add lemon juice, toss to coat and leave aside for now.
2. Line a heatproof dish with some parchment paper, grease with some oil and dust with some flour.
3. Sprinkle some sugar on the bottom and arrange sliced apple on top.
4. In a bowl, mix the egg with cheese, sugar, vanilla extract and oil and stir well.
5. Add flour, baking powder and soda and cinnamon and stir again.
6. Add chopped apple, toss to coat and pour everything into the pan.
7. Place the pan in the steamer basket of your instant pot, add the water to the pot, seal the instant pot lid and cook at High for 20 minutes
8. Quick release the pressure, carefully open the lid; turn cake on a plate and serve warm.

Fruit Compote

(**Prep + Cooking Time:** 20 minutes | **Makes:** 4 cups)

Ingredients:
- 1/4 cup freshly squeezed orange juice
- 1 ½ cups sugar
- 6 cups mixed berries

Directions:
1. In the Instant Pot, combine the berries, sugar and orange juice.
2. Lock the lid and turn the steam release handle to Sealing. Using the Manual function, set the cooker to High Pressure for 3 minutes
3. After completing the cooking time, turn off the Instant Pot and let the pressure release naturally for 10 minutes; quick release any remaining pressure
4. Remove the lid carefully. Select Sauté Medium. Stir the berry mixture and cook for 5 to 10 minutes (depending on how much liquid there is) so some of the excess liquid evaporates
5. Switch to Low if it's spattering too much. When you've reached the desired consistency, let the compote cool a bit before enjoying.

Ginger and Pineapple Risotto

(**Prep + Cooking Time:** 22 minutes | **Servings:** 4)

Ingredients:
- 1/4 cup candied ginger; chopped.
- 1 ¾ cups risotto rice
- 20 oz. canned pineapple; chopped.
- 4 cups milk
- 1/2 cup coconut, shredded.

Directions:
1. In your instant pot, mix milk with rice, coconut, pineapple and ginger; then stir well. seal the instant pot lid and cook at High for 12 minutes.
2. Release the pressure naturally, carefully open the lid and serve your dessert

Pecan-Cinnamon Coffee Cake

(**Prep + Cooking Time:** 56 minutes | **Servings:** 8)

Ingredients:
- 1½ cups almond flour or almond meal
- 3 eggs, at room temperature
- ½ cup finely chopped pecans
- ¾ cup coconut sugar
- 2 tbsp. melted coconut oil
- 1 tsp. ground cinnamon.
- ½ tsp. baking soda
- ¼ tsp. fine sea salt

Directions:
1. Lightly grease a 7-inch round pan and line it with parchment paper. Take a large bowl, combine the almond flour, coconut sugar, baking soda, salt and cinnamon and whisk to break up any lumps

2. Add the eggs and melted coconut oil and mix with a spatula until smooth. *If your eggs are cold from the fridge, the mixture will be thick and difficult to stir, but the cake will still bake well.
3. Pour the batter into the pan and smooth the top with the spatula. Sprinkle the pecans over the batter
4. Pour 1 cup water into the Instant Pot and arrange the trivet (Which comes with your instant pot) on the bottom. Place the pan on top of the trivet and cover it with an upside-down plate or another piece of parchment to protect the cake from condensation
5. Now, Lock the lid and Turn the steam release valve to "Sealing" Position. Select *Manual/Pressure* Cook to cook on *High* pressure for 30 minutes
6. Once the cooking cycle is completed, let the pressure naturally release for 10 minutes, then move the steam release valve to Venting to release any remaining pressure.
7. When the floating valve drops, remove the lid. Use oven mitts to lift the trivet and the pan out of the pot. Let the cake cool in the pan for 30 minutes before cutting and serving

Peach Jam Recipe

(Prep + Cooking Time: 15 minutes | Servings: 6)

Ingredients:
- 4 ½ cups peaches, peeled and cubed
- 1 box fruit pectin
- 6 cups sugar
- 1/4 cup crystallized ginger; chopped.

Directions:
1. Set your instant pot on Simmer mode, add peaches, ginger, and pectin, stir and bring to a boil
2. Add sugar; then stir well. seal the instant pot lid and cook at High for 5 minutes.
3. Quick release the pressure, carefully open the lid, divide jam into jars and serve.

Instant Pot Sweet Carrots

(Prep + Cooking Time: 25 minutes | Servings: 4)

Ingredients:
- 2 cups baby carrots
- 1/2 cup water
- 1/2 tbsp. butter
- 1 tbsp. brown sugar
- A pinch of salt

Directions:
1. Set your instant pot on Sauté mode; add butter and melt it.
2. Add sugar, water and salt, stir and cook for 1 minute.
3. Add carrots, toss to coat, seal the instant pot lid and cook at High for 15 minutes. Quick release the pressure, carefully open the lid;
4. Transfer carrots to plates and serve

Candied Lemon Peel

(Prep + Cooking Time: 40 minutes | Servings: 80 pieces)

Ingredients:
- 5 big lemons
- 2 ¼ cups white sugar
- 5 cups water

Directions:
1. Wash lemons, slice them in half, reserve juice for another use, slice each half into quarters, take out the pulp and cut peel into thin strips
2. Put strips in your instant pot, add 4 cups water, seal the instant pot lid and cook at High for 3 minutes.
3. Release pressure fast, carefully open the lid; strain peel, rinse and put in a bowl.
4. Clean your instant pot and add 2 cups sugar and 1 cup water in it.
5. Add lemon strips; then stir well. set pot on Simmer mode and cook for 5 minutes.
6. Seal the instant pot lid, cook at High for 10 more minutes and release pressure naturally for 20 minutes
7. Strain peels again, spread them on a cutting board and leave them to cool down for 10 minutes. Keep them in jars until you serve them.

Samoa Cheese Cake Recipe

(Prep + Cooking Time: 1 hour 15 minutes | **Servings:** 6)

Ingredients:
For the crust:
- 1/2 cup chocolate graham crackers, crumbled.
- 2 tbsp. butter, melted

For the filling:
- 1/4 cup sour cream
- 1/4 cup heavy cream
- 1/2 cup sugar
- 12 oz. cream cheese, soft
- 1 ½ tsp. vanilla extract
- 1 tbsp. flour
- one egg yolk
- 2 eggs
- 1 cup water
- Cooking spray

For the topping:
- 1/4 cup chocolate; chopped.
- 12 caramels
- 3 tbsp. heavy cream
- 1 ½ cups coconut, sweet and shredded.

Directions:
1. Grease a spring form pan with some cooking spray and leave it aside
2. In a bowl, mix crackers with butter; then stir well. spread in the bottom of the pan and keep in the freezer for 10 minutes.
3. Meanwhile, in another bowl, mix cheese with sugar, heavy cream, vanilla, flour, sour cream and eggs and stir very well using a mixer.
4. Pour this into the pan on top of crust, cover with tin foil and place in the steamer basket of your instant pot.
5. Add 1 cup water to the pot, seal the instant pot lid and cook at High for 35 minutes
6. Release the pressure naturally for 10 minutes, then release remaining pressure by turning the valve to 'Venting', carefully open the lid; take the pan, remove tin foil and leave cake to cool down in the fridge for 4 hours.
7. Spread coconut on a lined baking sheet, introduce in the oven at 300 degrees F and bake for 20 minutes, stirring often
8. Put caramels in a heatproof bowl, introduce in the microwave for 2 minutes, stir every 20 seconds and then mix with toasted coconut
9. Spread this on your cheesecake and leave aside for now.
10. Put chocolate in another heatproof bowl, introduce in your microwave for a few seconds until it melts and drizzles over your cake. Serve right away

Coconut Rice Pudding

(Prep + Cooking Time: 35 minutes | **Servings:** 5)

Ingredients:
- 1 cup jasmine rice; rinsed and drained
- 1 (14-ounce) can full-fat coconut milk
- 1/4 cup sugar
- 2 cups water
- 2 tsp. ground cinnamon
- 1 ½ tsp. vanilla extract
- 1/2 tsp. ground nutmeg
- 1 tsp. salt or as your liking
- Nondairy milk, to thin after cooking
- Coconut flakes; for topping
- Raisins; for topping
- Maple syrup; for topping

Directions:
1. In the Instant Pot, combine the rice, coconut milk, water, cinnamon, vanilla, nutmeg, salt and sugar. If needed, whisk to break down any chunks from the canned coconut milk
2. Lock the lid and turn the steam release handle to Sealing. Select the Porridge function. This will automatically cook for 20 minutes

3. After completing the cooking time, let the pressure release naturally for 10 minutes; quick release any remaining pressure
4. Remove the lid carefully and stir in the milk if you want a thinner pudding. Keep in mind it will thicken as it cools, so if you're planning to reheat it later you'll likely need more milk.

Holiday Pudding

(**Prep + Cooking Time:** 50 minutes | **Servings:** 4)

Ingredients:
- 4 oz. dried cranberries, soaked in hot water for 30 minutes, drained and chopped.
- 1 cup white flour
- 3 tsp. baking powder
- 1 cup raw sugar
- 15 tbsp. butter
- 3 tbsp. maple syrup
- 1 tsp. ginger powder
- 2 cups water
- 4 eggs
- 1 carrot, grated
- 4 oz. dried apricots; chopped.
- A pinch of cinnamon powder
- A pinch of salt
- A drizzle of olive oil

Directions:
1. Grease a heatproof pudding mould with a drizzle of oil and leave aside for now
2. In a blender, mix flour with baking powder, sugar, cinnamon, salt and ginger and pulse a few times.
3. Add butter and pulse again.
4. Add maple syrup and eggs and pulse again.
5. Add dried fruits and carrot and fold them into the batter
6. Spread this mix into the pudding mold, place this in the steamer basket of your instant pot and add 2 cups water in the pot as well
7. Set the pot on Sauté mode and steam your pudding for 10 minutes.
8. Cover your pot, cook pudding at High for 30 minutes.
9. Release the pressure naturally for 10 minutes, then release remaining pressure by turning the valve to 'Venting', carefully open the lid; take pudding out and leave it aside to cool down before serving it

Instant Pot Baked Apples

(**Prep + Cooking Time:** 20 minutes | **Servings:** 6)

Ingredients:
- 6 apples, cored
- 1 cup red wine
- 1/4 cup raisins
- 1/2 cup raw sugar
- 1 tsp. cinnamon powder

Directions:
1. Put the apples in your instant pot
2. Add wine, raisins, sugar and cinnamon, close the lid and cook at High for 10 minutes.
3. Release pressure naturally, carefully open the lid; transfer apples and their cooking juice to plates and serve.

Lemon Crème Pots

(**Prep + Cooking Time:** 35 minutes | **Servings:** 4)

Ingredients:
- 1 cup whole milk
- 2/3 cup sugar
- 6 egg yolks
- 1 cup fresh cream
- 1/2 cup fresh blackberries
- Zest from 1 lemon
- 1 cup water
- Blackberry syrup for serving

Directions:
1. Heat up a pan over medium heat, add milk, lemon zest and cream; then stir well. bring to a boil, take off heat and leave aside for 30 minutes
2. In a bowl, mix egg yolks with sugar and cold cream mix and stir well
3. Pour this into ramekins, cover them with tin foil, place them in the steamer basket of your instant pot, add 1 cup water to the pot, seal the instant pot lid and cook at High for 5 minutes.
4. Release the pressure naturally for 10 minutes, then release remaining pressure by turning the valve to 'Venting', carefully open the lid; take ramekins out
5. leave them to cool down and serve with blackberries and blackberry syrup on top

Apple Bread

(**Prep + Cooking Time:** 1 hour and 20 minutes | **Servings:** 6)

Ingredients:
- 3 cups apples, cored and cubed
- 1 cup sugar
- 2 eggs
- 1 tbsp. baking powder
- 1 tbsp. apple pie spice
- 2 cups white flour
- 1 stick butter
- 1 tbsp. vanilla
- 1 cup water

Directions:
1. In a bowl mix egg with 1 butter stick, apple pie spice and sugar and stir using your mixer.
2. Add apples and stir again well.
3. In another bowl, mix baking powder with flour and stir.
4. Combine the 2 mixtures, stir and pour into a spring form pan.
5. Place in the steamer basket of your instant pot, add 1 cup water to the pot, seal the instant pot lid and cook at High for 1 hour and 10 minutes.
6. Quick release the pressure, leave bread to cool down, cut and serve it.

Delicious Apple Crisp

(**Prep + Cooking Time:** 18 minutes | **Servings:** 4)

Ingredients:
- 5 apples, cored and cut into chunks
- 2 tsp. cinnamon
- 1/2 tsp. nutmeg
- 1/4 cup brown sugar
- 1/4 cup flour
- 3/4 cup old fashioned rolled oats
- 1/2 cup water
- 1 tbsp. maple syrup
- 4 tbsp. butter
- A pinch of salt

Directions:
1. Put the apples in your instant pot.
2. Add cinnamon, nutmeg, maple syrup and water.
3. In a bowl, mix butter with oats, sugar, salt and flour and stir well.
4. Drop spoonfuls of oats mix on top of apples, close the lid and cook at High for 8 minutes.
5. Release the pressure and serve warm

Zucchini Nut Bread Recipe

(**Prep + Cooking Time:** 30 minutes | **Servings:** 6)

Ingredients:
- 2 cups zucchini, grated
- 1/2 cup baking cocoa
- 1 tsp. baking soda
- 1/4 tsp. baking powder
- 1 cup applesauce
- 3 eggs, whisked
- 1 tbsp. vanilla extract
- 2 cups sugar
- 1/2 cup walnuts; chopped.
- 1/2 cup chocolate chips

- 1 tsp. salt
- 2 ½ cups white flour
- 1 tsp. cinnamon
- 1 ½ cups water

Directions:
1. In a bowl, mix zucchini with sugar, vanilla, eggs and applesauce and stir well
2. In another bowl, mix flour with salt, cocoa, baking soda, baking powder, cinnamon, chocolate chips and walnuts and stir.
3. Combine the 2 mixtures; then stir well. pour into a Bundt pan, place pan in the steamer basket of your instant pot, add the water to the pot, seal the instant pot lid and cook at High for 25 minutes.
4. Release the pressure naturally, carefully open the lid; transfer bread to a plate, cut and serve it.

Ricotta Cake Recipe

(**Prep + Cooking Time:** 60 minutes | **Servings:** 6)

Ingredients:
- 6 oz. dates, soaked for 15 minutes and drained
- 1 lb. ricotta
- 2 oz. honey softened
- 4 eggs
- 2 oz. sugar
- 17 oz. water
- Orange juice and zest from ½ orange
- Some vanilla extract

Directions:
1. In a bowl, whisk ricotta until it softens.
2. In another bowl, whisk eggs well.
3. Combine the 2 mixtures and stir very well.
4. Add honey, vanilla, dates, orange zest and juice to the ricotta mixture and stir again
5. Pour the batter into a heatproof dish and cover with tin foil
6. Place dish in the steamer basket of your instant pot, add water to the pot, seal the instant pot lid and cook at High for 20 minutes
7. Quick release the pressure, carefully open the lid; allow cake to cool down, transfer to a platter, slice and serve.

Peach Compote

(**Prep + Cooking Time:** 13 minutes | **Servings:** 6)

Ingredients:
- 8 peaches; chopped.
- 6 tbsp. sugar
- 1 vanilla bean, scraped
- 2 tbsp. grape nuts cereal
- 1 tsp. cinnamon, ground.
- 1 tsp. vanilla extract

Directions:
1. Put peaches in your instant pot and mix with sugar, cinnamon, vanilla bean and vanilla extract. Stir well, close the lid and cook at High for 3 minutes.
2. Release pressure for 10 minutes, add grape nuts, stir well, transfer the compote to bowls and serve

Quick Raspberry Curd

(**Prep + Cooking Time:** 25 minutes | **Servings:** 4)

Ingredients:
- 12 oz. raspberries
- 2 tbsp. butter
- 2 egg yolks
- 1 cup sugar
- 2 tbsp. lemon juice

Directions:
1. Put raspberries in your instant pot.
2. Add sugar and lemon juice; then stir well. seal the instant pot lid and cook at High for 2 minutes.
3. Release pressure for 5 minutes, carefully open the lid; strain raspberries and discard seeds
4. In a bowl, mix egg yolks with raspberries and stir well.

5. Return this to your instant pot, set it on Sauté mode; simmer for 2 minutes, add butter, stir and transfer to a container. Serve cold.

Poached Pears with Caramel Sauce

(Prep + Cooking Time: 12 minutes | **Servings:** 4)

Ingredients:
- 1 whole vanilla bean, split and scraped
- 4 Bosc pears, ripe but not soft
- 1 batch Easy Caramel Sauce, warmed
- 1 lemon, halved
- 2 cups sugar
- 3 cups water
- 2 cups white wine
- 1 cinnamon stick

Directions:
1. Select the "Sauté" Low mode on your instant pot. When the display reads "Hot," add the water, white wine, sugar, vanilla bean and seeds and cinnamon stick, stirring well
2. Cook for 1 to 2 minutes; or until the sugar dissolves completely. Cancel Sauté and select Keep Warm.
3. Gently peel the pears. If presentation is important, keep the stems intact. Rub the pears with the lemon halves to prevent browning and add the pears to the Instant Pot
4. Lock the lid and turn the steam release handle to Sealing. Using the Manual function, set the cooker to High Pressure for 3 minutes
5. After completing the cooking time, quick release the pressure. Remove the lid carefully and remove the pears. Set aside to cool.
6. Save the sauce and pour it over the pears once cooled. Serve, warm or at room temperature, topped with caramel sauce

Banana Bread

(Prep + Cooking Time: 40 minutes | **Servings:** 6)

Ingredients:
- 2 bananas, mashed
- 3/4 cup coconut sugar
- 1/3 cup ghee, soft
- 1 tsp. vanilla
- 1/2 tsp. baking soda
- 1/3 cup cashew milk
- one egg
- 1 ½ tsp. cream of tartar
- 2 cups water
- 1 tsp. baking powder
- 1 ½ cups flour
- A pinch of salt
- Cooking spray

Directions:
1. In a bowl, mix milk with cream of tartar and stir well.
2. Add sugar, ghee, egg, vanilla and bananas and stir everything.
3. In another bowl, mix flour with salt, baking powder and soda
4. Combine the 2 mixtures, stir well, pour this into a cake pan which you've greased with some cooking spray and arrange pan in the steamer basket of your instant pot
5. Add the water to your pot, seal the instant pot lid and cook at High for 30 minutes
6. Quick release the pressure, carefully open the lid; take bread out, leave aside to cool down, slice and serve it.

Coconut Rice Pudding

(Prep + Cooking Time: 35 minutes | **Servings:** 5)

Ingredients:
- 1 cup jasmine rice; rinsed and drained
- 1 (14-ounce) can full-fat coconut milk
- 1/4 cup sugar
- 2 cups water
- 2 tsp. ground cinnamon
- 1 ½ tsp. vanilla extract
- 1/2 tsp. ground nutmeg
- 1 tsp. salt or as your liking

- Nondairy milk, to thin after cooking
- Coconut flakes; for topping
- Raisins; for topping
- Maple syrup; for topping

Directions:
1. In the Instant Pot, combine the rice, coconut milk, water, cinnamon, vanilla, nutmeg, salt and sugar. If needed, whisk to break down any chunks from the canned coconut milk
2. Lock the lid and turn the steam release handle to Sealing. Select the Porridge function. This will automatically cook for 20 minutes
3. After completing the cooking time, let the pressure release naturally for 10 minutes; quick release any remaining pressure.
4. Remove the lid carefully and stir in the milk if you want a thinner pudding. Keep in mind it will thicken as it cools, so if you're planning to reheat it later you'll likely need more milk

Fruit Compote

(Prep + Cooking Time: 20 minutes | Makes: 4 cups)

Ingredients:
- 1/4 cup freshly squeezed orange juice
- 1 ½ cups sugar
- 6 cups mixed berries

Directions:
1. In the Instant Pot, combine the berries, sugar and orange juice
2. Lock the lid and turn the steam release handle to Sealing. Using the Manual function, set the cooker to High Pressure for 3 minutes.
3. After completing the cooking time, turn off the Instant Pot and let the pressure release naturally for 10 minutes; quick release any remaining pressure
4. Remove the lid carefully. Select Sauté Medium. Stir the berry mixture and cook for 5 to 10 minutes (depending on how much liquid there is) so some of the excess liquid evaporates.
5. Switch to Low if it's spattering too much. When you've reached the desired consistency, let the compote cool a bit before enjoying

Sticky Rice and Fruit

(Prep + Cooking Time: 31 minutes | **Servings:** 4)

Ingredients:
- 1 cup full-fat coconut milk
- 1/4 cup sugar
- 1 cup sweet rice; rinsed and drained
- 2 ¼ cups water; divided
- 1/2 tsp. salt or as your liking
- Sliced fresh fruit; for serving

Directions:
1. In a small saucepan over low heat, make the coconut sauce by combining the coconut milk, sugar and salt.
2. Cook for 2 to 3 minutes, stirring frequently, don't let it boil-until the sugar dissolves. Remove from the heat
3. Pour 1 cup of water into the Instant Pot and place a trivet into the inner pot. In a medium glass or stainless steel bowl, combine the remaining 1 ¼ cups water and the rice, ensuring the rice is completely covered.
4. Place the bowl atop the trivet. Lock the lid and turn the steam release handle to Sealing. Using the Manual function, set the cooker to High Pressure for 14 minutes
5. After completing the cooking time, let the pressure release naturally for 10 to 12 minutes; quick release any remaining pressure
6. Remove the lid carefully and add half the coconut sauce. Cover the cooker and let sit for at least 5 minutes so the rice absorbs the liquid. Top each serving with fruit and additional coconut sauce

Brownie Cake Recipe

(Prep + Cooking Time: 60 minutes | **Servings:** 6)

Ingredients:
- 1 cup borlotti beans, soaked for 8 hours and drained
- 4 cups water

For the cake:
- 1/4 cup almonds, sliced
- 1/2 cup cocoa powder
- 1/8 tsp. almond extract
- 1/2 cup raw sugar
- 3 tbsp. extra virgin olive oil
- 2 eggs
- 2 tsp. baking powder
- A pinch of salt

Directions:
1. Put beans and water in your instant pot, close the lid, cook at High for 12 minutes, release pressure, carefully open the lid; strain beans, transfer them to a blender and puree them.
2. Discard water from the pot and keep 1 cup
3. Grease a heatproof bowl with some olive oil and leave it aside for now.
4. Add cocoa powder, almond extract, honey, salt, eggs and oil to your blender with the beans and puree everything for 1 minute.
5. Transfer mix to greased bowl, spread, place bowl in the steamer basket of your pot, add reserved water from cooking the beans,
6. Seal the instant pot lid and cook at High for 20 minutes.
7. Quick release the pressure, take cake out of the pot, leave it aside for 15 minutes,
8. Transfer to a plate, sprinkle almonds on top, slice and serve.

Oatmeal Raisin Cookie

(Prep + Cooking Time: 50 minutes | **Servings:** 8)

Ingredients:
- ½ cup 100 percent white whole-wheat flour
- ¼ cup melted coconut oil or butter
- ½ cup quick-cooking oats
- ½ cup raisins
- ½ cup coconut sugar
- 1 egg
- 1 tsp. ground cinnamon.
- ½ tsp. pure vanilla extract
- ¼ tsp. fine sea salt
- ¼ tsp. baking soda

Directions:
1. Grease a 7-inch round pan and line it with parchment paper. Take a large bowl, stir together the flour, sugar, salt, baking soda and cinnamon. Add the egg, coconut oil and vanilla and stir until a smooth batter forms. Fold in the oats and raisins
2. The batter will be thick and sticky. Transfer the batter to the prepared pan and use a spatula to smooth the top.
3. Pour 1 cup water into the Instant Pot and arrange the trivet (Which comes with your instant pot) on the bottom. Place the pan on top of the trivet and cover it with an upside-down plate or another piece of parchment to protect the cookie from condensation
4. Now, Lock the lid and Turn the steam release valve to "Sealing" Position. Select *Manual/Pressure* Cook to cook on *High* pressure for 25 minutes.
5. Once the cooking cycle is completed, let the pressure naturally release for 10 minutes, then move the steam release valve to Venting to release any remaining pressure.
6. When the floating valve drops, remove the lid. Use oven mitts to lift the trivet and the pan out of the pot. Let the cookie cool completely, about 1 hour, before cutting and serving

Made in the USA
San Bernardino, CA
17 February 2020